Springer Proceedings in Business and Economics

More information about this series at http://www.springer.com/series/11960

Kesra Nermend • Małgorzata Łatuszyńska
Editors

Selected Issues in Experimental Economics

Proceedings of the 2015 Computational Methods in Experimental Economics (CMEE) Conference

Springer

Editors
Kesra Nermend
Faculty of Economics and Management
Institute of IT in Management
University of Szczecin
Szczecin, Poland

Małgorzata Łatuszyńska
Faculty of Economics and Management
Institute of IT in Management
University of Szczecin
Szczecin, Poland

ISSN 2198-7246 ISSN 2198-7254 (electronic)
ISBN 978-3-319-28417-0 ISBN 978-3-319-28419-4 (eBook)
DOI 10.1007/978-3-319-28419-4

Library of Congress Control Number: 2016932401

Printed on acid-free paper

This Springer imprint is published by Springer Nature
The registered company is Springer International Publishing AG Switzerland

Preface

The field of experimental economics is rapidly evolving. Recent research includes experiments conducted both in the laboratory and in the field, and the results are used for testing and better understanding of economic theories. This book focuses on providing a deep insight into main topics of experimental economics and on presenting the recent trends in this area of expertise.

The book includes the papers of researchers who are interested in this subject and represent a certain level of experience regarding the field. Its main objective is to exemplify the links between various domains of knowledge which are part of experimental economics.

The book is divided into three parts:

1. Theoretical aspects of experimental economics
2. Methods and tools of experimental economics
3. Practical issues: case studies

Each of these parts begins with an introduction outlining its subject and summarising each of its chapters. The purpose of the introduction is to help the reader navigate through the chapters contained in the given part. The authors of the introductions are their thematic editors.

As its title suggests, the first part of the book presents theoretical foundations of experimental economics. It outlines the historical background of experimental economics, the types of economic experiments, the procedures in experimental studies in economics as well as several other issues referring to the experimental economics. The thematic editor of this part is Danuta Miłaszewicz (professor of the University of Szczecin, Poland).

In every stage of an economic experiment, from its design to the data analysis, the researcher has to choose among a vast range of methods and tools. Therefore, the second part of the book contains a broad outline of instruments that support experimenters in various phases of their studies. The outline presents both the methods commonly used by experimenters (such as statistical ones) and those typically less associated with experimental economics (e.g. artificial intelligence, computer simulation, computer graphics, cognitive neuroscience techniques or multicriteria decision support methods) pointing to their potential application in economic experimenting. Showing the variety of these methods and their possible applications in the book is meant to widen the scientific toolkit of experimental economics researchers. The thematic editor of this part is Mariusz Borawski (associate professor, West Pomeranian University of Technology, Szczecin, Poland).

The last part of the volume, titled 'Practical issues: case studies', presents the examples of broadly understood experiments in economics. They refer to different areas and utilise various methods which were described in methodological chapters of the book. The third part of this book presents only selected experiments and approaches to experimental economics. It outlines, however, the wide range of topics and methods that can be used within this field of study. Recent advancements in technology allow for designing increasingly advanced and interesting experiments. Therefore it can be assumed that experimental economics will develop dynamically in the future. A thematic editor of this part is Anna Borawska (assistant professor, University of Szczecin, Poland).

The issues addressed in the monograph do not exhaust the subject of experimental economy. Yet, in the opinion of the editors, it shows well the diversity of areas, problems, methods, techniques and domains concerning this subject.

Szczecin, Poland

Kesra Nermend
Małgorzata Łatuszyńska

Contents

Part I
Theoretical Aspects of Experimental Economics

Introduction

Danuta Miłaszewicz

Part one of the book on "Selected Issues of Experimental Economics" introduces the reader to the theoretical aspects of experimental economics. Each chapter in this part of the book is dedicated to selected issues related to this topic. The main aim of this introduction is to present the contents of each of the five chapters of the theoretical part of the book.

Chapter 1 introduces to the reader the theory of experimental economics as well as both complements the chapters in the first part of the book on experimental economics. The definitions of experimental economics outlined in this chapter define its very essence which is a theme of the subsequent chapters. Chapter 1 also supplements methodological considerations included in Chaps. 2 and 4—situating experimental economics in modern economic science and comparing its methodology with conventional mainstream economics. What binds all the chapters in the first part of the book are, both included in Chap. 1, the description of principal attributes of a good experiment and the list of ten principles to be followed by the theorists of economics and experimental economists.

Chapter 2 shows theoretical background for experimental economics. Presenting the origins of experimental economics, it provides a good insight into the factors which determined the application of experiments in economics thus giving origins to experimental economics. It first shows the widely accepted modern definition of

D. Miłaszewicz
Department of Macroeconomics, Faculty of Economics and Management,
Institute of Economics, University of Szczecin, Mickiewicza 64,
71-101 Szczecin, Poland
e-mail: dmilasz@wneiz.pl

economics, and later describes methodological foundations of research within mainstream economics and their consequences to the use of experiments in economics. This chapter offers also a subjective depiction of the history of experimental economics. Starting with the description of the first experiments, the St. Petersburg paradox and Chamberlin's market experiment, the chapter characterises two paths in the history of development of experimental economics and shows how it has contributed to the development of both microeconomic and macroeconomic theory.

Chapter 3 in the theoretical part of the book provides the reader with an insight into the essence of experiment as a research method and the nature of economic experiments. It describes the main elements and characteristics of the economic experiment, applications and theoretical background as well as the strong and weak points of its practical use. It also presents classifications of experiments by the conditions and techniques used as well as by the area of study. Next, the chapter discusses various classifications of areas of application of the experimental method in economics. The three synthetically described classifications are helpful in experiment preparation using showed methods. The chapter stresses also the relationship between the theory of economics and economic experiments, and the potential for their mutual stimulation. The diversity of economic experiments presented in this publication confirms the opinion that experimental economics is wrongly considered equivalent solely to laboratory experiments.

The issues discussed in Chaps. 2 and 3 are further developed in Chap. 4. With reference to the methodology of economic sciences and recent discussions on this topic, this chapter presents the benefits related to the application of the experimental method in economics. It also offers a synthetic presentation of selected types of experiments and areas of their application with reference to the classifications of economic experiments discussed in Chap. 3. In addition to the considerations on the methodology of experimental research as a set of rules evolving with the wider use of this method and important from the viewpoint of the reliability of experimental works, Chap. 4 presents also an outline of the recommended research procedure. It proposes universal yet essential stages to properly conduct an experimental study. Emphasising the role of experiments in the causal analysis in economics, the chapter also briefly describes five methods of causal inference which are most frequently used as analytical methods (propensity score, differences in differences estimator, regression discontinuity, instrumental variable estimator, simulation methods). It is a good introduction to the second part of the book.

The experimental method is used to analyse major macroeconomic problems—to explain the aggregated macro behaviour, for inferring unobservable behaviour such as expectations formation, for studying the implications of different public policies and regulations. In this field of economics mostly model-based experiments and natural experiments are used. The essence of the latter is discussed in Chap. 4, which presents also their advantages and disadvantages. Selected examples of natural macroeconomic experiments, in turn, are described in Chap. 5. These experiments were carried out in different periods in different countries and regions and address various macroeconomic problems: cultural determinants of understanding the concept of justice and an equitable distribution, the case of new money Bitcoin and Gresham law, causal effect of institutional order on economic outcomes, the impact of external shocks on the output and income in low-income economies, migration flows from Central and Eastern European Countries after the EU enlargement in 2004, the programme of regional development that was realised in Poland in 2007–2013.

Chapter 1
Preface to the Theory of Experimental Economics

Danuta Miłaszewicz

Abstract Chapter 1 presents different definitions of experimental economics expressing its essence, features of a good experiment and guidelines for theorists of economics and experimental economists. The main aim of this chapter is to supplement some of the remaining chapters of the first part of the book "Selected Issues of Experimental Economics". This chapter also works as a link between the other four chapters.

Keywords Experimental economics definition • Good experiment features

1.1 Introduction

Experimental economics, the topic of this book, may be generally defined as an element of modern economics which employs various experiments to provide deeper understanding and contribute to the economic knowledge of how the real world operates. It is sometimes known also as laboratory economics, although next to laboratory experiments it also relies on field experiments and natural experiments. Experimental economics is defined by the research method it applies rather than its object of study. According to Croson (2002), "experimental economics uses controlled human experiments to answer research and policy questions". Levine (2009) emphasises that "experimental economics has certainly taught us where the theory needs strengthening—as well as settling some long-standing methodological issues". Svorenčík (2015, 58), on the other hand, points out that "experimental economics is pervaded by the gradual application of its method to new, previously experimentally unexamined, and often very well-known issues within economics".

Santos (2011) is even more straightforward, claiming that "experimental economics is part of recent mainstream economics, sharing with other emergent research programmes the rejection of fundamental assumptions and commitments of the previously dominant neoclassical economics research programme".

D. Miłaszewicz (✉)
Department of Macroeconomics, Faculty of Economics and Management,
Institute of Economics, University of Szczecin, Mickiewicza 64, 71-101 Szczecin, Poland
e-mail: dmilasz@wneiz.pl

K. Nermend, M. Łatuszyńska (eds.), *Selected Issues in Experimental Economics*,
Springer Proceedings in Business and Economics, DOI 10.1007/978-3-319-28419-4_1

Croson and Gächter (2010) emphasise that experimental economics provides realistic assumptions and regularity to behaviours of individuals, whereas mainstream economics, by means of its own methods, strives to construct interesting models on that foundation so as to describe individuals, groups, markets and economies. Wilkening (2011), on the other hand, argues that "one of the main contributions of experimental economics has been to highlight the importance of adapting institutions, conventions and rules to meet the needs of economic systems".

Beyond defining experimental economics—what was done above—the main aim of this chapter is to supplement some of the remaining chapters of the first part of the book "Selected Issues of Experimental Economics". This chapter also works as a certain link between the other four chapters.

1.2 Additional Remarks to Methodological Considerations

The considerations presented in Chaps. 2 and 4 should be completed with a remark that experimental economics is one of the development directions in behavioural economics which "has come of age" (Croson and Gächter 2010). Its brief history implies that it cannot boast a canon with a long tradition; we have been witnesses to the process of its formation. It is different from traditional economics in the methodology it uses. Traditional economics, despite being a social science, formulates context-free (i.e. without accounting for any institutional, social or cultural factors) analytical theories based on primary unrealistic assumptions. By means of deduction, more and more complex and elegant models were then developed based on these theories. The models were later used to formulate verifiable hypotheses, yet the models themselves were used to test the underlying assumptions. The assumptions are, however, such a narrow depiction of micro-foundations that the models based on them do not provide a good description of reality; they neither show nor explain a variety of real phenomena and choices made. They also proved inefficient in their predictive function. The discrepancy between the actual behaviours and phenomena with such models was explained for a long time as anomalies. It was also argued, as emphasised in Chaps. 2 and 4, that economics could not be an experimental science and should be limited solely to observations and pure theories.

Experimental economics, on the other hand, is based on experimental research. Controlled experiments used as a research method can simulate certain conditions in which economic decisions are made. Natural experiments, too, are experiments performed under certain conditions. Research within experimental economics, just like in the majority of empirical studies, should be oriented at the applicability of its results in the practice of functioning of the economy, society and state. Knowledge which can be used in practice, however, usually involves an interdisciplinary approach, i.e. combination of issues studied by a number of sciences. Experimental economics is no exception—it derives from psychology, sociology, political sciences and other schools of behavioural economics. Economic experiments offering verifiability of the existing economic theories allow construction of more realistic theories and models on the one hand and their verification on the other. As a consequence, experimental economics broadens the research area of traditional economics, enabling researchers to study how cultural and social factors as well as institutional environment affect the functioning of individuals and the entire economy (Miłaszewicz 2011).

Traditional economics defended its research method for a long time and considered experiments as an impossible way of investigating economic reality, whereas experimental economics was seen as one of nonmainstream directions of minor significance. Nevertheless, in spite of all this scepticism, experiments turned out to be useful tools in economics, and since the 1980s experimentalists have made numerous attempts to investigate various problems concerning human behaviour (Sugden 2009, 857). At the beginning, economic experiments (the first ones are discussed in the second part of Chap. 2 presenting a brief history of experimental economics) were not conducted within the great economic models, yet they addressed their foundations, proving that it was possible to perform empirical tests of basic hypotheses concerning individuals. They allowed studying individual human behaviours which were difficult to observe in natural environment; in other words, they referred to the model assumptions of *homo oeconomicus*. This fact is strongly emphasised by Beinhocker (2006) in his book on transformations essential in economics. At the same time, he points out that even though it would be difficult to perform experiments on entire economies, it is possible to experiment "on economies in miniature". He argues that experimental research may be used to study "groups of people and have them bargain with each other, bid in auctions, play economic games, invest in simulated stock markets, go shopping in fake stores, and participate in all sorts of contrived situations to capture specific aspects of economic behaviour" (Beinhocker 2006) This part of his considerations seems to address only laboratory experiments, and so it does not account for the variety of types of economic experiments. Natural experiments may involve the economy as a whole. Examples of such experiments are provided in Chap. 5, including the Volstead Act introducing prohibition in the United States in 1919 (which remained in place till 1933) and known as the Noble Experiment and the ban on the sale of alcohol before 1 p.m. in Poland introduced in 1982 (which remained in place till 1990). Political and economic transition of post-Soviet countries and the German reunification can also be considered as special types of natural experiments on entire economies.

In the last years, the number of laboratory experiments related to economics has been increasing, and they usually tend to go well beyond studying individual decisions. The areas of potential experimental research studies in economics, presented in Chap. 3, show the vast potential for the application of the experimental method in this science. They also indicate departure from the so-called economic imperialism, which is mentioned in Chap. 2 and the change of its relation with other social sciences in the direction of the so-called cooperation, which offers potential benefits related to the tendency of various sciences to diffuse (Brzeziński et al. 2007).

1.3 Features of Good Economic Experiments

The first part of Chap. 3, describing the essence of experiment as a research method in economics, points to its two essential features: intentionality and controllability. Both of these features convey the necessity to diligently design and conduct the experiment so as to obtain results that reliably represent the causal relationships under examination. Krawczyk regards the controllability of variables in the experiment as the first of the principal features of a good experiment (Krawczyk 2012, 22). Also Guala (2008) describes it as a fundamental idea of the experiment and indicates that the control takes place in two important areas:

1. Control over a variable that is changed or manipulated by the experimenter
2. Control over other (background) conditions or variables that are set by the experimenter

Experiments enable the researchers to rigorously control the factors of their choice thus intentionally creating a situation where they can conduct observations in order to test their hypotheses. Therefore, in the course of experimentation, the characteristics of an examined phenomenon are manipulated so that their causal relationships with the remaining characteristics of this phenomenon can be determined and the experimenter can attempt to eliminate the by-factors that can disturb the surveyed relationship (Czarny 2007).

In other words, the essence of the experiment is to measure the influence of an independent variable on a dependent variable, the former typically taking a form of an experimental stimulus. Practically, the number of dependent and independent variables to be used in experimenting is unlimited. Due to the fact that the experiments are focused on determining causal relationships, they should be used for explanatory purposes rather than the descriptive ones (Babbie 2004, 246).

The intentionality of experiments and the controllability of variables are important but just the two of many features of a good experiment. A properly conducted experiment should also ensure the controllability of preferences and random assignment to a treatment group as well as the repeatability, anonymity, abstractness, simplicity and transparency of the experiment itself (Krawczyk 2012, 23–28).

In almost every experiment aimed at testing some theory or hypothesis, it is vital to guarantee the tools to control the agents' preferences.[1] The main difficulty in conducting an experiment is biased, peculiar to every participant (idiosyncratic), evaluation of gains and losses that the experimenter is not directly aware of. Chamberlin, who was the first to face this problem, suggested incentivising agents with payoffs in cash so that their decisions and behaviour on the experimental market could be stimulated only by the adequate monetary rewards they were expecting to receive. Such a way of incentivising the experiment agents called the

[1] The induced-values methodology is employed in economic experiments conducted in laboratories. This methodology is limited by requiring the experimenter to know subjects' motivations, which is impossible in field experiments (Harstad 2011) described in Chap. 3.

induced-values method was applied for the first time by V. Smith (1976) and, in his mind, was a cornerstone of experimental economics (Friedman 2010). The method, subsequently improved by Smith, has become today a standard tool of experimental economics. The use of financial (monetary) stimuli in experimental economics is considered its fundamental principle (Ried 2011). Yet three conditions need to be satisfied in order to make the induced-values methodology bring expected effects (Krawczyk 2012, 24):

1. The monotonic nature of preferences, which means that the agents prefer a reward in cash which is larger rather than smaller
2. Salience, which means that the decisions made by the agents in the course of the experiment are intelligibly for them and directly related with the payments
3. Domination, meaning that the payment received during the experiment is more relevant for the agent than other stimuli

Random assignment of individuals to a treatment group, or randomisation, is another characteristic of a good experiment, and, simultaneously, it is a condition for obtaining reliable results. Laboratory experiments encompass at least two groups of agents, one of them being a treatment group, while the second one is a control. The groups are compared on the basis of a statistical analysis of data obtained in the course of the study. However, for the data to meet the requirement of correct reasoning concerning the causal relationship, the condition of noncorrelation between the experimental variable and the remaining relevant variables must be satisfied. The experimenter is able to ensure the independence of many variables describing the agents' decision-making environment but what is beyond their control are so-called hidden variables which cannot be observed. Their first of all concern is the agents' individual characteristics. The solution to this problem is randomisation which guarantees a high level of probability that in both groups (treatment and control) hidden variables have identical values. The probability that the differences among the surveyed individuals in groups as well as between the groups will be small is growing as the sample is growing in size. It should be noted, however, that randomisation may not be possible in field experiments that differ from laboratory experiments with nonstandard samples (*artefactual field experiments*); application of nonstandard tasks, objects or information (*framed field experiments*); or the requirement that the agents are not aware that they are being tested (*natural field experiments*) (List 2011).

The third feature of a good experiment is its replicability. It means that a given economic experiment can be repeated, and its results will remain comparable to the original findings so that their stability can be confirmed. To this end, the whole research procedure must be recorded (so as to be replicated in future experiments), a specialist software should be used (as it regulates the manner of the agents' interactions), and the participants should be introduced into the nature of the experiment by means of written-down instructions (which exclude any gestures or words uttered by the experimenter that would influence their findings) (Krawczyk 2012, 26). According to List and Rasul (2011, 126), "The ability of other researchers to reproduce quickly the experiment, and therefore test whether the results can be independently verified, not only serves to generate a deeper collection of comparable data but also provides incentives for the experimenter to collect and document data carefully". Yet, it should be emphasised once again that, for purely objective reasons, full replicability of field experiments is not possible.

In the majority of cases, human decisions are conditional upon the question whether they affect the situation of people whose identity is known or unknown to the decision-maker. Therefore, in economic experiments, the assumption should be made that the disclosure of experiment participants' identity, including the experimenter themselves, can have a considerable effect on their behaviour. Hence, the anonymity of both agents taking part in the experiment and the experimenter is another characteristic of a good experiment. This rule also refers to money paid to the participants, which has to be done by third parties. It is driven by a concern to ensure the replicability of the experiment as well as to reduce the experimenter's influence on individuals participating in the experiment (Barmettler et al. 2011). It is particularly important in a relatively common situation when the agents are students who know the experimenter. Yet, it is not in all economic experiments that this condition must be complied with, and research has been conducted on how varying degrees of anonymity and social distance determine decision-making (Charness and Gneezy 2008).

According to Smith (1976), the condition of salience of the induced-values methodology, meaning that the decisions made by the agent in the course of the experiment are comprehensively for them and directly related with their payoff, should result from the simplicity and transparency of the experimental design. These two characteristics of a good experiment imply that the experimenter is confident that the experiment itself is apprehensible to the agents, i.e. that they know the mechanism of the experiment and all the aspects of the decisions they are expected to make. It usually allows to exclude many other explanations of the agents' behaviour without the necessity to explain to them the adopted hypotheses and to suggest the choices they are expected to make (Krawczyk 2012, 27).

Abstraction, or depriving economic experiments of their context, is their traditional and important characteristic. According to many economists, abstraction provides three important benefits: generalisation of experimental results (i.e. greater external validity), better theory testing and better replication (Huff 2014). But contextuality is increasingly essential in experimental research, particularly in so-called applied experiments intended to improve the institutional performance. Another argument for the need to abandon the principle of correctness in experimental economics is economic experiments aiming at explaining human behaviour in areas formerly reserved for sociologists or psychologists and at revealing the diversity of contextually dependent decision-making behavioural patterns. It does not mean, however, that, just like in psychological experiments, the agents can be intentionally deceived.

All the above-mentioned characteristics of a good experiment render the experimental research procedure (its main stages are outlined in Chap. 4) rather complicated. Yet, if the experimental design remains in compliance with this procedure, the results of the experiment raise no objections as for their validity.

Due to the advancement in information technology, the economic experimentation, used to analyse and solve economic problems, is becoming an increasingly popular method of research into most complex economic phenomena.

1.4 Summary

As it has been pointed out in Chap. 4, experiments are regarded as one of the most valuable inference methods in causal analysis. They support causal relationship seeking because the possibility to control the decision-making factors additionally allows to manipulate them in order to determine if and how the induced changes influence the agents' decisions and the research results. Yet, this view, just like many attributes of a good experiment outlined in the previous section, refers to laboratory experiments that, according to Guala (2008), are to some extent "artificial" reality in comparison to what can happen in the "natural" or real world. Croson and Gächter (2010) are of a similar opinion that "like theoretical models, experiments are simplifications of the world. They are equally (or sometimes more) descriptively inaccurate than economic models (. . .) That said, just as descriptively inaccurate theories are useful, descriptively inaccurate experiments are useful as well". This is why the studies focusing solely on laboratory experiments and ignoring the relevance of field experiments of various kinds do not seem to exemplify a proper scientific attitude as it restricts the cognitive potential of the experimental method.

According to Croson and Gächter (2010), economic experiments should be considered a controlled process of generating data, fuelled by economic questions and designed to deliver answers to those questions. These authors argue that economic experiments may be used:

1. To address theories (experiments test predictions, provide behavioural models, refine theories, suggest/construct new theories and serve as measurement tools)
2. To examine regularities from the field (observational data) in a controlled, abstracted setting (can highlight which observed regularities or anomalies are particular to a specific field context and which are generalisable and should be observed in other settings)

Roth (2015), in turn, points out that experimentation would facilitate and improve three kinds of work in economics, which are interestingly called:

1. Speaking to theorists, in other words testing the empirical scope and content of theories (including especially formal theories that might depend on factors hard to observe or control outside the lab) and in particular testing how well and on what domains their quantitative and qualitative predictions might serve as (at least) useful approximations
2. Searching for facts, in other words exploring empirical regularities that may not have been predicted by existing theories, and might even contradict them, but

whose contours, once they had begun to be mapped by experiments, could form the basis for new knowledge and new theories
3. Whispering in the ears of princes, in other words formulating reliable advice, as well as communicating, justifying and defending it

Potential applications of economic experiments indicated by these authors almost entirely overlap with areas of experimental research described in 1998 by Smith (as shown in Chap. 3). It may imply that potential areas of application of economic experiments were defined long ago (given the "length" of the history of experimental economics); the experiments can be used in (nearly) all areas studied within micro- and macroeconomics, and new potential uses emerge within neurosciences (neuroeconomics), biology or physics (Economics needs other sciences 2014; Roth 2015, 31).

Nevertheless, despite the validity of economic experiments as a research method and a certain popularity of their application, Levine and Sheng (2010) finds it impossible that experimental economics has somehow overturned years of theoretical research. What should be emphasised, however, is the existence of strong links between theoretical and experimental research in economics. The application of both methods which expand economic knowledge (next to other forms of research studies, such as observations, simulations or case studies) contributes significantly to our understanding of economic phenomena, decision-making in economic context and analysis of economic policy. A tolerant and constructive dialogue between theorists and experimentalists in economics offers more benefits and generates more knowledge and scientific progress than isolation of the two groups of researchers. In order to raise the quality of this dialogue, Croson and Gächter (2010) developed a list of ten "commandments" for economics, which should be obeyed by both experimentalists and theorists. These principles include (Croson and Gächter 2010) the following:

1. Experimentalists shall not hypothesise after the results are known.
2. Experimentalists shall not criticise theory without suggesting (informally or formally) an improved alternative.
3. Experimentalists shall choose experimental parameters and designs that provide true tests of theories, ideally differentiating them from competing theories.
4. Experimentalists shall replicate and encourage replications, including making your data, instructions and software publically available.
5. Theorists shall not develop models in vain—no one needs a new model for every experimental or observational result.
6. Theorists shall not reject or criticise an experiment simply because its results do not support their theory.
7. Theorists shall respect optimisation and equilibria—not because they are true (as quite a lot of research on bounded rationality has shown) but because they are unique to economics and should not be lightly put aside.
8. Theorists shall consider trade-offs between parsimony and accuracy—we can write extremely accurate theories by adding many degrees of freedom, including saying that "context matters" or "social norms matter", but these theories

need loads of information in order to make a prediction (e.g. what is the social norm) and are thus difficult or impossible to falsify.
9. All economic scientists (theory, experimental or empirical) shall not oversell their results.
10. All areas of science (economics included) need to be tolerant of multiple methodologies.

Harrison (2011) argues that the main merit of experimental economics is that as a result "economics has been improved by being reminded of the heterogeneity of economic behaviour, and the fact that much of the behaviour observed does not fit well with existing models. However, now begins the more serious task of restating, reapplying, and extending the tools of traditional economics".

Experimental economics is in its essence one of the many research methods used in economics. According to Roth (2015), "experimental economics is thriving. It is living up to its promise, although we are also learning, by doing experiments, more about what experiments promise for economics". Since experiments are mutually complementary and are also completed by other forms of economic research, they should gradually become a standard tool used by economists.

References

Babbie E (2004) Badania społeczne w praktyce. Wydawnictwo Naukowe PWN, Warszawa

Barmettler F et al (2011) Big experimenter is watching you! Anonymity and prosocial behaviour in the laboratory. IZA Discussion Paper, 5925

Beinhocker ED (2006) The origin of wealth. The radical remaking of economics and what it means for business and society. Harvard Business School Press, Boston. http://olms1.cte.jhu.edu/olms/data/resource/2631/bein.pdf. Access 11 Sept 2015

Brzeziński M et al (2007) Między imperializmem a kooperacją. Ekonomia a inne nauki społeczne na początku XXI wieku. Paper submitted to the 8th Congress of Polish Economists, Warsaw. http://coin.wne.uw.edu.pl/mbrzezinski/research/KEPfinal.pdf. Accessed 12 Sept 2015

Charness G, Gneezy U (2008) What's in a name? Anonymity and social distance in dictator and ultimatum games. J of Economic Behaviour & Organization 68:29–35. doi:10.1016/j.jebo.2008.03.001

Croson R (2002) Why and how to experiment: methodologies from experimental economics. Illinois Law Review 4:921–946

Croson R, Gächter S (2010) The science of experimental economics. J of Economic Behaviour & Organization 73:122–131. doi:10.1016/j.jebo.2009.09.008

Czarny B (2007) Metodologiczne osobliwości ekonomii. Bank i Kredyt 7:67–77

Economics needs other sciences (2014) An interview with P. Ormerod by S. Stodolak. http://www.obserwatorfinansowy.pl/tematyka/rynki-finansowe/ekonomia-potrzebuje-innych-nauk/. Accessed 14 Aug 2015

Friedman D (2010) Preferences, beliefs and equilibrium: what have experiments taught us? J of Economic Behaviour & Organization 73:29–33. doi:10.1016/j.jebo.2008.09.011

Guala F (2008) Experimentation in economics. In: Mäki U (ed) Elsevier handbook of the philosophy of science, vol 13. Amsterdam, pp 597–640. http://users.unimi.it/guala/Handbook%20Elsevier3.pdf. Access 15 Aug 2015

Harrison GW (2011) The methodological promise of experimental economics. J of Economic Methodology 18(2):183–187. doi:10.1080/1350178X.2011.580135

Harstad RM (2011) Behavioural efficiency I: definition, methodology and demonstration. Discussion Paper 818

Huff SC (2014) When economic experiments can help consumer research. International Business Research 7(5):91–102

Krawczyk M (2012) Podstawy: filozofia metody eksperymentalnej w ekonomii. In: Krawczyk M (ed) Ekonomia eksperymentalna. Wolters Kluwer Polska, Warszawa, pp 17–32

Levine DK (2009) The relationship of economic theory to experiments. http://dklevine.sscnet.ucla.edu/papers/theory-experiment.pdf. Accessed 19 Sept 2015

Levine DK, Sheng J (2010) The relationship of economic theory to experiments. http://dklevine.sscnet.ucla.edu/papers/theoryandexperiment2.pdf.pdf. Accessed 12 Aug 2015

List JA (2011) Why economists should conduct field experiments and 14 tips for pulling one off. J of Economic Perspectives 25(3):3–16

List JA, Rasul I (2011) Field experiments in labor economics. In: Card D Ashenfelter O (ed) Handbook of labor economics, 4A:103–228

Miłaszewicz D (2011) Dylematy polityki ekonomicznej w świetle ustaleń ekonomii eksperymentalnej i neuroekonomii. In: Sokołowski J, Sosnowski M (ed) Polityka ekonomiczna, Prace Naukowe Uniwersytetu Ekonomicznego we Wrocławiu, vol 166. pp. 494–502

Riedl A (2011) Experimental economics. Economic and game theoretic principles in experimental research in the social sciences. Netspar Discussion Papers, 12/2011-109:1–26

Roth AE (2015) Is experimental economics living up to its promise? In: Frechette GR, Schotter A (eds) Handbook of experimental economic methodology. Oxford University Press, Oxford, pp 13–42

Santos AC (2011) Behavioural and experimental economics: are they really transforming economics? Cambridge J of Economics 35(4):705–728. doi:10.1093/cje/beq049

Smith V (1976) Experimental economics: induced value theory. American Economic Review 66 (2):274–79

Sugden R (2009) Can economics be founded on 'indisputable facts of experience'? Lionel Robbins and the pioneers of neoclassical economics. Economica 76:857–872. doi:10.1111/j.1468-0335.2009.00793.x

Svorenčík A (2015) The experimental turn in economics: a history of experimental economics. University of Utrecht, Utrecht School of Economics Dissertation Series, 29. http://papers.ssrn.com/sol3/papers.cfm?abstract_id=2560026&download=yes. Accessed 10 Sept 2015

Wilkening T (2011) Review experimental economics: rethinking the rules. The Economic Society of Australia, Economic Record 87(276):178–181

Chapter 2
Origins of Experimental Economics

Danuta Miłaszewicz

Abstract This chapter addressed the determinants of the formation and development of experimental economics. Its first part discussed the widely accepted definition of economics proposed by Robbins and its consequences to the methodology of economics. Emphasis was placed on those which referred to the applicability of experiments as a method to expand knowledge on economics. The second part of the chapter presented the short history of experimental economics. When describing the first experiments, the development path of experimental economics was carefully analysed, and emphasis was put on its contribution to the theories of both micro- and macroeconomics. The chapter is concluded with a brief summary pointing to the relevance of experimental economics.

Keywords Experimental economic theory • Methodological background

2.1 Introduction

Experiments as a research method and a separate method of empirical study of the real world have been at the foundation of acquiring knowledge in many disciplines of science for more than four centuries. In this context, the tradition of using the experimental research method in economics[1] is relatively new since "the proper construction of a counterfactual control group was not given foundations until the early twentieth century" (List and Rasul 2011).

[1] An interesting approach to presenting the history of experimental economics was proposed by Roth (1993), Guala (2008a, b) and Svorenčík (2015).

D. Miłaszewicz (✉)
Faculty of Economics and Management, Department of Macroeconomics,
Institute of Economics, University of Szczecin, Mickiewicza 64, 71-101 Szczecin, Poland
e-mail: dmilasz@wneiz.pl

K. Nermend, M. Łatuszyńska (eds.), *Selected Issues in Experimental Economics*,
Springer Proceedings in Business and Economics, DOI 10.1007/978-3-319-28419-4_2

Experimental economics derives from both traditional economics and criticism of its assumptions, so when describing the process of formation of experimental economics, one should begin with a brief presentation of economics and its paradigm. The purpose of this chapter is to present determinants of the formation of experimental economics and its short history.

2.1.1 Determinants of the Formation of Experimental Economics

In broad terms, economics may be defined as one of the social sciences which explains how the real world works, its phenomena and economic categories. Among the plethora of definitions of economics, one is particularly noteworthy in its perception of individuals as the subjects and objects of study of this science. This definition, "analytical"[2] in its nature, was formulated by Robbins, who in his essay of 1932 wrote, "Economics is the science which studies human behaviour as a relationship between ends and scarce means which have alternative uses" (Robbins 1932).

This simple, one-sentence definition not only emphasised the relevance of scarcity of resources (means) and effects of shortages, which in those times were at the centre of interest of economics and affected understanding of economic laws and their origins. It also stressed the necessity and purposefulness of choice-making which entailed incurring related opportunity costs. At the same time, this definition pointed to two elements determining the essence of making a choice—alternative character of ends and means (resources). It enabled the normative economics, which had so far been results oriented,[3] to indicate within economic policy alternative ways of affecting economic processes at various stages of the choice-making process.

What is most important from the viewpoint of this study, however, is that in his definition Robbins emphasised the necessity to consider human behaviour as the common foundation for all economic considerations. And although this approach is nothing new in modern definitions of economics, it should be pointed out that Robbins made thus a reference to early views of A. Smith who considered human beings as the main subject of study whose choices were determined by moral and psychological factors. Nonetheless, with the development of economics, Smith's concept of economic man affected by moral sentiments was abandoned in favour of

[2] This definition described economics by indicating a method of analysis rather than pointing to the subject scope. The second method addressed by Backhouse and Medema (2009) was defined by the authors as "classificatory".

[3] It resulted mostly from the former perception of the subject and method of political economics developed by Mill (1966), which in its a priori approach reduced human beings solely to those aspects of their activities which were related to accumulating wealth.

the focus on an individual's benefit as a motive of his or her actions, which—paired with rationality—formed a solid foundation for the development of economics as a science. Nevertheless, it was not the concept of *homo oeconomicus* alone, one of the major paradigms of economics, but also the way of interpreting human behaviour predominant in economic research that became a foundation for methodological discussions and led to a split of this science into orthodox and heterodox economics.

Robbins also made a significant contribution to this. His redefinition of the subject of economics, paradoxically, did not affect the views on the ways of studying human behaviour used in his times. In his essay, Robbins argued that since in reality economic phenomena were very complex and determined by a variety of factors which could not be isolated and measured, observations and experiments could not be treated as a source of economic knowledge (Robbins 1932, 74–79). He also claimed that the basic theses of economic theory should be deduced from the assumption that individuals acted in a rational way in accordance with their consistent preferences[4], and this indisputable fact based on experience did not need to be validated in controlled experiments (Sugden 2009). It follows, therefore, that when explaining how people make choices in reality, there is no need for economic research to refer to results of psychological tests.

Robbins's methodological approach placed him among economists who consider economics as a formal discipline (a priori science based on deduction), where it is deduction that serves as a method to acquire new knowledge and contribute to scientific development rather than induction and experiments which are attributed to natural sciences (empirical sciences based on induction).[5] In the second, extended version of his essay of 1952, Robbins put even more stress on these issues, indicating that propositions of economic theories, similarly to all "pure" scientific theories, should be deduced from a variety of assumptions. According to Hands (2009), who interpreted Robbins's approach, "economics does not study a 'kind' of behaviour but rather studies a particular 'aspect' of almost all human behaviour" (Hands 2009). It follows that the type of ends is irrelevant. They are taken as given. "The ends may be noble or they may be base. They may be 'material' or 'immaterial' - if ends can be so described" (Robbins 1932, 24, 25). In both editions of his essay, Robbins emphasised that knowledge on individual agents is not derived from objective scientific observations from controlled experiments available in sciences but is rather of intuitive, experimental and intersubjective nature.

The above definition of economics was introduced in the time when economics remained under a strong influence of Marshall's economics and the US economy

---

[4] It has become the foundation for standardisation of rationality of actions as the following axioms: completeness (order), reflexivity, transitivity and monotonicity of preferences (Varian 1997, 66–78). These axioms allowed formalisation of economic considerations and have become a foundation for constructing consistent logical models of economic reality, disregarding, however, the real motives behind choices.

[5] This distinction between the two paths to scientific advancement was first made in the seventeenth century by Descartes and Bacon and has been used ever since.

was dominated by institutionalism which derived from empiricism an emphasis on the social and historical aspects determining the course of economic processes. The two trends offered different approaches to understanding and development of economic science. The first one focused on methodological individualism, axiomatisation of rational human behaviours and a normative approach to exploring human behaviour (neoclassical economics and other schools and approaches based on the neoclassical paradigm referred to as orthodox economics). The second trend, which dates back to Smith, was guided by methodological holism and a positive approach to research (Veblen and post-Veblen institutional economics and more contemporary economics of complexity, behavioural economics and experimental economics).

In the time when Robbins proposed his definition, it was met with radical comments approving or criticising both his approach to the role of economics as a science and methodological conclusions drawn from it; it was something entirely different from the contemporary "classificatory" approach. It was the subject matter of most vivid discussions during development of neoclassical economics when marginal analysis was first introduced and "economists began to see themselves as modellers" as a result (Backhousew and Medema 2009). They formulated their models, however, based on unrealistic assumptions.

According to Lypsey (Lypsey 2009), long after Robbins had published his essay, economics was seen as he saw it—as a science on the real world (and choices made in this world) and yet based on intuitively obvious assumptions. Robbins was regarded by many economists as a defender of economics against empiricism (the actual one as opposed to the "armchair empiricism", "common sense empiricism") (Backhousew and Medema 2009). This best-known definition of economics nowadays was not immediately accepted by economists, and it was not until 1960 that it gained broader, although not universal, approval[6] and the economists began to employ their methods to explain problems traditionally considered to be noneconomic (Backhousew and Medema 2009).

The methodological individualism approach presented by Robbins in his essay, characteristic of neoclassical economics and completed by methodological instrumentalism and emphasis on behaviour analysis under equilibrium conditions, was adopted by all approaches within mainstream economics.[7] Nonetheless, neither economic theories arrived at by deduction nor an impressive and technically sophisticated array of models developed and derived from them did meet the predictive function attributed to each science. This isolation of axiomatic foundations of theories and models from reality led to disregarding other noneconomic

[6] Robbinsian definition of economics underlying the formalisation of the theory of economics contributed to the so-called economic imperialism which "is the claim of some economists that the methodology of neoclassical economics has superior scientific qualities and should be adopted by most or all social sciences" (Rothschild 2008). This term was first used by Ralph William Souter in 1933 in response to L. Robbins's essay.

[7] They were named "meta-axioms" and have become a foundation for all the approaches within mainstream economics (Arnsparger and Varoufakis 2008, 19).

factors which did not fit with the concept of rational behaviour of extremely calculating individuals. According to Fine and Milonakis (Milonakis and Fine 2009), mainstream economics focusing on explaining only one type of human behaviour (rational, driven by economic motives) suffered from desocialisation and dehistoricisation.[8] It was met with opposition from many economists promoting a more holistic approach to analysing human behaviour.

According to Hands (2009), Robbins's essay "...is one of the most influential methodological works in twentieth century economics". On the one hand, Robbins's definition implied returning to placing the individual in the centre of the theory of economics. On the other hand, however, the views on subject-related and methodological assumptions, particularly the potential for using experiments, were a reference to Mill, who distinguished social (moral) sciences emphasising that "it is seldom in our power to make experiments in them" (Mill 1836, 146–147). According to Milonakis and Fine (2009), Mill emphasised that, granted that the experimental (a posteriori) method is not available in political economy, the latter has to recourse to deductive (a priori) method. Mill identified also several practical obstacles to using conclusive experiments in economics (Guala 2008a). It was in accordance with the findings of Marshall who contributed to popularisation of mathematics in economics and explained that the dynamics of variables makes it impossible to conduct empirical tests as it is impossible to create experimentally an environment where certain factors are stabilised and the whole system is investigated only in relation to one variable. As a result, the experimental method was found to be impractical, ineffective and—as such—irrelevant in economics. According to Guala (2008b), this approach was commonly accepted till at least the 1980s.

2.1.2 *Birth and Development of Experimental Economics*

Despite a short history, precise identification of the turning point widely recognised as the beginning of using experiments in economics and the date when experimental economics was born seems to be impossible.

Some researchers believe that the first isolated experiment of economic relevance and underlying one of the directions of experimental economics dealing with behavioural aspects of decision-making was a lottery game which inspired the formulation of the so-called St. Petersburg paradox in 1738. It was Nicolas and Daniel Bernoulli who contributed to the decision theory through conducting the experiment on themselves. The experiment (a game of chance) involved tossing a coin.

---

[8] The authors, when revising the evolution of the theories of economics from the times of Ricardo and Smith to contemporary writings, reveal the reasons behind "desocialisation" and "dehistoricisation" of this science (Milonakis and Fine 2009). For more on this topic, see also (Jackson 2013).

The researchers proved that individuals not always made choices which maximised their gains, and they showed the relevance of subjectivism in the evaluation of the same events by different individuals (Zaleśkiewicz 2011, 99). It also laid foundation for formulation of the utility theory and the hypothesis concerning the shape of the utility function and related approach to risk (Kroll and Vogt 2009). This relevance of the St. Petersburg paradox to the development of experimental economics is emphasised by Neugebauer (2010) who shows that it has inspired academics to validate it in various areas of economics for nearly three centuries.

The discussion on the St. Petersburg paradox attracted also von Neumann and Morgenstern, authors of the theory of games and the book *Theory of Games and Economic Behavior* (1944)—fundamental to the development of experimental economics. The problem of rationality of choices presented in this book in the context of the theory of games was based on a set of neoclassical axioms concerning behaviours of an economic man striving to maximise expected utility. This publication is widely recognised as extremely relevant not only to the origins of experimental economics but also to its further changes and to developments in the theory of games and the decision theory. Guala (2008b) argues that it resulted from the fact that the theory of games not only had a significant contribution to the theory of economics but had also been used by many researchers developing various research approaches and methods "to solve scientific, policy, and management problems across the disciplinary boundaries—from conflict resolution in international relations, to group psychology, cybernetics, and the organization of the firm, to name just a few".

Based on the results of numerous experiments conducted using the theory of games, researchers frequently formulated rules later incorporated into the theory of expected utility. The aim of those experiments was to show the reality of decision-making by individuals, i.e. investigate individual preferences and choices. The results usually pointed to a number of inconsistencies in the behaviours of players with the theoretical patterns of optimal behaviour. They also became the foundation for formulating examples which did not validate the postulates of the expected utility hypothesis (e.g. Allais paradox or Ellsberg paradox) nor alternative decision theories. The development of the theory of games resulted also in formulation of so-called business games which have become a significant part of experimental education.

Experimental research was also preceded by the formulation of the prospect theory by Kahneman and Tversky (1979). Their theory explains decision-making under risk, and it questions rationality standards adopted by neoclassical economics and hence also the expected utility hypothesis (Giza 2014). The formulation of the prospect theory laid foundation for development of behavioural finance and won Kahneman a Nobel Memorial Prize in Economic Sciences. He received the prize for integration of findings from psychological studies with economic sciences, particularly those referring to human judgement and decision-making under risk (The Sveriges Riksbank Prize in Economic Sciences in Memory of Alfred Nobel 2002).

The first typical economic experiment which defined the second path to the development of experimental economics is attributed to Edward Chamberlin. While observing imperfections of the market in the process of adaptation to shocks during the Great Depression, he did not stop at publishing in 1933 his *The Theory of Monopolistic Competition*. In order to validate certain theoretical assumptions made in the study, he carried out an experiment among his students (Holt 1993). It involved introducing a certain structure to the market through grouping students taking part in the experiment into buyers and sellers. Providing buyers with private information (written on pieces of paper distributed to students) on the price of placing an order for a good and sellers with information on the costs of its production, he determined the maximum purchase price and the minimum sale price for transactions made by the students. Since the number of transactions was usually above the number defining market equilibrium, the experiment seemed to suggest the invalidity of the neoclassical theory of market equilibrium and proved the existence of imperfectly competitive markets. Chamberlin's experiment is regarded as one of the first experiments testing economic theories.[9] The literature of the subject perceives it as extremely relevant as it opened the door to the importance of induced values and market institutions in experimental economics (Friedman and Cassar 2004). It also contributed to the origin of experimental research in the field of industrial organisation (Holt 1993).

At the beginning of the 1960s, based on the experiment conducted by Chamberlin, Vernon Smith carried out a number of market experiments, introducing to them public information about rates and offers. Buyers and sellers were able to make offers at the same time (the so-called double auction) and were learning throughout the repeated sessions of the experiment (Smith 1962). The results he obtained seemed to prove the validity of the neoclassical theory of prices (Schmidt 2009), and—fascinated by the results—he initiated a long-term revolution, introducing experimental methods to the mainstream economics (Kopaczewski 2013, 113). Next experiments by Smith concerned the operation of other market forms than perfect competition. They also served the purpose of testing various market institutions and regulations. His introduction of "double auction" to market experiments became a model solution used by many later experimental economists (Landreth and Colander 2012).

In one of his publications (1989), Smith admitted to having conducted his first experiment in January 1956. He pointed out, however, that he was neither the first nor the only researcher to have done it, as there had been others conducting experiments at the same time or even earlier. He named several researchers from the United States and Germany whom he considered to be pioneers of experimental economics; they worked independently and almost simultaneously and yet were unaware of each other's work. Next to Chamberlin (Harvard), he also recognised

---

[9] According to Schmidt, however, the experiment was used by Chamberlin as an educational tool revealing imperfections of the neoclassical theory of prices rather than as a strict method to validate the theory (Schmidt 2009).

Hoggatt (Berkeley), Sauermann and Selton (Germany), Shubik (Yale), Siegle and Fouraker (Pennsylvania State) and Friedman (Yale).

Market experiments initiated by Chamberlin and continued by Smith and other experimental economists served testing new instruments of market regulation and contributed significantly, first and foremost, to the development of the microeconomic theory. Smith's achievements were widely recognised, and in 2002 he and Kahneman were awarded a Nobel Memorial Prize in Economic Sciences for employment of laboratory experiments as tools of empirical economic analysis, particularly to investigate alternative market mechanisms (The Sveriges... 2002). V. Smith's contribution to experimental economics is even more substantial. He also contributed to studies on the mechanism of delivery of public goods and promotion of computer technologies—at that time in the phase of development—thus increasing effectiveness of economic experiments, and indicated seven major reasons for using experiments in economics (discussed in detail in Chap. 3) (Smith 1989). It is widely believed that the Nobel Memorial Prize awarded in 2002 established the position of experimental economics and the role of experiments in economic research. Nevertheless, the two Nobelists of 2002 "have different approaches to modelling economic behaviours: Kahneman focuses on the analysis of individual behaviours whereas Smith pays more attention to the aspects of interactions between individuals, establishment of social institutions and collective thinking" (Kopaczewski 2013).

Macroeconomics turned out to be the last bastion of economics resistant to the influence of new tendencies in the use of the experimental method to economic research. Laboratory experiments were not recognised as an appropriate method to validate macroeconomic theories since it was impossible to control the economy so as to analyse the effects of alternative institutions and policies. As recently as the late 1990s, opinions were popular that the experimental method could not be successfully applied to macroeconomics on a large scale. According to Sims (1996), "Economists can do very little experimentation to produce crucial data. This is particularly true of macroeconomics". And in his famous textbook on macroeconomics published one year later, Blanchard (1997) indicated even that "macroeconomists, who want to find out, for example, how changes in the money supply affect aggregate activity cannot perform such controlled experiments; they cannot make the world stop while they ask the central bank to change the money supply".

It turns out, however, that macroeconomists use the laboratory method to investigate problems which have been so far described by theories and complex formal economic models which are validated empirically through observation of real economies. As a consequence, contemporary economic theory separates experimental macroeconomics as a relatively new discipline which "is aimed to use controlled laboratory method to test predictions and assumptions of macroeconomic models and to analyse aggregate economic phenomena" (Chytilova 2013).

According to Duffy (2008), precise origins of macroeconomic experiments are rather not clear, yet he is inclined to believe that they can be traced back to "Lucas's 1986 invitation to macroeconomists to conduct laboratory experiments to resolve macro coordination problems that were unresolved by theory". Chytilova (2014), on the other hand, argues that development of experimental macroeconomics would not have been possible without prior "rational expectation revolution" initiated by Lucas. She also emphasises that "experimental macroeconomics shouldn't be omitted as one of the possible methods in economics, since individual and aggregate outcomes might be assessed".

Expectations play a crucial role in macroeconomics, monetary economics, fiscal policy and finance, and as a result the last decade witnessed a significant increase in the number of laboratory experiments performed to study individual expectation formation, the interactions of individual forecasting rules and the aggregate macro-behaviour they cocreate.[10] In the last two decades, economic experiments were used, in turn, to analyse such major macroeconomic problems as strategic behaviour, coordination issues, optimal lifetime consumption and savings decisions, theories of money, commitment versus discretion and fiscal and tax policies. The experimental method is well suited for studying the implications of different public policies and for inferring unobservable behaviour such as expectations formation (Amano et al. 2014). Selected macroeconomic experiments are presented in Chap. 5.

2.2 Summary

In a relatively short period following Robbins's publication of his essay, set against the effects of the Great Depression and—later—World War II, economics experienced a Keynesian revolution (when writing about "animal spirits", its initiator emphasised the relevance of psychological factors to market behaviours) and an increased significance of the econometric movement (relying on a large number of observations and statistical material derived in this way) and the rapid development of heterodox economics.

Although the mainstream economists strongly defended their research[11] method, the development of unorthodox economics gradually contributed to extending the scope of economic research and eventually also to using experiments to acquire new knowledge in economics, transforming this discipline into one where major advancements and breakthroughs are based on the data gathered from experiments. Guala (2008a, b) found it to be one of "the most stunning methodological revolutions in the history of economics" and considered experimental economics as the protagonist in this revolution.

[10] A more recent review of the literature on this topic and description of certain results of such experiments is offered by Assenza et al. (2014).

[11] Wojtyna believes it resulted from considering certain unorthodox concepts as part of mainstream economics (Wojtyna 2009).

Despite its short history, experimental economics contributed to a fast development of the economic theory, particularly within its behavioural foundations and microfoundations of macroeconomic considerations. At present, experimental economics is considered as one of heterodox approaches to economic research originating in the erosion of traditional economics and forming one school of behavioural economics (Tomer 2007). It is also believed that experimental economics will not formulate its separate paradigm nor will it oust the mainstream economics, yet its results cannot be underestimated (Noga and Noga 2014). It has already given origin to other concepts which are considered part of the mainstream economics (Wojtyna 2009), and the experimental method may become a standard tool for economists.

References

Amano R et al (2014) Recent developments in experimental macroeconomics, Bank of Canada review. www.bankofcanada.ca/wp.../11/boc-review-autumn14-amano.pdf. Accessed 21 Aug 2015

Arnsparger C, Varoufakis Y (2008) Neoclassical economics: three Identifying features. In: Fullbrook E (ed) Pluralist economics, Zed books, London. Cited in: Wojtyna A (2011) Czy w wyniku kryzysu finansowego ekonomia otworzy się bardziej na psychologię? Kozłowski P (ed) Węzeł polski. Bariery rozwoju z perspektywy ekonomicznej i psychologicznej, Instytut Nauk Eko-nomicznych PAN, Instytut Psychologii PAN, Warszawa

Assenza T et al (2014) Experiments on expectations in macroeconomics and finance. In: Duffy J (ed) Experiments in macroeconomics, research in experimental economics, vol 17. Emerald Group Publishing Limited, Bingley, pp 11–70

Backhousew RE, Medema SG (2009) Defining economics: the long road to acceptance of the Robbins definition. Economica 76:805–820. doi:10.1111/j.1468-0335.2009.00789.x

Blanchard OJ (1997) Macroeconomics. Prentice Hall, New Jersey. Cited in: Ricciuti R (2008). Bringing Macroeconomics into the Lab, J of Macroeconomics 30(1):216–237, doi: 10.1016/j.jmacro.2006.06.001

Chytilova H (2013) Methodological considerations of macroeconomic experiments. www.iises.net/download/Soubory/soubory-puvodni/Chytilova.pdf. Accessed 19 Aug 2015

Chytilova H (2014) Experimental macroeconomics, a challenge for the future?. European Scientific J, SPECIAL edition:243–251

Duffy J (2008) Macroeconomics: a survey of laboratory research. Working Papers 334, Department of Economics, University of Pittsburgh

Friedman D, Cassar A (2004) Markets. In: Friedman D, Cassar A (eds) Economics lab: an intensive course in experimental economics. Routledge, London and New York

Giza W (2014) Normatywny wymiar koncepcji homo oeconomicus. In: Zagóra-Jonszta U and Pęciak R (ed) Dokonania współczesnej myśli ekonomicznej: racjonalność - efektywność - etyka. Cz. 1, Problemy teoretyczne. Uniwersytet Ekonomiczny w Katowicach, Studia Ekonomiczne 180:46–54

Guala F (2008a) Experimentation in economics. In: Mäki U (ed) Elsevier handbook of the philosophy of science, vol 13. Amsterdam, pp 597–640. http://users.unimi.it/guala/Handbook%20Elsevier3.pdf. Accessed 15 Aug 2015

Guala F (2008b) Experimental economics, history of. www.2.econ.iastate.edu/tesfatsi/HistoryOfExpEcon.FGuala2008.Palgrave_Long.pdf9. Accessed 16 Aug 2015

Hands DW (2009) Effective tension in Robbins' economic methodology. Economica 76:831–844. doi:10.1111/j.1468-0335.2009.00791.x
Holt CA (1993) Industrial organization: a survey of laboratory research. In: Kagel JH, Roth AE (eds) Handbook of experimental economics. Princeton University Press, Princeton
Jackson WA (2013) The desocialising of economic theory. International J of Social Economics 40 (9):809–825
Kahneman D, Tversky A (1979) Prospect theory: an analysis of decision under risk. Econometrica XLVII:263–291
Kopaczewski T (2013) Recenzja książki Vernona Smitha 'Racjonalność w ekonomii'. Decyzje 20:111–118. doi:10.7206/DEC.1733-0092.14
Kroll EB, Vogt B (2009) The St. Petersburg paradox despite risk-seeking references: an experimental. FEMM Working Paper 4. www.fww.ovgu.de/fww_media/femm/femm_2009/2009_04.pdf. Accessed 18 Aug 2015
Landreth C and Colander (2012) Historia myśli ekonomicznej. PWN, Warszawa
List JA, Rasul I (2011) Field experiments in labor economics. Chap. 2. In: Card D, Ashenfelter O (eds) Handbook of labor economics. Elsevier 4A:103–228
Lypsey RG (2009) Some legacies of Robbins' an essay on the nature and significance of economic science. Economica 76:845–856. doi:10.1111/j.1468-0335.2009.00792.x
Mill J (1836) On the definition of political economy: and on the method of investigation proper to it. Cited in: Milonakis D, Fine B (2009) From political economy to economics. Method, the social and the historical in the evolution of economic theory. Routledge, New York. http://pauladaunt.com/books/From_Political_Economy_to_Freakonomics.pdf. Accessed 15 Aug 2015
Mill JS (1966) Zasady ekonomii politycznej. PWN, Warszawa
Milonakis D, Fine B (2009) From political economy to economics. Method, the social and the historical in the evolution of economic theory. Routledge, New York, http://pauladaunt.com/books/From_Political_Economy_to_Freakonomics.pdf. Accessed 17 Aug 2015
Neugebauer T (2010) Moral impossibility in the St. Petersburg paradox: a literature survey and experimental evidence. LSF Research Working Paper Series 10(174):1–43
Noga M and Noga B (2014) Kultura a ekonomia behawioralna. Studia i Prace Wydziału Nauk Ekonomicznych i Zarządzania 35:155–167
Robbins L (1932) An essay on the nature and significance of economic science. Macmillan, London, https://mises.org/system/tdf/Essay%20on%20the%20Nature%20and%20Significance%20of%20Economic%20Science_2.pdf?file=1&type=document. Accessed 10 Aug 2015
Robbins L (1952) An essay on the nature and significance of economic science, 2nd edn. Macmillan & Co, London [reprint of 2nd ed 1935]
Roth AE (1993) Introduction to experimental economics. In: Kagel JH, Roth AE (eds) The handbook of experimental economics. Princeton University Press, Princeton
Rothschild KW (2008) Economic Imperialism. Analyse & Kritik 30:723–733
Schmidt KM (2009) The role of experiments for the development of economic theories. Discussion Paper 252. http://www.sfbtr15.de/uploads/media/252.pdf. Accessed 18 Aug 2015
Sims CA (1996) Macroeconomics and methodology. J of Economic Perspectives 10:105–120, http://sims.princeton.edu/yftp/jep/mthdlgy.pdf. Accessed 19 Aug 2015
Smith VL (1962) An experimental study of competitive market behaviour. J of Political Economy 70:111–137
Smith VL (1989) Theory, experiment and economics. J of Economic Perspectives 3(1):151–169
Sugden R (2009) Can economics be founded on 'indisputable facts of experience'? Lionel Robbins and the pioneers of neoclassical economics. Economica 76:857–872. doi:10.1111/j.1468-0335.2009.00793.x
Svorenčík A (2015) The experimental turn in economics: a history of experimental economics. Utrecht School of Economics Dissertation Series no. 29. University of Utrecht. http://papers.ssrn.com/sol3/papers.cfm?abstract_id=2560026&download=yes. Accessed 11 Aug 2015

The Sveriges Riksbank Prize in Economic Sciences in Memory of Alfred Nobel 2002. http://www.nobelprize.org/nobel_prizes/economic-sciences/laureates/2002/index.html. Accessed 16 Aug 2015
Tomer JF (2007) What is Behavioral Economics? J of Socio-Economics 36:463–479
Varian HR (1997) Mikroekonomia. Kurs średni. Ujęcie nowoczesne. PWN, Warszawa
Wojtyna A (2009) Współczesna ekonomia – kontynuacja czy poszukiwanie nowego paradygmatu. In: Fiedor B, Hockuba Z (eds) Nauki ekonomiczne wobec wyzwań współczesności, VIII Kongres Ekonomistów Polskich, t. II, PTE, Warszawa
Zaleśkiewicz T (2011) Psychologia ekonomiczna. Wydawnictwo Naukowe PWN, Warszawa

Chapter 3
Sorts and Types of Experiment

Barbara Kryk

Abstract This chapter presents the essence and characteristics of the economic experiment as well as the strong and weak points of its practical use. Moreover, three most commonly applied classifications along with their subclasses are synthetically described. This methodological overview gives the idea how fast this underestimated scientific method has been developing, thus contributing to the advancement of experimental economics. That the constantly changing reality generates demand for new solutions and for new cognitive methods, so the scientific world strives to meet this demand by coming up with new types of experiments or discovering innovative applications of the existing ones.

Keywords Economic • Scientific experiment

3.1 Introduction

The purpose this chapter is presentation the essence and characteristics of the economic experiment as well as the strong and weak points of its practical use. Moreover, three most commonly applied classifications along with their subclasses are synthetically described. This methodological overview gives the idea how fast this underestimated scientific method has been developing, thus contributing to the advancement of experimental economics.

3.1.1 The Essence of Experiment

An experiment is one of the research methods used to verify scientific hypotheses. It is a method that enables researchers to prove their theories empirically. According to Brzeziński (1978), "what proves the maturity of a given empirical

B. Kryk (✉)
Faculty of Economics and Management, Department of Socio-Economic Policy and European Regional Studies, Institute of Economics, University of Szczecin, Mickiewicza 64, 71-101 Szczecin, Poland
e-mail: krykb@wneiz.pl

K. Nermend, M. Łatuszyńska (eds.), *Selected Issues in Experimental Economics*, Springer Proceedings in Business and Economics, DOI 10.1007/978-3-319-28419-4_3

discipline is the extent to which its hypotheses can experimentally tested". Yet, it should be noted that as long as in exact and natural science the (laboratory) experiment is an elementary, effective and reliable research method as well as a primary source of knowledge, in social science, it has long been of marginal importance. As it has been said above, not until recently has the experiment been recognised as a scientific method that can be successfully applied in economics.

The experiment is a procedure providing researchers with an insight into a phenomenon they have manipulated or into changes in these phenomena occurring under controlled conditions in order to draw conclusions concerning its specific properties (Babbie 2013; Karpiński 2006). Hence, the experiment is conducted with a view to learn about facts, objects, phenomena or processes (Czaja et al. 2012). In other words, "the experiment is a process that is designed and created with the aim of observation or the one due to which the observed phenomenon is taking place and the experiment changes its course. To experiment means to operate within such phenomena which we can give rise to or which we can manipulate" (Wendeker 2009; Durlauf and Blume 2010).

In simple terms, the experiment is such a scientific procedure where the researcher attempts to influence the natural course of events or the state of things by modifying their setting on a voluntary and coordinated basis with the intention to observe if and how that course of events has changed following the manipulation with factors. In experimental economics the scientific contact does not end with observation, but it has a considerable effect on the observed reality. Scientists manipulate the reality either directly or indirectly and then register the effects of their intervention. This is related to the fact that the experiment is based on manipulation with some variables, called factors (independent variables), and on observation/measure of dependent variables that, according to the experimenter, can be influenced by this factor (Karpiński 2006). The experimental model is founded on:

- Manipulation with one or more independent variables
- Controlling additional and confounding variables that can affect the results
- Measuring one or more dependent variables which, to the experimenter's mind, is under the influence of a manipulated variable (independent variable)

According to Smith (1998), a Noble prize winner in experimental economics, experiments can be used for:

1. Testing the predictive capacity of theoretical models and finding differences amongst them
2. Finding the reasons for a prediction failure by means of a theoretical model
3. Finding empirical regularities which can become a ground for new economic theories
4. Comparing behaviour patterns in different environments in order to determine the boundary conditions for the applicability of a given theory

5. Comparing institutions
6. Simulating the cause and effect of changes in economic policies
7. Experimenting with new institutions

Generally speaking, experiments can be applied (Krawczyk 2012):

- In basic research aimed at finding permanent and fundamental attributes of human nature (such as the experiments exploring common good-driven human propensity to pay for clean natural environment or in-play strategic interactions)
- In research into more specific questions (e.g. in marketing studies or in testing the effectiveness of individual institutions, such as local governments, courts of law, stock exchanges or market-based instruments, e.g. e-administration)

The above possibilities that experiments offer in scientific studies indicate that there is a strong relationship between these possibilities and the theory of economics, namely, that new hypotheses lead to new experiments, whilst their results set new directions for the development of scientific theories. Experiments may also play a role of a computer simulator, i.e. to suggest a result when we cannot find a solution to a given model.

An experiment features the following advantages (Kuc 2014):

- In the course of an experiment, we can accurately record and observe the triggered phenomena, because when we consciously make them happen, we can take the right measures beforehand to prepare ourselves for the observation.
- In an experimental situation, we can change the conditions, configuration and sequences of these changes, isolate the important factors from others, etc. and, thanks to careful observation of the consequences, single out the factors that are relevant for maintaining some states, thus proving theorems about cause-and-effect relationships.
- An experiment can be replicated, which allows for intersubjectivity and control of the results.

Taking the above into consideration, we can say that in economics, the experiment is in fact the only research technique that permits testing a hypothesis assuming a cause-and-effect relationship.[1] In social studies, however, the experiment is very problematic to conduct due to (1) difficulty in manipulating social phenomena, as such manipulation is an essential condition for an experiment to be successful, and (2) impossibility of replicating an experiment under identical conditions, as replicability is a principal rule in exact and natural sciences.

---

[1] Cause-and-effect relationships between events are relationships that, under conditions of a controlled experiment, lead to an observed sequence of events outlined by a given experiment design (Nowak 1957).

3.1.2 *Types of Economics Experiments*

The main goal of experimental research is to create a situation in which two objects can be compared and then to draw conclusions concerning the similarities or to find the differences between two things. Depending on the degree to which these goals can be accomplished, a distinction is drawn amongst the types of experiments. One of the classification criteria is the environment in which they are conducted. According to this classification, there are two basic types of experiments: the laboratory and the field ones (Fig. 3.1).

In a laboratory (classical) experiment, respondents make economic decisions in controlled circumstances, which is a vital condition of methodological soundness. Such a survey is conducted in an artificial setting which has been solely created for the purpose of a given study. In the strictest approach, it means that decisions are made anonymously and players cannot communicate. To avoid a framing effect, they choose amongst artificial alternatives that are presented almost by the book. What is characteristic of this type of study is the fact that no real market entities or elements are involved. The situation created is purely hypothetical and reminds a game where a scientist is seeking appropriate values of parameters and their interrelations that will allow them to move as close as possible towards their goal. Having completed the experiment, the players receive a certain sum of money, the amount of which is determined by the quality of the player's decisions, which means the better the decisions, the larger the money.[2] This type of experiment offers the strictest control over the environment and the institutions, i.e. over the effects of the experiment.

A classical experiment is based on a causal response. The variable Y is compared between two groups Z1 and Z2 that are observed in two time periods t1 and t2. Between t1 and t2, one of the groups is exposed to manipulation.[3] The groups are selected in such a way that in the time t the differences regarding the analysed

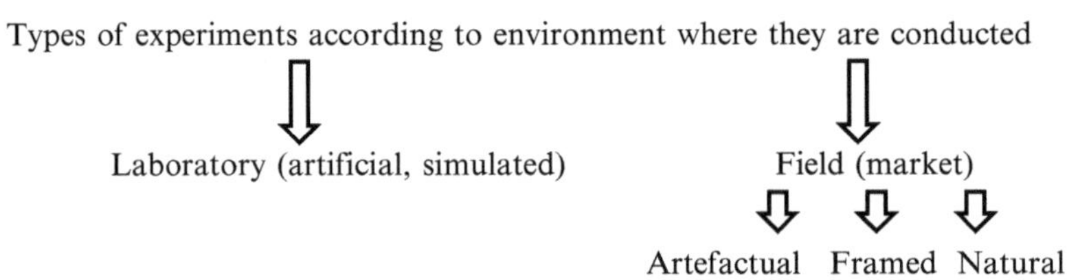

Fig. 3.1 Classification of experiments according to their environment (Source: own study based on (Harrison and List 2004; Kopczewski and Malawski 2007).

[2] It is worth remembering that the goods used in laboratory experiments are usually artificial, abstract and virtual and that their value is determined by the investigator.

[3] Observation of two groups is conducted in order to compare them in reference to Y, whilst observations in two time periods enable the experimenter to find out if a properly conducted interference with the factor X has caused a change in the treatment group.

variables are the least significant. Such unification, as well as reliable results, are achieved through randomisation, or random assignment to reference groups (of specified characteristics) and experimental settings, according to the probability theory. Owing to this, both groups are regarded as representative for the same population. It also eliminates the contamination of uncontrolled variables with a dependent variable. In this type of test, scientists strive to unify the real-life environment of the experiment.

According to Smith (1994), the laboratory experiment is defined by three elements:

- Environment (controlled economic setting), including initial funding and specified costs that motivate a respondent to take part in the exchange. Control is administered by means of money rewards in order to obtain a specific configuration of costs and values.
- A group of institutions that define the language of communications exchanged in an artificial laboratory environment that imitates the real-life market. It is a set of rules providing information how to structure, accept an offer, conclude a deal, etc.
- The observed behaviour which is a function of variables defined by the two aforementioned elements, i.e. the environment and the institutions.

What is an advantage of the laboratory experiment is the fact that it can be replicated in an identical form.[4] If the effects remain the same, the results are thereby confirmed. Also, if the experiment is conducted in several time intervals, these effects become a regularity, and the ongoing changes are easier to study.

This type of scientific observation is very time-, cost- and labour-intensive. However, if methodological soundness has been maintained, the experiment findings will provide evidence for refuting or establishing the validity of a hypothesis. Despite its advantages, the laboratory experiment is not always appropriate to the situation that it is supposed to explain. For example, in development studies on underdeveloped countries, where institutions are weak and the behaviour of market participants is far from the *homo oeconomicus* standards, the classical experiment may prove ineffective and fail to provide reliable results. This is where field experiments come in.

Field experiments are conducted in settings that are natural for the sampled individuals, whilst being well defined and controlled. Ideally, a field experiment should be designed so as to keep its subjects unaware of their participation. The observed decisions are made in a natural environment and everyday context. Such a setting allows the situation to be more realistic—more elements specific for the simulated social situation can be preserved, which is important when the investigation does not aim at verifying some general theory but its purpose is to optimise an existing institution or to make the best possible decision in the existing circumstances. Field

[4] The experimenter is obliged to guarantee the same experiment conditions and the same level of factors used for manipulation.

experiments usually give access to a more diversified sample. What is more, field experimenters can offer higher compensation to participants than in laboratory tests.[5] The advantage of field experiments over the laboratory ones is the fact that their outcomes are more reliable when relating to a specific context, which makes conclusions concerning the nature of a given economic reality much easier to be drawn. Additionally, in the case of market studies, the problem of selection bias disappears as the subjects are integral parts of the observed environment.

One of the categories of field experiments is artefactual field experiments which are the same as laboratory experiments, but instead of a randomised sample, their subjects are individuals associated with the observed environment.

Another type of field experiments is framed experiment which is set within the field context. The examples would be social experiments or valuation of goods with no market price by means of the economic value. Finally, there is the third type of market experiments called natural field experiments that combine the benefits of real-life observations with randomisation. Their subjects voluntarily undertake tasks assigned by experimenters, often not knowing that they are the participants in an experiment. Natural field experiments are used to create institutional policies supporting socio-economic development (Czaja et al. 2012; Friedman and Sunder 1994).

Preparation of a field experiment requires from scientists more intellectual effort in comparison to a laboratory experiment which is conducted according to a fixed pattern. What is more, the very execution of a field experiment can be challenging as (a) subjects' behaviour can be less observable than in a laboratory, (b) the course of field testing (e.g. the subjects' behaviour) is less controlled and (c) there is a risk of ethical dilemmas. On the other hand, the costs of a market experiment are lower, and a target group is easier to reach.

Experiments can also be classified according to testing techniques. This classification encompasses two groups of experiments: with one or with many variables. Both of them can be divided further into subgroups, as seen in Fig. 3.2.

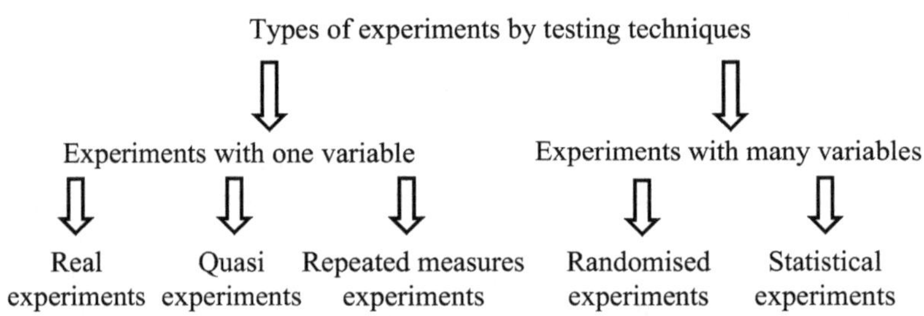

Fig. 3.2 Classification of experiments according to testing techniques (Source: own study based on (Babbie 2013).

[5] It is worth noting that in the case of a field experiment, the experimenter deals with real goods of a certain natural value, usually not known to them, such as satisfaction from supporting earthquake survivors or from making a handmade patchwork quilt.

Real experiments are procedures with a real number of measures. In contrast to quasi-experiments, they offer a chance of eliminating the interference of random factors into the investigated phenomenon because measures are taken before and after the introduction of an independent variable. This provides an opportunity to define precisely how this variable affects the phenomenon. Real experiments fall into several categories:

- One-group with two measures—e.g. measuring effects of changing prices or packaging; they are prone to error.
- Two-group, stimulated—used in advertising studies; an independent variable is an advertising campaign, and measures are performed by means of surveys and interviews. The measured characteristic is the buyer's attitude towards a given product. This type of experimental design is sensitive to uncontrolled factors and subjects' response.
- Two-group with four measures—just as the two experimental designs mentioned above, they are used to examine such issues as the effectiveness of price modifications, promotions, sales techniques, packaging, etc. Thanks to the number of measures this experiment type is more accurate. The use of a control group eliminates all the errors, except for the one resulting from changes made in the constitution of the control group.

A quasi-experiment is an experimental design which lacks random assignment to treatment, thus not being a "proper" experiment. For a study to be experimental, its participants must be granted an equal chance to experience the same treatment conditions (designed by the experimenter), and the assignment to a given treatment condition should depend solely on a random choice. This rule, however, is often ignored. Such an experimental design is called a quasi-experiment. There are several types of quasi-experiments:

- One-group with one measure, e.g. the measure of the effectiveness of promoting a given good by determining the fluctuations in its sales; such a measure is susceptible to many errors associated with the interference of external factors.
- Two-group with two measures, used for, e.g. examining the effectiveness of an advertising campaign or, less frequently, for measuring the modification of prices, packaging or sales methods. In this case the most serious mistake is to change the composition of the group.

Repeated measures experiments differ from the real experiments in the number of measures. The more measures, the less interference of adventitious factors. Due to a larger number of comparisons, the conclusions from the study are more precise and less contaminated with errors. This type of experimental design can take a form of:

- One-group repeated measures experiments used in panel research. In contrast to one-group/two-measure models, the measures are taken before and after the introduction of a variable.

- Two-group repeated measures experiments used, for example, to examine buyers' preferences or the changes in the market share as well as in areas similar to those addressed by real and quasi-experiments. This experimental design is a variation of the two-group/four-measure model. Due to an extended number of measures, they provide very accurate conclusions.
- Solomon design (controlled, ideal design) used in situations similar to a two-group/four-measure experiment. It is one of the best tests, yet it is not very popular due to its time-consuming character and high costs of implementation.

Randomised experiments are the experiments that can be replicated. They are based on the probability theory and can follow:

- A fully randomised design where treatment and control groups are large; we can introduce an independent variable in the control group. Some examples include its use in marketing studies.
- A stratified randomization design where a collective entity is divided into homogenous strata according to specific criteria or bound variables. Treatment and control groups are randomly selected in such proportions so that their structure can reflect the structure of the whole collective entity. Due to the abundance of criteria, such experiments are used in, e.g. marketing studies, studies on the quality of life or on consumer behaviour.

Statistical experiments can take a form of:

- The Latin square,[6] which makes it possible to simultaneously control two bound variables, thus leading to a certain distribution of independent variables. When designing this type of experiment, it is essential to make sure that both the bound variables are divided into an identical number of groups. The Latin square as a statistical method can be used in a great variety of economic studies.
- The factorial design[7] is used when there is a need of measuring two or more independent variables having several values each. The purpose of such an experiment is to reduce a large number of random variables to a smaller set, which can be achieved by assuming that some groups of random variables represent the variability of the same factors, i.e. random variables in a given

[6] A Latin square of order n is a square matrix of order n with numbers given by a set $\{1,2,3,\ldots,n-1,n\}$, where no row or column contains the same number twice. Latin squares are used in statistical experimental planning. Sometimes, instead of a set of $\{1,2,3,\ldots,n\}$ we talk about n values. The Latin square analysis was pioneered by Leonhard Euler, who used Latin characters as symbols (Penszko 2011).

[7] The factorial analysis is a statistical method used to find structures in a set of random variables. Two kinds of approach are used in this analysis: the exploratory factor analysis (AFA), where initially unknown factors are determined by means of an analysis of random variable values, and the confirmatory factor analysis (CFA), where we assume the existence of a specific set of factors and, thanks to the analysis of random variable values, we test whether our assumption is viable. Then we estimate the parameters of our model (StatSoft 2006).

group are interdependent to some extent. This design is used in marketing, product management or in the decision theory.[8] The factorial design is associated with structural equation modelling, i.e. with the class of multivariate, parametric statistical models which allow testing scientific hypotheses of great potential complexity of relations amongst variables.[9]

Taking into consideration the scope of investigation, Kopczewski and Malawski (2007) distinguished several types of experiments involving:

1. Individual decisions—their purpose is to confirm and describe deviations from the principal economic concept of *homo oeconomicus*.[10] "The most significant forms of irrational behaviour include basing a decision on the framing of the decision problem, and the certainty effect, which means that in the presence of risk exaggerated importance is systematically and irrationally given to minor changes in likelihood that is close to zero or to one, while the same changes are ignored in the case of high likelihood".
2. Small games (simple games)—games involving a few participants and typically having a simple structure (prisoner's dilemma or extensive-form games). Related laboratory experiments show that the course and results of these games diverge from theoretical predictions as the players are driven not only by the amount of payment (the principle of reasonableness) but also by its comparison to payments received by other players.
3. Social dilemmas—where the analysed objects are public good games (referring to, for instance, theory of common goods by Ostrom) and the free riding phenomenon. The existing experiments in this field have shown that real-life human behaviour of people sponsoring public goods stand in contradiction to the standard economic theory.
4. Market—in the meaning of market effects understood generally rather than as individual decisions.

The very fact that there are so many classifications of economic experiment types implies how fast these methods develop, even though until recently they were regarded useless in economic studies. We can say that the constantly changing reality generates demand for new solutions and for new cognitive methods, so the scientific world strives to meet this demand by coming up with new types of experiments or discovering innovative applications of the existing ones.

---

[8] The factorial design is very popular in psychological studies, especially in the events structure analysis conducted by means of surveys.

[9] The strong points of this approach are the opportunity to reflect freely path dependencies amongst the variables as well as to reflect the theoretical construct as a delayed variable (Bagozzi and Yi 2012).

[10] We may consider Laibenstein's Homo RS model as the pioneering experiment of this type.

3.2 Conclusion

The very fact that there are so many classifications of economic experiment types implies how fast these methods develop, even though until recently they were regarded useless in economic studies. We can say that the constantly changing reality generates demand for new solutions and for new cognitive methods, so the scientific world strives to meet this demand by coming up with new types of experiments or discovering innovative applications of the existing ones.

References

Babbie E (2013) Podstawy badań społecznych. PWN, Warszawa
Bagozzi RP, Yi Y(2012) Specification, evaluation, and interpretation of structural equation models, Vol. 40. Issue 1: 8–34
Brzeziński J (1978) Elementy metodologii badań psychologicznych. PWN, Warszawa
Czaja S, Becla A, Włodarczyk J, Poskrobko T (2012) Wyzwania współczesnej ekonomii. Difin, Warszawa, pp 107–118
Durlauf SN, Blume LE (2010) Behavioural and experimental economics. Palgrave Macmilian, New York
Friedman D, Sunder S (1994) Experimental methods. A primer for economists. Cambridge University Press, New York
Harrison GW, List JA (2004) Field experiments. J Econ Lit 42:1009–1055
Karpiński J (2006) Wprowadzenie do metodologii nauk społecznych. Wydawnictwo WSPiZ, Warszawa
Kopczewski T, Malawski M (2007) Ekonomia eksperymentalna: wprowadzenie i najnowsze badania. Decyzje 8:79–100
Krawczyk M (2012) Podstawy: filozofia metody eksperymentalnej w ekonomii. In: Krawczyk M (ed) Ekonomia eksperymentalna. Wolters Kluwer Polska, Warszawa
Kuc BR (2014) Badania empiryczne i ich znaczenie w pracy naukowej. http://wydawnictwoptm.pl/blog/wp-content/uploads/2014/01/B.-R.-Kuc-Badania-empiryczne-i-ich-znaczenie.pdf. Accessed 20 Jun 2015
Nowak S (1957) Casual interpretation of statistical relationship in social research. Academic Press, New York
Penszko M (2011) Czekoladki i zbiory krytyczne. Świat Nauki 9(241):70–72
Smith VL (1994) Economics in the Laboratory. J Econ Perspect 8(1):113–131
Smith VL (1998) The two faces of Adam Smith. Southern Economic J 65(1):2–9
StatSoft (2006) Elektroniczny Podręcznik Statystyki PL. Krakow. WEB: http://www.statsoft.pl/textbook/stfacan.html. Accessed 10 July 2015
Wendeker A (2009) Badania eksperymentalne. http://wiedzaiedukacja.eu/archives/19548. Accessed 20 June 2015

Chapter 4
Concept and Inference Based on Experiments in Economics

Jerzy Boehlke and Magdalena Osińska

Abstract The chapter concerns the concept of experimentation in economics. The perspective of economic methodology is taken as a starting point for the experiment design. Then types of experiments are discussed along with their advantages and disadvantages. The role of the concept of causality in experimentation in economics is pointed out. A natural experiment is of our main interest. Hence, the methods of inference within natural experiments are briefly discussed. Some examples illustrate the methodological background.

Keywords Experimental economics

4.1 Experimentation in Economics: The Methodological and Historical Background

Experimental economics is the application of experimental methodology to study economic issues. Its rapid growth since the second half of the twentieth century is, on the one hand, the consequence of the still ongoing dispute among philosophers and research methodologists over the status of the humanities and social sciences and their relationship with the natural sciences, while on the other hand, of the substantial progress of quantitative research as well as of the statistical and econometric tools of analysis, mathematics and computer simulation methods applied in it. A dominating opinion in the subject literature is that in the last few decades both of these reasons have played a significant role in the light of research practice.

J. Boehlke
Department of Economics, Faculty of Economic Sciences and Management, Nicolaus Copernicus University in Toruń, Gagarina 13a, 87-100 Toruń, Poland
e-mail: jurekbo@umk.pl

M. Osińska (✉)
Department of Econometrics and Statistics, Faculty of Economic Sciences and Management, Nicolaus Copernicus University in Toruń, Gagarina 13a, 87-100 Toruń, Poland
e-mail: emo@umk.pl

K. Nermend, M. Łatuszyńska (eds.), *Selected Issues in Experimental Economics*,
Springer Proceedings in Business and Economics, DOI 10.1007/978-3-319-28419-4_4

According to Guala, experimental economics is a methodological revolution in this scientific discipline (Guala 2012, 528). Therefore, it ought not be combined with the next direction of economic thought encompassing new areas for research or alternative approaches to traditional problems of economics. It is a reflection on the role, opportunities, conditions, types and results of the application of an experiment in economic research. The starting point for this reflection is always seeking answers to the question of whether economics, as an empirical science, is also an experimental science, that is a science in which the experiment is a tool of scientific cognition. As is commonly known, until the second half of the twentieth century economics used to be considered as a non-experimental discipline, though this fact should not be related merely to its affiliation with social sciences. It should be emphasised that for a long period of time also biology, physics and astronomy were considered to be non-experimental. Within research methodology the answer to the above formulated question usually involves a discussion on the dominant in the twentieth-century empirical sciences cognition model based on the acceptance of the following views: critical realism (experience is not a determining criterion of truth) and critical rationalism (there is no complete and certain knowledge in the understanding of the classic definition of truth). What is meant here is the hypothetico-deductive model of scientific explanation. It was developed as a result of the criticism by Poincaré, Duhem, Quine and, above all, by Popper (1959) of the positivist approach to the philosophy of science. In literature it is usually associated with the version presented by Hempel and Oppenheim (1948, 1965). This model rejects inductionism, which manifests itself in denying induction as a legitimate tool of scientific knowledge due to its incompleteness (there is always a relatively small number of observations in relation to the potentially possible number) and assigning its auxiliary role at the stage of organising facts with a view to formulating the premises for the hypothetico-deductive method. It is proposed that inductionism should be replaced by hypothetism and reductionism, while verificationism, in turn, is opposed to falsificationism (Filozofia a nauka 1987, 226–235; Hajduk 2007, 116–118 and 163). In addition, the Hempel-Oppenheim model assumes the thesis that all processes of scientific cognition have a common logical structure. As Blaug claims (1995), every scientific explanation includes at least one general law and a description of significant initial and boundary conditions (i.e. the explanans) that are the premises which, with the application of the rules of deductive logic, always provide the explanandum—the claim relating to the fact to be explained. A general law is universal and is a statement taking the following form: every time when phenomena A occur, they are accompanied by phenomena B. It may take a deterministic form of phenomena concerning individual B or statistical, relating to the classes of phenomena B (Blaug 1995, 39–40). A scientific explanation can be accepted only when explanans are true. Hempel and Oppenheim suggest that it follows the same rules of deductive logic that forecasting does (the thesis of symmetry). The only difference is that explanation, in contrast to forecasting, is lagged relative to the phenomenon studied. In the case of explanation, the starting point is the phenomenon being explained and finding at least one universal law that along with the initial or boundary conditions, is the logical premise of its statement. As regards forecasting, the starting point is a universal law and a set of initial conditions under which, applying the rules of deductive logic, statements are drawn up relating to the unknown phenomenon. Therefore, in both cases the explanans are related to the occurrence of the explanandum within a general law. It should be stressed that general laws are not a consequence of inductive generalisations of a limited number of cases studied, they are hypotheses being verified within the testing process of forecasts relating to specific facts. As turned out in research practice, identifying initial conditions or limitations that make up the explanans is of significant importance. According to a well-known Duhem-Quine thesis, in the cognitive process every theory must be tested considering restrictive conditions. This means that, in contrast to the traditional approach to validating laws, hypotheses, rules and scientific theories must be tested as a whole. So you cannot refute a single theory in an exclusive way. All tests applied to a theory require auxiliary hypotheses that are necessary to be able to interpret observations as their tests. Therefore, every theory test is a combination of the test of the main hypothesis and of auxiliary hypotheses, which prevents direct falsification of any implications of the theory under test. And conversely, every positive test of the theory might be undermined by an appropriate revision of the grounds on which the theory has been built (Smith 1994, 126–128). This holistic point of view was the basis for the rejection of the idea of the existence of the so-called experimentum crucis (a cross experiment, a conclusive one) that would allow choosing a true theory from a set of alternative theories (a positive experiment) or indicating a false theory (a negative experiment). It should also be noted that the authors and proponents of the hypothetico-deductive model accepted to a lesser or greater extent the main idea of conventionalism, according to which the recognition of statements (theory) de-pends on the terminology agreements adopted previously, i.e. conventions. These conventions are accepted not because they are true but for other reasons, such as, for instance, simplicity and elegance of developed theories, and organisation of thinking threads. Due to conventions, axioms and theoretical rules are definitions of the terms contained therein. However, conventions are not arbitrary agreements. They are not only explicitly compelled by the facts. Prominent philosophers of science, such as Carnap, Neurath, Popper, Kuhn, Lakatos, Fayerabend accepted conventionalism to some extent, which on the basis of the hypothetico-deductive model is now considered essential for the proper interpretation of empiricism.

For the proponents of the hypothetico-deductive model a scientific theory is always a tool of explanation and prediction, and not a tool used to describe the world (Woleński 2000, 150). The main concern is not an objective picture of reality, but the relation of the scientific theory to the image of the world and its properties. There is no theory beyond the facts. This opinion is referred to even as the fundamental hypothesis of science (Hollis 2003, 82). As is commonly known, Friedman (1953, 33) formulated and justified it for the purpose of economics. The choice of a theory that is better than others results from its greater explanatory power, simplicity, elegance, language and accurate forecasts. Acceptance of the hypotheses being one possible interpretation of events is the result of tests carried out and concerning attempts to reject them on the basis of accepted experience data. Hypotheses are the creation of the mind intending to explain a certain phenomenon, and not empirically verifiable truths about the world. According to Popper, the model in question does not apply the criterion of authenticity.

It was not a coincidence that this reflection on the conditions and the role of the experiment in the process of scientific cognition developed when strengthening and then in the period of the domination of the hypothetico-deductive model accepted in the philosophy of science as a methodological standard in research practice of empirical science. Based on this model methodological postulates and directives relative to the applicability of experiments in empirical sciences, including economics, are derived and justified. The consequence of the Duhem-Quine thesis for the considerations on experiments in science are nowadays frequent references made to causality analysis (Guala 2012, 536–539). It is worth recalling that although the experiment as an instrument of knowledge, in particular as a criterion for the settlement between hypotheses, appeared in the writings of Galileo and Newton (i.e. a cross experiment—two different hypotheses remain in such a relationship that when one of them is validated, the other is disproved). Also Mill, Herschel followed Galileo and Newton in that respect, and its classic concept presented by Bernard. However, only in the second half of the twentieth century, methodologists of economics gave a wider support for the opportunities and the need for using experiments in the process of cognition. As Kalinowski rightly says (2008, 237–241), the earlier lack of strong acceptance of experiments in economics is mainly due to disputes concerning methodological monism. Supporters of applying the experiment as an explanation tool should be in favour of methodological monism calling for the unity of cognition methods in science. While the proponents of this position recognise the need for the empirical verification of the effects of cognition, its opponents, referring to the arguments justifying the methodological differences of the humanities and social sciences, emphasise the inadmissibility of an empirical test of forecasts built on the basis of economic theories. Traditionally, the main argument in favour of methodological dualism is the doctrine of Verstehen recognised by the neo-Kantian philosophy. It says that the social sciences are based on the cognition of direct participants of the events that constitute the subject of their research. For this reason, the weakness of experiments in economics is the deformation of the cognition effects through the interference of the knowing subject (Hajduk 2007, 119).

Disputes between supporters of methodological monism and dualism have a strong tradition in the history of economic thought. A compromise proposal that is compatible with the hypothetico-deductive model was introduced by the already mentioned Friedman (1953). Using the division of normative and positive economics proposed by Hume he concluded that the latter can provide objective knowledge about the world in the sense adopted by the natural sciences. Therefore, there are reasons for recognising methodological monism (Friedman 1953, 2–5). According to Friedman, the only acceptable verification of the probability of hypotheses is their confrontation with experience data. Therefore, there is room for experiments, be it a natural experiment. A moderate view on the applicability of experiments in economics is represented by Machlup (1978, 139–141). It seems that the opinion expressed by Kalinowski should be doomed reasonable. Kalinowski states that a supporter of the use of experimental economics should be at least a moderate opponent of methodological dualism and may not be an orthodox empiricist, assigning the experiment the role of a summative falsifier of hypotheses posed in economic terms (Kalinowski 2008, 240). This position is shared today by most proponents of the use of experiments in economic research. They accept that the experimental method is not a sufficient criterion for assessing the logical consistency and correctness of the theory. It can, however, help to identify the degree of the resistance of a specific theory to the deviations from its adopted explicit and implicit behavioural, institutional and formal assumptions.

As regards the indicated earlier second reason for the use of experiments in the empirical sciences, particularly in economics, that is the development and application of methods of mathematical statistics, econometrics and computer simulations, it should be pointed to increasing numbers of laboratories, academic journals on experimental research, scientific publications and reports on conducted experiments. This has led to an increase in the prestige of experimental economics, as evidenced by the Nobel Prize awarded to Smith and Kahneman. The experiment makes it possible to answer a precisely formulated question and the development of quantitative and simulation methods, and laboratory practices cause certain detachment of research practice from methodological disputes on it. The obtained results of experimental research are the driving force of their further development. It is also an important opportunity to conduct experimental research of interdisciplinary nature (e.g. economics and psychology). As stated by Kalinowski, an empirical test of an empirical model does not determine its truth or falsity, but its power, understood in the sense of relevancy in the context of a broad class of games, or in terms of economic and statistical significance, which is manifested in the fact that the factors on which the model was based have a significant quantitative impact (Kalinowski 2008, 241).

Plott (1991, 901–919) indicates six phenomena which are a manifestation of the already-mentioned at the beginning of the chapter "methodological revolution" in economics that has occurred in recent decades and which causes the increasing use of the experiment both in theoretical and applied research:

1. Changes in the way of formulating questions by economists—the inspiration for the new studies goes beyond theory and increasingly these are ambiguous results of previous experimental studies and difficult to understand non-laboratory observations in space and time.
2. Making several significant scientific discoveries (e.g. Kahneman and Tversky's Prospect theory) is a stimulus for the intensification of experimental research.
3. The advancement of economic theories, in particular the recognition of information as a key variable in economic models.
4. The development of laboratory experiments confirming the usefulness of theory and research applications.

5. The discovery of various paradoxes of thinking and human behaviour in decision-making (e.g. The Ellsberg Paradox).
6. The Say's law of experimental methods (the emergence in practice of experimental research within certain methods creates demand for new ones).

4.2 Types of Experiments in Economics

Generally, in economics two ways of observing data are applied, i.e. traditional observation (such as, for instance: survey, census, statistical observation) and experiments. The advantage of experimental methods includes the possibility of the isolation of a variation of exogenous factors ("treatment variables") and observing their impact on the output in interest. In contrast to observational methods, in which changes in exogenous and endogenous variables are frequently simultaneous, a well-defined experiment allows isolating a treatment variable (Cameron and Trivedi 2005, 48–49). However, a very cautious approach should be adopted when the results of experiments in economics are interpreted. The reason is that, excluding a few situations, an experiment in economics cannot be repeated under the same conditions. This is due to the human factor and due to the changing environment. Over 20 years ago Davis and Holt (1993) pointed out three main sources of experimentation in economics. These are the following: market experiments, game theory and individual decision-making. Although they do not cover all possible areas, it may be useful to realise that experiments were first introduced in microeconomics. Their application was also extended to macroeconomic issues.

Several ways of experimentation are possible. One of them is a laboratory experiment when a small group of volunteers are examined for economic behaviour, but the limitations of such an approach in economics are obvious. The second way is a randomised controlled experiment when the treated and control groups are chosen to show the impact of a treatment variable when a treated group is compared with a control one. The experiment can be randomised in such a sense that those individuals who want to participate in the experiment are located in one of two groups by random. Sometimes, however, the circumstances exhibit natural conditions for economic experimentation. Such a case is called a natural experiment.

A natural experiment is defined as an observational study where assignment to treatment or control is as if randomised by nature (Freedman 2009, 6). Natural experiments occur when "nature" gives a good basis for identification. Thus, they are considered basically in terms of the policy discontinuities, external shocks and disasters. In the opposite to the experimental methods such as randomised controlled trials or quasi-experimental design studies researchers must rely on a natural choice of the treatment groups and the control groups, which are examined as an effect of natural experimentation. It is very important than in natural experiments the observed changes are considered as exogenous. This fact simplifies the methodology applied for inference for the impact of a given change on the defined output.

Shadish et al. (2002, 12) defined five types of experiments and called them "the vocabulary of experiments".

1. Experiment: a study in which an intervention is deliberately introduced to observe its effects.
2. Randomised experiment: an experiment in which units are assigned to receive the treatment or an alternative condition by a random process such as the toss of a coin or a table of random numbers.
3. Quasi-experiment: an experiment in which units are not assigned to conditions randomly.
4. Natural experiment: not really an experiment because the cause usually cannot be manipulated.
5. Correlation study: usually synonymous with a non-experimental or observational study; a study that simply observes the size and direction of a relationship among variables.

On this basis another classification may be proposed. Due to the object of experimentation, the experiments in economics can be divided into two groups: "real life" experiments: the experiments designed for individuals (consumers, producers, firms, investors, decision-makers and so on) when human decisions are observed and model-based experiments; the experiments using models (deterministic or stochastic) as tools of observing what may happen in real life when specified conditions are changed. The former group is a limited one when the problem of repeatability is concerned, and it generates ethical problems with experimentation while the latter is free of such boundaries. Yet, it involves another problem when the limitations of the model as a reflection of real processes are examined.

This simple classification is very helpful in defining and distinguishing a type of an experiment in economics. It seems to cover all types of experiments that are present in economics. However, some researchers use these terms in a misleading way when the observational studies are called "an experiment" (see Meyer 1995 for a comment).

4.3 Experiments and Causal Inference

For many years economics has been perceived as a non-experimental science. Although the process of economic cognition was sometimes developed in a way of an experiment, in the dominating mainstream economic thought it was usually skipped or excluded. As Shadish et al. (2002, 17) indicate, the role of a natural experiment in economics has decreased after two studies published by Fraker and Maynard (1987) and Lalonde (1986) on the effects of job training programmes. The studies showed that the adjustments produced estimates that were not close to those generated from a randomised experiment and were unstable across the tests of the model's sensitivity. Hence, in their search for alternative methods, many economists came to do natural experiments. One of the widely known is that prepared by

Card (1993) who studied the effects that occurred in the Miami job market when many prisoners were released from Cuban jails and allowed to come to the United States of America. The experiments related to the subsidized training programs and their efficiency for unemployed in the US were widely discussed by Card and Sullivan (1988).

In the seminal paper by Smith (1994) the motivation for conducting experiments by economists is discussed. The most important reasons include the following:

1. To test the theory or discriminate between theories.
2. To explore the causes of a theory failure.
3. To establish empirical regularities as a basis for new theory.
4. To compare environments using the same institutions.
5. To compare institutions.
6. To evaluate policy proposals.
7. To test ground for institutional design in the laboratory.

One can see that causality analysis constitutes the basis for most of the reasons given above. In the causality analysis in social sciences the experiment is considered as the one of the most valuable ways of inference (Cartwright 2007). Causality in economics is being defined in different ways (Osińska 2008) and the role of an experiment in generalised causal inference is also different (Shadish et al. 2002). The pioneer of a modern cause–effect analysis in economics was Herbert Simon (1953). He defined the causality as a logical characteristic of a deterministic model that describes a chosen part of real economic life. Let us assume that the model takes the form of a linear operator that transforms the space of R^m external variables onto the space of R^n internal variables where $m \geq n$. The structural model is then as follows:

$$y = Ay + Bx, \tag{4.1}$$

where: A is a $(n \times n)$ matrix with zeros on the main diagonal; B is a $(n \times m)$ matrix. Additionally $(I - A)^{-1} = C$, and the reduced form of the model is $y = CBx$.

Simon's impact on the theory consists in defining the causal order in the model (4.1) for two internal (endogenous) variables, say y_1 and y_2. He says that y_1 causes y_2 $(y_1 \rightarrow y_2)$, if y_1 is recursively ordered ahead y_2 assuming asymmetry of a cause–effect relationship. Such an approach, although logical, has a certain disadvantage because in some cases it is difficult to identify what is a cause and what is an effect.

Let us consider the following recursive system as an example of model (4.1)

$$y_1 = b_{11}x_1 + b_{12}x_2 \tag{4.2}$$

$$y_2 = a_{21}y_1 + b_{23}x_3. \tag{4.3}$$

If $a_{21} \neq 0$ then $y_1 \rightarrow y_2$. It is easy to show (Hoover 2008) that Simon's definition is not sufficient for the identification of causal order because simple algebraic transformation of the form:

$$y_2 = a_{21}(b_{11}x_1 + b_{12}x_2) + b_{23}x_3 \tag{4.4}$$

shows that neither y_1 nor y_2 is in the causal relationship. This is due to the fact of over identification in Eq. (4.4) resulting in the situation where inference about causal ordering depends on a given vector of parameters. In the contrary to conservative economic thought Simon proposed the solution of the problem of selection between two sets of parameters in the way of an experiment, either controlled or natural. Thus, Hoover (2008) defines Simon's idea as a bridge between structural modelling and experiment based inference. Hoover (1990, 2001) generalises Simon's approach to the type of nonlinear systems of equations found in modern rational-expectations models. He shows that Simon's idea of natural experiments can be operationalised by coordinating historical, institutional or other non-statistical information with information from structural break tests. Consequently, he extends the model (4.2) and (4.3) with lagged dynamics (Hoover 2008). Hoover points out the role of non-statistical information of the qualitative nature. The information comes from a historical analysis, an institutional analysis or from searching for structural changes. He indicates the key role of intervention in causality analysis, assuming that an intervention is exogenous given the process in interest. His concept is close to the concept of super exogeneity introduced by Engle et al. (1983) and developed by Favero and Hendry (1992). If two processes: X_t and Y_t are considered, super exogeneity of X_t requires that firstly, the knowledge of Y_t is not necessary for efficient estimation of the marginal model of X_t and secondly, the change of marginal model of X_t does not influence the conditional model of Y_t. Super exogeneity is defined given any form of intervention (Osińska 2008, 47). Although the concept of super exogeneity is defined in the context of the econometric modelling of time series data and it belongs to a type of the observational study, it may be helpful in statistical identification of structural breaks and in determining exogenous and endogenous variables that will be a subject of further discussion. It is worth emphasising that a causality analysis in microeconomics has brought researchers to the concept of an experiment, particularly to the natural experiment that was developed independently of Simon (see, for example, Angrist and Krueger 2001).

The history of natural experiments in economics is quite long and the examples described date back to the nineteenth century. Although not so developed as nowadays, the idea remained the same: to answer the question about the impact of a given change on the economic and social environment on the process in hand. Some of the early examples of natural experiments are given by Freedman (2009). More recent examples of natural experiments can be found in Dunning (2008) and Fuchs-Schündeln and Hassan (2015). There are also plenty of examples of randomised experiments and quasi-experiments in economics. The literature on examples of quasi-experiments is briefly summarised in Lee and Lemieux (2010). Shadish et al. (2002) present examples of experiments in economics from both historical and current perspectives.

4.4 Steps of Experimentation in Economics

The experimentation in economics may be considered in different ways depending on the type of experiment and the type of inference (Krawczyk 2012). However, some elements seem to be necessary and universal for proper experimentation.

Here we propose the following scheme:

1. The aim of an experiment. It is important to determine the motivation of experimentation in economics and the expected results of the experiment. The reasons defined by Smith (1994) can be taken into account.
2. Hypotheses to be tested. These are not necessarily statistical hypotheses in terms of H0 or HA but rather statements that need further exploration; the unknown that should be uncovered. The questions that must be answered after the experiment should be formulated at this stage.
3. Return to the theory. At this stage the so far knowledge must be summarised. It is also worth finding out what kind of departure from the theory is expected.
4. Design of the experiment. The design includes the following:
   (a) Sample size.
   (b) Choice of the treated and control groups.
   (c) Treatment variable(s).
   (d) Time period of the experiment.
   (e) Type of the experiment.
   (f) Possible replication of the experiment in similar conditions.
   (g) Method of collection the data and selection of an appropriate software device.
   (h) Method(s) of analysis.
   (i) Validation method(s).
   (j) Possible threats of the designed experiment.
5. Statistical and qualitative elaboration of the results of the experiment.
6. Conclusions and comparison with the results obtained by the others.

4.5 Advantages and Disadvantages of a Natural Experiment

Advantages and disadvantages of data coming from natural experiments can be then summarised (see: http://www.gov.scot/resource/doc/175356/0091395.pdf). One of the advantages is expressed in terms of costs; they can be cost-effective when data are already available in national data sources. The other types of experiment can be rather expensive. The second one is that they can provide an opportunity to answer research questions that may not be possible to be addressed in any other way (particularly given the ethical and practical constraints of "randomisation"). And finally, thanks to isolation they provide an identification of effective interventions to improve different types of equalities (including microeconomic and macroeconomic) and find a useful tool for policy evaluation. An additional advantage—not mentioned in the cited text—is that the isolation of exogenous treatment variable significantly simplifies the inference about the results of natural experiment.

The disadvantages come directly from the fact that natural experiments are observational studies, not true experiments and the researcher has little (if any) control over the social or economic conditions of the experiment. Meyer (1995) emphasises that the absence of an actual randomisation device determining treatment assignment to treatment and control may present important concerns in the analysis of many natural experiments. This fact can limit drawing clear casual inferences. The process by which subjects are assigned to the treatment or control groups is rarely truly random and many extraneous factors may influence the selection. Subjects may even self-select in ways that are unobserved or unmeasured but are correlated with the outcome of interest. Another important problem is that there may be baseline differences in economic, social or other prognostic factors between the two groups. Finally, the boundaries of geographical and social populations may be difficult to define and may change and overlap in unpredictable ways.

Summing up, it can be stated that the natural experiment combines the characteristics of both the observational study, since it was not designed by researchers as "an experiment" and the data are collected in the national or regional data sources, and the experimental study because the treatment and control groups revealed in a specific way. The approach to examining causality based on natural experiments is subject of criticism. Some researchers claim that it requires lot of investigation in the underlying economic mechanism, and not only on theoretical grounds but also in historical prospective. The simplicity of the inference based on a single experiment may be misleading. The question is how to find the period of intervention excluding the impact of other possible changes that might happen in the period in interest. Extra statistical information, such as the change in government policies, institutional policies, etc., and other qualitative data are necessary. Purely statistical or econometric information is unlikely to be sufficient to identify an intervention. Hoover (2001) mentions that the intervention in interest should be traced in historical prospective and then statistical tests should also be carried out to validate whether intervention is there. However, an opposite viewpoint is also present in the subject literature. Shadish et al. (2002, 489) argue that these criticisms are in fact misplaced since experiments do not require well specified programme theories. Experiments make a contribution when they simply probe whether an intervention-as-implemented makes a marginal improvement beyond other background variability. Still, the preceding facts can reduce statistical power and, in consequence, bias causal inference. We may agree with the viewpoint of the experiment promoters but it is worth emphasising that the inference about the results of experiments must be treated with care and compared with other studies to prevent misleading conclusions. The recommendation made by Shadish et al. (2002, 489) is to prepare experiments using large samples, to reduce the influence of extraneous variation and, finally, to study implementation quality.

4.6 Measurement of the Impact of an Intervention in Experiments

The methodology of identification of causal relations via experiment consists of several methods which are usually described in particular studies, or in statistical and econometric textbooks, such as, for instance, written by Cameron and Trivedi (2005). These methods were the subject of many variants and modifications. In this chapter we simply take a glance at different methods in their simplest versions giving a guideline of ideas for a deeper search for an appropriate technique of experimental causal inference. The following methods are the most often used in experiments in economics, while each of them is often but non-necessarily devoted to a particular method of experimentation:

- Propensity score (PS)—suitable for an observational data or to the treatment defined by some observable variables.
- Differences in differences estimator (DD)—a method of analysis the cause–effect impact in a natural experiment
- Regression discontinuity (RD)—a method applicable in a quasi-experiment
- Instrumental variable estimator (IV)—a most popular method of analysis of experimental data
- Simulation methods—Monte Carlo (MC) and Bootstrap—methods used in the model-based experiments.

4.7 Propensity Score (PS)

It is appropriate to the situation when treatment participation is not by random assignment but depends stochastically on a vector of observable variables **X** (e.g. age, gender, socio-economic status). The PS is widely known and frequently applied in statistical analysis (Cameron and Trivedi 2005, 864–865).

The method is based on the conditional probability measure of treatment participation given **x** of the form:

$$p(\mathbf{x}) = \text{Prob}\left(D = 1 \middle| \mathbf{X} = \mathbf{x}\right) \tag{4.5}$$

Several assumptions are necessary when PS method is applied. One of them is the balancing condition:

$$D \perp \mathbf{x} \middle| p\ (\mathbf{x}) \tag{4.6}$$

That means that for the individuals with the same propensity score the assignment to treatment is random and should be identical like their **x** vector.

Another assumption corresponds to Rosenbaum and Rubin (1983) conditional independence given $p(\mathbf{x})$

$$y_1, y_0 \perp D|\mathbf{x} \Rightarrow y_1, y_0 \perp D|p(\mathbf{x}) \tag{4.7}$$

The assignment done by the propensity score can be modelled using logit or probit models (Cameron and Trivedi 2005; Gruszczyński 2010).

4.8 Difference in Difference (DD) Estimator

Freedman describes (2009) an approach to analysis of the causes of poverty in England made by Yule in 1899. Two types of policy were applied at the time. Yule analysed the impact of policy choices on the number of paupers. To study this problem he proposed the following equation:

$$\Delta Paup - a + b\,Out + c\Delta Old + d\Delta Pop + e \tag{4.7a}$$

where: *Paup* is the percentage of paupers, *Out* is the out-relief ratio *N*/*D*, while *N* denotes the number on welfare outside the poorhouse and *D* is the number on welfare inside, *Old* is the percentage of the population of age over 65 years, *Pop* is the population and *e* is an error term. Yule studied the problem within different geographical regions qualifying them into four groups: rural, mixed, urban and metropolitan having different results for the years 1871–1881 and 1881–1891. The equation proposed by Yule focused on the changes in the output (the number of poor people) due to the changes in exogenous variables, where ΔOut is the most important because it is related with the proportion of poor people being outside and inside the poorhouses that implies different policies applied for these two groups of paupers. Yule applied a standard single-equation regression model to measure the impact of the changes in exogenous variables on the change of the endogenous variable and this application was very important for developing other methods.

One of the simplest ideas underlying the measurement of changes is applied in Difference in Differences estimator. The standard case is one where outcomes are observed for two groups in two time periods. The first group (the treatment group) is exposed to a treatment only in the second period, while the second group (the control group) is not exposed to the treatment during either period. Let the control group denote as "A" and the treatment group as "B". The structure can apply to repeated cross sections or panel data.

4.8.1 1⁰ Repeated Cross Section Case

Let us consider the regression of the form

$$y = \beta_0 + \beta_0 dC + \delta_0 d2 + \delta_1 d2dC + e \tag{4.8}$$

where y is the outcome of interest, *dC* captures possible differences between the treatment and control groups prior to the policy change, *d2* captures aggregate factors that would cause changes in y over time even in the absence of a policy change. The difference-in-differences (DD) estimate is as follows:

$$\widehat{\delta_1} = \left(\overline{y_{B,2}} - \overline{y_{B,1}}\right) - \left(\overline{y_{A,2}} - \overline{y_{A,1}}\right) \tag{4.9}$$

where $\overline{y_{i,j}}$, $i = \{\mathrm{A}, \mathrm{B}\}$, $j = \{1, 2\}$ denotes the average output variable for a given group and a given period of time. The $\widehat{\delta_1}$ is called the estimator of treatment effect.

4.8.2 2⁰ Individual-Level Panel Data

Let w_{it} be a binary indicator, which is equal to 1 when unit i participates in the programme at time t and 0 otherwise. Consider the formula

$$y_{it} = \alpha + \gamma d2_t + \varphi w_{it} + c_i + e_{it}, t = \{1, 2\} \tag{4.10}$$

where $d2_t = 1$ if $t = 2$ and zero otherwise, c_i is an observed effect and φ is the treatment effect. Remove c_i by first differencing:

$$(y_{i2} - y_{i1}) = \gamma + \varphi(w_{i2} - w_{i1}) + (e_{i2} - e_{i1}) \tag{4.11}$$

which is equal to

$$\Delta y_1 = \gamma + \varphi \Delta w_i + \Delta e_i. \tag{4.12}$$

If $\mathrm{E}\left(\Delta w_i \Delta e_i\right) = 0$ then OLS applied to the estimation of the equation is consistent.

Standard inference concerning the parameter estimates within the OLS framework is well known. The assumptions underlying the DD method are not very demanding. To ensure the consistency of the DD estimator, it is assumed that the time effects are the same across treated and untreated individuals. Further conditions can be found in Cameron and Trivedi (2005, 770).

4.9 Regression Discontinuity (RD)

This method is an example of a situation in which the probability of receiving a treatment is a discontinuous function of one (or more) variable. It should be understood as a certain data generating process. It arises when a treatment is triggered by an administrative or organisational rule. The examples of such situations can be indicated in education, see: for example Angrist and Lavy (1999), political economy, i.e. votes share in election, see: Lee (2008) or labour market, see: Chen and van der Klaauw (2008). A brief overview of the methodology related with RD is given in Cameron and Trivedi (2005), while an extended study is offered by Lee and Lemieux (2010).

The simplest RD design allows assigning the individuals to one of the treatment or control group on the basis of a continuous variable called the selection or assignment variable. This is a sharp RD design. There exists also a fuzzy type of RD assignment. The interest in RD designs lies in the fact that causal inferences from RD designs are potentially more credible than those from typical natural experiment strategies (Lee and Lemieux 2010). In the sharp RD the cutoff level is established as a threshold value. The individuals that are above a threshold value receive treatment.

The decision rule is then as follows:

$$D_i = 1\left[S_1 \geq \overline{S}\right], \tag{4.13}$$

where D is a dummy and S_i is an assignment variable with a threshold value $\overline{S}$.

The simplest linear regression appropriate in this case is as follows:

$$Y = c + \alpha D + S\beta + \varepsilon, \tag{4.14}$$

where ε is the usual error term that can be viewed as a purely random error generating variation in the value of Y around the regression line $c + \alpha D + S\beta$.

It is often pointed out that a graphical presentation of a RD design is very helpful and informative. The example of a design can be seen in Fig. 4.1.

In Fig. 4.1 one can see discontinuity in threshold $\overline{S}$ and on the left (low) the control and on the right (high) the treatment groups are shown. The difference between an average level of the treatment group and an average level of the control group measures the causal effect.

Assuming that the relationship between Y and X is otherwise linear, a simple way of estimating the treatment effect α is fitting the linear regression. The main problem is estimating values in the neighbourhood of the threshold value $\overline{S}$. It is usually assumed that the individuals in the small neighbourhood of the cutoff have essentially the same S value. This means that the conditional mean $E\left(\alpha\middle|S\right)$ is continuous at $\overline{S}$ where u is the error in the output equation. Furthermore, the mean treatment effect $E\left(\alpha\middle|S\right)$ is right continuous at $\overline{S}$. As a consequence, α is a consistent estimator of a treatment effect (Cameron and Trivedi 2005, 880–881).

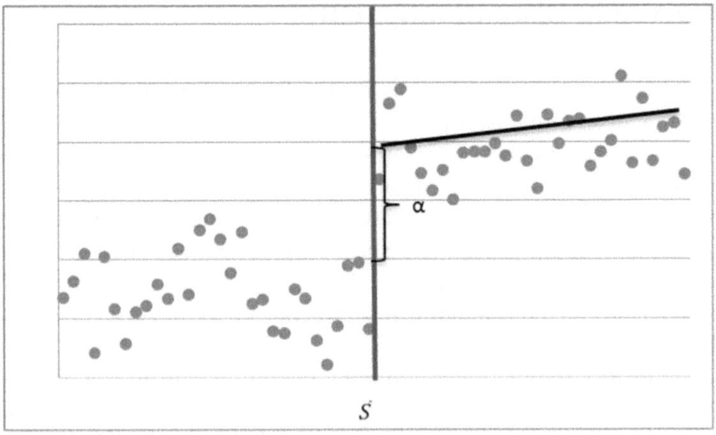

Fig. 4.1 Sharp RD design

In practice the following regression is OLS estimated:

$$Y = c_l + \alpha D + \beta_l(S - \overline{S}) + (\beta_r - \beta_l)D(S - \overline{S}) + \varepsilon, \tag{4.15}$$

where l and sub-indices correspond to the left-hand side and the right-hand side of the RD design. The problem with constraining the slope of the regression lines to be the same on both sides of the cutoff ($\beta_r = \beta_l$) is best illustrated by estimating the separate regressions from the left and from the right side of the cut-off. If we were to constrain the slope to be identical on both sides of the cut-off, this would amount to using data on the right hand side of the cut-off to estimate α_l, and vice versa. This constraint is not necessary in general (Lee and Lemieux 2010).

Furthermore, Lee and Lemieux (2010) suggest the way of parametric estimation of a treatment effect, where the relationship is non-linear, but they also recommend nonparametric methods in estimation of the RD design.

4.10 Instrumental Variables (IV)

In analysing the experiments in economics the literature typically employs the language of instrumental variables. Angrist and Krueger (2001) give an overview of the instrumental variables method from the historical perspective starting with Wright. In 1928, he showed various applications of IV method in natural and randomised experiments in economics. Angrist et al. (1996) advocate the IV method as a simple and efficient method of causality analysis when some assumptions are applied. The method has, however, a long tradition and is widely known and used in econometrics (Maddala 1983).

This approach is interesting when selection on unobservables is made. The idea can be illustrated with the following model:

$$y_{1i} = x_1^{'}\beta_1 + u_{1i} \tag{4.16}$$

$$y_{0i} = x_1^{'}\beta_0 + u_{0i} \tag{4.17}$$

$$D_i^{*} = z_i^{'}\gamma + \varepsilon_i \tag{4.18}$$

where D_i^* is a latent variable such as

$$D_i = \begin{cases} 1 & if \quad D_i^* > 0 \\ 0 & if \quad D_i^* \leq 0 \end{cases} \tag{4.19}$$

and $\mathrm{E}(\mathrm{u}_1|\mathbf{x},\mathbf{z}) = \mathrm{E}(\mathrm{u}_0|\mathbf{x},\mathbf{z}) = 0$. The variables **x** may overlap with **z** but there exists at least one z, say z_1 which is a unique and independent determinant of D. Then a variable z_1 is an instrumental variable that is correlated with the endogenous variable D but is uncorrelated with the outcomes y_1 and y_0 except through D. The variable D is then defined as endogenous, and the error term of the above system is assumed to be multivariate normal distributed with zero mean and the covariance matrix $\sum$.

The simplest version of the model (4.16)–(4.18) is as follows:

$$y_i = \beta_0 + \beta_1 D_i + u_i \tag{4.20}$$

$$D_i^{*} = \gamma_0 + \gamma_1 z_i + \varepsilon_i, \tag{4.21}$$

where D_i remains the same as in Eq. (4.19). Then β_1 represents the causal effect of D on Y. The estimation of the above system can be made using a maximum likelihood estimator or a two-step semiparametric procedure (see: Angrist et al. 1996; Cameron and Trivedi 2005 for details).

4.11 Simulation Methods in Economics

Simulation methods are very popular in economics, where a model-based experimentation is used. They are genuinely repeatable. Any possible errors are generated by the assumptions of the model. Two stochastic methods are mainly used, i.e. Monte Carlo (MC) experimentation and bootstrap.

Monte Carlo method is a general approach to mathematical problems by replacing them by equivalent stochastic problem and solving the latter. The distribution sampling is then only a part of MC method. It is an alternative to the analytical method. The simulation methods in mathematics were first defined by G. Comte de Buffon in 1777 in order to compute an integral. The Monte Carlo method was worked out in the 40s of the twentieth century by Von Neumann, Ulam, Metropolis, Feynman and others (see: Metropolis and Ulam 1949). Actually, MC technique is any technique that uses random numbers for solving a problem. A MC experiment is a laboratory experiment, where one replicates the real world study many (N) times. Every time, one draws a different sample of size M from the original population. Thus, one can calculate the estimate many times and any estimate will be a bit different. The empirical distribution of these many estimates approximates the true value of the estimator (Christian and Casella 1999). This method can also be used for prediction. The only disadvantage of the MC method is its strong requirement for the distribution of which the random numbers are drawn. The rudiments for MC method are based on probability theory and include the following: the law of large numbers, the central limit theorem and the stochastic convergence concept.

The bootstrap method is considered as a variant of the MC method. The difference consists in that instead of generating random numbers basing on the distribution assumption, it uses the residuals coming directly from the estimated model. The bootstrap relies on multi resampling from the original sample. Broadly speaking, the advantage of the bootstrap is that the unknown distribution function F is replaced by its empirical estimator. Thus, the only thing it requires is the properly specified and estimated model. The bootstrap is then less restrictive than the Monte Carlo method. The method was defined and developed by Efron (1979). Brown and Mariano (1984) show that in the case of a very large number of replications the mean squared error of prediction based on the bootstrap is similar in a magnitude to the mean squared error of prediction computed on the basis of the Monte Carlo method.

4.12 Threats of Experimentation in Economics

All the methods required validity checking. The validity of the inference drawn by experimental methods is a subject of a wide discussion, for example in Meyer (1995). The list of threats is quite long and includes two groups: threats to internal validity when within the context of the study the differences of the dependent variables were caused by the differences in the relevant explanatory variables and threats to external validity which deals with whether effects found in an experiment can be generalised to different individuals, contexts and outcomes. The former group contains the following problems: omitted variables problem, trend in outcomes, misspecified variances, mismeasurement, simultaneity, selection, attrition and omitted interactions. The latter group consists of the following three threats: the interaction of selection and treatment, interactions of setting and treatment and interactions of history and treatment.

References

Angrist JD, Krueger AB (2001) Instrumental variables and the search for identification: from supply and demand to natural experiments. J Econ Perspect 15(4):69–85

Angrist JD, Lavy V (1999) Using Maimonides' rule to estimate the effect of class size on scholastic achievement. Q J Econ 114(2):533–575

Angrist JD, Imbens GW, Rubin DB (1996) Identification of causal effects using instrumental variables. J Am Stat Assoc 91(434):444–455
Blaug M (1995) Metodologia ekonomii. Wydawnictwo Naukowe PWN, Warsaw
Brown BY, Mariano RS (1989) Prediction in dynamic nonlinear models: large sample behaviour. Economet Theor 5:430–452
Cameron AC, Trivedi PK (2005) Microeconometrics. Methods and applications. Cambridge University Press, New York
Card D (1993) Using geographic variation in college proximity to estimate the returns to schooling. Working paper 483, National Bureau of Economic Research
Card D, Sullivan D (1988) Measuring the effect of subsidized training programs on movements in and out of employment. Econometrica 56(3):497–530
Cartwright N (2007) Hunting causes and using them (approaches in philosophy and economics). Cambridge University Press, New York
Chen S, van der Klaauw W (2008) The work disincentive effects of the disability insurance program in the 1990s. J Econometrics 142(2):757–784
Christian R, Casella G (1999) Monte Carlo statistical methods. Springer, New York
Davis DD, Holt CA (1993) Experimental economics. Princeton University Press, Princeton, NJ
Dunning T (2008) Improving causal inference strengths and limitations of natural experiments. Polit Res Q 61(2):282–293
Efron B (1979) Bootstrap methods: another look at the Jackknife. Ann Stat 7(1):1–26
Engle RF, Hendry DF, Richard JF (1983) Exogeneity. Econometrica 51:277–304
Favero C, Hendry DF (1992) Testing the Lucas critique, a review. Economet Rev 11:265–306
Filozofia a nauka (1987) Zarys encykopedyczny. Zakład Narodowy im, Ossolińskich—Wydawnictwo
Fraker T, Maynard R (1987) The adequacy of comparison group designs for evaluation of employment-related programs. J Hum Resour 22:194–227
Freedman DA (2009) Statistical models. Theory and practice. Cambridge University Press, New York
Friedman M (1953) Essays in positive economics. University of Chicago Press, Chicago
Fuchs-Schündeln N, Hassan TA (2015) Natural experiments in macroeconomics. http://www.hoover.org/sites/default/files/fuschs-schundeln-hassan-papernaturalexperimentsmacro_mar16.pdf. Accessed 27 July 2015
Gruszczyński M (ed) (2010) Mikroekonometria. Wolters Kluwer, Netherlands
Guala F (2012) Experimentation in economics. In: Gabbay DM, Thagard P, Woods J, Mäki U (eds) Handbook of the philosophy of science: philosophy of economics, vol 13. Elsevier, Amsterdam
Hajduk A (2007) Ogólna metodologia nauk. Wydawnictwo KUL, Lublin
Hempel CG, Oppenheim P (1948) Studies in the logic of explanation. Philos Sci 15:135–175
Hollis M (2003) The philosophy of social science. An introduction. Cambridge University Press, New York
Hoover KD (1990) The logic of causal inference: econometrics and the conditional analysis of causality. Econ Philos 6:201–234
Hoover KD (2001) Causality in macroeconomics. Cambridge University Press, New York
Hoover K (2008) Causality in economics and econometrics. In: Durlauf SN, Blume LE (eds) The new Palgrave dictionary of economics, 2nd edn. Palgrave Macmillan, New York
Kalinowski S (2008) Konkurencja lub współpraca. Studia eksperymentalne nad funkcjonowaniem rynków. Wydawnictwo Akademii Ekonomicznej w Poznaniu, Poznaniu
Krawczyk M (2012) Ekonomia eksperymentalna. Wolters Kluwer, Netherlands
Lalonde R (1986) Evaluating the econometric evaluations of training programs. Am Econ Rev 76:604–620
Lee DS (2008) Randomized experiments from non-random selection in U.S. House elections. J Econometrics 142(2):675–697
Lee DS, Lemieux T (2010) Regression discontinuity designs in economics. J Econ Lit 48:281–355

Machlup F (1978) Methodology of economics and other sciences. Academic, New York
Maddala GS (1983) Limited-dependent and qualitative variables in economics. Cambridge University Press, New York
Metropolis N, Ulam S (1949) The Monte Carlo method. J Am Stat Assoc 44(247):335–341
Meyer BD (1995) Natural and quasi-experiment in economics. J Bus Econ Stat 13(2):151–161
Osińska M (2008) Ekonometryczna analiza zależności przyczynowych. Wydawnictwo Naukowe UMK, Toruń
Plott CR (1991) Will economics become an experimental science? South Econ J 57(4):901–919
Popper K (1959) The logic of scientific discovery. Harper-Torch-books, New York
Rosenbaum P, Rubin DB (1983) Assessing sensitivity to an unobserved binary covariate in an observational study with binary outcome. J Roy Stat Soc B 45:212–218
Scottish Government Social Research Group, Social Science Methods Series, Natural experiments. http://www.gov.scot/resource/doc/175356/0091395.pdf. Accessed 24 July 2015
Shadish WR, Cook TD, Campbell DT (2002) Experimental and quasi-experimental designs for generalized causal inference. Houghton Mifflin Company, Boston, MA
Simon HA (1953) Causal ordering and identifiability. In: Hood WC, Koopmans TC (eds) Studies in econometric method, Cowles Commission Monograph no 14. Wiley, New York
Smith V (1994) Economics in the laboratory. J Econ Perspect 8(1):113–131
Woleński J (2000) Epistemologia. Tom I. Zarys historyczny i problemy metateoretyczne. Areus, Kraków

Chapter 5
Examples of Experiments in Macroeconomics

Jerzy Boehlke and Magdalena Osińska

Abstract The considerations in the chapter are related to the examples of experiments that were conducted in macroeconomics in various economic areas, in different periods and under different conditions. Due to the specific characteristics of macroeconomics, these are mainly natural experiments and model-based experiments, comparable to laboratory experiments. The subject matter is very promising and gives some insights into the usefulness and possible applications of the so-called "experimental macroeconomics".

Keywords Experimental economics • Macroeconomics

5.1 Experiments in Macroeconomics

The development of behavioural economics observed in recent decades has caused a significant increase in the interest of economists in applications of psychology to explain the behaviour of economic entities not only at a microeconomic level, but also to try to strengthen the macroeconomic knowledge base on management processes. As is known, the greatest achievements of cognitive economics are noted in the area of macroeconomic research. However, since the creation of the Keynesian theory, the thesis about the accuracy of diversity of human behaviour at the macro level compared to the rules governing individual behaviour has been commonly accepted. Therefore, formulated macroeconomic theories may not constitute a sufficient basis for explaining individual behaviours and vice versa. In recent decades, attempts to connect macro and micro analyses were made on the grounds of macroeconomic psychology and experimental economics. Natural and

J. Boehlke
Department of Economics, Faculty of Economic Sciences and Management,
Nicolaus Copernicus University in Toruń, Gagarina 13a, Toruń 87-100, Poland
e-mail: jurekbo@umk.pl

M. Osińska (✉)
Department of Econometrics and Statistics, Faculty of Economic Sciences and Management,
Nicolaus Copernicus University in Toruń, Gagarina 13a, Toruń 87-100, Poland
e-mail: emo@umk.pl

K. Nermend, M. Łatuszyńska (eds.), *Selected Issues in Experimental Economics*,
Springer Proceedings in Business and Economics, DOI 10.1007/978-3-319-28419-4_5

model-based (laboratory) experiments carried out within the latter area became an important source of cognitive successes in modern economics. The major objective of macroeconomic experiments, as defined by Tyszka—these are experiments carried out at an aggregated level (Tyszka 2004, 31), is testing abstract economic theories, rather than actual choices made by individuals or groups. The dominant group here are natural experiments. They are implemented under real market conditions and individuals being researched are not aware of their participation in the experiment. Macroeconomic experiments allow primarily determining the cognitive capacity of an economic theory, understood as resistance to projections for derogation from assumptions that were formulated on its basis.

5.2 Examples of Natural Experiments in Macroeconomics

Natural experiments in macroeconomics are typically used to verify the assumptions of the theory, the quantification of the parameters of economic models, as well as to identify the mechanisms whose effects are the observed macroeconomic factors (Fuchs-Schúndeln and Hassan 2015, 1). Macroeconomic experiments are, therefore, instruments of cognition. It should be remembered that they are not a way to verify the logical integrity of an economic theory.

The spectrum of examples of natural experiments in macroeconomics is very broad. For the purposes of the chapter the following examples will be discussed:

1. Multicultural interpretations of justice from the ultimatum and dictator games point of view, as described by Zaleśkiewicz (2011),
2. A Bitcoin case and Gresham law reflecting the money circulation and its stability discussed by Bergstra and de Leeuw (2013) and Smith (2013),
3. The impact of an institutional order and macroeconomic policy on economic outcomes (the cases of Ghana and Argentina during the post-war period) discussed by Acemoglu et al. (2003),
4. Migration flows from Central and Eastern European Countries after the EU enlargement in 2004 discussed in Pedersen and Pytlikova (2008) and extended in this chapter by the analysis of the unemployment rates in CEEC,
5. A case of regional development based on the Operational Programme Development of Eastern Poland realised in 2007–2013.

5.2.1 Social Justice in Different Countries: The Ultimatum and Dictator Games

An example of an experiment in macroeconomics, whose aim was to identify and compare the cultural, that is also institutional, determinants of ways of interpreting social justice in different countries is the ultimatum game. Its creators are W. Guth,

R. Schmittberger and B. Schwarze. The game is designed for two players. The first one (a) has at his/her disposal a certain amount of money which should be divided between himself/herself and the other anonymous player (b) in the proportions decided personally by him or her. The anonymous player may accept the amount assigned to him/her and then both players receive the amount of money proposed by the holder or reject it, which means that none of the players receives any money. This experiment showed that the behaviour of both players does not conform to a model in which individuals maximise their utility, because in their actions they seek to carry out a fair distribution. The ultimatum game was used to search for the answer to the question of intercultural stability of choices made by players in various countries which considered the criterion of equitable division. It turned out that studies, among others, by Roth in the USA, Japan, Israel and in Slovenia, showed a high level of sustainability of human behaviour in the ultimatum game. As turned out, the modal offer of type A players took the values ranging from 40 % of the initial amount (Israel and Japan) up to 50 % of the initial amount (Slovenia and the USA). As regards the percentage of rejections, the highest one was noted in Japan (29 %) and was followed by the USA and Israel (28 %); the lowest percentage was noted in Slovenia (22 %). Thus, the similarities are much greater than the differences, which leads to the conclusion that the quest for equitable distribution of wealth is more strongly conditioned by the nature of man than the culture in which he lives. In contrast, based on the review of studies made by Zaleśkiewicz (2011, 386–388) on using the ultimatum game, or its mutation, which is the dictator game (rules of the game are similar to those in the ultimatum game with one difference—player B cannot reject payments from player A), it can be considered that a way of understanding the concept of justice and an equitable distribution is culturally conditioned. This conclusion is consistent with the findings of the new institutional economics.

5.2.2 Bitcoin: New Money

The ultimatum and dictator games also proved to be useful in experiments conducted on electronic money which is Bitcoin. This very well-known money is defined as an example of technical informational money. It is very often classified in a more extreme way: exclusively information money (Bergstra and de Leeuw 2013). Bergstra and de Leeuw have experimented with the second notion of Bitcoin. They emphasise its experimental status, novelty as a software development project and business utility. The circulated quantity of Bitcoin is not controlled by any conventional money authorities. All Bitcoin software problems must be solved by the Bitcoin community which has its way to create and maintain a power hierarchy. Probably, the most important economic questions about Bitcoin as an example of informational money concern functionality and sustainability. Experiments based on the ultimatum and dictator games could be treated as a source of information about the participants' preferences to Bitcoin and conventional money.

Results of these games are also a base for Bitcoin's demise or acquire scenarios. Behaviour of participants depends on external Bitcoin's evaluation informational money. Assuming game participants full rationality (utility maximisation), if the external value is significant, the moment that it is estimated at zero euro means that this existing informational money will be replaced by euro. In experiments done by Bergstra and de Leeuw the external estimated value of a Bitcoin was at 50 euros.

5.2.3 The Gresham Law

The Bitcoin example presented above may also be considered in a more general way. Such an approach was adopted by Smith (Smith 2013, 76–77) who analysed Gresham's law as an example of an experimental market in which the theoretical predictions of Cournot–Nash equilibrium are incompatible with the effective results of its operations. He reminds us that for the two available currencies, A and B, of which A is a value in itself, and B is only a fiat currency, this theory predicts displacement of B by A. Assuming the rationality of behaviour of all subjects, it should be assumed that they will accept only money A, which will become the dominant medium of exchange money at the same time displacing B. As the Smith says, experimental studies have confirmed, in fact, the compliance of the rationalist (theoretical) behaviour model with a model of the observed ecological behaviour, but only for those cases in which both A and B currencies are available. However, in situations where economic entities first use money B, as the only available means of exchanging and obtaining the benefits of this exchange, then the fiat money will continue to dominate. This is a consequence of the faith of exchange participants that other entities will accept within this exchange money B. This trust is reinforced by their past experience. In addition, V. Smith states that the experiments conducted have shown that if currency B is the only currency, then it will be used in the exchange, even when it is replaced by another fiat currency over a specified time horizon. The collapse of the real economy occurs only in a situation where the public sector prints fictitious money (i.e. money without coverage) to acquire real goods from the private sector (Smith 2013, p. 77).

5.2.4 An Institutional Order and Economic Outcomes

A very interesting example of macroeconomic experiments was investigated by Acemoglu et al. (Acemoglu et al. 2003, 49–123). They interpreted the causal effect of an institutional order on economic outcomes in countries where European colonists faced high mortality rates more than 100 years ago. This colonial past influences high volatility and economic crises after post-war history. At the beginning Acemoglu et al. assumed that macroeconomic policies appear to have only a minor impact on volatility and crises, so that distortionary macroeconomic policies are more likely to be only symptoms of underlying institutional problems rather than the main causes of economic volatility. To document this relationship, they used an instrument for investigating the historically determined component of institutions in a cross-section of countries. More specifically, they treated differences in mortality rates faced by European settlers during colonial times as a source of variation in the historical development of institutions among former colonies. It is very well-known that European colonisation processes starting in the fifteenth century comes close to a "natural experiment" in creating and shaping different institutions. Usually, in places where colonists faced high mortality rates, they followed a different colonisation strategy, with more extractive institutions, while they were more likely to set up institutions protecting private property and encouraging investments in areas where they settled (Acemoglu et al. 2003, 51).

To identify the relationship between institutions, macroeconomic policy and economic performance they decided to the consider the following three measures of macroeconomic policies: the average size of government consumption, inflation and real exchange rate evaluation. To measure institutions they tried to identify the extent of constitutional limits on the exercise of arbitrary power by the executive Historically determined component of institutions was analysed on based on the Ghana and Argentina cases. In their baseline regressions, the basic time period was from 1970 to 1997. Two main reasons for such an approach were important: data availability and a desire to start the analysis at a point in time where the countries for which they have data could be treated as all independent nation states. Finally, they documented a strong relationship between institutions and volatility (as well as a link between institutions and crises or growth).

5.2.5 *External Shocks and Economic Performance of Low-Income Countries*

Another example of a natural experiment in macroeconomics was described by C. Raddatz (Raddatz 2007). He decided to quantify the impact of comprehensive set of external shocks on the output and income in low-income economies and assess their ability to explain the large cyclical fluctuations, considering also internal circumstances. According to Raddatz, external shocks included terms-of-trade shocks, natural disasters, volatility of the international economy, international interest rates and changes in aid flows. Raddatz asked not only the question of the limit to which the changes of output in low-income economies could be attributed to external factors, but also which of these factors are the most important. According to his opinion, the effect and importance of different shocks was a reason for using a vector autoregression model. In this model external shocks were assumed to be exogenous to country-level variables. This approach considered the dynamics of all variables and, therefore, allows estimating overall variance of real GDP per capita. The results of this natural experiment showed that, on the one hand, external shocks have a small but economically meaningful impact on low-income economies GDP per capita. On the other hand, it is necessary to know, that this kind of shocks could explain no more than 11 % of overall variance of real GDP per capita. It means that 89 % of overall variance must be associated with endogenous shocks. Raddatz (Raddatz 2007) formulated the following results of his experiment:

- A one standard deviation positive shock to either per-capita GDP of high-income countries, commodity prices (our main measure of terms of trade), or per-capita aid flows results in an approximately 1 % significant increase in the GDP per capita of low-income countries.
- Climatic disasters (which include floods, droughts, extreme temperatures and wind storms) and humanitarian disasters (which include famines and epidemics) result in declines in real GDP per capita of 2 and 4 %, respectively.
- Real interest rate shocks and geological disasters do not have a significant impact on real activity. Although these magnitudes may look modest in absolute value, they are significantly larger than the mean and median growth rates of low-income countries during the last decade (0.2 and 0.4 %, respectively).
- Among the external shocks, changes in commodity prices are the most important source of fluctuations (explaining 37 % of the 11 % explained by all external shocks), followed by aid shocks (25 %), climatic disasters (14 %), humanitarian crises (12 %), and fluctuations in the GDP of high-income countries and the international interest rate (10 and 3 %, respectively).

5.2.6 Migration Flows from CEEC After 2004

In recent years one of the wide scale natural experiments in the European Union has been observed. The experiment consisted in entering the EU structures by thirteen new member states between 2004 and 2013, mainly from Central and Eastern Europe (CEE). This resulted in opening labour markets all over the European Union which, in turn, caused large migration flows from the new member states to the Western and Northern parts of Europe. Figure 5.1 shows the unemployment rates in the EU15 and ten CEE countries. A significant decrease in the unemployment rate in each country can be seen between 2004 and 2008. The absolute difference between 2004 and 2008 amounted to −1.1 for the EU15 group of states, while in Poland the scale was apparently bigger and ranged almost twelve percentage points. The second biggest reduction of the unemployment rate in Slovakia reached 8.8 pp. In the Czech Republic it reached almost four percentage points. Only Hungary denoted an increase of 1.7 pp. in the unemployment rate in this period. Of course, the data although official can be biased because of a procedure of registration in labour offices while working abroad which was quite common, at least in Poland. That is why the evaluation of a “pure” unemployment rate in Poland in this period has been a challenging work.

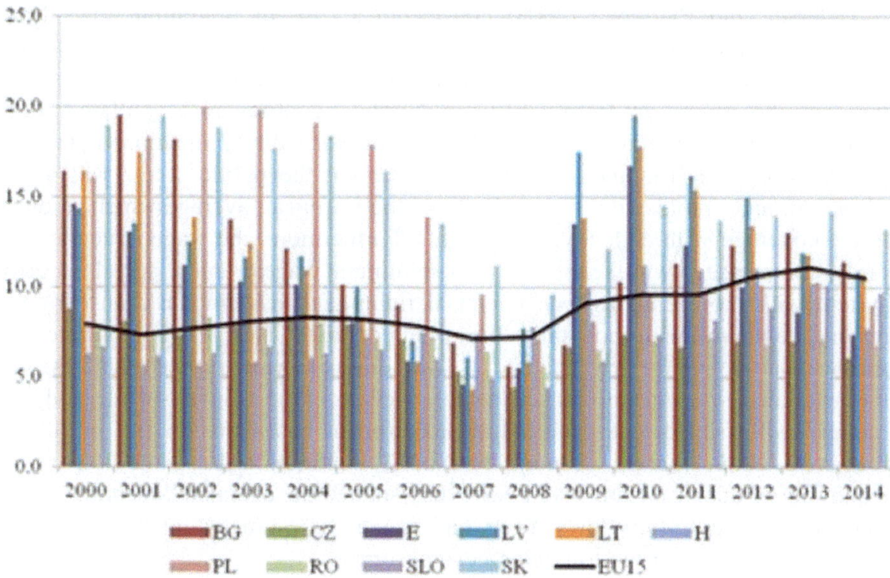

Fig. 5.1 Unemployment rate in CEEC and EU15 in 2000–2014 (source: data from Eurostat)

A positive impact of the EU enlargement on the unemployment rate indicator was particularly due to:

- An increase of investments including investments financed by the EU funds,
- Positive incentives for economic developing of the new member states thanks to an increase in foreign trade,
- Labour market openness and migration flows from Central and Eastern Europe to the "old" European Union and the European Economic Area members.

It is worth mentioning that some of the "old" EU members, such as Great Britain, Ireland and Sweden, have accepted new immigrants on their labour markets just at the moment of the EU enlargement, the others, i.e. Greece, Finland, France, Spain, Portugal, the Netherlands, Luxemburg, Italy and Iceland applied a 2 or 3-year transition period. Several countries such as Austria, Belgium, Denmark, Germany and Norway restricted their labour markets and opened it either conditionally or for selected professions only. The series of reports on migration flows from Poland after May 1st, 2004 prepared by researchers from the Centre for Migration Research in the University of Warsaw (see: Grabowska-Lusińska and Okólski 2008; Mioduszewska 2008) analyse different sources of the data to estimate the scale and directions of migration flows indicating that using different data sources can bring about various results. Thus, a very careful study considering the data and its interpretation is required. In general, after 2004, Poles immigrated mainly to Great Britain, Ireland, the Netherlands, Italy, Spain and Norway. The dynamics of migration to Germany decreased in this period.

Pedersen and Pytlikova (2008) considered a case of migration flows from 10 Central and Eastern European Countries (CEEC) to five Nordic countries which became one of the important destinations over the years 1985–2007. Assuming that the migration from CEEC to Nordic countries is job related, they characterised the Nordic labour markets. They particularly mentioned that the participation rates for married women were high, the public sector was a big employer, and unionisation was well above the European average which resulted in the coverage with collective agreements. Furthermore, the wage structure was fairly compressed, with relatively high minimum wages, and a social security system with more emphasis on universal rights and less emphasis on earnings history, compared with most other European countries. That is why Nordic countries were attractive for new "incomers". The authors indicated some problems with the actual data sets and emphasised the possible bias of the estimates while studying migration flows. However, the natural experiment based on the fact of full or restricted labour market opening by Nordic countries caused the interest in exploiting of this occasion. That is why they studied the eventual "opening" effect to explain the migration flows. They applied the DD estimator for the panel data econometric model of the following general form:

$$\begin{aligned}\text{lnmigr}_{ijt} &= \beta_0 + \beta_1\text{TreatCountry} + \beta_2\text{PostTreatPeriod} \\ &\quad + \beta_3\text{TreatCountry* PostTreatPeriod} + \varepsilon_{\text{ijt}}\end{aligned} \tag{5.1}$$

where lnmigr_{ijt} denotes flows of migrants from country i to country j divided by the population of the country of origin i at time t in natural logs. This model was a basic one, and it was extended by adding some economic variables such as GDP p.c. and distance in kilometres between the country of origin and the country of immigration. In their study, Pedersen and Pytlikova applied both gross and net migration flows. The net flows variable was defined as a difference in stocks of foreigners living in country j and coming from i country of origin, i.e. $\text{netmigr}_{ijt} = \text{stock}_{ijt} - \text{stock}_{ijt-1}$. The results using a differences-in-differences estimator showed that the estimated effect on migration of the opening of Swedish, Finish and Icelandic labour markets in the first round of EU enlargement towards the East was not significantly different from zero. However, the results regarding the opening towards the 2007 EU entrants were different. The estimated effect from opening of the Swedish and the Finish labour markets towards Bulgaria and Romania was positive and significantly differed from zero for both: gross and net flows model specifications.

Following analysis of migration flows we examine the changes in CEEC unemployment rates concerning three dates of the EU labour markets opening, i.e. 2004 and 2006 for the Czech Republic, Estonia, Hungary, Latvia, Lithuania, Poland, Slovenia and Slovakia, and 2007 for Bulgaria and Romania. We compare it with the unemployment rates in EU25. The following dynamic panel model was then estimated:

Table 5.1 The DD estimates for the unemployment rate of CEE countries starting from 2004 to 2006 to 2007

Country group—EU25	2004	2006	2007
$\widehat{\beta_0}$	0.020 (0.031)	−0.043 (0.060)	−0.002 (0.034)
$\widehat{\beta_1}$	−6.609 (1.626)	−6.372 (1.166)	−3.476 (1.205)
$\widehat{\beta_2}$ (DD)	0.515 (0.140)	0.581 (0.120)	0.407 (0.099)
$\widehat{\beta_3}$	0.531 (0.127)	0.538 (0.104)	0.755 (0.052)

$$\begin{aligned}\mathrm{ur}_{it} = \beta_0 + \beta_1 \mathrm{PostTreatPeriod} + \beta_2 \mathrm{TreatCountry}^{*}\ \mathrm{PostTreatPeriod} \\ + \beta_3 \mathrm{ur}_{it-1} + \varepsilon_{it}\end{aligned} \tag{5.2}$$

where ur_{it}—is the unemployment rate in country i in time t, TreatCountry was defined as the group of 8: the Czech Republic, Estonia, Hungary, Latvia, Lithuania, Poland, Slovenia and Slovakia since 2004 and 2006 and Bulgaria and Romania since 2007. PostTreatPeriod variables were defined as follows: 2004–2014, 2006–2014 and 2007–2014, respectively. Due to the fact that unemployment rate counts a stock of people who search for jobs and cannot find them, we lagged the endogenous variable to cover this part of unemployed people who did not find their jobs. The results of difference in differences estimator are given in Table 5.1.

An empirical analysis of the unemployment rates within the CEE countries confirms a significant decrease in three specified periods after the EU enlargement ($\widehat{\beta_1}$) but no permanent effect occurred in the longer time period ($\widehat{\beta_2}$). This impermanence resulted mainly from the recession that started in Europe in 2008 that worsen the conditions on labour markets in all European countries. The Baltic States registered a particular increase in the unemployment rates in 2010 (see Fig. 5.1). The average unemployment rate in the EU15 group of countries was also higher and in 2009 exceeded a limit of 9 %, while in 2013 it was above 11 %.

5.2.7 *Natural Experiment in a Regional Scale: Development of Eastern Poland*

Let us consider the case of the programme of regional development that was realised in Poland in 2007–2013. The programme was aimed to accelerate the social and economic growth ratio in the provinces (voivodships) of the so-called Eastern Wall of Poland (the lubelskie province, the podkarpackie province, the podlaskie province, the świętokrzyskie province and the warmińsko-mazurskie province). The projects realised as a part of the *Operational Programme Development of Eastern Poland* (OP DEP) are co-financed by the European Regional Development Fund. The funds granted for this aim amount to over 2.2 billion euros (see: http://en.parp.gov.pl/). Here we considered the effects of the programme

Table 5.2 DD estimator of treatment effect in Eastern Poland

Variable	East-Central	East-South	East-N-West	East-S-West	East-North
GDP pc	0.775	0.425	0.795	0.19	0.92
un_rate	0.87	0.925	2.265	2.64	2.12
Inv	−4,623,906	−701,865	2,204,505	6,573,294	891,931

held in the Eastern part of Poland in comparison to other regions. We applied DD estimator to compare two separate periods, i.e. 2004–2007 and 2008–2012, while the treated group was formed by Eastern region and non-treated groups consist of Central, Southern, North-Western, South-Western and Northern regions of Poland. The sub periods correspond to the business cycle phases, the former means the phase of economic growth and the latter is related to an economic recession. The following variables were taken into account: the regional GDP per capita, the unemployment rate and investment made. Chow test applied for the data shows significant structural breaks in all three series in Eastern region in 2008. The results of difference in differences estimator are shown in Table 5.2.

The results show positive effects of the programme aimed at the development of Eastern Poland taking into account both GDP p.c. and the unemployment rate. Only investment when compared with Central and Southern Poland was negative. The reasons of such a state of arts are complicated. The first one may be due to the fact that enterprises located in Eastern Poland are poorer than those located in Central and South regions and their investments are insufficient in comparison to Central and South regions. The second reason is that despite of pumping additional funds for the development of Eastern Poland, it still remains not very attractive for investment. There is yet another possible interpretation. Although the European Union is interested in the realisation of the cohesion policy covering all regions, it is insufficient for the incentives for investment in some regions, i.e. in Eastern Poland. And the final possible reason is related to the domestic policy for creating and supporting business in Poland, but this one is not diversified regionally. It is worth noting that in the period of the economic recession in the years 2008–2009, the incentives for investment were weaker than in the period of prosperity.

Analysing the case of the Programme Development of Eastern Poland, it is interesting to compare the results of the model based on the observations and the results of the natural experiment. To show the difference we considered the panel data model describing the unemployment rate conditionally on the magnitude of investment and regional GDP p.c. growth rate in six regions of Poland in the years 2004–2012. A fixed effect estimator was applied, since the regions exhibited significant diversity (see Tables 5.3 and 5.4).

Individual effects are shown in Table 5.4.

The observational perspective indicates that growth of investment and growth of the regional GDP per capita caused a decrease in the unemployment rate in Eastern Poland. Thus, the results of the Operational Programme may be thought as positive from the perspective of the desired changes. But when the level of the unemployment rate is considered, the results are not so optimistic. Individual effects show the

Table 5.3 The impact of treatment effect in Eastern Poland on the unemployment rate

	Estimate	Est. std error	t-Student	*P* value
Inv	−3.153e-07	5.199e-08	−6.064	2.32e-07
GDP p.c.	−0.265	0.111	−2.382	0.021
LSDV $R^2 = 0.701$ within $R^2 = 0.558$ DW = 0.64				

Table 5.4 Individual effects in the unemployment rate across the regions of Poland

Region	Central	South	East	N-West	S-West	North
Estimate	4.452	−0.791	−1.172	−0.967	−3.014	1.491

distance between average unemployment rates in particular regions in comparison to the average unemployment rate in Poland. Only two regions, i.e. Central and Northern, had lower unemployment rates in comparison to the average level, while four remaining regions had their unemployment rates above the average. In the case of Eastern region it was 1.17 % higher.

Applying the dynamic panel model for the unemployment rate gave the following results: better statistical characteristics of the residuals (no autocorrelation), insignificant effect of investment and GDP p.c. and adding lagged value of the unemployment rate which occurred significant. When the DD estimator was applied where y_i is the unemployment rate in treated and non-treated regions and w_i is a treatment variable, such as it takes the value 1 in the treatment period, i.e. 2008–2012 based on natural experiment was estimated for the case of Poland's Eastern region, the estimate of the parameter φ estimate was equal to –0.001 and it was significant at 10 % level. This may imply a slight efficiency of the Operational Programme Development of Eastern Poland and, also, the confounding impact of the economic recession of 2008–2009. Then the results of the regional experiment were lower than expected. Otherwise, the observational study gave an insight into regional differences.

All of the presented above results of natural experiments in macroeconomics show the importance of discussion developed by Hayek (Hayek 1978) on constructivist and ecological rationality in economics and the Duhem-Quine problem in methodology.

5.3 Model-Based Experiments in Macroeconomics

Econometric models constitute one of the most important backgrounds for experimentation and simulation in macroeconomics. Since the earliest models of the economy were constructed, these tools have developed significantly not only due to the improvement of economic theories but also as an effect of developing computers, packages and methods of analysis. In this part two types of experiments are considered. The first one is related to forecasting based on simulation using the

Table 5.5 Forecast errors comparison for MC method and simple extrapolation (source: Osińska (2007)

Series	MAPE for MC (median)	MAPE for extrapolation
WIGbanki	3.84	2.71
WIGbud	1.63	2.54
WIGinfo	1.27	2.66
WIG20	3.04	3.73

Monte Carlo method when the Stochastic Unit Root Model was used, presented in Osińska (2007). The second one covers the scenarios of Polish economy development prepared on the basis of the model W8D-2002 and published by Welfe et al. (2004).

5.3.1 Forecasting Using Model-Based Experiment

Osińska (2007) considered a stochastic unit root model for forecasting financial time series (see Granger and Swanson 1997). The simplest STUR representation is as follows.

$$y_t = \alpha_t y_{t-1} + \varepsilon_t, \tag{5.3}$$

where:

$$\alpha_t = \alpha_0 + \delta_t \tag{5.4}$$

$$\delta_0 = 0. \tag{5.5}$$

$$\delta_t = \rho\delta_{t-1} + \eta_t, \tag{5.6}$$

and $\alpha_0 = 1$ as well as $|\rho| \leq 1$. Furthermore, $\varepsilon_t \sim N(0, \sigma_\varepsilon^2)$ and $\eta_t \sim N(0, \omega^2)$ are independent of each other. For the reason of time varying unit root, the model is fairly complicated for practical use.

The data came from the Warsaw Stock Exchange and covered the period from 02 January, 2001 to 15 November, 2005. The data set cover selected sub-indices of the WSE (called WIGx). The data were checked for the presence of a stochastic unit root and respective models were estimated. The forecast errors values based on the Monte Carlo experiments using 10,000 replications (the median was computed) and on simple extrapolation (daily data, in-the sample forecasts) are shown in Table 5.5. Lower (better) values of errors are bolted.

The illustration of the results for WIFinfo is shown in Fig. 5.2.

The results meet the expectation that reasonable results can occur only when the non-linear mechanism generating the conditional mean of returns is recognised. The STUR models seem to be one step closer to reaching this aim. The usefulness of the MC method in economic forecasting was then fully confirmed.

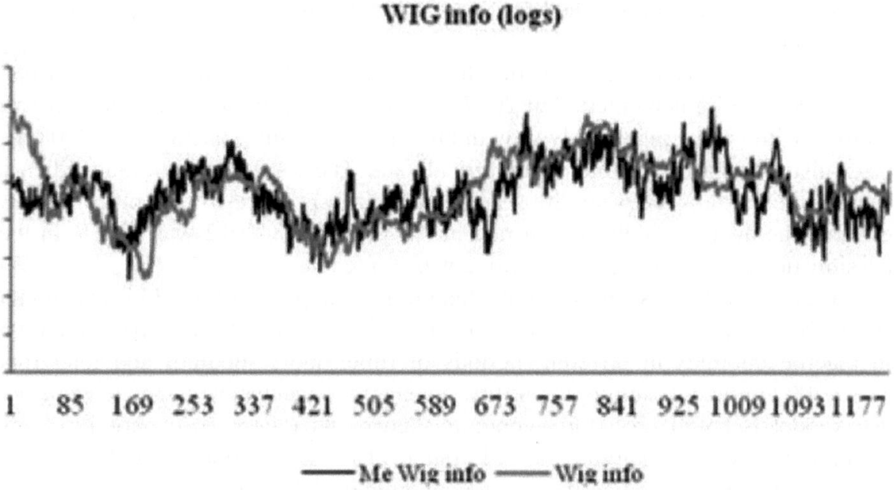

Fig. 5.2 Median of forecasts of WIGinfo series and the original series

5.3.2 Scenarios of the Economic Development of the Polish Economy in the Long-Run

Welfe et al. (2004) proposed an experiment concerning different scenarios of the development of the Polish economy after the EU enlargement. The macroeconomic model W8D-2002 was a basis of the analysis. The W8D-2002 model is a medium-sized model which in its simulation version includes 216 equations, i.e. 80 stochastic equations and 136 identities. The model allows generating final demand and its elements, and production potential and its determinants. Further, it enables analysing inflationary processes, financial flows and possible tensions in macro-balances. The full description of the model is given in Welfe et al. (2004).

Here the most meaningful assumptions that formed the basis of the simulations are presented. The assumptions of the long run values of the following variables were taken: the share of investments in GDP [%], share of FDI in GDP [%], net transfers from the European Union [billion USD], exports of goods and services [rate of change, %], share of expenses for education in GDP [%], share of expenses for R&D in GDP [%] and the elasticity of absorption from abroad changes [%]. Six scenarios were assumed taking into account different values of the mentioned variables. Two of them were optimistic, two other were moderate and the last two were really restrictive. An additional assumption of the growth supporting the long-run policy in Poland was taken despite of the political option represented by the government. At the same moment the expansionary fiscal policy was excluded and the neutrality condition of monetary policy was assumed. The assumptions were fully compatible with those of the Polish government policy assumptions presented in different documents.

The forecast horizon reached the year 2025, although shorter sub-periods were of the special interest, too.

The results proved quite realistic, though between 2004 and 2015 at least two scenarios were implemented. Till 2007 an optimistic scenario of fast growth was realised with the average yearly growth rate of 5.5 %, while starting from 2008 the pessimistic scenario became an empirical fact. The recession was planned in a pessimistic scenario between 2009 and 2011 but in practice it took place 2 years earlier. The average GDP growth rate in the years 2008–2012 was 3.4 %. In the pessimistic scenario its simulated value was 3.6 %.

The example of the scenarios of the long run development of the Polish economy shows that an appropriate macroeconomic model can be a useful in experimentation in macroeconomics in different periods of time: short, medium and long run. W8D-2002 proved its simulation utility. Yet another conclusion can be formulated. The model is based on a fair economic theory and related to economic policy assumptions. Thus, it captures a wide range of possible scenarios and it is very useful from the perspective of a macroeconomic decision-making process.

5.4 Conclusions

Experiments in macroeconomics are mainly an instrument of scientific cognition that allows examination of causality, quantification of model parameters and the identification of active social and economic mechanisms. A large number of experiments confirms the high utility of this tool. Examples of experiments conducted are provided also by Fuchs and Hassan (Fuchs-Schündeln and Hassan 2015, 95–100). Experimenting in macroeconomics is undoubtedly the result of the development of economic psychology (usually being associated with behavioural economics), in particular, of macroeconomic psychology. Both natural and laboratory experiments find their applications. It should be noted that experiments in macroeconomics may concern both short and long term dependence. Resource, organisational, social and cultural dependence taken into account while conducting macroeconomic research constitutes the subject of experimentation.

References

Acemoglu D, Johnson S, Robinson J, Thaicharoen Y (2003) Institutional causes, macroeconomic symptoms: volatility, crises and growth. J Monetary Econ 50:49–123

Bergstra JA, de Leeuw K (2013) Questions related to Bitcoin and other Informational Money (2013) Informatics Institute. University of Amsterdam, Amsterdam

Development of Eastern Poland. http://en.parp.gov.pl/. Accessed 20 July 2015

Fuchs-Schündeln N, Hassan TA (2015) Natural experiments in macroeconomics. http://www.hoover.org/sites/default/files/fuschs-schundeln-hassan-papernaturalexperimentsmacro_mar16.pdf. Accessed 8 Aug 2015

Grabowska-Lusińska I, Okólski M (2008) Migracja z Polski po 1 maja 2004 r.: jej intensywność i kierunki geograficzne oraz alokacja migrantów na rynkach pracy krajów Unii Europejskiej. CMR Working Paper 33/91

Granger CWJ, Swanson NR (1997) An Introduction to Stochastic Unit–root Process. Journal of Econometrics 80:35–62

Hayek FA (1978) New studies in philosophy, politics and the history of ideas. Routledge & Kegan Paul, London/Henley

Mioduszewska M (2008) Najnowsze migracje z Polski w świetle danych Badania Aktywności Ekonomicznej Ludności. CMR Working Paper, 36/94

Osińska M (2007) Prognozowanie na podstawie modeli STUR. In: Osińska M (ed) Procesy STUR. Modelowanie i zastosowanie do finansowych szeregów czasowych. Dom Organizatora TNOiK, Toruń

Pedersen PJ, Pytlikova M (2008) EU enlargement: migration flows from Central and Eastern Europe into the Nordic countries – exploiting a natural experiment. University of Aarhus Working Paper 08-29

Raddatz C (2007) Are external shocks responsible for the instability of output in low-income countries? J Dev Econ 84:155–187

Smith VL (2013) Racjonalność w ekonomii. Wolters Kluwer Polska S.A., Warszawa

Tyszka T (2004) Psychologia ekonomiczna. Gdańskie Wydawnictwo Psychologiczne, Gdańsk

Welfe W, Florczak W, Welfe A (2004) Scenariusze długookresowego rozwoju gospodarczego Polski. Wydawnictwo Uniwersytetu Łódzkiego, Łódź

Zaleśkiewicz T (2011) Psychologia ekonomiczna. Wydawnictwo Naukowe PWN, Warszawa

Part II
Methods and Tools of Experimental Economics

Introduction

Mariusz Borawski

The second part of this book focuses on different methods that are presently used to support experiments in economics. Moreover, it includes also contributions that present methods whose potential in experimental economics is not yet explored, but is very promising in the future.

Presented methods could be applied on various stages of economic experiment—starting from its design, through the execution, up to the data analysis. Therefore, following chapters could be treated as a "toolbox" for every scientist that conducts his research in experimental economics. The better and greater set of methods researchers have, the more reliable data they can obtain. As a consequence, they can extract more useful information, and therefore draw accurate and precise conclusions.

Methods of experimental economics, that are currently used, often are very advanced and require complex and tedious calculations. Hence, it is necessary to utilise a specialised software. Particularly important in economic experiments are, in this context, statistical methods which allow for correct planning of the experiment, and provide tools for data analysis concerning the considerable random factor that is an integral part of it. More on this topic can be found in Chaps. 6 and 7.

Experience of many researchers in the field and overview of the studies conducted show, that almost all economic experiments are conducted with the involvement of human subjects—in the laboratory or in the field. Participants in such studies perform different tasks that are required by researchers and answer

M. Borawski
Faculty of Computer Science and Information Technology,
West Pomeranian University of Technology, Szczecin, Poland
e-mail: mborawski@wi.zut.edu.pl

their questions. Contemporary trends in this kind of research are focused not only on conscious answers and behaviours of examined subjects, but also on much deeper level of their unconscious reactions that can reveal some new information. Examples of methods that can be used in this scientific approach are presented in Chaps. 8, 9 and 10. The first of these three chapters focuses on measuring implicit attitudes with the use of Implicit Association Test. The second describes methods and tools of cognitive neuroscience in the scope of experimental economics. The last one in this triple is devoted to the topic of reading facial expressions to understand human emotions and experience in order to gain a better understanding of study participants.

If we already have an example of an experiment performed without the participation of human subjects, it is often realised with the application of computer simulation. It allows to simulate the behaviour of objects (humans) on a computer. To be credible it requires a reliable model of the surveyed object. Such models are created based on already existing knowledge, observations and previous experiments. The simulation can also be a very useful tool in laboratory studies. These aspects of simulation are discussed in Chap. 11. Simulation allows to imitate the real world as well. When it is merged with algorithms of computer graphics it could also create lifelike simulated world on the computer screen. This realism can be further enriched using elements of virtual reality. As a result, examined subjects can perform tasks in a simulated environment without the need of imagining certain situations. To increase interest in the study performed activities can be carried out in the form of the game in the virtual world. Unfortunately, such solution is very expensive. To solve this inconvenience non-computer games can be combined with elements of virtual reality. An example of the use of virtual reality in economic experiment and the concept of games dedicated to this type of research is presented in Chap. 12.

In expanded simulations, simulating objects controlled by humans, such as shops, manufacturing and service enterprises require the use of appropriate methods of decision-making. This involves methods for modelling human decisions such as AHP, ANP, Electre, PVM and many others. They allow for creating a model of human decision-making on the basis of the questions asked to the persons surveyed. In some more complicated situations in this context, artificial neural networks that can learn specific patterns of human behaviour can be also used. These methods are widely discussed in Chaps. 13–16.

The content of this part of the book could be considered as an overview of possibilities and approaches that can be used in experimental economics. Presented methods do not exhaust the topic, but they lay solid foundations for every researcher that is interested in conducting economic experiments from different points of view.

Chapter 6
Basics of Statistical Research

Małgorzata Tarczyńska-Łuniewska

Abstract Experimental study in economics can be a good contribution for a better knowledge and understanding of the economic theory or the processes occurring in it. These studies can be conducted both in the laboratory setting and in the field. It depends on the kind of experiment being carried out and its specifics. In the course of the conducted study certain information emerges that should be properly developed and analyzed. Therefore, appropriate methods to bring a certain order in this regard should be applied. Operationalization and conceptualization as well as measurement, analysis, and development of its results become important. However, in order to be able to use appropriate statistical methods certain operations that allow this need to be carried out. Application of methods requires, as a first step, some preparation, i.e., determining the investigated variables, the type of the statistical regularity, defining the sample, the method of measuring variables, information on the statistics. This chapter discusses these issues. This chapter has theoretical character.

Keywords Stages of a statistical study • Study construction • Measurement • Measurement scales • Operationalization • Quantitative • Qualitative • Dependent/independent and controlled variables

6.1 Introduction

Conducting experimental studies in economics can be a good contribution for a better knowledge and understanding of the economic theory or the processes occurring in it. Experimental studies can be conducted both in the laboratory setting and in the field, depending on the kind of experiment carried out and its specifics. The process of conducting an experiment and its description are precisely determined. In the course of the conducted study certain information emerges that should be properly developed and analyzed. It is crucial, i.e., from the point of view of the

M. Tarczyńska-Łuniewska (✉)
Department of Statistics, Faculty of Economics and Management, Institute of Econometrics and Statistics, University of Szczecin, Mickiewicza 64, Szczecin 71-101, Poland
e-mail: m.tarczynska@wneiz.pl

K. Nermend, M. Łatuszyńska (eds.), *Selected Issues in Experimental Economics*, Springer Proceedings in Business and Economics, DOI 10.1007/978-3-319-28419-4_6

outcome of the conducted experiment, success or failure of actions or past events that are the subject of the experiment. Thus, this information should be gathered and developed in an appropriate manner. Study results are in fact closely related to the results obtained by conducting the experiment. Operationalization and conceptualization become important and so do measurement, analysis, and development of its results. Statistical methods are helpful in this regard, the use of which introduces a certain order to the record-keeping of experimental study results, their development or analysis. Statistical methods also provide guidelines for the design of the experimental study, which may facilitate the process of planning the experiment. The emerging study results recorded and developed using appropriate statistical methods also allow the process of inferring the success of the experiment.

The investigator has the opportunity to choose from a variety of statistical methods (quantitative or qualitative). The selection of the appropriate method should be determined not so much by the kind of experiment itself, but by information obtained in the course of its performance. From the point of view of the application of statistical methods what becomes also important is the issue of data quality that may emerge as a result of an already conducted experiment or one being carried out or as a result of conducting comparative studies in this area. This is supported by a number of publications that refers to basic of statistical issue.

6.2 Operationalization, Conceptualization, Data Quality

The development of results obtained from the conducted experiment is one of the essential elements of experimental studies. It is a very important issue from the point of view of application of statistical methods in the development or measurement of these results. However, in order for it to be possible one needs to know what is to be investigated and what scheme will be adopted by the investigator. Conducting experimental studies also requires a certain action schedule, which in principle is somewhat convergent with the stages of the study design. When establishing the study design step-by-step actions that need to be taken in order to meet the stated objectives and to verify the set research hypothesis are known. The study design should include the following elements:

- Objectives and assumptions of the experimental study, including research hypothesis,
- Operational definitions of most important terms that will be used in the study need to be specified (e.g., glossary of terms),
- Descriptions of research methods and instruments the application of which will facilitate the process of development of information and results,
- Description and discussion of the sample so that it is clear who or what the subject to investigation is or what the surveyed population is,
- Specifying the method of analysis, including presentation of experimental study results,
- Study implementation timetable together with costs.

Application of statistical methods also requires that the analyst establishes a certain pattern. In this regard there are some similarities between the study design and the stages of the statistical study. A study design has a wider scope since it includes all stages of the experimental study or simply a study, regardless of whether or not it will be required to apply specified statistical methods. As a result, the investigator knows how to proceed when conducting the study and can operate task-based in order, as a consequence, to bring about the realization of the pursued objective and verification of hypotheses. The action schedule appearing in the case of statistical methods is a formal requirement for their application. A schedule of such a study most often proceeds as follows, e.g., Kolanko (1981, 17), Hozer (1996, 30):

- Designing (preparation) the statistical study, including determination of the purpose and scope of the study, adoption of relevant research hypotheses. When planning an experimental study the set research hypothesis may give rise to the employment of selected statistical methods for their verification. At this stage, the type of investigated statistical regularity and population, unit and statistical characteristics/variables to be investigated are defined. Elements referred to, taken into account as principal guidelines for the conducted experiment, are already preset at the stage of devising the study design,
- Statistical observation involving data collection. In the case of experimental studies where statistical methods appearing in the course of the experiment are applied, information is the data subject to appropriate development with the use of these methods,
- Development of the collected statistical data indicates that the collected statistical material (statistics) must be properly grouped, segregated and presented. In order to do so, the selected form, appropriate to the particular statistical material, needs to be applied: statistical series or statistical tables,
- Analysis of results and their presentation—this phase entails analysis of the statistical material and use of certain statistical methods. The specificity of statistical methods results in the fact that obtained partial results need be correlated and analyzed keeping in mind the purpose of the study and the set hypotheses. The element facilitating this process is adequate and clear presentation of results, e.g., in the form of tables or graphs.

The construction of the study design or stages of conducting the statistical study is fairly well in line with the concept of the notion of conceptualization. Conceptualization (e.g., Blaikie (2009, 116), Babbie (2003, 144–148), Babbie and Rubin (2011, 172)) is a procedure which aims at defining the research problem, terms, concepts, and indicators used in its description as well as determining methods, techniques, and instruments by means of which the study will be carried out. In this perspective, we can say that the selected and adopted statistical methods make the realization of the stated research objective possible. Nevertheless, they are seen as a tool used at a certain stage of tests realized as part of the experiment. Their application takes place if it is necessary or appropriate. As a rule, it is defined and recorded in the study design.

Experimental studies are a specific type of studies not only due to the way they are carried out but also the type of information obtained. Experimental studies in economics at various levels of aggregation should be treated as a certain kind of scientific study. The scientific approach to this problem requires a description of economic reality using specific information. This is also crucial for the construction of measures of state or assessment in simple and complex (multidimensional) terms. In the first case, the investigated problem can be defined clearly in a one-dimensional set-up, whereas in the second case the problem is dealt with in many aspects (dimensions) when the investigated phenomenon cannot be defined unambiguously, e.g., economic potential, intellectual capital.

Previous considerations have led to the conclusion that certain information (statistics) obtained in the course of the conducted experiment will be processed and analyzed in accordance with the adopted procedure (applied statistical or non-statistical method). This means that the investigator should specify what information or, for example, variant of response will be obtained in the course of the conducted experiment. Information type depends on the type of the conducted experiment, assumptions adopted and the principles of performing the experiment. Nevertheless, from the point of view of statistical methods application, such information constitutes statistics.

Formally, statistics data Luszniewicz and Słaby (2008, 25–27) are all information which may be obtained and developed (analyzed), in a mind-based or computer-based manner, constituting a source of information regarding the studied phenomenon or issue. The information may form a basis for constructing the assessment measure of the phenomena or issues (e.g., economic and financial indicators). The data may be divided into two categories of factors: quantitative and qualitative, and—from the perspective of applying specific methods of measurement—quantitative and qualitative variables, respectively.

The information (factors, variables) may be applied to different planes or contexts. It is a consequence of the aim and scope of the conducted survey or analyses. The important element is application of a properly selected set of data and variables in the experiment. It should be emphasized that reliable, properly delivered, obtained, developed, and interpreted information is crucial for correct inference. It is essential for each type of economic investigation, regardless of the full use statistical-econometric methods for analytical purposes. Such elements apply in the development of both quantitative and qualitative as well as quasi-quantitative variables.

Depending on the specific nature of the conducted experimental study, it may be necessary to operationalize the variables in order to prepare them for further development and analysis. Operationalization De Vaus (2001, 24) is a process of transforming the abstract concepts referring to the subject of the study into specific variables which can be measured empirically. Another definition Wieczorkowska (2004, 18) denominates operationalization as indication of the operation which needs to be performed in order to assess the value of the variable. In other words, operationalization of theoretic variables is based on defining how the observations (information) obtained in the course of the experiment (or, in broad terms, from our surroundings) may be translated and recorded in a manner enabling the analysis. This allows obtaining the data constituting the basis for analyses. Such operations on variables very often prove necessary in case of economy-based experimental studies.

The statistics should be of good quality. There are several indicators of data quality Nowak (1990, 23), Grabiński (1995), Kukuła (2000, 45–47):

- Credibility, i.e., reliable source of the data,
- Accessibility—the data should be available—in a statistical sense—it should not be classified information available only to selected group of individuals,
- Comparability—related to data conformity, so as to enable proper performance of studies and analyses and ensure that the inference follows the logic of economics. Areas of comparability should be taken under consideration in this regard. Data can be compared in the following terms: temporal (dynamic)—data should be of the same periods of time and/or refer to periods which raise no formal or substantive reservations; subject, referring to data conformity in terms of form and substance regarding the aim and scope of the conducted analysis, as well as application of conceptual consistency and consistency of interpretation in statistics; spatial—areas should be comparable, e.g., within company, companies, between companies; units of measurement—it should be remembered, while examining multivariate phenomena, to develop (unify) the data properly, in accordance with formal conditions applicable to particular method from the WAP group; statistical Kordos (2007, 28) related to application of particular statistical methods appropriate for the type of the conducted survey or analysis. It applies, among others, to obtaining statistical material—that is data collection, determining the sample and its selection method, development of the obtained statistical material in the form of appropriate series and/or charts in order to allow application of appropriate measurement instruments,
- Method of presentation—related to the use of appropriate types of series, charts for presenting and recording specific quantitative, qualitative, or quasi-quantitative statistics, in compliance with the type of statistical regularity and the type of study they refer to.

Formal conditions regarding data quality are of significant importance and their role grows when statistical-econometric measurement methods are applied in the study. From statistical methods perspective, the quality of data itself affects the final results of the analyses. Moreover, data quality may become a factor determining the possibility of its application. Thus, it is necessary to take the following actions Tarczyńska-Łuniewska (2013, 134):

- Establish what knowledge regarding the studied phenomenon the data are to deliver, as well as the context of their usage—thus, it is essential to select variables taking into consideration the substantive elements, i.e., aim and

scope of the study, logical links between variables, theorems and theses consistent with the general economic theory,
- Make a preliminary formal assessment of the set of variables, indicating key trends, but without details. In this respect, the main and secondary factors occur, determining occurrence of specific statistical regularities and thus affecting the application of specific measurement instruments,
- Present the statistics in an appropriate form, i.e., adequate statistical series allowing application of appropriate method and analytical tools, or check if the form of presenting data is correct formally appropriate for conducting studies and analyses,
- Ensure a proper type of measurement scale to present statistics, influencing the type of applied measurement method and correctness of the operations carried out on variables (more in Walesiak (1988, 63–71; 2002, 11–25), Gatnar (2000)).

In practice, certain properties are attributed to quantitative and qualitative variables in the analyses: quantitative data are considered objective or more objective than qualitative data which are considered subjective. Such division may result from the specificity of the data, sources and methods of acquisition. Quantitative variables occur in the form of a numeric sequence that is considered unambiguous. In the case of qualitative data, there is no such unambiguity. Recording and defining data may be difficult, sometimes even impossible. For example, it is difficult to assess or directly record the management quality in a company, even if it is commonly known that the company is well-managed. The method of recording or description often depends on the competence of the person performing the task—thus, the issue of subjectivity of qualitative variables arises. In the case of qualitative data, variables should not be sought "at a push"; instead, information used should present—in a general, but precise manner—the qualitative determinants possible to achieve in the course of experiment. It should also be possible to record this information in a quantitative or quasi-quantitative form, so as to allow measuring and/or including the information in the applied measurement methods. Certain generalizations whose introduction significantly facilitates performance of studies and analyses, and thus the application of measurement methods, may be adopted.

Therefore, there are two aspects of data quality to be considered:

- Data quality in statistical terms,
- Data quality in view of the aim and scope of the conducted studies and analyses.

Both have a strong impact on the results of the analyses, as well as on the constructive conclusions. The results of the conducted experiment may also constitute the measurable outcome of data quality, thus determining the success or failure of the experiment.

In respect of statistical-econometric methods, apart from quality of the statistics, it is essential to use data collected and presented in the form of appropriate statistical series or tables when conducting the study. It is usually determined by the nature of the studied statistical regularity or type of obtained data, number of observations or specificity of the study. Two general forms of presenting statistical material may be distinguished:

- Tabular– presenting statistical material in a form of statistical series or tables,
- Graphic—presenting statistical material with a proper graph.

Moreover, depending on the methods of measurement used, the data may be presented in univariate or multivariate series.

6.3 Measurement, Measurement Scales

By means of quantification, statistical methods allow recording many problems and processes in a numerical form and in a specific manner. In this context, operationalization-related actions carried out by the analyst may prove contributive. In the case of experimental studies, measuring the achieved results may determine success of the experiment. Obviously, due to the type of variables appearing in the course of the study (quantitative, qualitative, or quasi-quantitative variables), the measurement process may be hindered. Recording variables on the appropriate scale implies a possibility to apply specific measurement methods and often determines the method of data development.

Measurement Ackof (1969, 226), Zeliaś (1991, 27), Walesiak (1996, 19), Steczkowski and Zeliaś (1997, 17), Ostasiewicz (2003, 17), Gatnar and Walesiak (2004, 19) refers to assignment of certain symbols or numbers to characteristics of statistical units and surveyed items, while maintaining relations between them and actions carried out on these units. The comparison is made compliant with the preset rules of the measured item with an appropriate model, equipped with a certain scale, allowing the analyst at least to identify the measured item. According to Steczkowski and Zeliaś (1997, 17), two types of figures are the outcome of the measurement: one informing about the count of a certain set of items, and the other informing about the degree of intensification of the phenomena occurring in these items.

In the field of experimental studies in economics, statistical methods are rather an instrument facilitating the achievement of set goals and verification of hypotheses. Their potential application, however, makes it necessary for the analyst to be familiar with issues related to measurement of variables arising from the conducted experimental study. Statistical methods or quantitative methods in general are highly varied. There is a large number of methods which may be applied in the analysis of economic phenomena; however, situations may occur where the analyst faces certain limitations in their application. The limitations may be of formal nature, e.g., Tarczyńska-Łuniewska (2013, 140):

- Describing phenomena with a certain type of variable or variables, nature of the phenomenon (e.g., social vs. economic),

- Applied data-recording method constituting basis for creating a database with regard to particular phenomenon, in order to enable application of statistical methods,
- Related to potential application of quantitative methods,
- Aim and scope of the conducted analyses.

The abovementioned elements are quite compatible with the conditions of applying quantitative methods, thus determining their application. Defining preliminary parameters of the conducted analysis contributes to the adjustment and selection of appropriate test instruments. Thus, the preliminary parameters should be defined at the very beginning of the study. In principle, such an approach to the problem correlates well with the elements of the study design and:

- Stages of statistical surveys,
- Steps of developing econometric models and decision models,
- Stages of multivariate comparative analysis.

Recording on a proper measurement scale is crucial in the case of variables which may appear in the course of experimental studies. It must be said that there are many information about measurement scale in the literature, e.g., in Mynarski (2000, 80), Gatnar (2000), Gatnar and Walesiak (2004, 20ff.). This publication contains only basic information, crucial for the essence of the measurement. It is the measurement scale assigned to a particular variable which allows performing proper operations on the variables. Consequently, this impinges on the possibility of applying appropriate methods of analysis, both quantitative and qualitative. Marketing research, for example, uses mainly the following scales: nominal, ordinal, interval, and ratio. They were introduced in 1959 by Stevens S. (Stevens (1959)). Application of measurement scales in economic research is related to the nature of the examined phenomenon, its description and recording in the form of an appropriate variable: quantitative or qualitative, hence the application of the aforementioned types of scales in this area.

It should be emphasized that the general division of measurement scales is the following: metric and nonmetric, assigned respectively to quantitative (measurable) and qualitative (nonmeasurable) variables (characteristics). Metric scales, contrary to the nonmetric ones, are considered so-called strong scales. It is a result of their specific properties. Regardless of the type of conducted research or field of analysis, (market, company, region), the analyst should be aware that every transformation on a weaker scale is also allowed on a stronger scale. The opposite relation, however, does not exist. Table 6.1 presents the properties of measurement scales, their division and allowed operations on variables.

Understanding the principle of a measurement scale for variables is essential for the successful analyses with the application of statistical methods. It is especially important when recording variants or values of the variables gathered during experimental studies. The issue of recording variables on appropriate scales allows proper application of analytical methods (measurement methods) and inference based on the results of the analysis. Failure to use adequate measurement scale

Table 6.1 Basic measurement scales (Gatnar and Walesiak 2004, 21)

Scale type	Mathematic transformations allowed	Relations allowed	Arithmetic operations allowed
Nominal	$z = f(x)$, $f(x)$—arbitrary biunique transformation	Equality ($x_A = x_B$) Inequality ($x_A \neq x_B$)	Events count (number of equality, inequality relations)
Ordinal	$z = f(x)$, $f(x)$—arbitrary strictly monotonically increasing function	The above and relations of the greater than ($x_A > x_B$) and the less than ($x_A < x_B$)	Events count (number of equality, inequality, the greater than, the less than)
Interval	$z = bx + a$ ($b > 0$), z∈R for all x included in R, zero value in this scale is usually arbitrary or conventional	The above and equality, inequality and intervals ($x_A - x_B = x_C - x_D$)	The above and addition and subtraction
Ratio	$z = bx + a$ ($b > 0$), z∈R for all x included in R_+, zero value is a natural beginning of ratio scale	The above and equality of ratios ($x_A/x_B = x_C/x_D$)	The above and multiplication and division

when recording the variable may be a manifest non sequitur in the conducted survey and analysis using statistical methods. A consequence of such a situation may be, for example, deriving erroneous conclusions from the conducted survey, which may determine the success or failure of the conducted experiment. The characteristics of measurement scales help to understand and, as a result, properly record the variables, hence Chojnicki and Czyż (1973, 18), Mynarski (1992, 28), Mynarski (2000, 80), Gatnar and Walesiak (2004, 19–31):

- Nominal scale—a nonmetric scale used for measuring the value of qualitative characteristics, whereas this measurement should be considered identification of specific characteristics, enabling to distinguish between the studied items; numbers used in this scale serve only for identification in order to distinguish the classes of items and no mathematical operations may be performed on that basis. Due to the nature of this scale, mathematical operations are not allowed. The values of variables on this scale have no obvious order (e.g., place names, company names), only equality/inequality relations. An equality operation may be used in order to compare two values on a nominal scale. A nominal scale with only two variants (two values), e.g., yes/no answers or 0 and 1 (in which case the variables take zero-one names) is called dichotomous; consequently, the use of the method of multivariate statistical analysis to survey the items is limited. When recording variables on the nominal scale, variate values for a variable need to be defined, in order to enable their precise indication,
- Ordinal scale—a nonmetric scale, allows measurement on the level of relational equation, the values have clear "order" (rank); ranging occurs, i.e., assigning sequential values of natural numbers of ordinal numbers in an ascending or descending order to items, depending on the strength of a particular

characteristics; intervals between characteristics are not given, and thus it is impossible to determine the degree of difference between two items; however, it is possible to determine which item is greater than, less than, or equal to the other, e.g., education, determining economic condition on the market, management quality. The ordinal scale may be used when conducting a macroeconomic, situational or sector analysis, where it is necessary to use an appropriate record method, e.g., for economic condition. Different groups of items may be compared on the ordinal scale, provided that the set of items is the same,

- Interval scale—a metric scale, allows to directly compare items by establishing distance between them based on the analyzed characteristics; sensible interpretation of differences between the characteristics is possible, but not the interpretation of their ratio, e.g., dates, time. Ranging transforms the interval scale into the ordinal scale with an arbitrary zero point. As it is a numeric scale, mathematic operations like addition, subtraction, and determination of arithmetic mean are possible. Financial result (profit–loss), where crossing the zero point defines the financial result achieved by the company is an example of a variable measured on the interval scale,
- Ratio scale—a metric scale where not only differences but the ratios as well have a sensible interpretation. The scale enables measurement at the level of proportionality of the items based on analyzed characteristics. It defines the probability of completing specific condition/action. All mathematic operations are allowed. Variables measured in a ratio scale are, for example, income or company expenses in monetary units,
- Absolute scale—only one sensible method of coding measurement results exists for a given variable, e.g., number of occurrences of a given variate value of a variable in a set.

There are also other types of measurement scales, e.g., Likert, Stapel, Thurstone, Guttman scales) (see for example Zeliaś (1991, 27), Walesiak (1996, 26–33), Ostasiewicz (2003, 19–23), Sagan (2004, 79–92), Gatnar and Walesiak (2004, 19–31)). Some of them require conducting surveys or research with the use of graphic elements.

Likert scale is involved in methodology of social studies, especially psychological research. It is a nominal scale containing many items. It is used in survey questionnaires and structured interviews. The scale is structured in a way facilitating the response related to the degree of acceptance of a certain phenomenon, view, etc. Ordinal (usually five-level) scales of intensity are subordinated to every position of the scale.

Stapel scale is a modification of a semantic differential scale used to measure opinion and impression regarding the studied phenomenon. Checklist responses and degree of satisfaction should be given on the scale. Ratings of the nominal scale constitute a set of unipolar scales, ten—or eleven-degree. The ratings on Stapel scale may have values ranging from –5 to 5 (there is no neutral (zero) point, which means it is a forced scale). By default, the scale poles are marked by adjectives describing the extreme characteristics of the assessed approach, item, or phenomenon.

Guttman scale (Guttman (1950), Robinson (1972, 260–267)) is used to measure attitude or acceptance of socially controversial phenomena. It comprises a series of hierarchically structured questions, referring to the same issue. The characteristic feature of this scale is that a positive response to the first question should result in a positive response to all questions that follow.

Thurstone scale (Thurstone (1928, 529–554)) has been designed to measure attitude. However, due to specific construction it is very seldom used in social studies.

Should the analysis employ statistical methods, especially quantitative, the variables should be measured on the same measurement scale to avoid any substantive or methodological dilemmas regarding application of statistical methods. In the case of different measurement scales, the scales may be transformed, if necessary. Such operations should enable application of statistical methods to analyze and assess the phenomenon. It is also possible to change from the stronger to the weaker scale; however, it may result in partial data loss.

6.4 Description of Selected Statistical Terms

Statistical methods cannot be learnt at random. In order for these methods to be appropriately applied in studies, their basics need to be known and understood, including basic concepts which appear in them. There is a lot of elaboration in literature that addresses the science of statistic. In general, all concepts and definitions that appear in the framework of statistics are the same Zając (1994), Hozer (1993, 1996), Sobczyk (1998), Ostasiewicz et al. (1998), Zeliaś (2000), Frątczak and Korczyński (2013), Wieczorkowska (2004). In general, the starting factor enabling the use of statistical methods is the occurrence of statistical regularities. If a statistical regularity occurs, we can examine it using methods appropriate for it. It is also possible to use statistical methods in order to detect a statistical regularity. Therefore, what is a statistical regularity? A statistical regularity is repeatability of items, phenomena or events occurring in mass processes. That is when the surveyed population is numerous. The regularity cannot be seen in individual cases. In turn, a mass process occurs in a large mass of events where there is an interaction of two kinds of reasons for determining the occurrence of a statistical regularity. These are constant causes—subject to which are all units of the surveyed population, and accidental; causes—which affect selected, often individual units of the surveyed population. Accidental causes disturb the course of the statistical regularity. There are three types of statistical regularities, to which certain study methods are assigned:

- Regularities in terms of the structure of the distribution of phenomena,
- Interdependencies (relationships) occurring between phenomena in time and space,
- Dynamics and fluctuations (changes over time) of phenomena.

A number of important concepts occur in the framework of statistical studies:

- Universe—collection of all measurements the investigator is interested in,
- Sample—a subset of measurements results selected from the population. The sample is as a rule taken at random, i.e., each element of the population has an equal chance of entering it,
- Statistical population—it is a set of nonidentical units (set of people, items, phenomena) covered by the study, having at least one common characteristic, relevant to the purpose of the study. The population should be both homogenous and unambiguously defined—e.g., company in a given sector, employees of a given company,
- Statistical unit—a single element of the surveyed statistical population,
- Statistical characteristic or variable—certain qualities that are borne by units forming the population.

In terms of characteristics or variables different types may occur, which determines the possibility of using suitable methods. In general, characteristics can be classified into:

- Constant—characteristic of all units of the surveyed population,
- Variable—differentiate units of the surveyed population and it is them that are subject to investigation.

Characteristics, variables can be classified as:

- Quantitative, measurable—numerical values are assigned to them. They can be expressed using units of measurement in a certain scale. These characteristics are divided into: continuous and discontinuous (discrete). Continuous characteristics are those that can take on numerical values form a specific finite numerical interval (e.g., investment expressed in monetary units). Discontinuous characteristics on the other hand are characteristics that can take on numerical values from a finite or enumerable set (e.g., the number of companies),
- Qualitative, nonmeasurable—they cannot be characterized using figures. They can be described using words,
- Quasi-quantitative—they are ordinal characteristics and allow organization or prioritization of the results of observations. They are defined by means of grading adjectives (e.g., weak, strong, heavy).

It is also worth mentioning that in statistical methods, in addition to the concept of a statistical characteristic, the concept of a random variable also occurs. The random variable is an equivalent of the statistical characteristic, with the proviso that a variable is defined not only by the set of possible realizations but also by an appropriate probability distribution function. A discontinuous random variable is a variable whose set of values that it can take on is finite or countable. A random variable is called continuous if the set of values that it can take on is uncountable.

The classification of characteristics into qualitative and quantitative determines the application of different statistical methods in the study. When dealing with qualitative characteristics or variables, we should use methods for investigating qualitative phenomena. In the case of quantitative characteristics/variables quantitative methods (statistical, econometric or multivariate) may apply. The selection of measurement and analysis methods for quasi-quantitative characteristics/variables results from the specific nature of recording them.

The purpose of the study presets what set of people, items, or phenomena will be included in the statistical population. In order to perform this "inclusion" into the surveyed population, the process of sampling selection needs to be carried out. The sampling frame is material reflecting the surveyed statistical population. It is a complete list of units of the surveyed statistical population which are allocated appropriate identification symbols (usually numbers) in order to select a sample. The primary role of the sampling frame is to ensure that each unit of the population is reached, to enable each unit to enter the sample and to avoid double testing of some units. There are different ways of sampling (e.g., Korol (2006, 31–32), Witkowski (2010, 11–13)):

- Independent sampling or sampling with replacement—maintaining the same conditions during the drawing of subsequent sample units (with replacement),
- Dependent sampling or sampling without replacement—the result obtained in the first sampling selection changes the conditions of subsequent sampling, i.e., it changes the probability of occurrence of events in subsequent sampling,
- In large samples the results of sampling (dependent and independent) return practically the same results,
- Cluster sampling—when the population is made up of parts that are characterized by less variability of surveyed characteristics compared to the variability of the entire population. The sampling involves first dividing the population into parts, and then a sample is taken from each part. The number of units drawn from each "level" should be proportional to the number of parts and standard deviation. The cluster sampling feature: optimal sampling, proportionate sampling.

Other types of sampling include multi-stage sampling, multi-phase sampling, and systematic selection.

Which sampling scheme will be adopted is determined by formal conditions for the carried out study. The sampling scheme, and thus the method of selection of statistical units, is determined prior to commencing the study. In the case of conducting experimental studies on the ground of economics the method of selecting units results from the principles and guidelines of the conducted study.

A separate issue is the numbers (size) of the sample Steczkowski and Zeliaś (1997) to be examined. It is required that the sample is representative enough (large enough), i.e., that it describes the population with the adopted accuracy (that it is its miniature). The representativeness of the sample is decisively influenced by two factors: the sample selection method and its size. The size of the sample affects the so-called statistical power of the obtained results. This situation is related to the verification of hypotheses and the issue of related errors. It may concern an erroneous adoption of hypotheses: e.g., adoption of a false hypothesis or rejection of a true hypothesis (the issue of hypotheses and related errors is found further below.) Such a situation occurs in particular when the investigated sample is too small. There is also the question of a sample that is too large (too numerous). A sample that is too large can affect the increase in the cost of the study, which is crucial not only for experimental studies but for research in general. However, this situation is also negative from a statistical point of view. Importance in this respect is also held by principles arising from the law of large numbers. The law of large numbers interacts in such a way that if the study is conducted with a sufficiently large sample (number of people, surveyed units) we obtain a significant result even for an apparent dependence. Therefore, this situation is a signal for every investigator of how important selection of appropriately sized sample is. The analyst should be aware of the importance of sample size for the success of the conducted study. What should also be borne in mind is the impact of the numbers on drawing study conclusions. In order to determine the appropriate size of a sample certain statistical procedures are of help. By using appropriate methods in the field of statistical inference (e.g., a formula for the required sample size or adopting adequate precision of specified parameter estimation), the analyst can check whether the sample is large enough and whether, therefore, no errors that could affect the final results and conclusions from the conducted study have been made. In the case of experimental studies, sampling may determine the success of the experiment, and therefore this issue should be carefully considered by the analyst before the experiment commences. In many economic and non-economic studies sampling is left out. It is a non sequitur of a study. The analyst is working on data which are results obtained from the sample. It is therefore necessary to ensure that the test sample is representative and reflects the essence and character of the population from which it is derived. There is one more issue in the case of experimental studies. A situation may occur (provided for in the experiment) where the sampling took place in a targeted manner, so that it is possible to verify (carry out) the experiment. Such a situation may on the one hand give rise to concerns of a formal nature for conducting studies with the use of statistical methods, but it is permitted. Then, however, caution needs to be applied in building study conclusions, taking into account the issues of the method of selecting the sample for the study.

References

Ackof R (1969) Decyzje optymalne w badaniach stosowanych. PWN, Warszawa

Babbie E (2003) Badania społeczne w praktyce. PWN, Warszawa, pp 144–148

Babbie E, Rubin A (2011) Research methods for social work. Cengage Learning, USA

Blaikie N (2009) Designing social research. Polity Press, Cambridge

Chojnicki Z, Czyż T (1973) Metody taksonomii numerycznej w regionalizacji geograficznej. PWN, Warszawa

De Vaus DA (2001) Surveys in social research. Routledge, London

Frątczak E, Korczyński A (2013) Staytsyka od podstaw z systemem SAS, Oficyna Wydawnicza SGH

Gatnar E (2000) Wpływ skali pomiaru zmiennych na konstrukcję drzew klasyfikacyjnych. In Walesiak M (ed) Pomiar w badaniach rynkowych i marketingowych. PN AE w Wrocław Nr 856, Wrocław
Gatnar G, Walesiak M (2004) Metody statystycznej analizy wielowymiarowej w badaniach marketingowych. AE Katowice, Katowice
Grabiński T (1995) Informacyjne aspekty statystyki międzynarodowe. Wiadomości Statystyczne No 9
Guttman L (1950) The basis for scalogram analysis. In: Stouffer et al. Measurement and prediction. The American Soldier Vol. IV. Wiley, New York
Hozer J (1993) Mikroekonometria, PWE, Warszawa
Hozer J (ed) (1996) Statystyka – opis statystyczny. University of Szczecin, Szczecin
Kolanko E (ed) (1981) Statystyka. Technical University of Szczecin, Szczecin
Kordos J (2007) Statystyczne badanie zjawisk społecznych. In: Panek T (ed) Statystyka społeczna. PWE, Warszawa
Korol M (2006) Statystyka w zarządzaniu. AWE Gorzów Wlkp, Gorzów Wlkp
Kukuła K (2000) Metoda unitaryzacji zerowej. PWN, Warszawa
Luszniewicz A, Słaby T (2008) Statystyka z pakietem komputerowym statistica PL. Teoria i zastosowania. C. H. Beck, Warszawa
Mynarski S (ed) (1992) Badania przestrzenne rynku i konsumpcji, PWN, Warszawa
Mynarski S (2000) Praktyczne metody analizy danych rynkowych i marketingowych. Zakamycze, Kraków
Nowak E (1990) Problem informacji w modelowaniu ekonometrycznym. PWN, Warszawa
Ostasiewicz S, Rusnak Z, Siedlecka U (1998) Statystyka elementy teorii i zadania, Wyd. AE we Wrocławiu, Wrocław
Ostasiewicz W (2003) Pomiar statystyczny. AE we Wrocław, Wrocław
Robinson JP (1972) Toward a more appropriate use of Guttman scaling. Publ Opin Q 37 (2):260–267
Sagan A (2004) Badania marketingowe. Podstawowe kierunki. AE Wrocław, Wrocław
Sobczyk M (1998) Statystyka, Wydawnictwo Naukow PWN, Warszawa
Steczkowski J, Zeliaś A (1997) Metody statystyczne w badaniu zjawisk jakościowych. AE Kraków, Kraków
Stevens SS (1959) Measurement, psychopchisics and utility. In: Churchman CW, Ratoosh P (eds) Measurement: definitions and theory. Wiley, New York
Tarczyńska-Łuniewska M (2013) Metodologia oceny siły fundamentalnej spółek (giełdowych i pozagiełdowych). Zapol, Szczecin
Thurstone LL (1928) Attitudes can be measured. Am J Sociol 33:529–554
Walesiak M (1988) Skale pomiaru cech (w ujęciu zwężonym) a zagadnienie wyboru postaci analitycznej syntetycznych mierników rozwoju. PN AE Wrocław, Wrocław
Walesiak M (1996) Metody analizy danych marketingowych. PWN, Warszawa
Walesiak M (2002) Pomiar podobieństwa obiektów w świetle skal pomiaru i wag zmiennych. PN AE Wrocław nr 950, Wrocław
Wieczorkowska G (2004) Statystyka. Wprowadzenie do analizy danych sondażowych i eksperymentalnych. WN Scholar, Warszawa
Witkowski M (ed) (2010) Statystyka matematyczna w zarządzaniu. UE Poznań, Poznań
Zając K (1994) Zarys metod statystycznych. PWE, Warszawa
Zeliaś A (1991) Ekonometria przestrzenna. PWE, Warszawa
Zeliaś A (2000) Metody statystyczne, PWE, Warszawa

Chapter 7
Selected Statistical Methods in Experimental Studies

Waldemar Tarczyński

Abstract Statistical methods have a wide range of applications, including various types of experimental studies. They can be used in the analysis of both quantitative and qualitative phenomena as well as the uni- or multivariate ones. Their application introduces a certain order in record-keeping, development, and analysis of study results. Statistical methods also provide guidelines for experimental study design, which may facilitate the process of planning the experiment. The chapter gives a general overview of the selected statistical methods, thus allowing identification of the essence of their application as one of the stages of developing the results of experimental studies. The chapter has theoretical character.

Keywords Test methods of statistical regularities • Structure • Dynamics and volatility • Correlations

7.1 Introduction

Statistical methods have been employed in a wide context of application in the studies of social phenomena, including various types of experimental studies. This is supported by a number of publications in the field of usefulness of statistical methods, e.g., Adamkiewicz (1996), Walesiak (1996), Steczkowski and Zeliaś (1997), Aczel (2000), Bielecka (2005), Stanisz (red.) (2005), Moczko and Bręborowicz (2010), and Lissowski et al. (2011). They can be used for examining both quantitative and qualitative phenomena. In this context, their application is determined by the type of the studied characteristics or variables (quantitative, qualitative, or quasi-quantitative characteristics/phenomena) and type of the conducted analysis. The previous chapter has shown that the choice of statistical methods of analysis depends on the type of data describing the studied phenomenon and the method of recording them. With regard to specificity of the phenomena, the analyst may be dealing with uni- or multivariate phenomena. Moreover, some of the

W. Tarczyński (✉)
Department of Insurance and Capital Markets, Faculty of Economics and Management, University of Szczecin, Mickiewicza 64, Szczecin 71–101, Poland
e-mail: wtarc@uoo.univ.szczecin.pl

K. Nermend, M. Łatuszyńska (eds.), *Selected Issues in Experimental Economics*, Springer Proceedings in Business and Economics, DOI 10.1007/978-3-319-28419-4_7

phenomena may be defined as simple and the other as complex. From the point of view of the measurement of such phenomena, it is necessary to apply adequate methods serving this purpose. In principle, in order to apply statistical methods, the conditions of their application should be fulfilled. Statistical methods, both quantitative and qualitative, uni- or multivariate, allow synthesizing information regarding the studied phenomenon (phenomena), and thus the design and development of the final conclusions. Using such methods introduces a certain order in record-keeping of the study results, their development, or analysis. These methods also provide guidelines for designing an experimental study which may facilitate the process of planning the experiment.

The fact that most statistical methods have been programmed significantly facilitates the process of development of the study results. The Statistica software package is particularly helpful in this regard; however some simple analyses can be conducted using appropriate functions of the Excel spreadsheet application. Moreover, the analyst does not have to know calculation formulas, but he should be aware of what they relate to, what the interpretation of study results is, and how significant they are from the point of view of statistics. Those elements should also include the aim and scope of the conducted experimental study.

The experimenter is able to choose from many statistical methods (quantitative or qualitative). It should be the information obtained in the course of the experiment and not the type of experiment itself that should determine the selection of the appropriate method. From the statistical methods perspective, the issue of the quality of data which may appear due to the conducted experiment or comparative research in this scope becomes significant.

7.2 Statistical Methods of Analysis

There is a lot of elaboration in literature that addresses the statistical methods. In general, statistical methods that appear in the framework of statistics are the same: Lange (1952), Krzysztofiak (1974, 1981); Zając 1994; Hozer (ed.) (1994), (1996); Ostasiewicz et al. (1998); Ostasiewicz (1999); Sobczyk (2000); Zeliaś (2000), Aczel (2000); Bielecka (2005); Paradysz (2005); Jóźwiak and Podgórski (2006). Within the framework of statistical methods, the person developing the results of the experimental study may apply the methods of analyzing statistical regularities. Due to the instrument apparatus used, these methods allow for the following:

- Learning about the nature of the studied phenomenon and the structure of its distribution
- Observation and analysis of the changes and temporal volatility
- Investigating and detecting the relations which may occur between the examined phenomena

The studies' results obtained in the course of the experiment are developed and the results constitute variables to be examined. Their nature, type, and kind determine the application of appropriate methods. The analyst has the following options to choose from in terms of the methods of examining statistical regularities:

- Examining and detecting regularities of structure and distribution
- Analysis of dynamics and volatility
- Analysis of interdependences in time and/or space

Analysis of structure regularities refers to examining the structure and distribution of the surveyed population in a static and/or dynamic design. The first occurs when a definite period of time is examined, e.g., analysis of the phenomenon in 2010. The dynamic design refers to a preset period of time, e.g., analysis for the period 2000–2010. When studying the structure, the population may be presented in the following ways:

- Graphic—in the form of a graph (graphs)
- Tabular—presenting data in tables
- By means of an appropriate statistical series—detailed (ordered, non-ordered), frequency distribution (point, interval), or any other appropriate for the type of analyzed data

The type of available statistical material (type of data or method of recording) affects the method of presentation. The experimenter also often decides about the form of presentation, however taking into consideration the guidelines regarding the aim and scope of the analysis.

In the methods of structural regularities the examined population has strictly defined distribution (structure). The type of structure and its characteristics have decisive impact on the direction of the conducted analysis and the choice of appropriate parameters serving the purpose of describing the statistical population. Knowledge about the distribution helps to avoid formulating false or erroneous conclusions and thus prevents the incorrect assessment of the population Krzysztofiak (1981, 121). Many studies expect that distributions of the studied variable are symmetric and unimodal and have features of a normal distribution. Such a situation allows the analyst to apply a wide range of instruments from the field of descriptive and/or mathematical statistics. It should be noted that normality of the distribution of the examined variable(s) is assumed in many analytical methods applied in modern economics, that significantly facilitates the process of measurement and analysis. The fundamental action, however, should be examining the type of distribution being dealt with. Only then may appropriate measurement methods for the examined phenomenon be applied.

In many studies carried out for the cognitive use of simple tools of descriptive statistics on the regularity of the structure (Table 7.1) may be sufficient. More on this subject, e.g., in Krzysztofiak (1981), Woźniak (1994), Zając (1994), Hozer (ed.) (1996), Luszniewicz and Słaby (1996), Adamkiewicz (1996), and Starzyńska (2004).

Table 7.1 Selected descriptive parameters of structure

Classical parameters	Location parameters
I. Average (location) measures	
Arithmetic mean—x'	Median—M Mode—D Quantiles—$Q_{r.s}$
II. Measures of dispersion (spread, variation)	
Standard deviation—S_x Coefficient of random variation—V_S	Quartile deviation—Q Coefficient of variation—V_Q R—range
III. Measures of asymmetry (skewness)	
Classical coefficient of skewness—A_1	Location coefficient of skewness—A_2
Mixed coefficient of skewness—A_3	

Source: Tarczyńska-Łuniewska (2013) after Hozer (1996, 84)

Table 7.1 may be sufficient in many studies conducted for learning purposes. It may be concluded that the more statistical parameters are applied in the study, the more information regarding the population will be obtained. However, the number of established parameters and their type are not unequivocal. The stage of the analysis of the shape of distribution for particular examined characteristics (variables) as a starting point of the study may be very helpful in this regard and may also serve as a guideline for the selection and assignment of appropriate parameters to describe the surveyed population. The experience of the analyst conducting the survey may also prove significant. Such a person may be considered an expert taking decisions regarding the type or number of estimated descriptive parameters and providing guidelines for conducting the analyses, provided that the expert has received relevant information evidencing it during the course of study. Due to the specificity of experimental studies such a situation is highly probable.

Descriptive parameters of structure can be divided into:

- Parameters of location, defining the "position" of the unit in the surveyed population, determined on the basis of one or several units of the population that hold a special position in the community: The design of measures of location makes these measures insensitive to extreme values occurring in the population.
- Classical parameters, where all units of the surveyed population are taken into account during designation thereof: In contrast to the measures of position, classical measures are heavily influenced by extreme or atypical values.

Averages Tarczyńska-Łuniewska (2013, 167–168)—measures of central tendency—indicate the position of the value best representing all units forming the surveyed population. They are characterized by an average or typical level of variate value. These are the values all other values of the analyzed characteristic focus around.

Measures of dispersion are an approximate measure of a random component. These are measures of numerical estimation of the variability of the surveyed population. They allow one to determine the degree of variation of statistical units in terms of variate value. They show deviations from the average value. Great variation (high levels of measures of variability and variation) is not beneficial in the study of the fundamental strength of economic entities.

Measures of asymmetry allow indicating whether the prevailing number of surveyed units is above or below the average (arithmetic or positional, mainly median).

The use of descriptive parameters in the study (Table 7.1) on the one hand allows to know the structure of the population. Moreover, the level of statistical measures can be associated with the quality of the data on the basis of which the study was conducted. Statistics descriptive parameters allow answering the following questions:

- How did the investigated variables develop in a given period of time or for a particular item?
- What disparities can be observed in their development?
- What properties characterize them (what type of distribution they represent, do they feature high/low variation, asymmetry, etc.)?

The second type of regularities are the regularities of dynamics and volatility. Within the scope of investigation thereof, the methods of studying the dynamics and volatility apply. (Analysis of the dynamics and volatility is a vast field of statistics. For the purposes of this study only certain elements of this method will be discussed.) Within this group of methods it is required that the statistical data are presented in the form of time series for periods (information about the phenomenon in a particular period) or moments (information about the phenomenon at a given moment in time).

Only then is it possible to apply appropriate measurement and analysis instruments. One of these methods of analysis is the observation of the phenomenon over time. Graphic presentation of data recorded in a time series becomes important. When building a graph, one has to bear in mind that the OX axis represents the time axis (t), and the OY axis presents levels of the phenomenon (y_t).

The aims of this group of methods are:

- To learn how the investigated phenomenon developed or ran over time
- To study what direction did or will the changes of the phenomenon take
- Observation of changes of the investigated phenomenon over time

Some methods also provide for forecasting of the investigated phenomena. It needs to be kept in mind that time is not a cause of the change, but it represents the change in the surroundings (e.g., the environment) where the phenomenon occurs, e.g., Woźniak (1994, 205).

Table 7.2 Selected instrument of analysis of dynamics and analysis of variation

Simple indexes of relatives[a]	
Gains	
Absolute chain-base—$\Delta y_{\frac{t}{t-1}}$	Absolute fixed-base—$\Delta y_{\frac{t}{0}}$
Relative chain-base—$\Delta \frac{y_{\frac{t}{t-1}}}{y_{t-1}}$	Relative fixed-base—$\Delta \frac{y_{\frac{t}{0}}}{y_0}$
Indexes (indicators) of relatives—simple (individual)	
Chain-base—$i_{\frac{t}{t-1}}$	Fixed-base—$i_{\frac{t}{0}}$
Trend analysis	
Analytical approach, by means of a specified mathematical function—$y_t = f(t)$ where: $t = 1, 2, \ldots n$	Mechanically, by means of moving averages—$y_t = \sum_t^m = {}_1 w_t y_{t+1}$ where: w_i—defined set of weights meeting condition $\sum_i^m = {}_1 w_i = 1$ m—number corresponding to sub-set ($m < n$) of units of time $t = 1, 2, \ldots (n - m)$

Source: Tarczyńska-Łuniewska (2013, 169), Hozer (1996, 197)
[a]Due to the nature of the conducted research the study does not include aggregate indexes of relatives

In dynamics and volatility regularities, the following instruments of analysis of variation may be employed:

- Short term—most often simple indexes of relatives apply.
- Long term—most often the instruments of trend analysis apply.

Classification and types of instruments of analysis of dynamics and analysis of variation are presented in Table 7.2.

Absolute gains inform about the number of units the size of the investigated phenomenon increased (positive sign) or decreased (negative sign) during the investigation period compared to the base period. The gain of zero means no change in the investigated phenomenon over time. They may be used for phenomena measured in the same units of measurement.

Indexes of relatives (fixed base and chain base), similar to the gains, inform what changes occurred at the level of the phenomenon in the comparable period of time. Indexes are dimensionless quantities; they express a quotient of two quantities of the studied phenomenon, and hence they can be used to compare phenomena expressed in different units of measure. Most often they are interpreted in percentage; however, should the index be equal to 1 it means that a change in the investigated phenomenon occurred. There is an increase when the index is greater than one (e.g., $i_{\frac{t}{0}} = 1.05$ means an increase in the size of an investigated phenomenon by 5 % in the studied period compared to the base period). If the index is less than one it designates a decrease in the size of the investigated phenomenon in the studied period in relation to the base period (e.g., $i_{\frac{t}{t-1}} = 0.95$—there was a decrease in the size of the investigated phenomenon by 5 % in the studied period compared to the preceding period). When examining the dynamics of phenomena, it is useful to establish the average rate of change $\dot{T}$, determined with the geometric mean $1'_{\frac{t}{t-1}}$. (The method of estimating a geometric average in accordance with a specific formula needs to be selected; see, e.g., Hozer (1996, 215).) Then, we gain information on the percentage by which the investigated phenomenon changed on average (increase for $\dot{T} > 0$, decrease for $\dot{T} < 0$) from one period to another.

In the course of a study it is often necessary to know the structure of the time series. In this respect the methods of extracting its components apply: trend, cyclical fluctuations, seasonal fluctuations, and chance fluctuations. The phenomenon's changes over time of a systematic, unidirectional nature are called a trend; its separation determines the occurrence of a regularity. It should be noted that the components of the time series can be superimposed on the trend in an additive or multiplicative fashion (e.g., in Hozer (1996, 244–280), Krzysztofiak (1981, 318–328)), which determines the method of its separation.

The last group of methods for investigating statistical regularities are methods of interdependence regularities (in time and/or space). They have crucial importance in the study of phenomena in economics. They allow detecting the relationships and dependencies occurring in the economy between specific features or phenomena. They can be applied for various types of characteristics/variables, both quantitative and qualitative, describing the analyzed phenomenon or phenomena. Similar to the other methods of studying statistical regularities, the type of characteristics/variables and the way they are recorded (in the form of appropriate series or arrays) impose both the method of describing interdependences and the category of measures that may apply. As for the method of presentation, depending on the size of the surveyed population (sample), characteristics (variables) are recorded through a correlation (usually when numbers are small) or a correlation table (when the sample is large). Analysis of correlation is usually performed by the following:

- Graphical analysis of the dependencies between selected characteristics—fundamental importance in the analysis is carried by a graph (the so-called correlation diagram) in the *XY* coordinate system, where on the basis of mutual arrangement of points in the correlation system for a given dependence the occurrence of the dependence, its direction, and force are established,
- Analysis by means of measures of interdependence—in this case the measures (correlation coefficients) are applied by which the measurement of strength and direction on the dependence are measured. In the first case, the strength of the relationship or dependence is expressed by the level of the given measure. In the second case, the direction of the dependence is evidenced by the sign positioned next to the given measure. These measures are most often standardized. Moreover, attention needs to the paid to the properties of individual interdependence measures to ensure correct application. This may affect the conclusions of the carried out study.

Table 7.3 Selected measures of statistical relations

Measures of statistical relations	
Kendall's coefficient of concordance Q	
Tschuprow's coefficient T_{xy}	
Spearman's rank correlation coefficient R_{xy}	
Correlation ratio e_{xy}, e_{yx}	
iPearson correlation coefficient r_{xy}	
Regression Analysis	
$y_i^A = f(x_i)$	$y_i^A = f(y_i)$

Source: Tarczyńska-Łuniewska (2013, 172) based on Hozer (1996, 305)

- Regression analysis—a description of the relationship between two characteristics by means of an appropriate form of the regression function. In this case, the dependent and independent characteristic/variable needs to be distinguished, so as to properly construct a regression function and thus examine the dependence we are interested in.

All methods of interdependence have certain properties that should be known to the analyst prior to commencing the study. This is related to their proper application, interpretation of results, and constructing final conclusions of the carried out analysis. From the perspective of the specifics of experimental studies, particularly in terms of interdependence, this element is of crucial importance. In studying a dependence, its direction, and strength, different measurement instruments, presented in Table 7.3, may be employed.

The first two measures of statistical relations apply to nominal scales, the third refers to ordinal scales, and the others refer to interval and ratio scales. Regression analysis applies to the ratio scale.

The selected interdependence measures have been summarized below: *Kendall's Q* coefficient measures the concordance between two characteristics, whereas each of them only has two variants. Variability interval (0,1): It can apply to quantitative and qualitative characteristics/variables, but only for fourfold table.

Tschuprow's T_{xy} coefficient is based on a chi-squared test (χ^2) and indicates the strength of association. It takes values $<0,1>$ and is symmetric. It can apply to quantitative and qualitative characteristics/variables. Data for analysis should be presented in a correlation table.

Spearman's R_{xy} rank correlation coefficient—measures strength and direction of association, is characterized by symmetry, and applies to a small number of observations. It takes values $<-1,1>$. Statistical material should be presented in a correlation series. It can apply to quantitative and qualitative characteristics. In certain circumstances it is used interchangeably with the Pearson coefficient.

Correlation ratio e_{xy}, e_{yx}—is used to describe the strength of relationship, and may apply to measurable and non-measurable characteristics, where the dependent characteristic must be measurable. It takes values $<0,1>$. It may be used for linear and nonlinear correlations, and is not symmetric. Data for analysis should be presented in a correlation table.

Pearson linear correlation coefficient r_{xy}—measures the strength and direction of association. It applies to measurable characteristics; the correlation between characteristics must be linear. It takes values $<-1,1>$ and is symmetric. Data for analysis should be presented in correlation series as well as in a correlation table.

Regression analysis, in turn, allows examination of the relationship between characteristics by means of an appropriate mathematic function best describing the mutual relations between the two characteristics. Thus, a regression function may be linear or nonlinear. The direction of the relationship is evidenced by the directional parameter sign (a_y or a_x, depending on which of the characteristics, x or y, constitutes the dependent variable of the function).

Among the methods that can be analyzed in the context of research in experimental economics are the methods of the qualitative phenomena analysis. These phenomena are usually measured on a nominal or an ordinal scale. Among the statistical methods, the following can be distinguished (Steczkowski and Zeliaś, 1997, 47–69):

- Location measures—inform about the average size of particular characteristics in the surveyed population. Due to the type of scale for qualitative phenomena, positional averages are the most useful.
- Relative measures of variability (location or classical).
- Measures of asymmetry.
- Statistical indicators:
  - Structure—ratio of a part to the whole population expressed as a relative number.
  - Magnitude—illustrates the intensity of the studied phenomenon by expressing one quantity in units of different quantity which constitutes a point of reference for the first quantity.
  - Dynamics—describe the growth of the phenomenon over time by creating a relationship between the magnitude of this phenomenon during the studied period and the magnitude of the same phenomenon in the base period.
- Measures of relations for non-measurable characteristics.

In the analysis of qualitative phenomena, the appropriate presentation, the so-called visualization, is also critically important. In fact, this mode of analysis itself can be valuable for the conducted study and may provide a distinct research method. Observation of the chart allows analyzing and evaluating the studied problem. Conclusions based on these have greater cognitive value. Appropriately constructed tables or graphs are used in the presentation of qualitative phenomena. Their type depends on the method of recording and presenting the statistics.

7.3 Basics of Statistical Inference

In experimental studies application of methods of mathematical statistics is particularly important. Mathematical statistics deals with statistical inference methods where, based on the results observed in the sample, conclusions about the general population (universe) are formulated. The task of mathematical statistics is to develop methods that allow generalization of results obtained on the basis of the sample for the entire population. When an experiment is conducted on randomly selected study sample, a process of generalization of results can occur if it is justified by methods with the group of methods of mathematical statistics. There is a lot of elaboration in literature that addresses the statistical methods. In general, statistical methods that appear in the framework of statistics are the same, e.g., Pawłowski (1969, 1980); Greń (1974), Krysicki et al. (1999); Gajek and Kałuszka (2000); and Zeliaś (2000, 164).

There are several reasons for the application of statistical inference in studies:

- The sample was selected from the statistical universe, which was conditioned by the following:
  - The statistical universe is so numerous that the study would be too costly or would involve excessive lengths of time for conducting.
  - The study has a destructive nature.
  - It involves estimate results and there is no need to conduct a study involving all units of the surveyed population.
  - Results of the statistical study should be treated as the results of a sample survey.
  - The observed population is infinitely large, so that no set of observations selected from it exhausts it, e.g., experimental studies.
- In the case of exhaustive studies that include the entire statistical universe at the given time—then the results of surveying this population are treated as results of a sample randomly selected from a higher order population, e.g., investigating births.

Due to methodological assumptions, mathematical statistics is strongly associated with probability theory. This has its substantive justification. Probability theory involves studying the regularity of behavior of the so-called random events, that is, events that depend on chance. Thanks to the application of principles of probability theory it is possible to assess the order of deviation from the structure of relevant characteristics in the statistical universe and to infer about the precision of results of the conducted studies.

Statistical inference methods are divided into two groups of methods, comprising methods of estimation and verification of statistical hypotheses.

The theory of estimation aims to establish parameters and distribution of the statistical universe on the basis of results obtained from the sample randomly selected from the population.

The preliminary action is to determine the random sample to be examined. After drawing (randomly selecting) the sample from the statistical universe, the randomly selected statistical units are measured in the next stage in terms of the investigated attributes and form a statistical series, which is described by means of appropriate characteristics, e.g., the arithmetic mean, variance, standard deviation, or faction. These characteristics of the sample are called statistics. Based on the statistics from the sample, relevant unknown characteristics of the statistical universe, the so-called parameters, are assessed. As the actual (true) value of a given parameter in the statistical universe is not known, they are estimated with predetermined probability, based on the statistics obtained from the sample. An important notion functioning in the framework of mathematical statistics, including estimation theory, is the concept of estimator. Estimator (e.g., Jóźwiak and Podgórski (2006, 202–210))—a relevant function which, based on certain relationships, allows determining the values of the unknown parameter of the statistical universe with some acceptable probability of error and with specified accuracy. It needs to be remembered that the estimator maintains basic properties, i.e., it is consistent, unbiased, and most effective. The actual value that the estimator takes on is assessment of the parameter. Further discussion on statistical inference, including estimation theory, requires introduction of certain names:

- θ—parameter of the statistical universe on which the distribution of random variable X depends
- Tn—parameter's estimator
- tn—estimate of parameter Tn that is actual value that the estimator takes on in the randomly selected sample

Within the framework of estimation theory there is a classification into:

- Parametric estimation—proceedings leading to estimating parameters of the distribution of the statistical universe
- Nonparametric estimation—involves estimating the functional form of the distribution of the statistical universe

Depending on the way the value of a parameter is estimated, estimation can be divided into:

- Point estimates—method of estimation in which a specific value is assumed as the value of a statistical universe parameter, i.e., assessment of the estimator determined on the basis of a random sample. Such estimate is supplemented with a certain measure of the possible error Δ. The notation of results of point estimates is as follows:

$$\Theta = t_n \pm \Delta \tag{7.1}$$

- Interval estimates—involves constructing a numerical range which, with predetermined probability, covers the value of the estimated parameter of the statistical universe:

$$P(a < \Theta < b) = 1 - \alpha \tag{7.2}$$

where:

a and b—bear the name of the bottom and top limits of the confidence interval.

$1 - \alpha$—predetermined probability that the confidence interval will cover a given parameter value, which is called confidence coefficient. The confidence coefficient in practice is selected as arbitrarily large probability. Values most frequently adopted as 1 are the following numbers: 0.90; 0.95; and 0.99. The closer to 1 the confidence coefficient is, the wider the confidence interval we obtain.

It needs to be noted that the length of the confidence interval depends on the following:

- Directly proportional to the confidence coefficient, the higher, i.e., the closer to 1, the longer the confidence interval.
- Inversely proportional to the sample size—the larger the sample size, the shorter the confidence interval.

Furthermore, as regards the confidence coefficient, it is worth keeping in mind that the closer to 1 the confidence coefficient is, the wider the confidence interval (and thus the less accurate the estimated parameter) is. Therefore, coefficients of confidence that are too high should not be adopted without a special need. In addition, at a given confidence level, the larger the sample size, the shorter the confidence interval (i.e., the precision of the estimate increases). With a fixed sample size with an increase in the confidence level, the span of the confidence interval increases (i.e., the precision of the estimate decreases). These elements can be key in the process of development of experimental study results. What is also crucial is the fact that when constructing the confidence interval, it is possible to specify the probability with which the estimated interval includes the value of the unknown parameter. When using point estimates it cannot be specified.

In studies conducted using statistical inference there is a question of whether the obtained results can be generalized to the entire population. In this situation, the accuracy of the estimation needs to be determined. In order to determine it, a relative measure of estimation, the so-called *accuracy of estimates*, is employed:

$$\delta = \frac{|u_\alpha| \times D(T_n)}{t_n} \times 100\% \tag{7.3}$$

In the case of precision of the estimates, its level conditions whether results can be generalized or not. Therefore:

- If $\delta_{t_n} \leq 5\%$—the obtained estimation result may be generalized to the entire statistical universe without reservations.
- If $5 < \delta_{t_n} \leq 10\%$—the obtained estimation result may be generalized to the entire statistical universe with certain caution.
- If $\delta_{t_n} > 10\%$—generalizations shall not be made.

The process of estimation (point or interval) of unknown parameters of the surveyed universe consists of several stages:

1. Defining the parameter (i.e.: the arithmetic mean, variance, structure ratio, parameters of the econometric model).
2. Selecting the estimator and determining the probability distribution.
3. Establishing the confidence coefficient and the maximum estimation error.
4. Determining the minimum sample size.
5. Collecting statistical data.
6. Setting estimator assessment.
7. Construction of the confidence interval.

In addition to the estimation theory, the second primary area of the theory of statistical inference is the theory of statistical hypothesis testing. Understanding the procedures for verifying hypotheses requires knowledge of the related conceptual scope or procedures for the construction of hypotheses and methods of verification thereof. Naturally, given the nature of the verification methods one must not forget the basic principles of probability theory which are employed in this regard.

A statistical hypothesis is any judgment (presumption, assumption) relating to an unknown level of parameters or to an unknown form of distribution of random variables in the statistical universe (population).

Hypothesis is grouped into:

- Parametric hypotheses—concerning (assumptions, judgments of) parameter values of variable distribution in the given statistical universe (when the variable distribution is known). The purpose of parametric hypothesis testing is to specify the value of a distribution parameter of the statistical universe of a known type.
- Nonparametric hypotheses—presumptions about the shape of the distribution of the statistical universe and/or assumptions, judgments about the independence of variables or randomness. The aim of testing this group of hypotheses is to specify the type of variable distribution in a defined statistical universe and/or the occurrence of interdependences between variables or assumptions of randomness.

Hypotheses can be formulated interchangeably depending on the purpose of the conducted statistical analysis. It should also be remembered that in the framework of testing the analyst must operate on two categories of hypotheses:

- The null hypothesis (H_0)—a basic statistical hypothesis which is subject to verification—is tested. The testing process may lead to its rejection or to a conclusion that there are no grounds to reject it. In formulating H_0 it is assumed that the distribution has a certain property.
- The alternative hypothesis (H_1)—a "competitive" hypothesis with respect to H_0. It is formulated as an assumption that the distribution does not have a certain value specified in the null hypothesis, or that it has it in another variant.

If H_0 is rejected, H_1 is accepted.

Taking a formal course, the construction of hypotheses assumes the use of appropriate notation, allowing verification of a given problem. The division of hypotheses into parametric and nonparametric ones in consequence leads to the formulation of hypotheses in an appropriate manner. The following situations are possible:

- When the null hypothesis is parametric, alternative hypotheses can be formulated as follows:

  Two-tailed ($\neq$)—two-tailed critical region
  Right-tailed ($>$)—right-tailed critical region
  Left-tailed ($<$)—left-tailed critical region

- When the null hypothesis is nonparametric, alternative hypotheses are formulated solely in a two-tailed manner (opposite to H_0).

The method of formulating hypotheses depends not only on the purpose of the study, but also on the type of statistical information from the sample. Moreover, defining statistical hypotheses itself does not prejudge their verification. In this regard, appropriate tools in the form of statistical tests (parametric and nonparametric, respectively) need to be used. The statistical test is a rule of conduct, which, based on the results from the sample, is designed to lead to rejection or acceptance of the null hypothesis. There are a lot of statistical tests (Domański, 1979, 1990). The test validation (test statistic) is a random variable with a specified distribution. Distribution of test statistic depends on the researcher's assumptions and knowledge about the statistical universe, the size of the statistical sample available, and the null hypothesis. The test's critical value is the value of a random variable with a specified distribution, which with given probability constitutes the limits of the rejection area (the critical region). It can be two tailed, left tailed, or right tailed. There are many statistical tests suitable for testing hypotheses. Often selection thereof is dictated by the knowledge of the person conducting the study. However, there are test groups assigned to a particular type of studies, thus suggesting their use.

When testing the hypotheses, the value of the test validation is determined from the sample and compared with the critical values. If the test validation value falls within the critical area, it rejects the null hypothesis and accepts the alternative hypothesis. Otherwise, there is no basis to reject the null hypothesis.

Designating the critical region is related to:

- The type of alternative hypothesis
- The distribution of the statistics which constitute test validation (e.g., Student's t-test, chi-square test, F-test)
- The significance level
- The sample size and the number of estimated parameters, which affect test's critical value

Table 7.4 Types of error when testing hypotheses (source: own compilation based on Greń (1974))

Decision	H_0 is true	H_0 is false
Accept H_0	Correct decision	Incorrect decision—type II error
Reject H_0	Incorrect decision—type I error	Correct decision

When testing statistical hypotheses, errors relating to the acceptance or rejection of incorrect hypotheses may be made. In this situation, one can talk of two categories of errors:

- Type *I* error—rejecting H_0 when it is true
- Type *II* error—involves accepting H_0 when it is false and H_1 is true

The decision to accept or reject the hypotheses and types of error are presented in Table 7.4.

In the scope of hypothesis testing, the following stages of procedure can be outlined:

1. Formulating the null hypothesis (H_0) and the alternative hypothesis (H_1)
2. Selecting the test statistic serving verification of the null hypothesis
3. Specifying the value of the test validation
4. Setting the significance level and defining the critical region (rejection region) of the null hypothesis
5. Taking the decision about the specified probability of type *I* error

In the case of experimental studies the use of methods of statistical inference can be a key element. The idea of the methods themselves, associated with the possibility of generalizing the results from the sample to the statistical universe, becomes of particular importance in this regard. Experimental studies generally assume conducting certain activities on the selected (random) sample; hence methods of statistical inference are of such great importance.

References

Aczel AD (2000) Statystyka w zarządzaniu. PWN, Warszawa
Adamkiewicz HG (1996) Statystyka – zastosowania w ekonomii. ODDK, Gdańsk
Bielecka A (2005) Statystyka w biznesie i ekonomii. Teoria i praktyka. WSPiZ im. Leona Koźmińskiego, Warszawa
Domański C (1979) Statystyczne testy nieparametryczne. PWE, Warszawa
Domański C (1990) Testy statystyczne. PWE, Warszawa
Gajek L, Kałuszka M (2000) Wnioskowanie statystyczne. Modele i metody. WNT, Warszawa
Greń J (1974) Statystyka matematyczna. Modele i zadania, PWN, Warszawa
Hozer J (ed) (1996) Statystyka – opis statystyczny. University of Szczecin, Szczecin
Hozer J (ed) (1994) Statystyka. Opis statystyczny. University of Szczecin, Szczecin
Jóźwiak J, Podgórski J (2006) Statystyka od podstaw. PWE, Warszawa

Krysicki W, Bartos J, Dyczka W, Królikowska K, Wasilewski M (1999) Rachunek prawdopodobieństwa i statystyka matematyczna w zadaniach. Cz. II. Statysyka matematyczna. PWN, Warszawa
Krzysztofiak M (1974) Metody statystyczne. PWN, Warszawa
Krzysztofiak M (1981) Statystyka dla wyższych zawodowych studiów ekonomicznych. PWN, Warszawa
Lange O (1952) Teoria statystyki. Polskie Wydawnictwa Gospodarcze, Warszawa
Luszniewicz A, Słaby T (1996) Statystyka stosowana. PWE, Warszawa
Lissowski G, Haman J, Jasiński M (2011) Podstawy statystyki dla socjologów. Tom 3. Wnioskowanie statystyczne, Scholar
Moczko JA, Bręborowicz G (2010) Nie samą biostatystyką... OWN PAN, Poznań
Ostasiewicz S, Rusnak Z, Siedlecka U (1998) Statystyka elementy teorii i zadania. AE w Wrocław, Wrocław
Ostasiewicz W (ed) (1999) Statystyczne metody analizy danych. AE w Wrocławiu, Wrocław
Paradysz J (ed) (2005) Statystyka. AE Poznań, Poznań
Pawłowski Z (1969) Wstęp do statystyki matematycznej. PWN, Warszawa
Pawłowski Z (1980) Statystyka matematyczna. PWN, Warszawa
Sobczyk M (2000) Statystyka. PWN, Warszawa
Starzyńska W (ed) (2004) Podstawy statystyki. DIFIN, Warszawa
Stanisz A (2005) Biostatsytyka, Wydawnictwo Uniwersytetu Jagiellońskiego
Steczkowski J, Zeliaś A (1997) Metody statystyczne w badaniu zjawisk jakościowych. AE Kraków, Kraków
Tarczyńska-Łuniewska M (2013) Metodologia oceny siły fundamentalnej spółek (giełdowych i pozagiełdowych). Zapol, Szczecin
Walesiak M (1996) Metody analizy danych marketingowych. PWN, Warszawa
Woźniak M (ed) (1994) Statystyka ogólna. AE w Kraków, Kraków
Zając K (1994) Zarys metod statystycznych. PWE, Warszawa
Zeliaś A (2000) Metody statystyczne. PWN, Warszawa

Chapter 8
Implicit Association Test (IAT): Using Computer-Based Methods to Measure Consumer Implicit Attitudes

Dominika Maison

Abstract In this chapter is presented a computer-based method of measuring implicit attitudes (IAT—implicit association test) and its potential for experimental economics. For many years attitudes were understood as three-component constructs (cognitive, affective, and behavioral), with an assumption that the person has introspective access to his/her attitude, can verbalize it, and expresses it in a questionnaire. Since the 1980s scientists' attention has been drawn to the unconsciousness of attitudes and the automatic character of them. Introduced the concept of implicit attitude and the method of measuring them—the IAT, a computer-based method using reaction time (RT) as an indicator of attitude strength. At the beginning the IAT was used to study racial attitudes, self-concept, and self-esteem. Nowadays the IAT is used in many other areas, including consumer attitudes (toward brands or categories), both in academic research and in practical context. In this chapter are presented three empirical studies using IAT for researching consumer implicit attitudes: (a) implicit consumer ethnocentrism—implicit attitudes toward local vs. foreign brands ($n=92$); (b) implicit attitudes toward smoking depending on smoking experience ($n=82$); and (c) implicit attitudes toward erotic advertising—the difference between women's and men's reactions ($n=92$).

Keywords Implicit attitudes • Implicit association test • Automatic consumer attitudes • Reaction time

---

D. Maison (✉)
The Robert B. Zajonc Institute for Social Studies, Center for Psychological Research, Psychology Department, University of Warsaw, Stawki 5/7, Warszawa 00-183, Poland
e-mail: dominika@psych.uw.edu.pl

K. Nermend, M. Łatuszyńska (eds.), *Selected Issues in Experimental Economics*, Springer Proceedings in Business and Economics, DOI 10.1007/978-3-319-28419-4_8

8.1 Introduction

Economists are concerned with explaining and finding reasonable solutions to big social problems such as financial crises, pollution, inflation, and unemployment. Economists observe these issues in nature, derive theories from those observations (events as they occur in their complex natural settings), and evaluate their theories in light of additional evidence (Davis and Holt 1993). Many criticize this approach because this way of building and verifying theories is far from hard science: conditions of such studies are usually not fully controlled (because these are complex natural situations), and hypotheses are not verified; therefore conclusions drawn can be sometimes misleading. For a change, experimental economists are trying to study and explain the same economic phenomena using experimental methodology, taken from hard science such as physics or biology (Loewenstein 1999). However, very often experiments conducted in economics remind of psychological experiments (and not those from hard science): they are mostly laboratory experiments, and they are conducted in very artificial situations created only for the purpose of the study, and which hardly resemble natural situations (e.g., artificial shops or banks). Moreover, often the situations created in the experiments are based on the imaginations of the respondents ("imagine you have a loan", "imagine you are unemployed" or "imagine you have a lot of money to invest"), and also the respondents are often students (Davis and Holt 1993). This evokes a lot of criticism, both in psychology and in experimental economics. Nevertheless, this methodology is very promising, because by using modern scientific methods, it makes it possible to verify hypotheses with more control over variables that are usually uncontrolled, rather than just observing the phenomenon in the nature. Moreover, experimental methodology has become more and more popular with the growing popularity of computers, which allows researchers to use more advanced measurement tools and design more complex experiments.

Many economic experiments have, however, some weak point, at least from a psychological perspective; they concentrate only on observing behavior or declaration of behavior (e.g., intention to buy the product) as a consequence of the experimental manipulation (e.g., different price levels), while not being at all interested in individual factors, which can modify those relations. For example, reaction to different price levels can depend on attitude toward money or individual styles of spending money (Maison 2012) and not only amount of money which one has into his/her disposal. Taking into account individual factors such as attitudes, traditional relations observed by economists in economic experiments, "stimuli => behavior" should be modified into a new relation, which includes the individual variable: "stimuli => attitude => behavior" relation.

Attitudes in general are concepts of interest to psychologists and sociologists and neglected by economists. It is probably a consequence of the nature of attitudes: they are abstract concepts impossible to observe directly (only their consequences can be observed), and—probably more importantly—because their measurement is usually based on declaration, and is therefore questionable. In this chapter is described a new approach to attitude, so-called implicit attitudes, and new way of measuring them—the implicit association test (IAT), a computer-based method using reaction time as an indirect indication of attitude (Maison 2004).

8.2 Traditional Approaches to Measuring Attitude

Attitude is a classical term used not only in psychology and sociology. Even though it is not an area of interest in terms of the economy and economists, for marketing, and especially for marketing research and consumer studies, attitudes are very often the subject of the research. There are measured attitudes toward brands, advertising, product categories, concepts, etc. The predominant way of understanding attitudes in marketing followed way in which this concept was understood in psychology and sociology for many years—as a three-component attitude model composed of three factors: cognitive (what a person thinks about the attitude object), emotional (what a person feels toward the attitude object), and behavioral (how does the person behave in the context of attitude object; Allport 1935). This approach to attitudes assumes also that the person has introspective access to his/her attitude, can verbalize it, and expresses in a questionnaire. This understanding of attitude determined the way of studying it—mostly by asking direct questions related to three components of attitudes (cognitive, affective, behavioral) and using 5- or 7-point scale to answer the questions (e.g., from "definitely disagree" to "definitely agree" or from "very negative" to "very positive"). An example of three such questions measuring attitudes to BMW cars would be the following: "What is your opinion of BMW cars?" (very negative/very positive); "Do you like the BMW brand/car?" (definitely dislike/definitely like); "Would you like to have a BMW car?" (definitely no/definitely yes).

The main reason for measuring attitudes in the context of marketing is to ascertain the respondent's attitude toward the object (positive vs. negative) and consequently to predict behavior toward the object (e.g., whether he/she would buy it). However, many examples from marketing practice show that very often the relationship between attitude components is more complex: some people buy a product even though they know that it is not the highest quality, only because they like the brand. In other examples people don't like or don't have positive opinion about the product, but use it because of other, perhaps practical, reasons (e.g., low price, availability).

In the traditional approach to attitudes it is also assumed that the three mentioned components (cognitive, affective, and behavioral) are correlated. It means that, for example, if somebody thinks positively about the object, e.g., a particular brand of car, he/she should also evaluate its features positively, and would like to have this car. And as a consequence, the person also should buy and use this brand of car. However, this assumption often seems to be untrue (Fazio and Zanna 1981). The meta-analysis of 88 attitude-behavior studies carried out by Kraus (1995) delivered evidence of a low degree of relation between the three components of attitude. This analysis revealed that the average correlation between attitude and behavior is on the level of $r = 0.38$. Whether in a particular case this correlation will be very strong, or almost none, depends on a variety of different factors, on the type of the attitude and the kind of measures applied. For example, when measures of many behaviors are aggregated (and not observed just as a single behavior), it results in greater attitude-behavior consistency (Ajzen and Fishbein 1980). Another factor which influences the attitude-behavior consistency is the degree of detail in the questions about attitude—the more concrete and directly connected with behavior is the question, the more correlated it will be with the attitude (Davidson and Jaccard 1979).

8.3 A New Way to Understand Attitude and New Way of Measuring It

The weak relation between the attitude components and weak relation between attitude and behavior made psychologists to revise traditional understanding of attitude and look for new attitude concepts. Since 1980s scientists' attention has been drawn to the unconsciousness of attitudes (Murphy and Zajonc 1993; Zajonc 1980) and the automatic character of them (Bargh 2002; Bargh and Chartrand 1999). Research on subliminal stimuli conducted by Murphy and Zajonc (1993) showed that shortly presented (for a 4 ms) affective-type stimuli (in this particular case they were faces expressing positive or negative emotions) can influence the evaluation of objects that follow afterwards (in this case Chinese ideograms). The same ideogram preceded by a face expressing positive emotions, unseen on the conscious level, was liked more than that ideogram which was preceded by a face expressing negative emotions. This research gives proof that subliminally presented stimuli can activate related affective categories in the absence of conscious awareness. For the attitude theory it means that attitudes can be created without conscious awareness of the person.

More support for unconscious information processing and unconscious creating of attitudes came also from the studies on the effect of mere exposure (Zajonc 1980). In this case participants of the experiment were also shown a set of Chinese ideograms, but the conditions differed in that some ideograms were shown more than others. It turned out that ideograms displayed several times were more liked than those displayed only once or not at all. It should be stressed that this effect appeared regardless of whether the individual was aware that he/she had seen the given ideogram earlier. This result showed, also, that an individual does not always know why he/she likes something and that liking (or disliking) of the object don't have to be a consequence of the features of this object. It also means that a positive (or negative) attitude can be formed unconsciously and automatically, without any conscious (and related) opinion about the object.

Nowadays there is no doubt that the human brain is able to receive stimuli that are not registered on the conscious level. Psychological findings have been supported to some extent by neuropsychology, which delivered strong evidence that emotions can appear earlier than the conscious processes and independently of them (LeDoux 1998). This means that an affective reaction to stimuli may arise beyond any cognitive processing (so-called low-road affective reactions). Therefore, because affective and cognitive processes can be so independently created and processed, they do not necessary have to be so strongly related as it was assumed in traditional attitude theories.

In the context of those discoveries traditional understanding of attitude was no longer sufficient. In the 1990s in psychology were introduced two new concepts of attitudes: "dual attitudes" (Chaiken and Trope 1999) and "implicit attitudes". The dualism of attitudes assumes that the same person can at the same time have two different attitudes towards an object, a conscious one and the other one, which is beyond the consciousness (Chaiken and Trope 1999). Implicit attitude (Greenwald and Banaji 1995) is defined as introspectively unidentified (or inaccurately identified) traces of past experience that may influence reactions, even if the experience is no longer remembered and not available on the conscious level. Thus, the natural consequence of this is the commonly observed dissociation between explicitly self-reported attitudes and implicit attitudes. The attitude-behavior relation is also complicated by the existence of "ambivalent attitudes", which contain positive as well as negative components (Shiv and Fedorikhin 1999). In such a situation, every component of an attitude can be regarded as the true attitude, although they result in predicting different behaviors. One can lead to approaching the attitude object, while the other can lead to avoidance.

Those new concepts of attitudes could better explain many doubts noted in this area, like the weak relation between attitude and behavior observed in practice. The consequence of this new understanding of attitudes, as implicit and automatic processes (i.e., uncontrolled and inaccessible to consciousness and introspection), forced psychologists to search for new methods of studying attitudes, which went beyond declaration and introspection. The first change was a move away from measurements based on the self-descriptive questionnaire and respondent declarations toward indirect measures during which the respondent does not know what is being measured and the outcomes of which are independent of the subject's conscious control. The second change, being a consequence of growing popularity of computers, was use of reaction times (RTs) as indicators of the attitude (Fazio 1990; Fazio et al. 1986; Bargh 1996; Zárate and Smith 1990; Lalonde and Gardner 1989; Gaertner and McLaughlin 1983).

In general, two uses of RT can be distinguished: adjunctive and primary (Gregg and Klymowsky 2013). Their use is adjunctive when they are appended to a conventional direct measure of attitude. In particular, by measuring how long it takes respondents to answer to a question but at the same time without respondent knowledge that reaction time (or rather response time) is measured (Bassili 1996). For example, Fazio and Williams (1986) measured in a telephone survey the speed of answering questions about US presidential candidates. Participants of the survey who responded more quickly were more likely to vote in accord with their explicit attitudes.

In contrast, the use of RT is primary when it is part of a stand-alone indirect measure of attitude based on particular association task (e.g., attributes combined with attitudes object). The majority of methods using primary reaction time are based on the assumption that faster RTs are used to diagnose the presence of stronger association between a target object (object of attitudes) and relevant attributes (describing this object). Shorter RTs in the association object-attribute are interpreted as a stronger implicit attitude toward the object (Fazio 2007). At the moment several methods using RT in primary way exist, e.g.: Lexical Decision Task (Wittenbrink et al. 1997), Adjective Evaluation Task (Fazio et al. 1986), Category Inclusion Task (Dovidio et al. 1986), Extrinsic Affective Simon Task (EAST; De Houwer 2003), the Implicit Relational Assessment Procedure (IRAP; Barnes-Holmes et al. 2010), and probably the best known and the most widely used method—IAT (Greenwald et al. 1998).

8.4 Implicit Association Test: A Method of Studying Implicit Attitudes

The IAT is a method of studying implicit attitudes. It is a computer-based categorization task designed to measure relative strengths of association between concepts in memory. The IAT is easy to implement, generates large effect sizes, and possesses good reliability and those are reasons for its popularity in psychology and related fields.

Initial IAT research focused on racial implicit attitude measurement (Greenwald et al. 1998; Dasgupta and Greenwald 2001), self-concept (Farnham et al. 1999; Greenwald et al. 2003; Greenwald and Farnham 2000), self-esteem (Farnham et al. 1999; Greenwald et al. 2003), gender stereotypes (e.g., Rudman et al. 2001), and stigmatized behavior such as smoking (e.g., Swanson et al. 2001). Nowadays the IAT is also used as a method to research consumer attitudes, both in an academic research context and in a practical context.

The assumption underlying the interpretation of the IAT is that it is easier to give the same response to items in two categories when those categories are associated (for example have the same evaluative value) than when they are not. In this example, suppose flowers and insects have an equally strong association with positive evaluations. Then, there should be no difference in ease of performing the task, regardless of which target category (flowers or insects) is paired with pleasant words. However, suppose instead that the categories have differential evaluative associations (e.g., flowers are more strongly associated with pleasant words than are insects). In this case, it should be easier to perform the task that requires giving the same response to flower names and pleasant words. This would be indicative of a more positive attitude toward flowers than toward insects. The IAT task is described as an implicit measure because it does not depend on participants' awareness of the existence or strength of the associations being assessed. Moreover it captures automatic reactions, because the task is done under the time pressure and is very difficult to fake (Röhner et al. 2011).

The original IAT method consists of doing a computerized categorization task where reaction time is measured. Respondents categorize stimuli into four different categories: (a) two contrasted target concept categories (in the study of Greenwald et al. 1998, experiment 1, flowers and insects), and (b) two contrasted attribute categories (pleasant and unpleasant words). The categorization task consists of presenting a person with a stimulus, which he/she has to categorize quickly into one of the two groups (presented as labels on the left and on the right side of the computer screen).

An example of application of the IAT task into consumer studies can be an IAT task measuring implicit attitudes toward two global and well-known brands: Coca-Cola and Pepsi (Maison et al. 2001). In this example contrasted target categories are Pepsi and Coke and attribute categories are pleasant and unpleasant words (as in many standard IAT studies). The whole IAT task involves five blocks (tasks), from which three are training tasks to train the participants in the appropriate responses to a given set of stimuli (e.g., simple categorization where there are only two categories at the same time, e.g., Pepsi vs. Coke or "pleasant" vs. "unpleasant" words) and two blocks are crucial tasks for the analysis (where four categories are categorized at the same time—combined task), where the speed with which respondent categorizes stimuli belonging to the attitude object or attributes is measured. While the participant is performing the crucial task on each side (left and right) of the computer screen, the names of one of the target categories and the name of one of the attribute categories are presented (e.g., "Coke" and "unpleasant" on the left and "Pepsi" and "pleasant" on the right—see Fig. 8.1). At the same time stimuli belonging to each category (represented by words or pictures) appear in the middle of the computer screen, one at a time (in place of "XXXXX" in Fig. 8.1). These stimuli are exemplars of the four categories (e.g., pictures of Coke symbols, pictures of Pepsi symbols, positive and negative words: love, war, flower, death). The participants' task is to press (as quickly as possible) either the left- or right-hand key (often it is the "A" and "L" key), depending on the side of the screen on which the label of target or attribute category is displayed (e.g., "Coke," "Pepsi" "pleasant," "unpleasant") corresponding to the stimuli appearing in the middle. Two crucial combined tasks differ on side of the screen, on which are displayed the names of categories of attitude object (Pepsi and Coke). In one block participants would do one version of the task with the labels "Pepsi" and "unpleasant" on the left side of the screen and "Coke" and "pleasant" on the right side—initial combined task (as shown in Fig. 8.1) and in the second block participants would do another, reversed version of the task with the labels "Coke" and "unpleasant" on the left side and "Pepsi" and "pleasant" on the right side—reversed combined task.

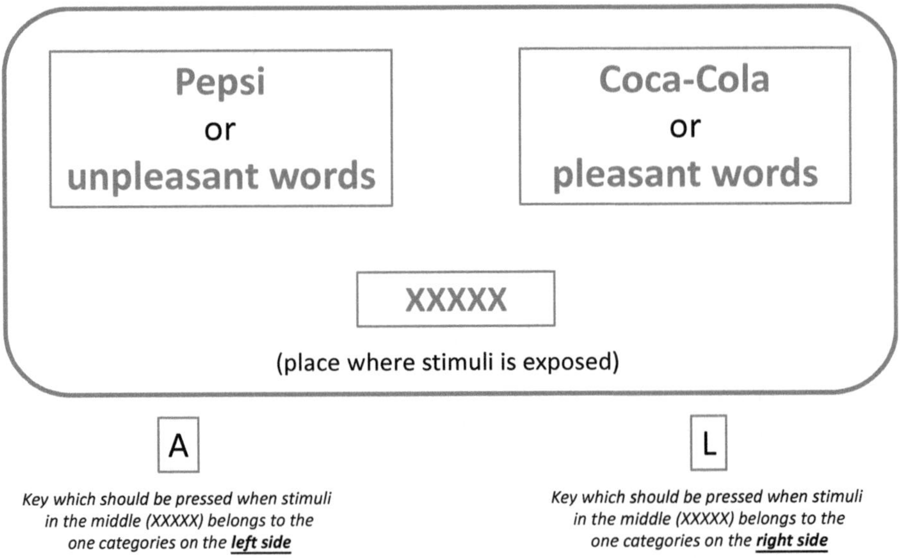

Fig. 8.1 Example of the IAT test to measure implicit attitudes toward two brands, Coca-Cola and Pepsi

The analysis is based on reaction times from the two tasks in which all four categories are presented on the screen (combined tasks). The IAT effect is computed as a difference in average response time between two blocks differing in the side of the screen where the attitude object (Pepsi and Coke) is displayed—the difference in time taken for the initial combined task and the reversed combined task (so-called IAT effect).

The respondent categorizes the item as quickly as possible by pressing the response key that represents its appropriate category. The ease or difficulty with which person is able to assign the same response to distinct concepts is interpreted as a measure of strength of the association between them. The assumption underlying interpretation of the IAT is that it is easier to give the same response to items in two categories when those categories have the same evaluative value (e.g., both are positive or negative) than when they are not (one in positive and one is negative). In this example, suppose Coke and Pepsi have an equally strong association with positive evaluations. Then, there should be no difference in ease of performing the task, regardless of which target category (Coke or Pepsi) is paired with pleasant words. However, when the categories have different evaluative associations (e.g., Coke has stronger positive associations than Pepsi) it should be easier to perform the task when Coke stimuli and pleasant words are at the same side of the screen, then opposite. This would be indicative of a more positive attitude toward Coke than toward Pepsi.

8.5 Implicit Consumer Attitudes: Use of the IAT Method to Answer Marketing Questions (Attitudes Toward Product Categories, Brands, and Advertising)

Consumer studies are an area where the IAT method has been used for more than 15 years to investigate and understand implicit consumer attitudes. At the beginning, IAT consumer studies were focused on validation of the method, where the IAT was used to measure implicit attitudes toward product categories (Maison et al. 2001). The first experiment compared implicit attitudes toward juices vs. sodas. Analysis revealed significant correlation between IAT-measured implicit attitudes and explicit measures of attitudes and behavior toward these product categories (correlations between 0.2 and 0.4 depending on the variable). The second experiment investigated implicit attitudes of females toward low-calorie products and high-calorie products. The implicit attitude toward low vs. high-calorie food measured by IAT correlated with dieting activity: women who had eating habits restricting high-calorie food intake showed implicit attitudes favoring low-calorie products. In later studies was investigated implicit attitudes toward different brands (Maison et al. 2004). In the first study the implicit attitude toward two leading and competing yogurt brands available in Poland (Danone—global brand and Bakoma—local brand) was measured. The second study investigated the relationship between implicit preferences, explicit preferences, and behavior toward two fast food restaurants: McDonald's (global brand) or Milk Bar (local brand). Crucial in this experiment was selection of the respondents based on their actual behavior (respondents had just eaten in one or another place). In the third experiment implicit attitudes toward two global brands (Coke vs. Pepsi) were investigated. Those three studies showed that users of particular brand also showed an IAT effect in the direction of positive implicit attitude toward the same brand. For example, users of McDonald's manifested a positive implicit attitude toward their brand, and users of Milk Bar to their brand (shorter reaction time when Milk Bar products were paired with positive attribute and McDonald's products with negative).

Both sets of experiments showed that IAT could be used to detect implicit attitudes in the consumer context. However, at the same time, they showed correlation with explicit attitude, which might evoke a question about the reason for using complicated IAT computer and reaction time procedures instead of simple direct questioning. Moreover, the correlation of the IAT effect with behavior was often lower than correlation of explicit measure, which might evoke another question—about the predictive validity of the method. Nevertheless, further research using IAT showed that this method can be successfully applied in many different consumer contexts and that IAT can provide knowledge impossible to discover based on declarations. However, the usefulness of the IAT method depends on the type of attitude and type of decision. Some consumers' attitudes are simple and easily accessible to introspection. In such a situation it can be expected that IAT will not add much to what can be provided by traditional attitude measurements, and methods based on reaction time can be omitted. However, other consumer attitudes are more complex, sometimes ambivalent, or even not accepted by a person. In such cases IAT should help to better understand the complexity of these attitudes. The same applies to predictive values of the IAT. In case of impulse behavior or decisions made under time pressure or information overload, IAT should better predict behavior, than in case of deliberate consumer decisions.

Friese et al. (2006) found that participants' choice of either a branded or generic product largely followed their self-reported preferences for one or the other. Among participants whose explicit and implicit preferences matched, explicit preferences predicted product choice roughly 80 % of the time, regardless of whether that choice was made reflectively (at participants' leisure) or impulsively (within a 5-s time limit). However, among participants whose explicit and implicit preferences mismatched, although explicit preferences again predicted product choice when that choice was made reflectively, they did not do so when it was made impulsively (in this case it was predicted less than half the time). Thus, under conditions where quick, more automatic decisions are made—the IAT added predictive value.

In general, when consumer brand choice is made under time-limited conditions implicit attitudes are more connected to behavior, while when consumers have more time available explicitly reported attitudes are more connected to behavior (Wänke et al. 2002). This was supported also by the study done by Friese and colleagues (Friese et al. 2006) who looked at the effect of time pressure on product choice. They found that implicit preferences regarding generic food products and well-known food brands were incongruent respondents were more likely to choose the implicitly preferred brand over the explicitly preferred one when choices were made under time pressure. The opposite results were observed when respondents had no time pressure to make their choice. Taken together, these findings suggest that cognitive resource limitations may lead people to base choices on implicit associations in memory, since they lack the cognitive resources to go through conscious deliberation.

Another factor which can influence whether implicit attitude measured by the IAT method could have predictive value for consumer behavior can be type of attitude, or rather type of attitude object. Some brands are stronger, some are weaker, some are more cognition based, and others more based on emotion and brand image. Toward some brands consumers are more emotionally attached, while others are irrelevant to them. Probably attitudes toward stronger brands, the more emotional ones, with stronger brand images, should be more easily predicted by the IAT method. Brunel et al. (2004) found that Apple Mac users, whose brand identity tends to be more pronounced, showed stronger implicit preferences in IAT test than Microsoft PC users (they showed shorter reaction time when Apple Mac symbols were paired with positive words and Microsoft PC with negative). Priluck and Till (2010) found that, although both self-reported and IAT scores distinguished high-equity from low-equity brands, only IAT scores distinguished between brands that were both high equity (Coke being implicitly preferred to Pepsi). Another confirmation that the IAT can be more connected with stronger attitude was provided by already mentioned study of Maison et al. (2004: Study 3). Participants reported how often they drank Coke vs. Pepsi, their explicit preferences for one or the other (using a scale), and their implicit preferences for one or the other (with the IAT). In general consumption behavior of Coke or Pepsi correlated with explicit preferences. However implicit preferences correlated with behavior only for those who could objectively distinguish Coke and Pepsi in a blind taste test—in other words only for those whose attitudes were more rooted in experience. They not only preferred the brand but also could really see difference in the product features.

A different set of studies explored domains where one might expect dissociation between explicitly and implicitly measured attitudes—ambivalent attitudes. One of these studies explored attitudes toward high- and low-calorie products (Maison et al. 2001). For these products, it was hypothesized that consumers (young women) hold ambivalent attitudes, perceiving high-calorie products as good in taste, but bad for their health and perceiving low-calorie products as bad in taste, but good for their health. When attitudes toward these food products were measured using traditional explicit measures, results suggested that young women preferred high-calorie products on some dimensions (e.g., taste). However, implicit attitude measures revealed that young women had more positive attitudes toward low-calorie products. What is more interesting was that the IAT effect was found to correlate with self-reported eating habits and feelings of guilt while eating high-calorie products. The IAT effect in favor of low-calorie products co-varies with choice of low-calorie products and at the same time with avoidance of high-calorie products. Also a more favorable implicit attitude toward low-calorie products is related to guilty feelings toward eating high-calorie products.

8.6 Study 1: Implicit Consumer Ethnocentrism: Implicit Attitudes Toward Local vs. Foreign Brands

In another study was found (Perkins et al. 2008) that Polish respondents, who generally report an explicit preference for foreign brands (e.g., Marlboro cigarettes), nonetheless expressed an implicit preference for domestic ones (e.g., Sobieski cigarettes). This finding can be associated with consumers' implicit ethnocentrism, which on an automatic level triggers preference for local products over foreign, although experience with better quality foreign cigarettes (which is what was objectively true at that time) created correction of the preference on explicit level.

The goal of the first study was to check the level of explicit and implicit preference of local (Polish) vs. global (foreign) brands in different product categories (not only cigarettes). While choosing the product consumers react to many different cues, some of them are intrinsic—directly connected to the product (e.g., taste, smell, consistency) and other extrinsic—not directly connected to the physical product (e.g., brand, country of origin; Watson and Wright 2000). It was assumed that in the case of brand preference a discrepancy could be observed between what people declare and what are their automatic, implicit preferences, depending on its local vs. foreign origin. In many developed countries a preference of local brands over foreign products is observed (consumer ethnocentrism; Watson and Wright 2000; Shimp and Sharma 1987); however in less developed countries people often prefer foreign products perceived as better quality (and often they are indeed of better quality). Quantitative surveys conducted on a representative nation-wide sample show that in general Polish consumers prefer foreign brands over local, especially in the context of technically developed products (Maison and Baran 2015). Therefore in this study it was predicted that a discrepancy between explicit and implicit brand preference of brands of different origin can be observed. Even though most people will explicitly prefer foreign brands, on the level of automatic, implicit brand preference, people will prefer local brands (as a consequence of automatic in-group preference).

Ninety-two people participated in the research (47 female and 45 male, aged 17–19). All of them filled in questionnaire where their preference for different brands was measured (chosen from a pair of two brands in the same category of which one was Polish, the other foreign) and after the IAT was measured with four categories used: (a) target categories—the same set of Polish and foreign brands as used in the explicit part; and (b) attribute categories: set of positive and negative words.

The results showed a very strong explicit preference of foreign brands over Polish (explicit allocentrism). On the contrary the IAT showed strong implicit automatic preference for Polish brands over foreign (implicit ethnocentrism). The IAT task when Polish brands were on the same side of the computer screen with positive words ([−]Foreign/PL[+]) was performed faster, than when they were reversed ([−]PL/Foreign[+]). The difference in implicit ethnocentrism was also observed depending on explicit preference of foreign brands (Fig. 8.2). Comparison of the IAT effect between extremely allocentric consumers (those who in explicit preference in case of all pairs preferred foreign brands) and those who preferred at least some Polish brands (mixed preference) showed that implicit ethnocentrism was not observed in the first group, only in the second.

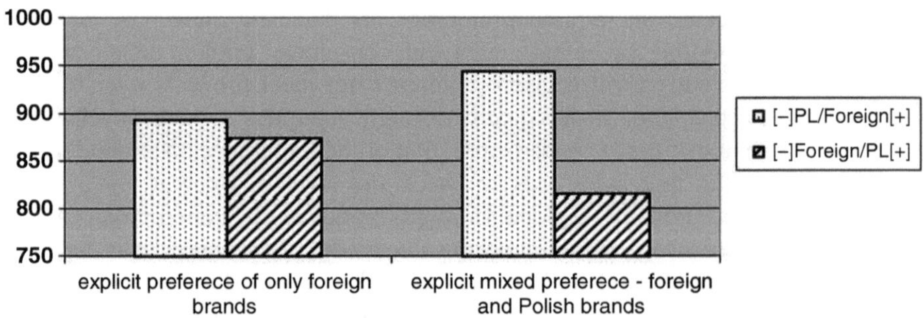

Fig. 8.2 Comparison of implicit attitudes toward local vs. global brands (IAT effect) among people who prefer on explicit level only foreign brands or those who preferred foreign and Polish brands (mixed preference). *Comparison between two tasks ([−]PL/Foreign[+] vs. [−]Foreign/PL[+]): $t[90] = 2.08$; $p < 0.04$. The difference in IAT effect between two groups of respondents (preferring only foreign brands or with mixed preference: Polish and foreign): $t[52] = 4.53$; $p < 0.0001$

The results of this study delivered new insights into knowledge about consumer ethnocentrism. It shows that consumer ethnocentrism is a very complex phenomenon where the discrepancy between explicit (declared) and implicit preference (IAT) can be observed—even though respondents showed explicit preference of foreign brands, on an implicit level they preferred Polish brands. The observed results can be a consequence of different roots of implicit and explicit attitudes toward brands. Explicit attitude is probably formed based on rational assumptions and experience. Implicit attitudes, on the contrary, are based on emotional cues, and automatic positive inclination for this which belongs to the in-group (in this case Polish in origin).

8.7 Study 2: Implicit Attitudes Toward Smoking Depending on Smoking Experience

The goal of the second research was to study the difference in explicit vs. implicit attitude toward ambivalent behavior—smoking cigarettes. Following earlier studies on implicit attitudes toward smoking (Swanson et al. 2001) it was predicted that people in general will have a negative implicit attitude toward smoking; however this attitude will be modified by experience with smoking. The strongest implicit negative attitude toward smoking will be observed among nonsmokers, but the weakest among regular smokers. It means that among smokers will be observed dissociation of attitude—positive on explicit level, however still negative on implicit level.

Eighty-two people participated in the study (56 female and 26 male). The respondents were selected based on purposive criterion—experience with smoking: (a) regular smokers (smoking minimum 10 cigarettes everyday, $n = 27$); (b) occasional smokers (not smoking everyday, smoking minimum 5 cigarettes per month, $n = 25$); and (c) nonsmokers ($n = 30$).

As was predicted the results showed that explicit attitude toward smoking was more positive among smokers than among nonsmokers (smokers - 3,24; occasional smokers - 2,94; nonsmokers - 2,41 Fig. 8.3—index created based on six questions; difference between three groups of smokers - $F[2.79] = 7.63$; $p < 0.001$). At the same time the result of IAT test showed strong negative implicit attitude toward smoking: the IAT task was performed faster when negative words were on the same side of the screen with smoking and positive words with nonsmoking ([−]smoking/nonsmoking[+]). Moreover this attitude depended on the experience with smoking. The strongest negative implicit attitude toward smoking was observed among nonsmokers, but the weakest among smokers (Fig. 8.3).

Summarizing, people in general have strong implicit attitudes toward smoking; however the strongest of these negative implicit attitudes toward smoking are among nonsmokers. However experience with smoking is to some extent reducing this automatic negative reaction, and causing less negative implicit attitude toward

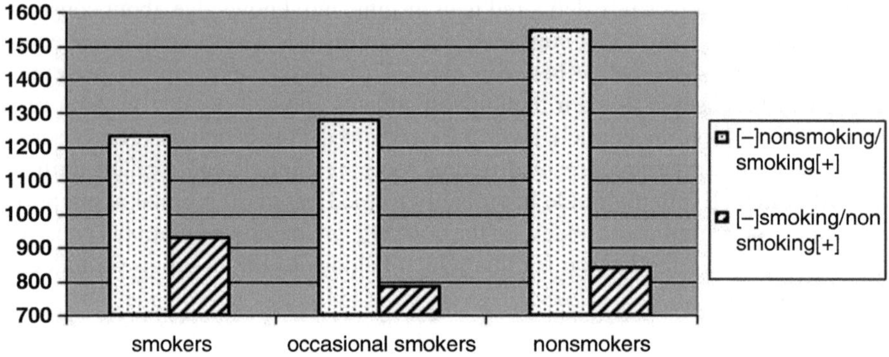

Fig. 8.3 Implicit attitude toward smoking among regular smokers ($n = 27$), occasional smokers ($n = 25$), and nonsmokers ($n = 30$). *The difference in reaction time (IAT effect) between three groups of smokers (one-way $F[2.79] = 11.17$; $p < 0.0001$)

smoking (probably because of the tendency for internal consistency). What is interesting was that smokers didn't have positive implicit attitude toward smoking, but still negative, only weaker. This shows that smokers have an ambivalent attitude toward smoking: positive on the explicit level, but still negative on implicit.

8.8 Study 3: Implicit Attitudes Toward Erotic Advertising

Another area where IAT can also be used in the consumer context is advertising research, where it can help to better understand real reactions toward advertising. Earlier study results showed that the IAT method helps in better understanding reactions toward ads with ethnically different spokespersons (Brunel et al. 2004). While explicit attitude toward tested advertising didn't show the differences in reaction of white respondents toward ads with white- or black-skinned spokespersons, implicit attitude (measured by IAT) showed bigger preference for ads with a white spokesperson than black spokesperson. Results of those studies show that using implicit measures can be very helpful in identifying factors influencing reactions to ads, especially those which one does not want or is not able to express.

The goal of the third research was to study implicit vs. explicit attitude of women and men toward erotic advertising. Erotic advertising is a very controversial type of ad, which evokes a lot of discussion especially about its effectiveness. Some people (usually working in advertising agencies) believe that it is effective because of attracting attention to the ad and evoking positive emotions (Whipple 1992). Others criticise it because it might distract attention from the product itself and can create negative emotions (some people might not like them). Therefore it was assumed that attitudes toward erotic advertising are ambivalent and a dissociation between explicit level (more deliberated and dependent on social norms—norm of tolerance) and implicit level (more individual and affective) can be expected. Moreover it was expected that women and men will react in different ways toward erotic advertising—women will have more negative implicit attitude toward erotic advertising with female models than men.

Ninety-two respondents (49 female and 43 male, aged 19–30, mostly students) participated in the study. At the beginning was measured the explicit attitude toward erotic advertising (11 questions) and afterwards respondents conducted the IAT. The target stimuli in the IAT were ads of a travel agency, modified in such a way that the same ad had two versions: (a) female model was clothed or (b) female model was partly naked (two sets of the same ads). The second category was a standard set of positive and negative adjectives.

As expected, explicit attitude showed positive attitudes toward erotic ads and more positive evaluation of ads used as stimuli in the IAT, when the model was naked. Moreover, as was predicted this positive attitude was stronger among men than women. However on the implicit level more positive reaction was observed in case of non-erotic ads, than erotic ads. The IAT task was performed faster when naked women were placed on the same side of the computer screen with negative words ([−]erotic/not erotic[+]), than opposite ([−]not erotic/erotic[+]). Moreover this effect (negative implicit attitude toward erotic ad) was much stronger among women than men (Fig. 8.4).

Summarizing, in case of attitudes toward erotic ads dissociation between explicit and implicit reactions can be observed. On the explicit level respondents (mostly young people and students) declared positive attitude toward erotic ads; however on the implicit level negative reaction was discovered—more negative implicit attitude toward ads with naked female model than toward ads with dressed model. This negative implicit attitude was especially strong among women than men.

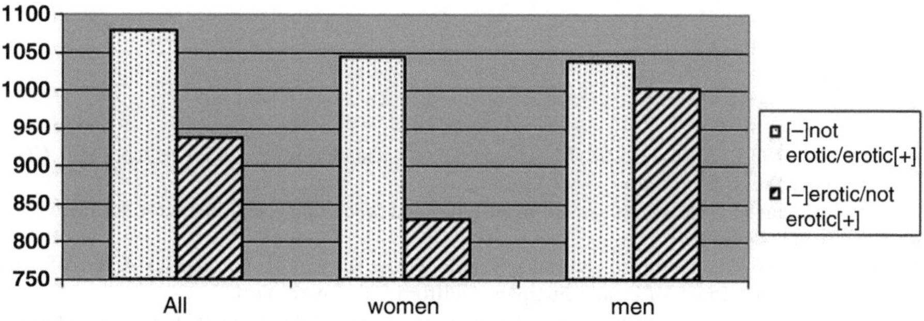

Fig. 8.4 Implicit attitude toward erotic vs. non-erotic ads (with naked female model vs. clothed) in the whole sample ($n=92$) and among women ($n=48$) and men ($n=43$). *The difference in reaction time between two IAT tasks for (**a**) the whole sample $t[91]=3.97$; $p<0.0001$; (**b**) for women $t[48]=5.62$; $p<0.0001$; and (**c**) for men—n.s. The difference between IAT effect between women and men: $t[90]=2.55$; $p<0.013$

8.9 Summary and Potential Uses of the IAT Method in Experimental Economics

The IAT is a relatively new, computer- and reaction time-based method, which has huge potential applications for the study of economic issues. Originally this method was invented to study phenomena, which are not accessible to introspection, are often unconscious, and are beyond control, where it was assumed that people are not always rational and don't behave in a predictable way. The IAT method was initially used to research subjects typical of social psychology (e.g., stereotypes, prejudices) or personality psychology (e.g., self-esteem). After some time, the IAT method attracted the attention of consumer researchers, who used it to study consumers' implicit attitudes toward brands, product categories, or advertising—all areas where it can be assumed that consumers have limited introspective access, some attitudes can be unconscious, and traditional methods were giving poor predictions of behavior.

Experimental economics is an area where, by using experimental methodology and tools developed by psychology, economic questions are answered. Therefore the IAT method should have also potential here, especially in the study of implicit attitudes toward subjects important to economy: financial issues, such as loans, credits, or money. There have already been some trials using IAT to study economic issues. Gasiorowska (2014) used it to study implicit attitude toward money and found that a positive attitude toward money was correlated with a symbolic but not instrumental approach to money. It means that people who perceived money in symbolic way (associating it with for example power, position, prestige) had a shorter reaction time when money symbols were paired with positive words than with negative. In other economic experiments, the IAT method could also be used as individual variables explaining part of the behavior studied in those experiments.

References

Allport GW (1935) Attitudes. In: Murchison G (ed) Handbook of social psychology. Clark University Press, Worcester

Ajzen I, Fishbein M (1980) Understanding attitudes and predicting social behavior. Prentice Hall, Engelwood Cliffs, NJ

Bargh JA (1996) Automaticity in social psychology. In: Higgins E, Kruglanski A (eds) Social psychology: handbook of basic principles. Guilford Press, New York

Bargh JA (2002) Losing consciousness: automatic influences and consumer judgment, behavior, and motivation. J Consum Res 29:280–285

Bargh JA, Chartrand TL (1999) The unbearable automaticity of being. Am Psychol 54:462–479

Barnes-Holmes D, Barnes-Holmes Y, Stewart I, Boles S (2010) A sketch of the implicit relational assessment procedure (IRAP) and the relational elaboration and coherence (REC) model. Psychol Rec 60:527–542

Bassili JN (1996) Meta-judgmental versus operative indices of psychological properties: the case of measures of attitude strength. J Pers Soc Psychol 71:637–653

Brunel FF, Tietje BC, Greenwald AG (2004) Is the implicit association test a valid and valuable measure of implicit consumer social cognition. J Consum Psychol 14:385–404
Chaiken S, Trope Y (1999) Dual-process theories in social cognition. Guilford Press, New York, NY
Dasgupta N, Greenwald AG (2001) On the malleability of automatic attitudes: combating automatic prejudice with images of admired and disliked individuals. J Pers Soc Psychol 81:800–814
Davidson AR, Jaccard JJ (1979) Variables that moderate the attitude-behavior relation: results of a longitudinal survey. J Pers Soc Psychol 37:1364–1376
Davis DD, Holt CA (1993) Experimental economics: methods, problems, and promise. Estudios Economicos 8:179–212
De Houwer J (2003) The extrinsic affective Simon task. Exp Psychol 50:77–85
Dovidio J, Evans N, Tyler R (1986) Racial stereotypes: the contents of their cognitive representation. J Exp Soc Psychol 22:22–37
Farnham SD, Greenwald AG, Banaji MR (1999) Implicit self-esteem. In: Abrams D, Hogg MA (eds) Social identity and social cognition, vol 17. Blackwell Publishers, Malden
Fazio RH (1990) A practical guide to the use of response latency in social psychological research. In: Hendrick C, Clarc MS (eds) Research methods in personality and social psychology. Sage Publications, London
Fazio RH (2007) Attitudes as object-evaluation associations of varying strength. Soc Cogn 25:603–637
Fazio FH, Sanbonmatsu DM, Powell MC, Kardes FR (1986) On the automatic activation of attitudes. J Pers Soc Psychol 50:229–238
Fazio RH, Williams CJ (1986) Attitude accessibility as a moderator of the attitude-perception and attitude-behavior relations: an investigation of the 1984 presidential-election. J Pers Soc Psychol 5:505–514
Fazio RH, Zanna MP (1981) Direct experience and attitude behavior consistency. Advances in experimental social psychology 14:161–202
Friese M, Wanke M, Plessner H (2006) Implicit consumer preferences and their influence on product choice. Psychol Market 23:727–740
Gasiorowska A (2014) Psychologiczne znaczenie pieniędzy [psychological meaning of money]. PWN, Warsaw
Greenwald AG, Banaji MR (1995) Implicit social cognition: attitudes, self-esteem, and stereotypes. Psychol Rev 102:4–27
Greenwald AG, Nosek BA, Banaji MR (2003) Understanding and using the implicit association test: I. An improved scoring algorithm. J Pers Soc Psychol 85:197–216
Greenwald AG, Farnham SD (2000) Using the implicit association test to measure self-esteem and self-concept. J Pers Soc Psychol 79:1022–1038
Greenwald AG, McGhee DE, Schwartz JKL (1998) Measuring individual differences in implicit cognition: the implicit association test. J Pers Soc Psychol 74:1464–1480
Gregg AP, Klymowsky J (2013) The implicit association test in market research: potentials and pitfalls. Psychol Market 30:588–601
Kraus SJ (1995) Attitudes and the prediction of behavior: a meta-analysis of the empirical literature. Pers Soc Psychol Bull 21:58–75
LeDoux J (1998) The emotional brain: the mysterious underpinnings of emotional life. Simon & Schuster, New York
Lalonde RN, Gardner RC (1989) An intergroup perspective on stereotype organization and processing. Br J Soc Psychol 28:289–303
Loewenstein G (1999) Experimental economy from the vantage – point of behavioural economics. Econ J 109:25–34
Gaertner S, McLaughlin J (1983) Racial stereotypes: associations and ascriptions of positive and negative characteristics. Soc Psychol Q 46:3–30
Maison D, Greenwald AG, Bruin R (2001) The implicit association test as measure of implicit consumer attitudes. Pol Psychol Bull 32:61–70

Maison D, Greenwald AG, Bruin RH (2004) Predictive validity of the implicit association test in studies of brands, consumer attitudes, and behavior. J Consum Psychol 14:405–415
Maison D (2004) Utajone postawy konsumenckie. Analiza możliwości wykorzystania metody IAT (implicit consumer attitudes. Possibilities for using implicit association test). GWP, Gdańsk
Maison D (2012) Polak w świecie finansów. [Pole in the financial world]. PWN, Warszawa
Maison D, Baran T (2015) Dobre, bo (nie)Polskie? O uwarunkowaniach i konsekwencjach etnocentryzmu konsumenckiego [Good because (not)Polish? About causes and consequences of consumer's ethnocentrism]. Marketing i Rynek 10:2–10
Murphy ST, Zajonc RB (1993) Affect, cognition, and awareness: affective priming with optimal and suboptimal stimulus exposures. J Pers Soc Psychol 64:723–739
Perkins A, Forehand M, Greenwald AG, Maison D (2008) The influence of implicit social cognition on consumer behavior: measuring the non-conscious. In: Haugtvedt C, Herr P, Kardes F (eds) Handbook of consumer psychology. Lawrence Erlbaum Associates, Hillsdale, NJ
Röhner J, Schröder-Abé M, Schütz A (2011) Exaggeration is harder than understatement, but practice makes perfect! Faking success in the IAT. Exp Psychol 58:464–472
Rudman LA, Greenwald AG, McGhee DE (2001) Implicit self-concept and evaluative implicit gender stereotypes: self and in-group share desirable traits. Pers Soc Psychol Bull 27:1164–1178
Priluck R, Till BD (2010) Comparing a customer-based brand equity scale with the implicit association test in examining consumer responses to brands. J Prod Brand Manag 17:413–428
Shimp T, Sharma S (1987) Consumer ethnocentrism: construction and validation of the CETSCALE. J Market Res 24:280–289
Shiv B, Fedorikhin A (1999) Heart and mind in conflict: the interplay of affect and cognition in consumer decision making. J Consum Res 26:278–292
Swanson JE, Rudman LA, Greenwald AG (2001) Using the implicit association test to investigate attitude-behavior consistency for stigmatized behavior. Cogn Emot 15:207–230
Wänke M, Plessner H, Friese M (2002) When implicit attitudes predict brand choice and when they don't. In: Zwick R, Ping T (eds) Asia pacific advances in consumer research, vol 5. Association for Consumer Research, Valdosta, GA
Watson JJ, Wright K (2000) Consumer ethnocentrism and attitudes toward domestic and foreign products. Eur J Market 34:1149–1166
Whipple TW (1992) The existence and effectiveness of sexual content in advertising. In: Danna SR (ed) Advertising and popular culture. Bowling Green State University Popular Press, Bowling Green
Wittenbrink B, Judd CM, Park B (1997) Evidence for radical prejudice at the implicit level and its relationship with questionnaire measures. J Pers Soc Psychol 72:262–274
Zajonc RB (1980) Feeling and thinking: preferences need no inferences. Am Psychol 35:151–175
Zárate MA, Smith ER (1990) Person categorization and stereotyping. Soc Cogn 8:161–185

Chapter 9
Neuroscience Techniques in Economic Experiments

Anna Borawska

Abstract Cognitive neuroscience is a new and rapidly developing field of research that brings together many different scientific domains. Although it emerged as a discipline only over the last two to three decades, it is widely used in many different applications. This chapter is intended to present briefly the concepts of cognitive neuroscience and to show how they are used in economics—especially when designing and performing experiments. It is done in the form of a synthetic review of the main trends in cognitive neuroscience tool applications in contemporary research publications. On the basis of this overview conclusions concerning possible future applications and trends are presented.

Keywords Cognitive neuroscience • Economic experiments

9.1 Introduction

Cognitive neuroscience is a new and rapidly developing field of research. It brings together many different scientific domains, chiefly psychology and neurobiology, but also philosophy, linguistics and many other sciences that incorporate study of the mind in their programs. Although cognitive neuroscience emerged as a discipline only over the last two to three decades, due to the advancement in technology, especially in neuroimaging and computational capabilities of processing the recorded signals, it is widely used in many different applications. These are not limited only to medical or biological ones, but also include domains that are seemingly quite distant. Because of merging cognitive neuroscience with many different areas of research, we observe now the development of numerous interdisciplinary sciences with the neuro-prefix. One of them, which is of special interest in

A. Borawska (✉)
Department of Computational Methods in Experimental Economics, Faculty of Economics and Management, Institute of IT in Management, University of Szczecin, Mickiewicza 64, 71–101 Szczecin, Poland
e-mail: anborawska@gmail.com

K. Nermend, M. Łatuszyńska (eds.), *Selected Issues in Experimental Economics*, Springer Proceedings in Business and Economics, DOI 10.1007/978-3-319-28419-4_9

this book, is neuroeconomics. It emerged as a fusion of behavioural and experimental economics around the 1990s and since then its popularity and recognition still grow (Glimcher et al. 2009).

This chapter is intended to present briefly the concepts of cognitive neuroscience and to show how they are used in economics—especially when designing and performing experiments. The next section aims to explain the origins of cognitive neuroscience and to describe some fundamentals of using it as a tool in economics. Then, in the following part, some core techniques of neuroscience are presented. At the end, there is an overview of various applications of cognitive neuroscience tools in economical experiments described in recent publications. The chapter ends with a short summary and a presentation of future possibilities that may support economics research.

9.2 Cognitive Neuroscience: General Concept and Origin of Its Application in Economics

Cognitive neuroscience emerged at the intersection of cognitive science and neuroscience. The first of the above-mentioned domains concerns mental processes and information processing associated with cognitive functions. The second one investigates mainly functional properties of the brain (Purves et al. 2013). Given this background, cognitive neuroscience covers quite a substantial range of research topics—from measuring brain functions and assessing cognition and behaviour to dealing with complexities of linking these elements together. This does not mean, however, that it is all about mapping the brain region's activation to psychological processes and looking for the so-called neural correlates of cognition (Purves et al. 2013). The latter notion is also very important, but cognitive neuroscience is mainly about creating biologically grounded models of cognitive functions. Such models support our knowledge about the brain, mostly thanks to imaging of brain activity and other techniques that allow to infer details about how the brain works (Camerer et al. 2005). Moreover, what is especially important in social sciences, cognitive neuroscience can help us to sort out the validity of different theories of human behaviour. In other words, cognitive neuroscience is the study of the neural mechanisms of cognition (Gazzaniga 2002).

The story of neuroscience in economics starts with decision-making problems. In the late 1980s a study on monkeys (Newsome et al. 1989) showed the correlation between neuronal activity and stochastic choice. It was also the first successful attempt to predict decisions from single-neuron activity. First research on humans was undertaken on the individuals with some brain damages (e.g. Bechara et al. 1994). However, better understanding of the relation between mental and neural functions in humans was not fully possible until the development of methods to image human brain activity non-invasively. These advances in technology in the field of cognitive neuroscience started then to be applied by behavioural and experimental economists to both test and develop alternatives to neoclassical/revealed preference theories (Glimcher et al. 2009). The examples of such research and the description of tools which are thereby applied are presented in the following parts of this chapter.

9.3 Techniques of Cognitive Neuroscience

The potential of cognitive neuroscience is primarily due to the development of brain activity measurement technologies (such as functional magnetic resonance imaging, fMRI) and adapting older technologies (including eye-tracking or electroencephalography) for new applications (Camerer 2007). Commonly used techniques of cognitive neuroscience can be divided into four main groups (Zaleśkiewicz 2008; Shiv et al. 2005):

- Neuroimaging of brain
- Neurophysiological techniques
- Examination of individual nerve cells
- Neuropsychological techniques (the study of neurological patients with brain damages)

In studies unrelated to medicine mainly neuroimaging and neurophysiological techniques are used. As it was already mentioned in the first part of this book, in economics research four major areas most often make use of experiments. These are studies concerning individual decision-making and eliciting preferences, game theory, social dilemmas and functioning of the market and its regulations. These are the core topics when it comes to experiments with the use of cognitive neuroscience tools as well. However, due to the specific way of recording the data and the equipment that is needed, the performed research is limited mostly to the issues of individual human beings. As a result, the dominating trends of neuroscientific experiments in economics are:

- Individual decision-making and intertemporal choice
- Risk attitudes
- Eliciting individual preferences
- Social dilemmas

The rest of this chapter is focused on research concerning these four areas and discusses the use of neuroimaging and neurophysiological techniques.

9.3.1 Neuroimaging of Brain

Neuroimaging is associated with a group of research methods used to study the structure and function of the brain. Among them there are electro- and magneto-physiological techniques, exploring the electrical and magnetic activity of neurons and tomographic methods in which it is proposed to infer about neuronal activity indirectly (Jaśkowski 2009). Generally, in the area of economic sciences the most applicable methods are electroencephalography (EEG) and functional magnetic resonance imaging (fMRI).

EEG is focused on the measurement of brain electrical activity recorded by electrodes placed on the scalp at specific locations (Purves et al. 2013). Because of its very good temporal resolution, this method is usually used to study changes in brain activity in time and to analyse reaction to external stimuli (Zaleśkiewicz 2008). Electroencephalography is not specific enough to determine exactly which areas of the brain are activated during performing certain tasks. In such applications, fMRI is much better suited. With its help, you can tell how much oxygen is delivered to specific parts of the brain and deduce their activity (Purves et al. 2004). Examples of experiments performed with the use of EEG and fMRI are shown in Tables 9.1 and 9.2.

Table 9.1 Exemplary research with the use of fMRI (source: own elaboration)

Work	Short description of research
Individual decision-making and intertemporal choice	
De Martino et al. (2006)	Authors investigated the framing effect by means of functional magnetic resonance imaging and a novel financial decision-making task concerning choice between two options in different contexts of gain and loss.
Grygolec et al. (2008)	Experiment investigates whether and how nature of social observability (private vs. social), degree of responsibility (external vs. personal) and their interactions influence the evaluation of outcomes in a simple decision problem.
Kable and Glimcher (2010)	The study investigates intertemporal decision-making and people's preferences concerning the delay of rewards.
Risk attitudes	
Minati et al. (2012)	The study provides the comprehensive evaluation of effective connectivity during risky decision-making (evaluation of gambles).
Eliciting individual preferences	
Alexopoulos et al. (2013)	The aim of the study was to investigate how the outcomes of the respective other are evaluated by participants who were treated fairly or unfairly themselves and to what extent agency influences concerns for fairness.
Social dilemmas	
Baddeley et al. (2012)	Research presents experimental evidence confirming that there are significant propensities to herd when people make financial choices. Moreover, evidence from fMRI data suggests that herding is a process of social learning.
Ramsøy et al. (2014)	The study suggests that empathy is related to the individual difference in the engagement of mentalizing in social dilemmas and that this is related to the efficiency of decision-making in social dilemmas.

Table 9.2 Exemplary research with the use of EEG (source: own elaboration)

Work	Short description of research
Individual decision-making and intertemporal choice	
Wang et al. (2006)	The study shows an attempt to explore human cognitive-affective interactions in strategic thinking through a neurocomputational modelling approach. Empirical justification of the model is carried out with a neuroimaging experiment using the ultimatum game.
Polezzi et al (2008)	On the basis of Ultimatum Game, the study supports the idea that economic decisions are significantly affected by non-rational factors, trying to narrow the gap between formal theory of economic rationality and the real decisional behaviour.
Risk attitudes	
Polezzi et al (2009)	The study highlights the idea that economic decision-making in case of risk attitude is not exclusively determined by payoffs but strongly affected by context.
Minati et al. (2011)	The study examines risk aversion of participants with the use of various gambles. Its findings provide potential biomarkers of choice in risky situations.
Eliciting individual preferences	
Ma and Hu (2015)	The study aimed to elucidate how the female subjects' facial attractiveness affected the male subjects' fairness and decision-making in social exchanges.

9.3.2 Neurophysiological Techniques

Techniques in this group are based on the correlation of brain function with physiological sensations (Zaleśkiewicz 2008). The most frequently used (especially in experiments on the effect of emotions on the actions and cognitive functions of respondents) are measurements of galvanic skin response (GSR), heart rate (HR) and eye-tracking (ET). The reason for their popularity is relatively simple registration and interpretation of signals.

Measuring GSR is based on detecting electrical changes in the skin (Dawson et al. 2007) and it is mostly performed on the skin of the hand (fingers). Heart rate measurement is performed on the wrist of the left hand or on the chest—the frequency of heart beats per minute is recorded (Dulleck et al. 2014).

Eye-tracking, on the other hand, is an effective tool for experimental research because of its abilities to detect eye position, gaze direction, sequence of eye movement and visual adaptation during cognitive activities. ET (with an appropriate software) provides both a quantitative and qualitative analysis of the gaze, which is very useful in understanding choice and decision-making behaviour (Popa et al. 2015).

Table 9.3 GSR measurement in economic experiments (source: own elaboration)

Work	Short description of research
Individual decision-making and intertemporal choice	
van't Wout et al. (2006)	The study aims to verify hypothesis that an emotional state, assessed on the basis of skin conductance, could allow for predicting the decision-making.
Adam et al. (2009)	The research states that the assessment of market participants' physiological arousal allows for a deeper understanding of how single facets of market design that affect market participants' emotional processing are essential for successful market engineering.
Social dilemmas	
Jaber-Lopez et al. (2014)	The study examines the behaviour and emotional arousal of the participants in an experimental auction, leading to an asymmetric social dilemma involving an auctioneer and two bidders.

Table 9.4 Eye-tracking in economic experiments (source: own elaboration)

Work	Short description of research
Risk attitudes	
Devetag et al. (2015)	The research analyses subjects' eye movements while they make decisions in a series of one-shot games. Results suggest that subjects apply bounded rational decision that involves best responding to the simplification of a decision problem.
Eliciting individual preferences	
Reutskaja et al. (2011)	The research deals with computational processes deployed by consumers during the search and decision processes and examines how these processes change with the number of options. Results are obtained on the basis of reaction times and eye movements of the participants during decision-making.
Khushaba et al. (2012)	The experiment explores the nature of decision-making by examining the associated brain activity with EEG and tracking the eye gaze with an eye-tracker. Decisions are designed to elicit the subjects' preferences.
Funaki et al. (2011)	In the study the participant's eye movements made during making choices are tracked. It is hypothesized that if an individual is actually motivated by a particular social preference, then he or she will acquire information accordingly, which will be reflected by a distinct pattern of eye movements.
Social dilemmas	
Colombo et al. (2013)	The aim of the research is to test how the perception that the responder is lying affects the proposers' offers in the Ultimatum Game. Results show that lie detection is crucial in economic decisions that involve interaction with other people.

Tables 9.3 and 9.4 show the exemplary research done in different scopes of experimental economics with the application of GSR measurement and eye-tracking.

Publications included in the tables do not cover all the research that is being done in experimental economics with the application of cognitive neuroscience tools. They present, however, an overview of the most popular issues that have been recently examined by experimental economists.

9.4 Conclusion

Experimental methodologies combined with imaging and other neuroscience tools can help us better understand the mechanisms of decision-making, choice, preference, risk seeking or avoidance and different approaches to gain and loss.

The analysis of publications presented in the tables shows that in most cases researchers use only one or two different cognitive neuroscientific tools. It is mainly due to various difficulties and the cost associated with acquiring data in such a way. Despite these obstacles, it can be assumed that in the future the experiments that use multiple tools at the same time will be more and more common. Such merger could offer deeper insight into neurophysiological foundations of people's economic behaviours.

Apart from that, there are more areas of research which have not yet been fully explored and could prove of further interest. Among them there is a field that has recently gained quite a lot of interest, namely the marketing research. Experiments within this domain and their benefits are described in more detail in the third part of this book.

References

Adam MPT, Gamer M, Hey S, Ketter W, Weinhardt C (2009) Measuring the impact of emotions on decision-making in electronic markets: a physio-economic approach. In Proceedings of the International Conference on Group Decision and Negotiation (GND), Toronto, Canada, June 14–17 2009

Alexopoulos J, Pfabigan DM, Göschl F, Bauer H, Fischmeister FS (2013) Agency matters! Social preferences in the three-person ultimatum game. Front Hum Neurosci 7:312

Baddeley M, Burke C, Schultz W, Tobler P (2012) Herding in financial behaviour: a behavioural and neuroeconomic analysis of individual differences, Cambridge Working Papers in Economics

Bechara A, Damasio H, Tranel D, Damasio A (1994) Deciding advantageously before knowing the advantageous strategy. Science 28:1293–1295

Camerer CF (2007) Neuroeconomics: using neuroscience to make economic predictions. Econ J 117(519):C26–C42

Camerer CF, Loewenstein G, Prelec D (2005) Neuroeconomics: how neuroscience can inform economics. J Econ Lit 43:9–64

Colombo B, Rodella C, Riva S, Antonietti A (2013) The effects of lies on economic decision making. An eye-tracking study. Res Psychol Behav Sci 1(3):38–47

Dawson ME, Schell AM, Filion DL (2007) The electrodermal system. In: Cacioppo JT, Tassinary LG, Berntson G (eds) Handbook of psychophysiology. Cambridge University Press, Cambridge

De Martino B, Kumaran D, Seymour B, Dolan RJ (2006) Frames, biases, and rational decision-making in the human brain. Science 313(5787):684–687

Devetag G, Di Guida S, Polonio L (2015) An eye-tracking study of feature-based choice in one-shot games. Exp Econ 18:1–25

Dulleck U, Schaffner M, Torgler B (2014) Heartbeat and economic decisions: observing mental stress among proposers and responders in the ultimatum bargaining game. PLoS One 9(9): e108218

Funaki Y, Jiang T, Potters J (2011) Eye tracking social preferences. Unpublished manuscript. Available via University of Pennsylvania. https://sites.sas.upenn.edu/behav-ethics/files/eye_tracking_social_preferences_2014-01-31-fjp.pdf. Accessed 15 Sep 2015

Gazzaniga M (2002) Cognitive neuroscience. WW Norton & Company, New York

Glimcher PW, Camerer CF, Fehr E et al (2009) Introduction: a brief history of neuroeconomics. In: Glimcher PW, Camerer CF, Fehr E et al (eds) Neuroeconomics: decision making and the brain, 1st edn. Academic, San Diego, pp 1–12

Grygolec J, Coricelli G, Rustichini A (2008) A neuroeconomic study of social observability and personal responsibility in decision making an fMRI experiment. Paper presented at the 2008 North American Summer Meeting of the Econometric Society, Carnegie Mellon University, Pittsburgh, 19 – 2 Jun 2008

Jaber-Lopez T, Garcia-Gallego A, Perakakis P, Georgantzis N (2014) Physiological and behavioral patterns of corruption. Front Behav Neurosci 8:434

Jaśkowski P (2009) Cognitive neuroscience. How brain creates mind? Vizja Press & IT, Warszawa [in Polish]

Kable JW, Glimcher PW (2010) An "As Soon As Possible" effect in human intertemporal decision making: behavioral evidence and neural mechanisms. J Neurophysiol 103:2513–2531

Khushaba RN, Greenacre L, Kodagoda S, Louviere J, Burke S, Dissanayake G (2012) Choice modeling and the brain: a study on the electroencephalogram (EEG) of preferences. Exp Syst Appl 39(16):12378–12388

Ma Q, Hu Y (2015) Beauty matters: social preferences in a three-person ultimatum game. PLoS One 10(5)

Minati L, Grisoli M, Franceschetti S, Epifani F, Granvillano A, Medford N, Harrison NA, Piacentini S, Critchley HD (2011) Neural signatures of economic parameters during decision-making: a functional MRI (fMRI), electroencephalography (EEG) and autonomic monitoring study. Brain Topogr 25(1):73–96

Minati L, Grisoli M, Seth AK, Critchley HD (2012) Decision-making under risk: a graph-based network analysis using functional MRI. NeuroImage 60:2191–2205

Newsome WT, Britten KH, Movshon JA (1989) Neuronal correlates of a perceptual decision. Nature 341:52–54

Polezzi D, Daum I, Rubaltelli E, Lotto L, Civai C, Sartori G, Rumiati R (2008) Mentalizing in economic decision-making. Behav Brain Res 190:218–223

Polezzi D, Sartori G, Rumiati R, Vidotto G, Daum I (2009) Brain correlates of risky decision-making. NeuroImage 49:1886–1894

Popa L, Selejan O, Scott A, Mureşanu DF, Balea M, Rafila A (2015) Reading beyond the glance: eye tracking in neurosciences. Neurol Sci 36:683–688

Purves D, Augustine GJ, Fitzpatrick D, Katz LC, LaMantia AS, McNamara JO et al (2004) Neuroscience. Sinauer, Sunderland

Purves D, Cabeza R, Huettel SA et al (2013) Principles of cognitive neuroscience. Sinauer, Sunderland

Reutskaja E, Nagel R, Camerer CF, Rangel A (2011) Search dynamics in consumer choice under time pressure: an eye-tracking study. Am Econ Rev 101(2):900–926

Ramsøy TZ, Skov M, Macoveanu J, Siebner HR, Fosgaard TR (2014) Empathy as a neuropsychological heuristic in social decision-making. Soc Neurosci 10:179–191

Shiv B, Bechara A, Levin I, Alba JW, Bettman JR, Dube L, Isen A, Mellers B, Smidts A, Grant SJ, McGraw PA (2005) Decision neuroscience. Mark Lett 16(3/4):375–386

van't Wout M, Kahn RS, Sanfey AG, Aleman A (2006) Affective state and decision-making in the ultimatum game. Exp Brain Res 169:564–568

Wang H, Coble C, Bello P (2006) Cognitive-affective interactions in human decision-making: a neurocomputational approach. In Proceedings of the 28th Annual Meeting of the Cognitive Science Society, Vancouver, BC, Canada, pp 2341–2346

Zaleśkiewicz T (2008) Neuroeconomics. Decyzje 9:29–56 [in Polish]

Chapter 10
Reading Facial Expression to Understand Human Emotions: Micro-Expressions Training Videos (METV): The New Tool for Experimental Economics

Kasia Wezowski and Dominika Maison

Abstract Micro-expressions are reliable indicators of individuals' true emotions and experience. Therefore, the ability to read and understand micro-expressions is important to individuals' social functioning and in many different professional areas. The goal of this study was to test the relationship between micro-expression recognition ability and emotional intelligence (EI), which can be perceived as the ability to function well in social life. The study used micro-expressions training videos (METVs), a new tool for detecting micro-expressions on faces filmed on videos, and the SIE-T test, which is a measure of emotional intelligence (Matczak et al. 2005). Social ability skills were measured through self-declaration. Forty students participated in the study. The results indicated a positive correlation between EI (SIE-T) and the ability to recognize facial expressions (METV). Moreover, METV performance was correlated with certain dimensions of social skills (declaration).

Keywords Body language • Emotional intelligence • Experimental Economics • Facial expressions • FACS • METT • METV • Micro-expressions • Non-verbal communication

K. Wezowski (✉)
Center for Body Language, Antwerp, Belgium
e-mail: kasia.contact@gmail.com

D. Maison
Center for Psychological Research, The Robert B. Zajonc Institute for Social Studies, Stawki 5/7, 00-183 Warszawa, Poland
e-mail: dominika@psych.uw.edu.pl

K. Nermend, M. Łatuszyńska (eds.), *Selected Issues in Experimental Economics*, Springer Proceedings in Business and Economics, DOI 10.1007/978-3-319-28419-4_10

10.1 Introduction

10.1.1 The Role of the Facial Expressions of Emotions in Recognizing Emotional Reactions

Understanding human features, particularly facial expressions, has always been essential in businesses seeking to hire manpower, as well as in investigations. In 1872, Darwin claimed that facial expressions are collective, common, and universal throughout cultures and species. He posited that emotional expressions are mostly unintentional and spontaneous in nature and that people cannot possibly constrain their emotions entirely or precisely formulate their emotional states at any given time. He further speculated that human behaviours and features are pure and basic mediums for understanding people's identities. For example, if a person is angry, his or her facial expressions will reveal this anger. Tomkins (1963) expounded on this perspective through the theory that people are emotionally driven by feelings and that it is a natural human state to feel according to given stimuli. Tomkins (1963) supported the idea that human beings are driven by diverse emotions and that such emotions are depicted on their countenances. Along with Tomkins (1963), Ekman and Friesen (1969) argued that "the emotions revealed by the human beings were seen through their faces" (p. 12). In other words, faces display the diverse forms of human emotions.

According to Tomkins (1963), the emotions demonstrated on the face are not socially learned; rather, they are the results of physical reactions triggered by various stimuli, situations, or occurrences. In fact, in one study, Ekman and Friesen (1971) modified their study framework, lengthening it to support their previous models and concepts. Their study framework included the theory that cultural differences are one significant determinant of how facial expressions are translated and assessed based on reactions to stimuli. Matsumoto and Hwang (2001) presented convincing evidence that the micro-expressions of emotion are significant clues to the mysteries of human features. Using the micro-expression recognition approach, they demonstrated that facial reactions occur in a fraction of a second and that they cover a diversity of emotions ranging from happiness to fear. Some behavioural experts have expressed uncertainty about the impact of facial recognition analysis, citing the need for further studies to support existing claims. However, according to Goldin et al. (2008), such experts were unsure of how the process worked or how the program could be utilized to study complex human emotions. Hence, further discussions are required to elaborate on the various methods (e.g. METT, METV, as described further in this text) for testing how emotions display on the face.

A related study by Matsumoto et al. (2008) confirmed that facial expressions are the by-products of the human response system. This result strongly indicates that, though human attitudes are complex, facial expressions reveal and manifest the real human nature. Matsumoto et al. (2008) expounded that the human behaviours are inherent to all humans and that they can only be manifested through various stimuli. Cole et al. (1989) found this theory challenging, but verified that facial expressions are innate and distinctive in nature. They also found that blind people present similar facial expressions when they receive appropriate stimuli from a given environment.

10.1.2 Micro-Expressions of Emotions: The Way to Recognize Hidden Emotions

The term "micro-expressions" was defined by Haggard and Isaacs (1966) and Ekman and colleagues (Ekman 2001; Frank and Ekman 1997). Micro-expressions, as previously noted, are split-second nuances of emotions that appear briefly and unexpectedly on an individual's face (Goldin et al. 2008). They are rapid and spontaneous and are triggered by various brain movements that correspond to emotional reactions. When an emotional reaction is experienced, it prompts the brain to fire off impulses that cause unconscious muscle contractions. Some micro-expressions have been known to occur for half a second, and they manifest when certain stimuli occur (Yan et al. 2013).

There are certain instances and situations that compel individuals to stifle their facial expressions in order to hide their emotions. For example, someone may smile and greet another person in a way that sounds optimistic and high spirited, despite genuinely not wanting to speak to or acknowledge the other person. In this case, the individual presents a false façade that is not detected by the other person. In certain instances, people are even driven to hide their true feelings because they do not want to expose what they are experiencing (Ekman 1971). This human condition typically occurs in social settings, when people do not like the social environment. Using the inhibition hypothesis, Ekman (1992) mirrored these micro-expressions and contended that it is nearly impossible for people to suppress their true emotions in their facial expressions. Ekman (1992) disproved declarations that people can hide their true feelings, showing that strong negative emotions, such as anger, fear, hatred, and disgust, are conspicuous. Even when experiencing positive emotions, such as happiness, joy, and surprise, people reveal what they feel through their faces. Ekman (1992) noted that micro-expressions, compared to normal facial expressions, are very difficult to hide or fake because they last only 5 s or less and are true representations of what we experience in the limbic system.

Micro-expressions are displayed on your face through visible movements of eyebrows, lips, noses, and mouths. People able to read micro-expressions using these movements can gain information that is accurate and reliable. According to Ekman (1992), micro-expressions can be quickly hidden, only to be immediately revealed again. People often believe that they can hold in their anger and rage for long periods of time; however, they fail to recognize that emotion appears naturally. Ekman (1992) confirmed the theory that people are unable to hide their emotions for long periods: instead, true emotions manifest once people reached their quota of patience. Ekman (1992) further believed that even when people are adept at hiding their emotions through their countenances, they can never hold facial expressions for extensively long periods of time. No matter how much people believe that they can conceal their emotions, it is possible to detect hidden emotions with a trained eye (Ekman 2001). For this reason, Ekman (1992) described micro-expressions as a symptom, a sign, or an indication of one's unpretentious human nature.

Moreover Tomkins (1963) challenged this certainty that people are expressively driven by their frames of mind and that the natural human states of feeling are innate for given stimuli. Ekman and Friesen (1969) illustrated human behaviours through experiments in both controlled research laboratory settings and in the field. Consequently, in their experiments, the differences in emotions among individuals remained definitive and conditional upon given situations and circumstances (Buck 1976; Rosenthal et al. 1979). In keeping with Tomkins' beliefs (1963), Ekman et al. (1969) maintained that "the human emotions, which were revealed by people, were seen through their appearances and gestures" (p. 12). Even if people try to conceal their emotions or use cosmetics to cover their visages so that they cannot be read, they will noticeably display emotions beyond their control. This is because people can sometimes demonstrate behavioural patterns separate from the dictates of their minds. These human emotions can be identified through their faces and appearances.

While human emotions are universal in nature, micro-expressions have proven difficult to recognize. In cases of crime and deep inquiries into evidence, exceptional skills and abilities are needed to distinguish whether criminals are telling the truth (Hurley 2012, 378). Some criminals have learned to hide their emotions during covert investigations, while others have been able to conceal their feelings while telling lies. For this reason, some agencies require facial expression analysis skills. In fact, facial expression readers have become integral parts of criminal investigations and are used in lie detection technologies (Schubert 2006; Weinberger 2010). They are used in investigations to help extract hidden information and uncover dangerous behaviours (Metzinger 2006; Schubert 2006; Weinberger 2010). Additionally, micro-expression recognition can be used in cases of the physical, mental, and emotional abuse of children and adults (Asla et al. 2011). Hall and Bernieri (2001) found that there are gender differences in terms of interpersonal sensitivity to the recognition of facial expressions of emotions. These suggest that females are better able than males to render accurate assessments of facial expressions; however, the results consistently showed that the positive outcomes of facial expressions could be read through certain measures and tools (Hall 1984).

Micro-expressions have been instrumental in removing the guesswork from determining people's intentions in social interactions with others while promoting a clear understanding of people's underlying intentions (Hurly 2011). Micro-expression recognition has vast, far-ranging capabilities with regard to discerning how individuals react in various situations. It can be used in situations ranging from assessing how customers react to different customer service situations to determining their reactions to advertisements and marketing (Wezowski and Wezowski 2012). Micro-expression recognition can even be relevant to in-depth and sophisticated investigations, such as those conducted after an unexpected terrorist attack (Weinberger 2010).

10.1.3 The Role of Reading Facial Expressions in Experimental Economics

Micro-expressions are especially important for experimental economics in relation to social outcomes. McArthur and Baron (1983) speculated that social outcomes are maximized when facial expression is precisely depicted. Marsh et al. (2005) also introduced some studies that relate to social functions. They asserted that reading facial expressions can be misleading, since people may exhibit different facial expressions and facial expressions might be received in different ways by different people (Keating et al. 1977; Marsh et al. 2005). In fact, they confirmed that various behavioural patterns may be unidentified or identified incorrectly because people have learned to control their emotions. Even when people use lie detector tests, the impacts of the test are unreliable because human emotions and facial expressions are complex (Keating et al. 1977; Marsh et al. 2005). Knapp and Hall (1997) assumed that understanding nonverbal cues would tend to provide an individual with an above-average accuracy in determining others' emotions and facial expressions of another.

Furthermore, there is evidence that professional observers may be more sensitive to the occurrence of micro-expressions and that laypeople can be easily trained to recognize them (Ekman and Friesen 1969; Matsumoto and Hwang 2011; Shen et al. 2012). As a result, in the context of the dyadic business relationship between a salesperson and a consumer, micro-expressions can play a role in the final outcome. Shapiro (2003) considered the dangers inherent in revealing one's true emotional state to a stranger; a person who reveals emotion too easily may become an easy target for manipulation (p. 738). On the other hand, increased sensitivity to non-verbal communication, as in the case of micro-expressions, may lead to increased satisfaction on both ends of a transaction (Puccinelli et al. 2013).

The role of emotions in business relationships is examined through the theories of emotional contagion and emotional labour. The first maintains that employees may influence the emotional states of customers by exhibiting emotions themselves. The second postulates that employees exhibit an expected range of emotions to customers, following different sets of display rules with varying degrees of authenticity. Hennig-Thurau et al. (2006) showed that emotional mimicry goes only so far in affecting the consumers' emotions, while the quality of employees' emotional labour is more successful.

10.2 How to Measure Micro-Expressions

Micro-expressions are considered involuntary facial expressions that result from experienced emotions and last only a few seconds. All of these expressions represent either positive or negative emotions experienced by an individual. Therefore, it is important to measure micro-expressions, and various methods have been developed to do so.

10.2.1 METT: Image-Based Program to Recognize Micro-Expressions of Emotions

In 1978, Paul Ekman and Wallace Friesen developed the idea of facial reading through photographs of human faces. Their work was based on the Facial Action Coding System rules, which are rules used to identify which facial muscles are responsible for which emotions. Based on these rules, they created the first micro-expression testing program, called the Micro-Expressions Training Tool—METT (Ekman 2002). According to Ekman (2002), the METT refers to an online micro-expression training tool with the ability to recognize micro-expressions based on context (Zhang et al. 2014). Interestingly, the two developers (Dr. Paul Ekman and Dr. David Matsumoto) of the METT decided to discontinue the technique; however, both went on to develop their own micro-expression training software programs, which are available on their respective sites. In addition to the METT, numerous other micro-expression recognition programs have been developed (Ekman and Friesen 2003). Notably, these other programs use 2D pictures (static stimuli) to describe human behaviours and study the human condition.

The METT has been used traditionally to teach micro-expressions (Ekman 2003). It has numerous applications. In the case of schizophrenia, a pilot study was conducted to investigate the effectiveness of micro-expression training. The study revealed that patients with schizophrenia made significant improvements in emotion recognition following training with this tool. The METT has also been used for remediation therapy for such patients (Russell et al. 2006). Further, METT training is very useful for health care practitioners and professionals, since it can help them identify patients withholding information or help to identify the intentions of suicidal victims and psychiatric patients (Endres and Laidlaw 2009).

The METT is also useful in training professionals to deal with theft and crime. It helps security and national security personnel understand people's true intentions. Subtle facial movements help to identify deceitful intentions or when individuals try to mask fake smiles (Pote 2012). METT training can also help police officers to identify person who attempt to conceal felt emotions through the expression of another emotion, thus helping in lie detection and criminal investigations (Metzinger 2006; Schubert 2006; Weinberger 2010).

10.2.2 METV: Video-Based Program to Recognize Micro-Expressions of Emotions

In addition to the METT, other testing programs, such as the Micro Expressions Training Videos (METV) program, have been developed (Wezowski and Wezowski 2012). The METV is a unique new program for identifying human features that does not utilize photographs or two-dimensional art, like Ekman's METT. Instead, it uses illustrative videos of people talking, listening, speaking, and carrying out other human activities to reveal human features in a natural setting (Wezowski and Wezowski 2012). The METV program uses videos to show facial expressions and the evolution of these expressions in natural interactions and under conditions natural for human beings (www.microexpressions.org).

Through the METV program, it is possible to reveal the process of how emotions emerge on the face. Thus, the METV program has great possibilities for training and facilitating learning and knowledge on this topic. The METV program enables users to view videos in slow motion or in an accelerated mode in order to focus on a specific angle or frame in order to enhance viewers' learning and to increase people's understanding of how the process of exhibiting reactions affects subjects' looks and appearance. Such understanding could not be accomplished with photo descriptions (e.g. as in the METT). Ultimately, the METV program was designed to support further learning on behavioural aspects and to assist government agencies and business sectors. It teaches the personal interaction skills necessary to understand human behaviours in organizations. Finally, the METV application was created specifically for practical applications: for example, to facilitate the learning and understanding of human behaviours and attitudes during job interviews, negotiations, and business meetings.

10.3 Study 1: The Relation Between Micro-Expression Recognition and Emotional Intelligence

10.3.1 Theoretical Background

The recognition of micro-expressions plays a very important role in human interactions. This may be due to the recognition of expressions of emotion, which is a part of emotional intelligence (EI). Importantly, EI can be described as the ability to understand and even respond to the emotions in normal daily life (Porter and ten Brinke 2010). Various studies reveal that EI is a learned and instinctual skill that can be cultivated in various ways. Such ways include learning more about EI, paying attention to EI, and reading previous research studies concerning EI (Gunderman 2011). Therefore, EI has significant importance in micro-expression studies.

The concept of EI represents a mixture of behaviours, abilities, and behavioural tendencies. EI describes the ability to perceive, manage, and understand one's own emotions and the emotions of others (Porter and ten Brinke 2010). The ability to evaluate emotion accurately, access emotionality through thought processes, and understand emotional responses promotes intellectual growth (Waal 2003). EI is divided into two major categories: (1) interpersonal, involving perceptions of others' emotions and empathy; and (2) intrapersonal, involving self-regulation, motivation, and awareness of emotions.

The other aspect of EI's importance concerns the real advantage that it provides in competitive micro-expression studies. According to Spencer (2001), economic competency involves any underlying characteristic of a person that is related to his or her effective performance in any given task. Other studies support the idea that EI helps individuals become competent in communication skills, thereby expanding their micro-expression abilities (Stubbs Koman and Wolff 2008). Interestingly, micro-expressions have also been shown to enhance EI—and, hence, the link between EI and micro-expressions. Importantly, EI ensures that an individual improves his or her micro-expression studies by improving his or her thinking skills and building better professional relationships (Stubbs Koman and Wolff 2008).

Micro-expression recognition is much more than simply reading mechanically the correct emotion from a face. It also involves the ways that we process this information and what we gain from it. Furthermore, it involves an understanding of human emotions and the ability to react—which, in effect, is EI. According to Goleman (1995, 1996), emotional intelligence and social intelligence are critical qualities that drive the performance of salespeople. Emotional intelligence, in this sense, is the ability to identify and respond to various emotions appropriately.

The METV advantage over other methods used to detect the micro-expressions is that the program does not use static pictures of faces; by contrast, METV uses videos to show facial expressions. In addition, METV videos show the evolution of expressions in actual interactions. Therefore, we assume that the METV is a good tool for detecting EI.

10.3.2 Goals of the Study

The main goal of this study was to understand the relationship between people's recognition of facial expression of emotions (micro-expressions) using the METV method and their EI, which can be perceived as their ability to function well in social life. We assumed that people who have a good ability to recognize facial emotions will also have high EI (i.e. the objective indicator of functioning in social life) and will perceive themselves to be high functioning (i.e. the subjective indicator of functioning in social life). In this study, the objective was to compare people's performances on the METV test with their performances on a non-verbal test of EI based on their recognition of complex emotions presented using pictures of faces (SIE-T, Matczak et al. 2005).

A secondary goal of this study was to determine whether people's performance on the METV would correlate with their self-declarations of interpersonal skills.

The study tested the following hypotheses:

H1: METV test scores will correlate with SIE-T test scores (objective measure). People who receive higher scores on the METV will also receive higher scores on the SIE-T.

H2: METV test scores will correlate with participants' self-declarations of interpersonal skills (subjective measure).

10.3.3 Methodology

10.3.3.1 Instruments and Procedure

In the research, participants were given two tests from the METV program: (a) normal speed, in which a variety of examples of emotions played at normal speed (Part C from the original program), and (b) double speed, in which videos played at double speed (Part D from the original program). This approach challenged participants to recognize emotions under difficult conditions. For research purposes, participants were exposed to a set of 20 videos randomly chosen from a set of 300 METV videos. The purpose of choosing the videos randomly was to avoid biases in the use of video materials to identify facial expressions. Since each picture included a description of the relevant emotions, respondents were able to identify and reveal emotions in a number of possible ways.

The SIE-T—Faces (Skala Inteligencji Emocjonalnej—Twarze) is a non-verbal test measuring people's ability to recognize expressions showing emotions, which is assumed to be one of the basic components of EI (Matczak et al. 2005). The test is composed of 18 photographs—nine of men and nine of women—that express different complex emotions. Six possible emotions are listed under each picture, and respondents must indicate which of the listed emotions (e.g. fear, joy, happiness, surprise, uncertainty, disrespect, admiration, rage, or anger) fits the emotion expressed by the face in the picture. Because the SIE-T tests people's recognition of complex emotions, the correct answer can include more than one emotion (e.g. a single face may express fear, anger, and sadness). The SIE-T has been validated in several studies that have shown that it has the potential to improve our understanding of human behaviour, particularly within organizations. The reliability of the test is high (Cronbach's alpha = 0.65).

Measurements of interpersonal skills were based on personal declarations. Specifically, each participant selected the degree (on a five-point scale) to which each of the following statements was true: (1) I perceive myself as an empathetic person; (2) I can correctly detect another person's mood; and (3) interaction with other people is or will be part of my professional activity.

During the study, participants completed in the following order: (a) the METV program; (b) the SIE-T test; and (c) the self-description of the level of interpersonal skill questionnaire (three questions).

10.3.3.2 Participants

The research sample was drawn from the population of psychology students at the University of Warsaw, Poland. The total number of participants was 40 ($n = 40$), including 20 females and 20 males, with an average age of 21.5 years old. It should be noted that none of these participants had previous exposure to the micro-expression measurement tools (METV).

10.4 Results

The first hypothesis (H1) assumed that those respondents who performed better on the METV would also perform better on the SIE-T test. As observed, the correlation tests were conducted between the SIE-T test and (a) regular and (b) double-speed METV videos. High and statistically significant correlations were found in both cases. The SIE-T correlated with both the regular METV ($r = 0.572, p < 0.001$) and the double-speed METV ($r = 0.656, p < 0.001$), indicating that the respondents who were able to correctly read facial expressions based on the METV also performed better in the SIE-T. These respondents were able to recognize behavioural patterns of certain depicted emotions in ways that showed that they had mastered such skills as identifying covert behaviours.

The second hypothesis (H2) assumed that those respondents who performed better on the METV would also declare higher interpersonal competences. The results showed some correlation between the METV and the declared interpersonal skills (shown in Table 10.1). However, the double-speed METV correlated only with participants' self-perceptions as empathetic people.

Table 10.1 shows the relationship between respondents' declarations of interpersonal skills and their regular and double-speed METV results. The table indicates that the correlation between respondents' METV performance and their declared interpersonal skills was statistically significant. The results also reveal that the three statements (i.e. declarations of interpersonal skills) were significantly correlated (two at the level of tendency) with the regular-speed METV. However, the double-speed METV correlated with only one statement: the one concerning participant's self-perceptions as empathetic people.

10.4.1 Discussion of Results

The data showed that the METV was correlated with the SIE-T. The METV program was authenticated by comparing respondents' METV scores with those of the SIE-T test, which was also based on facial expression recognition. The results showed that people who scored higher on the METV also scored higher on the

Table 10.1 METV (regular and double speed) correlation with declarations of interpersonal skills

	METV (regular)		METV (double speed)	
	r	*p*	*r*	*p*
I perceive myself as an empathetic person	0.284	0.075	0.365	0.02
I can correctly detect another person's mood	0.368	0.02	0.244	ns
Interaction with other people is (or will be) part of my professional activity	0.283	0.077	0.242	ns

SIE-T. This implies that people who are better at recognizing basic emotions from micro-expressions are also better at recognizing more complex emotions expressed on faces, which is assumed to be an indicator of EI.

The correlations between METV performance and respondents' declarations of interpersonal skills were positive, but not very high and not always statistically significant (Table 10.1). One of the reasons for the non-significance of the correlations could be the sample size ($n = 40$). With such a small sample, only high correlations can reach the level of significance.

However, there is another possible explanation for the limited correlation. First, the measure of interpersonal skill was based on declarations (rather than on an objective indicator). Self-knowledge might not always be correct, and people may hold beliefs that differ from reality. Thus, some people who believe that they are good at reading and observing personal interactions may not be in practice. Therefore, it is possible that the METV is, in fact, correlated with interpersonal skills; however, this possibility should be assessed through measurements, rather than declarations. In addition, the data showed that the METV results correlated with some participants' self-perceptions of their interpersonal skills.

In sum, this study has furthered our understanding of human behaviours. In this study, people who scored higher on the METV perceived themselves to be more empathetic and to possess a stronger ability to correctly recognize others' emotions.

10.5 Conclusions and Implications for Experimental Economics

This research established various critical findings. First, it was established that the METV can help to improve facial recognition skills required to recognize human behaviour. Therefore, the use of the METV program is recommended in scientific inquiries, investigations, business sectors, academic admissions, and many other applications. Furthermore, the understanding of human features, particularly facial expressions, is indispensable in many situations, including business, government, academia, and social groups. Thus, the understanding of human emotions is vital in many spheres of humanity. The application of the aspects associated with micro-expressions is very important, since such applications tend to focus more on the emotional aspects of human beings, particularly in the realm of experimental economics. Moreover, the METV is an important tool in the detection of the EI, which is also vital to understanding human micro-expressions—a critical component of experimental economics. This study conclusively showed the METV to be correlated with the SIE-T based on facial expression recognition.

Secondly, this study established the importance of micro-expressions in experimental economics. From the study results, it can be concluded that, in a contemporary business environment, micro-expressions have advanced to a level beyond what people can foresee. Specifically, the use of the micro-expressions in experimental research, as well as the number of studies carried out in the context of micro-expressions, is significantly increasing. These realities increase the importance of micro-expressions as an area that can significantly influence the outcomes of experimental economics topics. For example, in social studies, in the context of economic activities, micro-expressions related to the experiences of customers are key factors for determining whether a product will achieve sufficient sales revenue. In sum, this study illustrates the explicit benefits of studying micro-expressions, which may increase our understanding of human behaviours in the business context and affect the effectiveness of business meetings.

In every aspect of research conducted on any subject, certain basic elements are considered critical to achieving relevant and accurate results. In experimental economics, various aspects are considered necessary to ensure the successful application of a topic's experimental methods. Therefore, the concept of facial expressions—and, especially, METV—is an important aspect in the experimental economics. The development of the METV has resulted in the creation of new types of micro-expression recognition training, which is based on the Facial Action Coding System rules developed by Paul Ekman and Wallace V. Freisen (Ekman 2002). Finally, experimental economics is described as the application of experimental methods in order to study a given economic question (Guala 2005). Therefore this research can be an inspiration for further studies using the METV program and the concept of micro-expressions in experimental economics.

The relationship between the METV and its applications in experimental economics is a wide area that requires numerous comprehensive studies. Experimental economics has become a critical research area, covering such topics as markets, games, decision-making, bargaining, evolution game theory, field experiments, and social preferences, among others (Guala 2005). In addition, experimental design and actual study areas require comprehensive assessments of human emotions, as exhibited by facial expressions (Guala 2005). However, previous studies conducted on the METV have not explicitly indicated the role of or the relationship between the METV and experimental economics. This study addressed this knowledge gap by specifically exploring the relationship between the METV and the EI to understand human emotions.

The METT and METV can be used in various ways in experimental economics. The study of any experimental topic, such as field experiments, bargaining, social preferences, and customer satisfaction, among others, requires knowledge of the application of the METV or the METT. Specifically, the knowledge of micro-expressions is important for ensuring that a researcher gains an understanding and improved emotional intelligence of study participants (Ekman and Friesen 2003). In addition, the METV can help a researcher spot concealed emotions while, for example, conducting experimental economics that involve various company CEOs, as shown in the picture below (Fig. 10.1).

In this case, the researcher can ask study participants to rate the faces of the leaders above. The ratings can then be used to accurately draw correlations between the facial expression and the profits generated by the company leaders over a given

Fig. 10.1 Facial expressions (www.scienceofpeople.com)

period. Lastly, micro-expressions, when recognized through the use of the METV or the METT, are important for developing researchers' social skills in conducting experimental economics research involving participants on the autism spectrum (Ekman and Friesen 2003).

References

Asla NN, de Paul JJ, Perez-Albeniz A (2011) Emotion recognition in fathers and mothers at high-risk for child physical abuse. Child Abuse Negl 35(9):712–721

Buck R (1976) A test of nonverbal receiving ability: preliminary studies. Hum Commun Res 2:162–171

Cole PM, Jenkins PA, Shott CT (1989) Spontaneous expressive control in blind and sighted children. Child Dev 60(3):683–688

Chu E, Phillips ML, Russel TA (2006) A pilot study to investigate the effectiveness of emotion recognition remediation in schizophrenia using the micro-expression training tool. Br J Clin Psychol 45(Pt 4):579–583

Ekman P (1992) An argument for basic emotions. Cogn Emot 6(3/4):169–200

Ekman P (2001) Facial expressions, In: C. Blakemore & S. Jennett (Eds) Oxford Companion to the Body. London: Oxford University Press

Ekman P (2002) Micro-Expression Training Tool (METT). University of California, San Francisco

Ekman P (2003) Emotions revealed: recognizing faces and feelings to improve communication and emotional life. Times Books, New York

Ekman P, Friesen WV (1969) Nonverbal leakage and clues to deception. Psychiatry 321:88–106

Ekman P, Friesen WV (1971) Constants across culture in the face and emotion. Journal of Personality and Social Psychology 17: 124–129

Ekman P, Friesen WV (1978) Manual for the faction action coding system. Consultation Psychologists Press, Palo Alto, CA

Ekman P, Friesen WV (2003) Unmasking the face: a guide to recognizing emotions from facial clues. Ishk, Los Altos, CA

Ekman P, Sorenson ER, Friesen WV (1969) Pancultural elements in facial displays of emotion. Science 164(3875): 86–88

Endres J, Laidlaw A (2009) Micro-expression recognition training in medical students: a pilot study. BMC Med Educ 9(47):1–6

Frank, M. G. and P. Ekman (1997) The ability to detect deceit generalizes across different types of high stake lies. Journal of Personality and Social Psychology 72:1429–1439

Goldin PR, McRae K, Ramel W et al (2008) The neural bases of emotion regulation: reappraisal and suppression of negative emotion. Biol Psychiatry 63:577–586. doi:10.1016/j.biopsych.2007.05.031

Goleman D (1995) Emotional intelligence. Bantam Books, New York

Goleman D (1996) Social intelligence: the new science of human relationships. Bantam Books, New York

Guala F (2005) The methodology of experimental economics. Cambridge University Press, Cambridge

Gunderman RB (2011) Emotional intelligence. J Am Coll Radiol 8(5):298–299

Haggard EA, Isaacs KS (1966) Micromomentary facial expressions as indicators of ego mechanisms in psychotherapy. In: Gottschalk LA, Auerbach AH, editors. Methods of research in psychotherapy. New York: Appleton Century Crofts. pp. 154–165.

Hall JA (1984) Nonverbal sex differences: communication accuracy and expressive style. The Johns Hopkins University Press, Baltimore, MD

Hall JA, Bernieri FJ (eds) (2001) Interpersonal sensitivity: theory and measurement. Erlbaum, Hillsdale, NJ

Hennig-Thurau T, Groth M, Paul M et al (2006) Are all smiles created equal? How emotional contagion and emotional labor affect service relationships. J Marketing 70:58–73

Hurley CM (2011) The effects of motivation and training format on the ability to detect hidden emotions. PhD Thesis, State University of New York at Buffalo, New York, USA. 71: 38–53

Hurley CM (2012) Do you see what I see? Learning to detect micro expressions of emotion. Motivation and Emotion 26:371–381

Keating CF, Mazur A, Segall MH (1977) Facial gestures which influence the perception of status. Soc Psychol Qtr 40:374–378

Knapp ML, Hall JA (1997) Nonverbal communication in human interaction, 4th edn. Wadsworth, Thompson Learning, Belmont, CA

Marsh AA, Adams RB Jr, Kleck RE (2005) Why do fear and anger look the way they do? Form and social function in facial expressions. Personality and Social Psychological Bulletin 31:73–86

Matczak A, Piekarska J, Studniarek E (2005) Skala Inteligencji Emocjonalnej – Twarze (SIE-T) Podręcznik (Emotional Intelligence Scale – Faces Manual). Pracownia Testów Psychologicznych PTP, Warsaw, 150 p

Matsumoto D, Hwang H (2011) Evidence for training the ability to read micro expressions of emotion. Motivation and Emotion 35:181–191

Matsumoto D, Keltner D, Shiota MN et al (2008) What's in a face? Facial expressions as signals of discrete emotions. In: Lewis M, Haviland JM, Feldman Barrett L (eds) Handbook of emotions. Guilford Press, New York, pp 211–234

McArthur LZ, Baron RM (1983) Toward an ecological theory of social perception. Psychol Rev 90:215–238

Metzinger T (2006) Exposing lies. Sci Amer Mind 17(5):32–37. doi:10.1038/scientificamericanmind1006-32

Porter S, ten Brinke L (2010) The truth about lies: what works in detecting high stakes deception? Legal and Criminological Psychol 15(1):57–75

Pote EC (2012) True lies: who can learn to tell? Laurentian University, Sudbury, ON

Puccinelli NM, Andrzejewski SA, Markos E et al (2013) The value of knowing what customers really want: the impact of salesperson ability to read non verbal cues of affect on service quality. J Mktg Mgmt 293(4):356

Rosenthal R, Hall JA, DiMatteo MR et al (1979) Sensitivity to nonverbal communications: the PONS test. The Johns Hopkins University Press, Baltimore, MD

Russell Tamara A, Chu Elvina, Phillips Mary L (2006) A pilot study to investigate the effectiveness of emotion recognition remediation in schizophrenia using the micro-expression training tool.British journal of clinical psychology 45(4):579–83

Schubert S (2006) A look tells all. Scientific American Mind 17(5):26–31. doi:10.1038/scientificamericanmind1006-26

Shapiro DL (2003) Emotions in negotiation: peril or promise. Marq L Rev 87:737

Shen X-B, Wu Q, Fu X-L (2012) Effects of the duration of expressions on the recognition of micro expressions. J Zhejiang Univ Sci B 13:221–230. doi:10.1631/jzus.b1100063

Spencer LM (2001) The economic value of emotional intelligence competencies and EIC-based HR programs. In: Goleman D, Cherniss C (eds) The emotionally intelligent workplace: how to select, measure, and improve emotional intelligence in individuals, groups, and organizations. Jossey-Bass, San Francisco, pp 45–82

Stubbs Koman E, Wolff SB (2008) Emotional intelligence competencies in the team and team leader: a multi-level examination of the impact of emotional intelligence on team performance. J Mgmt Dev 27(1):55–75

Tomkins SS (1963) Affect, imagery, and consciousness (Vol. 2: The negative affects). Springer, New York

Waal FBM (2003) Darwin's legacy and the study of primate visual communication. In: Ekman P, Campos J, Davidson RJ et al (eds) Emotions inside out: 130 years after Darwin's The Expression of Emotion in Man and Animals. New York Academy of Sciences, New York, pp 7–31

Weinberger S (2010) Airport security: intent to deceive? Nature 465(7297):412–415. doi:10.1038/465412a

Wezowski K, Wezowski P (2012) The micro expressions book for business. New Vision, Antwerp, p 127

Yan W, Wu Q, Chen Y et al (2013) How fast are the leaked facial expressions: the duration of micro expressions? J Nonverbal Behav 37:217–230. doi:10.1007/s10919-013-0159-8

Zhang M, Fu Q, Chen Y-H et al (2014) Emotional context influences micro-expression recognition. PLoS One 9(4):e95018. doi:10.1371/journal.pone.0095018

Chapter 11
Experimental Research in Economics and Computer Simulation

Małgorzata Łatuszyńska

Abstract Thanks to continually developing information technology, experimental research in economics can be performed with increasingly more powerful support of computers. One of such computer methods that facilitate laboratory economics experiments is computer simulation. The analysis of properties of computer simulation used as a research method helps us distinguish two elementary directions of its applications in experimental economics: it can support or replace traditional lab experiments. These trends are the subject of the analysis in this chapter.

Keywords Computer simulation • Experimental economics

11.1 The Essence of Computer Simulation

The word simulation has been borrowed for the sake of science from everyday language. Colloquially, to simulate means to resemble the outlook of another thing as well as to imitate or reproduce this thing. In the case of computer simulation, we deal with the imitation of the entire system, or just a given situation, by means of computer programs.

In the narrow sense, the term of computer simulation refers to the use of a computer to solve an equation that we cannot solve analytically, or more generally—to explore mathematical properties of equations where analytical methods fail (e.g. Humphreys 1991, 501; Humphreys 2004, 49; Winsberg 1999, 275; Winsberg 2001, 444). In the broad sense, computer simulation refers to the entire process of constructing, using and justifying a model that involves analytically intractable mathematics (e.g. Winsberg 2001, 443; Winsberg 2003, 105; Humphreys 1991, 501; Humphreys 2004, 107). Following Humphreys (2004, 102–104), we call such a model a computational or a simulation model (Frigg and Reiss 2009, 596). This process embraces a combination of intentionally

M. Łatuszyńska (✉)
Department of Computational Methods in Experimental Economics, Faculty of Economics and Management, Institute of IT in Management, University of Szczecin, Mickiewicza 64, 71-101 Szczecin, Poland
e-mail: mlat@wneiz.pl

K. Nermend, M. Łatuszyńska (eds.), *Selected Issues in Experimental Economics*, Springer Proceedings in Business and Economics, DOI 10.1007/978-3-319-28419-4_11

selected stages designed to lead to an adopted research objective. In the first stage the range of the study and its objective are defined. This determines the choice of variables for a mathematical model to be constructed in the subsequent stage. In the next step of the procedure the model is computer programmed. The fourth stage consists in qualitative and quantitative tests of the model's formal and logical validity. In this stage the researcher is forced to repeatedly restate their initial assumptions and to repeat the previously completed stages again and again. In the fifth stage the experiments are designed so that the ultimate goal of the study can be achieved. Finally, the simulations are made and their results are interpreted (Gordon 1974, 37).

Historically speaking, computer simulation methods fall into two categories, namely (Pidd 1998, 21) into the methods that allow to illustrate discrete processes (discrete simulation) and the ones that allow us to model continuous processes (continuous simulation). However, when analysing the character of changes in the modelled system as well as the lapse of time during which the simulation is undergoing, one obtains four types of simulation models, i.e. models in which the system changes in the following ways (Pidd 1998, 27):

- Continuously at every moment of time, i.e. the values of variables change smoothly and not abruptly (in a discrete way) and are available at every moment during the simulation.
- Continuously but only at discrete moments of time—in this case the values of variables change smoothly, yet they are available only at certain moments (points in time) during the simulation.
- Abruptly at every moment of time, i.e. the values of variables are discrete, yet changes may occur at every point in time.
- Abruptly at discrete moments of time—in such a case changes may occur only at certain points in time.

The analysis covering the characteristics of the aforementioned types of simulation models enables one to distinguish the following three main types of computer simulation methods: continuous, discrete and mixed (hybrid) simulations.

It is typical of the continuous simulation methods to use continuous functions for a formal description of variables characterising the system state and the continuous or quasi-continuous ones for describing the lapse of time. In the case of the continuous simulation, the system state is generally represented as a system of differential equations in the function of a simulated time. Typical examples of the continuous simulation include the simulation of various physical phenomena, e.g. the change of weather or the flow of gases around a solid body such as a car body (Nowak 2009). The most popular simulation method is system dynamics (Forrester 1961) where continuity is achieved through determining the values of variables at many points in a simulated time with the use of a simulation based on the method of constant time increments (simulation with the smallest possible time step).

Discrete simulation methods involve discrete functions both to describe the variables characterising the system state in a formal way, and to describe the lapse of time. In this case, the change in the state of a simulated system occurs at certain moments, the so-called discrete moments of time. The system state is not subject to change in between these moments. The system may be perceived as 'stepping' from one state to another, which resembles the change of frames in a cartoon. As far as the discrete simulation is concerned, the literature on the subject often refers to a discrete event simulation (Banks et al. 2005), cellular space simulators (the so-called cellular automata) (Gilbert and Troitzsch 1999) and multi-agent simulation (North and Macal 2007).

Last but not least, the main type of computer simulation is a mixed (hybrid) simulation. It consists in using discrete and continuous functions for formal description of variables characterising the system state, and using discrete, continuous and quasi-continuous functions for describing the lapse of time.

Apart from the aforementioned classificatory approach (taking into account the change in the state of a modelled system and mapping the simulated time), the computer simulation is classified by a number of criteria. The literature generally provides the following criteria: (1) uncertainty (event predictability), (2) the level of aggregation of system elements that are subject to modelling, (3) the number of computers/processors in use, (4) the time devoted to simulation and (5) the aim of modelling and simulation (see more in Łatuszyńska (2012)).

Computer simulation has many advantages that make it an attractive analytic tool. First of all, it can 'condense' time to such extent that we are able to simulate several years of the system functioning within a minute or, sometimes, within a few seconds—depending on the complexity of the system or the power of our computer. This property enables the researcher to consider various scenarios in a short span of time, while in the real life such a trial would take very long or would not be possible at all. What is more, computer simulation enables the researcher to stretch the time in which the system is functioning as it offers the opportunity to study in great detail the structure of changes that are impossible to be observed in the real time. In contrast to laboratory experiments, each experimental simulation can be reproduced in the same conditions. The findings of experiments can be easily recorded and compared (Fishman 1981, 30–33). The benefits of computer simulations make them a popular scientific method utilised in order to address a vast variety of problems.

Nevertheless, a researcher using computer simulation should be aware of the fact that developing and launching a simulation program is a difficult task and that there is no guarantee that their effort invested in creating a model will pay off in a form of valuable results. There is always a risk that a model, being a simplified imitation of the reality, will not represent all the dependencies existing in the real-life system which are vital to the study.

11.2 Computer Simulation in Economics

In the last decades, as computers improved, the use of simulation has rapidly grown in the field of economics. The history of simulation in economics is a characteristic one. While being pioneered by scientists such as Norbert Wiener and John Von Neumann who exerted a great influence on economic theory and methodology, simulation started to spread to the sciences just when economics became addicted to theorems and proofs. While simulation has found steady employment in physics and biology, the accomplishment of the Samuelsonian project has relegated simulation to a secondary role (mainly, finding numerical solutions and conducting statistical analysis) with respect to qualitative mathematics. From the 1990s onwards, however, there has been a systematic attempt at promoting simulation as a methodology in its own right (Axelrod 1997) and as a tool to embody and experiment theories (Epstein and Axtell 1996). The distinction between the 'instrumental' and the 'theoretical' use of simulation is helpful in tracing its role in economics and trying to find evidence for the view that simulation represents an ongoing methodological 'revolution'. In addition, the propagation of the interpretation of economic phenomena as complex adaptive systems has provided the (micro) foundations for a wider use of simulation as a modelling method. Thus, another interpretation of our analysis could be that of reading evidence as an approximation of the relative positions of the complexity approach as compared to the traditional one (Fontana 2006).

For what concerns its scientific applications in economics, simulation has started to develop as an aid to find numerical solutions to complicated mathematical models. However, as more sophisticated and powerful programming languages were devised, it has assumed a multifaceted role. In fact, it now can be a way to explore the implications of a theory and to achieve a high level of richness in description. Within the simulation techniques, however, such properties are present in different degrees. It is therefore necessary to draw some distinctions between simulation as a mere instrument that extends the ability of mathematical modelling or statistical analysis and simulation as a theoretical statement. In addition, when focusing on simulation as an autonomous way of conducting a research, it must be considered that each technique implies different views of the functioning of modelled phenomena.

According to the reference literature (Behdani 2012; Borshchev 2013, 37), there are three most commonly used methods of computer simulation with dedicated computer tools and simulation languages:

- System dynamics
- Discrete even simulation
- Multi-agent simulation

A detailed investigation of the properties of each of the mentioned simulation methods is beyond the scope of this chapter; however their brief description seems necessary. In Table 11.1, which relies on Behdani (2012), the most important features of the kinds of simulations that will be the object of the following analysis are summarized and compared.

Table 11.1 General characteristics of properties of selected computer simulation methods (based on Behdani (2012))

System dynamics	Discrete event simulation	Multi-agent simulation
System oriented, focused on modelling aggregates	Process oriented, focused on details of a modelled system	Agent oriented, focused on modelling agents and their interactions
Homogeneous system elements; assumed similar characteristics of system elements; averaging of values	Heterogeneous elements	Heterogeneous objects (agents)
No representation on micro level	Elements on micro level are passive objects running through a system in an imitated process (they are attributed neither with intelligence nor with decision-making capacity)	Objects on micro level are active agents that cooperate with one another as well as with their environment and make autonomous decisions
Imitation of dynamic behaviour by means of feedback loops	Imitation of dynamic behaviour by means of events	Imitation of dynamic behaviour by means of agents' decisions and interactions
Mathematical formalisation based on concept of stocks-and-flows	Mathematical formalisation based on concept of event-action-process	Mathematical formalisation based on concept of agent-environment
Continuous or quasi-continuous functions used to describe time flow	Discrete functions used to describe time flow	Discrete functions used to describe time flow
Experimenting through changes in system structure	Experimenting through changes in a process structure	Experimenting through changes in agents' behaviour rules (internal/external rules) and in system structure
System structure is stable	Process is stable	System structure is not stable

The analysis of the properties of computer simulation methods shows that they can be utilised in experimental economics to:

- Support laboratory experiments by using:
  - A specific simulation model in order to generate data needed by the experiment participants for decision-making and/or to determine the effects of their actions
  - The existing simulation games
  - Interactive virtual simulation environment that imitates the real-life environment as closely as possible and can be applied to record the participants' answers, responses and actions
- Replace a conventional laboratory experiment

The above applications will be briefly summarised in the following sections of this chapter.

11.3 Simulation Models in Economics Experiments

The application of a specific simulation model in order to support the economics experiment is made through implementing models that mock individual economic processes/phenomena in a specialist experimental software. Among the diverse kinds of these programs three principal categories can be distinguished (Kowal et al. 2008): dedicated programs, experimental services and development environments. In each of these categories we can find applications/modules which use, to a limited extent, simulation models. Their examples are presented in Table 11.2.

Dedicated programs are applications created for the benefit of a given economics experiment with a precisely defined algorithm of its course. This group mainly includes applications written as Java applets or dynamic websites.

Table 11.2 Selected specialised experimental applications (source: own study on the basis of the websites quoted in the table)

Name	Author/ producer	Users	Area of application	Website
Dedicated programs				
JessX	School of Engineering Ecole Centrale de Lille	University of Lille	Simulation of selected financial markets, e.g. stock, bond or banking markets, thus allowing experiment subjects to participate in these markets	rb.ec-lille.fr/jessx/index.php
Rotman Interactive Trader	Rotman School of Management at the University of Toronto	University of Toronto	Simulation of order-driven market; experiments with stock markets and auctions	rit.rotman.utoronto.ca/software.asp
Experimental services				
EconPort	Georgia State University	University of Canterbury; Shanghai Jiaotong University; University of Haifa	Simulation of auctions in order to test consumer demand; testing the expected utility hypothesis	www.econport.org/content/experiments.html
Development environments				
z-Tree	Urs Fischbacher and Stefan Schmid, University of Zurich	Shanghai Jiaotong University; Florida State University; San Francisco State University; University of Munich; Yale University	Simulation of the market and various types of auctions in order to develop experiments either from scratch or with predefined application elements	www.iew.uzh.ch/ztree/index.php

(continued)

Table 11.2 (continued)

Name	Author/ producer	Users	Area of application	Website
LabSEE	Experimental Economy Laboratory, Warsaw University	Warsaw University	Developing and carrying out experiments with the use of predefined application elements, including simulations and decision games	labsee.pl/menu/id-10/labsee-xp.html
SWIEE	Riccardo Boero	University of Pavia; University of Torino; University of Piemonte	Using multi-agent simulations to design experiments for the purpose of social studies	swiee.econ.unito.it

Experimental services allow their users to choose from a number of available experiments. The users do not have the right to modify the application, but they can choose their own experimental parameters. They can also export the results and automatically generate charts that graphically demonstrate the course of the experiment.

The most advanced forms of experimental software are complete development environments for the experiment creation where the experimenter can implement their own ideas of experimental design. In such environments personalised scripts, which meet specific requirements of given experiments, are created by means of a dedicated or a widely known software language. Thanks to the application of such software the process of matching of the tool to the researchers' expectations is much more flexible.

11.4 Simulation Games

When carrying out an economics experiment, we can use simulation games available on the market. Obviously, we should not consider a laboratory experiment as equivalent to a simulation game (Kopczewski 2010), but it can aid us in creating a decision-making situation which in turn will allow us to test the conformity of the participants' decisions with our theoretical economic model.

Simulation games are a specific combination of three elements: a game (understood as a set of rules), a role (assigned to each participant) and a simulation. So, the term simulation game can be comprehended as a certain system whose principal element is a model of the reality (a simulation model) initiated (rules of the game) with the participants' decisions (players/roles) (see Rizzi and Woźniakiewicz 2008, 58; Wiącek-Janka 2011, 84). The games simulating economic processes and phenomena are called economic simulation games, business simulation games or management/decision-making simulation games. In principle, the economic simulation games are computer programs based on mathematical models that imitate, in a simplified way, specific economic processes or phenomena, such as business operation in a competitive environment (Wawrzeńczyk-Kulik 2013, 306–307). The examples of such games are to be found in Table 11.3.

The economic simulation games listed in the table above are just several examples of a large number of free or paid games available online. The Internet provides current popularity ranking of such games (Ranker 2015).

Table 11.3 Examples of economic simulation games [own elaboration on the basis of the following websites: Classroom Aid (2012), Ranker (2015) and Poszewiecki et al. (2012), Sterman (2014)]

Name	Producer/author	Description	Website
Marketplace	Innovative Learning Solutions, Inc.	A simulation program imitating a competitive and continually evolving market. The game shows the consequences of the player's financial decisions and their effect on a company in general. Each decision is followed by a change in the cash flow and with a specific financial outcome.	www.marketplace-simulation.com
Beat the Market	Steven Gold Saunders College of Business	A simulation of a captive market. Players are given the opportunity to make experimental decisions concerning company management under conditions of perfect competition.	www.goldsimulations.com
Global Management Challenge	SDG Simuladores E Modelos De Gestão, S.A.	A general management game. Its purpose is to faithfully imitate a day-to-day work of senior management in a company manufacturing three industrial products and selling them on three different markets.	www.worldgmc.com
Sim Venture	Venture Simulations Ltd.	Business areas being an object of the game include sales and marketing (market research, pricing policies, sales channels and promotions), operation (product design, supplies, manufacturing, quality control), finances, organisation (inventories, legal requirements, training policies, time management and efficiency).	simventure.co.uk
Industry Masters Realtime	Tycoon Systems Inc.	The game covers such business areas as strategic management, demand, supply, pricing mechanism, product life cycle, economy of scale, competition, cash flow or benchmarking. The simulation may cover several markets.	realtime.industrymasters.com

(continued)

Table 11.3 (continued)

Name	Producer/author	Description	Website
TOPSIM General Management II	TATA Interactive Systems GmbH	The game provides the opportunity to make experimental decisions in a team environment where the participants play different roles on a virtual market. Available in many variations—from general management to logistics, marketing, project management to manufacturing.	www.topsim.com
UGS® GAME STANDARD	UGS® ULM	The game simulates a newly set up business activity as well as the preparations for setting up a company in various business environments. There are ten scenarios where the players start or take over companies operating in different lines of business. The players also can design their own scenarios.	www.ugs.de
INNOV8	IBM	The games give insight into proper business process management practice.	www.ibm.com/innov8
Go Venture-World	GoVentureOasis.com	The game simulates business operation in a cooperative and competitive environment. The participants can play the roles of entrepreneurs, investors, bankers, lawyers or marketing managers.	www.goventureworld.com
SimCEO	Jetlag Learning based in Hendersonville	The players start companies, buy/sell shares and respond to everyday media coverage (real or fictitious), thus testing the effect of their decisions on the market.	www.simceo.org
Gazillionaire	LavaMind	The game simulates market demand and supply. The players make economic decisions concerning margins, balance, growth, investments, etc.	www.gazillionaire.com

11.5 Virtual Simulation Environments

Another, very promising, form of experimental support in economics is interactive virtual simulation environments known as virtual worlds—closely imitating the real-life reality and recording the experiment participants' answers, responses and actions.

In the general opinion the notion of virtual world is understood as a reality created by means of computer technology. However, it can be defined more precisely through describing its features which, in the present approach, are represented by a permanent, simulated and engaging environment that is available online and provides many players with communication tools, hence enabling them to act and interact within the created world in a real time (Girvan 2013). Thus defined reality is supported by numerous computer programs (e.g. graphic or acoustic software, communicators or simple editors) which simulate conditions similar to those existing in the real world. The attractiveness of a virtual world can be multiplied by various technical solutions, such as systems allowing to expose the user to different stimuli—virtual reality helmets, gloves, glasses/goggles, etc.

The exact number of virtual worlds available on the Internet is not known. According to some sources there are several dozens of them, while others report the number of several hundreds. One of the virtual world lists can be found in the publication by de Freitas (2008, 44–47). The most popular virtual worlds are in alphabetic order: Active Worlds (www.activeworlds.com), Blue Mars (www.bluemars.com), Open Sim (www.opensim.pl), Reaction Grid (reactiongrid.com), Second Life (secondlife.com), SmallWorlds (www.smallworlds.com) and czy World of Warcraft (www.warcraft.com). Additionally, it is worth noting that the Consumer Behaviour Simulator was created by researchers of the University of Szczecin (Łatuszyńska and Nermend 2008).

The scientific potential of virtual worlds was first recognised by Castronova (2001) at the beginning of the twenty-first century. In his report he described their potential usability in economics and social studies. Since then many reports have been published that present results of experiments conducted in the virtual environment. The examples of economics experiments described in the reference literature are shown in Table 11.4.

Table 11.4 Examples of economics experiments conducted in virtual worlds in 2006–2014

Application domain	Virtual world	Article title	Authors	Year
Classical economics experiments				
Coordination games	EverQuest Dark Age of Camelot	On the Research Value of Large Games: Natural Experiments in Norrath and Camelot	Castronova E.	2006
Virtual economic decision-making	Second Life	Inductive Metanomics: Economics Experiments in Virtual Worlds	Atlas S. A.	2008
Studies on reciprocity	World of Warcraft	Reciprocity and status in a virtual field experiment	Nicklisch A., Salz T.	2008
E-collaboration and e-commerce	Second Life World of Warcraft	E-collaboration and e-commerce in virtual worlds: The potential of Second Life and World of Warcraft	Kock N.	2009
Trust games with communication	Second Life	The lab versus the virtual lab and virtual field—an experimental investigation of trust games with communication	Fiedler M., Haruvy E.	2009

(continued)

Table 11.4 (continued)

Application domain	Virtual world	Article title	Authors	Year
Ultimatum bargaining, trust games, Monty Hall paradox	Second Life	Learning About Real Economics in Virtual Worlds	Abrams D.	2009
Ultimatum bargaining, dictator game, public goods games and other classical economics experiments	Second Life	Virtual World Experimentation: An Exploratory Study	Chesney T., Chuah S-H., Hoffmann R.	2009
Studies on trust and collaboration	Second Life	Cooperation in virtual worlds	Fiedler M.	2009
Trust games	Second Life	Trust among the Avatars: A Virtual World Experiment, with and without Textual and Visual Cues	Atlas S., Putterman L.	2010
Decision-making in virtual worlds (dictator game and other classical economics experiments)	World of Warcraft	Decision-making in virtual worlds: an experimental test of altruism, fairness and presence	Spann M., Hinz O., Hann I., Skiera B.	2010
Trust games, impact of social distance on economic decisions	Second Life	Social Distance in a Virtual World Experiment	Fiedler M., Haruvy E, Xin Li S.	2011
Trust games	Second Life	Trust and trustworthiness in anonymous virtual worlds	Füllbrunn S., Richwien K., Sadrieh A.	2011
Common-pool resources	OpenSim	The Determinants of Territorial Property Rights in a Spatial Commons Experiment	Twieg P., McCabe K.	2014
Ultimatum bargaining	Second Life	Is avatar-to-avatar communication as effective as face-to-face communication? An Ultimatum Game experiment in First and Second Life	Greiner B., Caravella M., Roth A. E.	2014
Studies on economic systems				
Law of demand	Arden (Aurora Toolkit)	A Test of the Law of Demand in a Virtual World: Exploring the Petri Dish Approach to Social Science	Castronova E.	2008
Price convergence	World of Warcraft	Price convergence in an online virtual world	Morrison M., Fontenla M.	2013

According to the reference literature, the virtual world that is most recognised in experimental economics is Second Life which, since it was launched by Linden Lab in 2003, has been embraced by millions of users. Bloomfield (2007) argues that Second Life is a perfect environment for experimental studies due to its rich virtual economy, naturally developing markets and a community of actively trading users. Moreover, Second Life is equipped with graphic and script tools that allow for constructing virtual laboratories which can recruit thousands of participants in experiments at a relatively low cost.

Controlled economics experiments in virtual worlds are an exciting idea presenting a number of advantages (see e.g.: Bainbridge 2007; Castronova 2006; Innocenti 2013). Virtual worlds have millions of users and at every moment plenty of them are online. What is more, their population is much more socially and economically diversified than any population sample in a standard laboratory experiment where the most likely participants are students (Duffy 2011). Other advantages of this scientific approach include the opportunity to conduct controlled macroeconomic experiments, since the macroeconomics of virtual worlds is very similar to the real-life one (Abrams 2009).

Data obtained in virtual worlds often outperform those that can be collected in real life, both in terms of quantity and quality. They come in a form of revealed rather than declared preferences, which brings them closer to the data obtained in natural experiments (Olds 2011). Also, it is very important that experiments in virtual worlds present the realism of field experiments, simultaneously allowing for the control that is typical of laboratory experiments (Abrams 2009). What is more, wrong decisions made in a virtual world have significantly weaker negative impact on real life than the same decisions in the physical world (Olds 2011). Last but not least, it is vital for experimenters that the cost of the participants' remuneration is low as it is paid in virtual currency of a given world (Atlas 2008).

Apart from their unquestionable advantages, economics experiments in virtual worlds have their drawbacks as well. One of the most often criticised aspects is their poor representativeness of study populations. Research shows that virtual worlds are generally populated with young people, mostly male (Abrams 2009). As it has been mentioned above, other frequent problems are inappropriate behaviour in virtual laboratories, repeated participation of one person in the experiment and contacts among individual participants (Chesney et al. 2009). There is also a risk that the experiment can be terminated at any time due to a server-side technical problem or a participant's getting bored (Duffy 2011).

In spite of all that, many of the above disadvantages can be eliminated or at least diminished. Moreover, when juxtaposed with a long list of advantages they do not seem to be relevant enough to discredit economics experiments in virtual worlds as a scientific method. Quite the contrary, this approach seems likely to develop dynamically in the near future.

11.6 Computer Simulation Rather Than Traditional Experiment?

As early as in 1967 Naylor et al. (1967, 1316) defined computer simulation as a numerical technique for conducting experiments with certain types of mathematical and logical models describing the behaviour of an economic system on a digital computer over extended periods of time. They also indicated that the principal difference between a simulation experiment and a traditional one is that with simulation the experiment is conducted with a model of the economic system rather than with the real-life economic system itself. Their definition is similar to the definitions provided in the modern literature, in which case simulation experiments are also called numerical, calculation or computer experiments (see Vallverdú 2014, 7; Parker 2009).

When observing the latest trends, we can see that computer simulation has become an essential part of modern scientific studies. There is also a clear tendency of the boundary between the experiment and the computer simulation to get blurred (Parke 2014), which has been noticed by science philosophers who have been paying increased attention to both the experiments (e.g. Hacking 1983; Franklin 1990; Radder 2003; Weber 2004) and the simulation (e.g. Humphreys 2004; Winsberg 2010; Weisberg 2013), as well as to methodological and epistemological differences and similarities between them (e.g. Barberousse et al. 2008; Guala 2002; Morgan 2003, 2005; Peck 2004; Grossklags 2007; Morrison 2009; Parker 2009; Winsberg 2009; Grüne-Yanoff and Weirich 2011; Peschard 2012; Vallverdú 2014; Roush 2014). Some of them ask if computer simulation should be perceived as an experiment as such, while the others see it as a substitute to scientific experiments.

Many science philosophers argue that despite the unquestionable relation between computer simulation and experiments, they still differ considerably at certain points (Grüne-Yanoff and Weirich 2011). The most important difference, signalled by Naylor et al. (1967, 1316) in their aforementioned definition, is the one in the similarity relationships of experiments and simulations in reference to the analysed actual systems (called target systems). Also Gilbert and Troitzsch (1999) point out that in a traditional experiment the researcher controls real objects, while what is controlled in the simulation is a model, not an actual object. Expanding on Simon's (1969) thought, Guala (2005, 214–215) points out to a similar problem and observes that in the traditional experiment we deal with the same material causes as in the real-life system, which is not true in the case of the simulation, and the relationship between a simulation model (which is not material) and a target system is merely abstract and formal.

According to Parker (2009), the criterion distinguishing the computer simulation from traditional experiments cannot be the 'identity' of the material used in different systems. The simulation is a kind of representation describing a time sequence of states, while the experiment is a type of scientific activity consisting in implementing an intervention into an experimental system. Even though the computer simulation may not be an experiment per se, simulation tests definitely are because they are also subject to interventions that are made in order to find out how the analysed properties of the system change as a consequence of this intervention. An experimental system, being an object of a direct intervention in the course of a simulation procedure, is a material system, i.e. a programmed computer. Therefore the computer experiments are, literally, material experiments.

Morgan (2002, 2003), while agreeing with the opinion that many simulation studies may qualify as material experiments, points out to the 'degree of their materiality' (Morgan 2003, 231) which renders traditional experiments more cognitively valuable than computer simulations. Morgan's opinion is criticised by Parker (2009) who claims that even if a target system and an experimental system are made of the same materials, they are not always identical in all relevant aspects. Hence, the conclusions regarding the target system can be unjustified. In certain cases the experimenters may have sufficient reasons to believe that the results of a computer experiment provide more reliable information about a target system than the results of a traditional experiment where both the experimental and the target system are made of the same materials.

Reiss (2011) is of similar opinion. Although he agrees that the systems used for conducting a computer simulation differ to a varying degree from the systems of traditional laboratory experiments, he also argues that this difference does not give reason against considering the simulation results valuable, because the value of a simulation depends on whether the conclusions drawn basing on findings of the simulation experiment and concerning the model's formal validity (verification—internal validity) as well as its relation to the target system (external validity) have been sufficiently justified. Also Winsberg (2009) advocates for the epistemological value of the computer simulation saying that the justification for the simulation experiment is based on our confidence in knowledge on which a simulation model has been built. Winsberg contradicts Morgan's opinion that traditional experiments have more cognitive value than the simulation. At the same time he insists that the knowledge needed to conduct a good simulation differs from the knowledge needed to carry out a good experiment. Parke (2014) is of the same opinion, concluding that the differences between the experiment and the simulation should not give grounds for making judgments about the epistemological power.

In the literature we can often find an opinion that simulation experiments simply have an advantage over laboratory experiments (e.g. Humphreys 2004, 115; Reiss 2011, 244). On the one hand, computer simulation provides an opportunity to study a larger group of empirical economic phenomena because it requires less restrictive idealisation. On the other hand, it is not subject to practical limitations that traditional experiments are exposed to, such as high costs, unethical practices or technical difficulties. Other advantages of the simulation over traditional experiments include:

- Replicability
- The possibility to change parameters that could not be modified in a real system
- More flexibility and changeable baseline of boundary conditions
- Significantly lower costs, both financial and ethical
- Swifter experiment implementation

The above considerations give solid ground for an opinion that the computer simulation should be seen as a valued method for the economics experimental studies and can be regarded as a true experiment.

11.7 Summary

Even though the number of experiments conducted by economists is growing every year and the experimental method has become for good a part of economics methodology (Reiss 2008, Chapter 5), it is not possible to do experiments on the economy as a whole and many economic phenomena cannot be subject to experimental manipulation for a variety of reasons—practical, ethical or technological. In such cases the computer simulation can support economics in achieving a status of a fully fledged experimental science (Reiss 2011, 243–244).

This support may not only mean the use of a specific simulation model for generating data necessary for the users' decision-making and/or for defining the effects of their actions, or the use of ready-made simulation games, but it may also mean experimenting by means of an interactive virtual simulation environment, also called a virtual world. In many instances the computer simulation can replace a traditional laboratory experiment because the methodological structure of a simulation resembles the experimental one (see: Hughes 1999; Norton and Suppe 2000) and its epistemology is similar to the epistemology of experiments (Peck 2004; Grimm and Railsback 2005, Chapter 9; Korb and Mascaro 2009; Reiss 2011). The computer simulation is even said to be an epistemological engine of our times (Ihde 2006; Tolk et al. 2013).

The computer simulation is based on well-established theoretical principles and, when used properly, provides information on the systems for which experimental data are rare (Winsberg 2003), thus being likely to become our best way to deal with the complexity of economic theory and practice.

References

Abrams D (2009) Learning about real economics in virtual worlds. http://economics.rutgers.edu/dmdocuments/DavidAbrams1.pdf. Accessed 4 Mar 2015

Atlas S (2008) Inductive metanomics: economic experiments in virtual worlds. J Virtual World Res 1(1):1–15

Atlas S, Putterman L (2010) Trust among the avatars: a virtual world experiment, with and without textual and visual cues. Working Papers. Brown University. http://www.brown.edu/academics/economics/sites/brown.edu.academics.economics/files/uploads/2010-18_paper.pdf. Accessed 4 Mar 2015

Axelrod R (1997) Advancing the art of simulation in social science. In: Conte R, Hegsel-mann R, Terna P (eds) Simulating social phenomena. Springer, Berlin, pp 21–40

Bainbridge WS (2007) The scientific research potential of virtual worlds. Science 317:472–476

Banks J, Carson J, Nelson B, Nicol D (2005) Discrete-event system simulation, 4th edn. Pearson, Upper Saddle River, NJ
Barberousse A, Franceschelli S, Imbert C (2008) Computer simulations as experiments. Synthese 169(3):557–574
Behdani B (2012) Evaluation of paradigms for modeling supply chains as complex socio-technical systems. In: Proceedings of the 2012 Simulation Conference WSC. Huntington, California, 9–12 December 2012, pp 1–15. doi:10.1109/WSC.2012.6465109
Bloomfield R (2007) Worlds for study: invitation. Working Paper. Cornell University. http://papers.ssrn.com/sol3/papers.cfm?abstract_id=988984. Accessed 18 January 2015
Borshchev A (2013) The big book of simulation modelling. Anylogic, North America
Castronova E (2001) Virtual worlds: a first-hand account of market and society on the cyberian frontier. CESifo Working Paper Series 618. http://ssrn.com/abstract=294828. Accessed 18 Jul 2015
Castronova E (2006) On the research value of large games: natural experiments in Norrath and Camelot. Games Cult 1(2):163–186
Castronova E (2008) A test of the law of demand in a virtual world: exploring the petri dish approach to social science. CESifo Working Paper Series 2355. http://ssrn.com/abstract=1173642. Accessed 18 Jul 2015
Chesney T, Chuah SH, Hoffmann R (2009) Virtual world experimentation: an exploratory study. J Econ Behav Organ 72:618–635
Classroom Aid (2012) Business simulation games could build hands-on business experience. http://classroom-aid.com/2012/11/09/15-business-simulation-games-could-build-hands-on-business-experience/. Accessed 18 Jan 2015
de Freitas S (2008) Serious virtual worlds. A scoping study. Serious Games Institute Cov-entry University Enterprises Ltd. http://webarchive.nationalarchives.gov.uk/. Accessed 18 Jan 2015
Duffy J (2011) Trust in second life. South Econ J 78(1):53–62
Epstein JM, Axtell R (1996) Growing artificial societies. MIT Press, Cambridge
Fiedler M (2009) Cooperation in virtual worlds. Schmalenbach Bus Rev 61(2):173–194
Fiedler M, Haruvy E (2009) The lab versus the virtual lab and virtual field – an experimental investigation of trust games with communication. J Econ Behav Organ 72:716–724
Fiedler M, Haruvy E, Xin Li S (2011) Social distance in a virtual world experiment. Games Econ Behav 72:400–426
Fishman GS (1981) Symulacja komputerowa. Pojęcia i metody. PWE, Warszawa
Fontana M (2006) Simulation in economics: evidence on diffusion and communication. J Artif Soc Soc Simul 9(2):8, http://jasss.soc.surrey.ac.uk/9/2/8.html. Accessed 17 Jul 2015
Forrester JW (1961) Industrial dynamics. MIT Press, Cambridge
Franklin A (1990) Experiment, right or wrong. Cambridge University Press, Cambridge
Frigg R, Reiss J (2009) The philosophy of simulation: hot new issues or same old stew? Synthese 169(3):593–613. doi:10.1007/s11229-009-9577-x
Füllbrunn S, Richwien K, Sadrieh A (2011) Trust and trustworthiness in anonymous virtual worlds. J Media Econ 24(1):48–63
Gilbert N, Troitzsch KG (1999) Simulation for the social scientist. Open University Press, Milton Keynes
Girvan C (2013) What is a virtual world? Definition and classification. Technical Report. Trinity College, Dublin
Gordon G (1974) Symulacja systemów. WNT, Warszawa
Greiner B, Caravella M, Roth AE (2014) Is avatar-to-avatar communication as effective as face-to-face communication? An Ultimatum Game experiment in First and Second Life. J Econ Behav Organ 108:374–382
Grimm V, Railsback S (2005) Individual-based modeling and ecology. Princeton University Press, Princeton
Grossklags J (2007) Experimental economics and experimental computer science: a survey. In: Proceedings of the Workshop on Experimental Computer Science (ExpCS'07), Part of ACM

Federated Computer Research Conference, San Diego, 13–14 June. doi:10.1145/1281700.1281711
Grüne-Yanoff T, Weirich P (2011) The philosophy and epistemology of simulation: a review. Simul Gaming 41(1):20–50. doi:10.1177/1046878109353470
Guala F (2002) Models, simulations, and experiments. In: Magnani L, Nersessian NJ (eds) Model-based reasoning: science, technology, values. Kluwer Academic Publishers, New York, pp 59–74
Guala F (2005) The methodology of experimental economics. Cambridge University Press, Cambridge
Hacking I (1983) Representing and intervening: introductory topics in the philosophy of natural science. Cambridge University Press, Cambridge
Hughes R (1999) The Ising Model, computer simulation, and universal physics. In: Morgan M, Morrison M (eds) Models as mediators. Cambridge University Press, Cambridge
Humphreys P (1991) Computer simulations. In: Fine A, Forbes M, Wessels L (eds) PSA 1990. Philosophy of Science Association, East Lansing, pp 497–506
Humphreys P (2004) Extending ourselves: computational science, empiricism, and scientific method. Oxford University Press, New York
Ihde D (2006) Models, models everywhere. In: Kuppers G, Lenhard J, Shinn T (eds) Simulation: pragmatic construction of reality, vol 25, Sociology of the Sciences Yearbook. Springer, Heidelberg, pp 79–86
Innocenti A (2013) Economic experiments in low immersive virtual environments. A methodological assessment. In: IV Joint Workshop Rutgers-Siena on Cognitive Sciences. Rutgers University Center for Cognitive Sciences, 21 May 2013. http://ruccs.rutgers.edu/tempdocs/Innocenti_Paper_Confirmed.pdf. Accessed 18 Jan 2015
Kock N (2009) E-collaboration and e-commerce in virtual worlds: The Potential of Second Life and World of Warcraft. In: Lytras M, Tennyson R, Ordóñez de Pablos P (eds) Knowledge networks: the social software perspective. Information Science Reference, Hershey, pp 308–319
Kopczewski T (2010) Eksperymenty ekonomiczne on-line w nauczaniu oraz w badaniach społecznych. In: Dąbrowski M, Zając M (eds) E-learning w szkolnictwie wyższym – po-tencjał i wykorzystanie. Fundacja Promocji i Akredytacji Kierunków Ekonomicznych, Warszawa, pp 63–71
Korb KB, Mascaro S (2009) The philosophy of computer simulation. In: Glymour C, Wei W, Westerstahl D (eds) Logic, methodology and philosophy of science: proceedings of the thirteenth international congress. College Publications, London, pp 306–325
Kowal P, Kopczewski T, Borowski R (2008) Oprogramowanie do tworzenia eksperymentów ekonomicznych online. Ekonomia 21:79–100
Łatuszyńska M (2008) Symulacja komputerowa dynamiki systemów. Wydawnictwo PWSZ w Gorzowie Wielkopolskim, Gorzów Wielkopolski
Łatuszyńska M (2012) Computer simulation methods in economics and management. Actual Prob Econ 5(2):174–175
Łatuszyńska M, Nermend K (2008) Badania marketingowe w Internecie przy użyciu sy-mulatora. In: Szewczyk A, Krok E (eds) Fenomen Internetu. Wydawnictwo Naukowe Uniwersytetu Szczecińskiego, Szczecin, pp 515–521
Morgan M (2002) Model experiments and models in experiments. In: Magnani L, Nerses-sian N (eds) Model-based reasoning: science, technology, values. Kluwer, New York, pp 41–58
Morgan M (2003) Experiments without material intervention: model experiments, virtual experiments and virtually experiments. In: Radder H (ed) The philosophy of scientific experimentation. University of Pittsburgh Press, Pittsburgh, pp 216–235
Morgan M (2005) Experiments versus models: new phenomena, inference and surprise. J Econ Methodol 12(2):317–329
Morrison M (2009) Models, measurement and computer simulation: the changing face of experimentation. Philos Stud 143(1):33–57

Morrison M, Fontenla M (2013) Price convergence in an online virtual world. Empir Econ 44 (3):1053–1064
Naylor TH, Burdick DS et al (1967) Computer simulation experiments with economic systems: the problem of experimental design. J Am Stat Assoc 62(320):1315–1337
Nicklisch A, Salz T (2008) Reciprocity and status in a virtual field experiment. Preprints of the Max Planck Institute for Research on Collective Goods, Bonn, http://www.coll.mpg.de/pdf_dat/2008_37online.pdf. Accessed 18 Jan 2015
North MJ, Macal CM (2007) Managing business complexity - discovering strategic solutions with agent-based modeling and simulation. Oxford University Press, New York
Norton S, Suppe F (2000) Why atmospheric modeling is good science. In: Miller C, Ed-wards P (eds) Changing the atmosphere: expert knowledge and environmental governance. MIT Press, Cambridge
Nowak M (ed) (2009) Symulacja sieci komputerowych. IITiS PAN, Gliwice
Olds N (2011) Virtual economics: research tools for economists. Economics - Research Papers, University of Ottawa
Parke EC (2014) Experiments, simulations, and epistemic privilege. Philos Sci 81(4):516–536
Parker WS (2009) Does matter really matter? Computer simulations, experiments, and materiality. Synthese 169(3):483–496
Peck SL (2004) Simulation as experiment: a philosophical reassessment for biological modeling. Trends Ecol Evol 19(10):530–534
Peschard I (2012) Is simulation an epistemic substitute for experimentation? In: Valenti S (ed) Simulations and networks. Hermann, Paris
Pidd M (1998) Computer simulation in management science, 4th edn. Wiley, Chichester
Poszewiecki A, Bizon W, Kulawczuk P (eds) (2012) Symulacje menedżerskie i studia przypadków. Wydawnictwo Uniwersytetu Gdańskiego, Gdańsk
Radder H (ed) (2003) The philosophy of scientific experimentation. University of Pittsburgh Press, Pitsburg
Ranker (2015) The best economic simulation games of all time. http://www.ranker.com/list/all-economic-simulations-list/reference?page=2. Accessed 18 Jan 2015
Reiss J (2011) A Plea for (good) simulations: nudging economics toward an experimental science. Simul Gaming 42(2):243–264
Reiss J (2008) Error in economics: towards a more evidence-based methodology. Routledge, London
Rizzi P, Woźniakiewicz J (2008) Perspektywy zastosowania gier symulacyjnych w eduka-cji – teoria i praktyka. Homo Communicativus 3(5):57–63
Roush S (2014) The epistemic superiority of experiment to simulation. In: Philosophy of Scientific Experimentation 4 (PSX4). Center for Philosophy of Science, University of Pittsburgh, Pittsburgh, 11–12 April
Simon HA (1969) The sciences of the artificial. MIT Press, Cambridge
Spann M, Hinz O, Hann I, Skiera B (2010) Decision making in virtual worlds: an experimental test of altruism, fairness and presence, Research Paper, 18th European Conference on Information Systems (ECIS). Pretoria, South Africa, 7–9 June 2010
Sterman J (2014) Interactive web-based simulations for strategy and sustainability: the MIT Sloan Learning Edge Management Flight Simulators, Part II. Syst Dyn Rev 30(3):206–231
Tolk A, Heath BL, Ihrig M, Padilla JJ, Page EH, Suarez ED, Szabo C, Weirich P, Yilmaz L (2013) Epistemology of modeling and simulation. In: Proceedings of the 2013 Simulation Conference WSC. Washington, 8–11 December 2013, pp 1152–1166. doi:10.1109/WSC.2013.6721504
Twieg P, McCabe K (2014) The determinants of territorial property rights in a spatial commons experiment. Working Paper No. 14-40. George Mason University, Department of Economics. Available at SSRN: http://ssrn.com/abstract=2503260
Vallverdú J (2014) What are simulations? An epistemological approach. Procedia Technol 13:6–15

Wawrzeńczyk-Kulik M (2013) Symulacyjna gra decyzyjna jako narzędzie wspomagające nauczanie w ramach przedmiotu "Podstawy przedsiębiorczości". Ekonomia 6(1):303–321
Weber M (2004) Philosophy of experimental biology. Cambridge University Press, Cambridge
Weisberg M (2013) Simulation and similarity, using models to understand the world. Oxford University Press, Oxford
Wiącek-Janka E (2011) Games & decisions. Poznań University of Technology, Poznań
Winsberg E (1999) Sanctioning models: the epistemology of simulation. Sci Context 12:275–292. doi:10.1017/s0269889700003422
Winsberg E (2001) Simulations, models, and theories: complex physical systems and their representations. Philos Sci 68(3):442–454
Winsberg E (2003) Simulated experiments: methodology for a virtual world. Philos Sci 70 (1):105–125
Winsberg E (2009) A tale of two methods. Synthese 169(3):575–592
Winsberg E (2010) Science in the age of computer simulation. University of Chicago Press, Chicago

Chapter 12
Games Using Virtual Reality as a Tool in Economics Experiments

Mariusz Borawski

Abstract The chapter demonstrates how the tabletop role-playing game has been combined with the elements of virtual reality for the purpose of experimental economics. The author describes the software employed in the experiments using virtual stores created for the project simulator of consumer market behaviour and demonstrates how it can be combined with the storyline of a tabletop role-playing game. Additionally, the chapter outlines the problems that can be encountered when conducting surveys with the use of virtual stores and proposes tabletop role-playing games as a solution to these problems.

Keywords Tabletop role-playing game • Virtual reality • Economics experiment

12.1 Introduction

Games have been known to people since the beginning of humanity. Even some playful animal behaviours can be considered as games. Games provide entertainment, but they also teach some behaviour and social skills that are useful in the workplace and in everyday life. So, no wonder that together with the first computers, the computer games soon followed. One of the first ones was a game written in 1951 by A.S. Douglas for the EDSAC computer. Its name was Noughts and Crosses (Jorgensen 2009).

Gradually, more genres of games appeared on the market. One of them, the simulation games, has been widely used in experimental economics. In the simulation games, the main focus is on replicating the real world as faithfully as possible. They have been developing in two directions: towards virtual reality, i.e. the best possible replica of the real world appealing to our senses, and towards the best possible representation of relationships undergoing in the real world. The examples of the former subgenre are Microsoft flight simulators

M. Borawski (✉)
Department of Multimedia Systems, Faculty of Computer Science and Information Technology, West Pomeranian University of Technology Szczecin, Żołnierska 49, 71-210 Szczecin, Poland
e-mail: mborawski@wi.zut.edu.pl

K. Nermend, M. Łatuszyńska (eds.), *Selected Issues in Experimental Economics*, Springer Proceedings in Business and Economics, DOI 10.1007/978-3-319-28419-4_12

(Microsoft 2015) such as MS Flight Simulator, Train Simulator by Dovetail Games (Dovetail Games 2015) or the everyday life simulator The Sims created by Will Wright for Maxis (Maxis 2015).

The Sims is particularly interesting as it allows the players to create and control the lives of human characters (the Sims) in a 3D artificial world resembling the real world: "Sims start their lives with a personality given by a player (or inherited from their parents). The personality develops under their own influence and under the influence of their own choices. During their lifetime Sims collect memories which determine their personality, decisions and behaviour. Their life experience can have either short- or long-term effect on the relationships among their family members or friends. Sims' childhood memories can determine their future lives and relationships. Sims, controlled by the player, can make best friends or worst enemies" (EA 2015).

The games aiming at the best representation of the real-world relationships first of all include decision games for management training. In such games, the accuracy of the graphic imitation is less relevant than the reconstruction of rules, dependencies and interactions. They are particularly popular in senior management training. The example is MAGNUS, a management game created by DecisionWare Simulations and Games Pte. Ltd. (DecisionWare 2015) for managerial training purposes. The game is used at the University of Antwerp in Belgium, the Hong Kong University of Science and Technology and the Ryutsu Keizai University in Japan. Other examples of this genre are EIS Simulation designed for HR training (Angehrn 2015) and the games offered with e-learning courses by Hall Marketing (Hall Marketing 2015). The above decision training games are simulators in which the trainee makes decisions and then tests their effect in simulated objects. Therefore, we can say that these games teach through experiments or, in the case of management games, through economics experiments. Decision training games can support data collection about human behaviour and interactions. Thanks to its education-oriented character, they reach large groups of people, which makes simulation results more reliable.

In the games used in economics experiments, it is crucial to make the players immerse in their enacted roles as much as possible. This can be done with the help of virtual reality. The term refers to a sophisticated human–computer interface which facilitates simulation in real time through multiple sensory channels such as vision, hearing, touch, etc. (Burdea and Coiffet 2003). The software makes players strongly identify with the mocked world. On the other hand, this world may influence people's responses which are then transferred to the real world. An example is simulators using virtual reality in training programs for pilots, maritime captains or military leaders. Behaviour trained there is moved to the real world. It can be seen in the Second Life (Linden Research 2015) where the virtual world started to work as an alternative reality. Just like in the real world, people buy and sell virtual goods, meet and even work and earn money. Virtual currency is exchangeable with the real one, so the players can support themselves with money earned in mock-up jobs. A game is not a game anymore and has become a part of the reality.

The combination of a decision game with the elements of virtual reality gives us the opportunity to collect information about human behaviour on a much larger scale than before. The study on human short-term decisions interfered with elements that are either distracting or subjectively irrelevant is difficult in when the researcher is not able to replicate the conditions when these decisions were originally made. Such situation is common in consumer behaviour studies. Scientists who examine consumer behaviour have more limited access to data than companies that can perform continuous observation of customers' response to specific incentives. Such data are not made available to the public due to strategic reasons. Consequently, the difficulty in accessing the data directly via company computer systems prevents the scientists from creating their own databases.

Social impact of the large multiples' marketing is enormous as a single hypermarket can be visited by thousands of shoppers a day. A chain can consist of dozens of stores; therefore, its impact is multiplied. Having at their disposal a precisely targeted database, large multiples can take experimental measures to develop their best marketing strategies. Theoretically, regular changes to the floor plan make customers spend more time moving through the aisles. From the practical point of view, this practice can be seen as experimenting to find the optimum floor plan so that the sales can grow. CCTV scattered all over the hypermarkets not only track shoplifters, but they can also be used to monitor customers' response to individual forms of marketing. Modern technology offers the opportunity to automatically collect this type of information even if the surveillance staff does not know anything about it.

The combination of a decision game with the elements of virtual reality offers the opportunity to gather data of the range similar to that available to large multiples, thus opening the possibility to studies on positive and negative social impact of various forms of marketing.

Decision games set in virtual reality are particularly useful in evaluating the effect of certain situations on customer behaviour. These situations consist of the following components (Foxall and Goldsmith 1998):

- Physical environment—the customer's position in the store, music, smells, floor plan, etc.
- Social environment—other people surrounding the customer
- Time perspective—time of the day and year, time devoted to decision-making
- The consumer's objective and attitude
- Situations preceding the purchase decision

The first two of the above elements are particularly useful for a simulation applying virtual reality. The store floor plan and size (Donovan and Rossiter 1982); the shelf layout, shape and size and the position of checkouts (Sommer et al. 1981); the access to shelves (self-service) (May 1965); and the way goods are presented (Buttle 1984) can significantly influence the behaviour of consumers. All these elements can be replicated by means of realistic 3D graphic design. The popularity of the FPP (first-person perspective) indicates that people easily identify themselves with the virtual world, which makes it a useful tool for obtaining data about consumers.

12.2 Consumer Data Collection by Means of Virtual Reality Elements

Consumer data collection can be based on computer games using the elements of virtual reality. For the obtained data to be reliable, the players must fully identify with their virtual counterparts. Therefore, the game must imitate as many elements of the real world as possible. The effectiveness of such an approach has been proved by the popularity of The Sims or by Second Life where the players strongly identify themselves with their counterparts in the game. Unfortunately, the costs of creating a complete replica of the real world in the virtual reality are very high, and the necessity to freely manipulate the rules governing this mock-up world makes it even more expensive. The researcher who is investigating certain regularities cannot be deprived of unrestricted access to such manipulation options. The solution to this problem is the combination of virtual reality with a noncomputer role-playing game (RPG).

The noncomputer games have an additional advantage as it allows for introducing role-playing, which is rare in computer games (Eladhari and Mateas 2009). This is a result of difficulty in transferring this element onto the computer platform. Role-playing requires the player to imagine how the fictional character would behave in a specific situation and to enact this behaviour. In reality, most players do not play the roles of fictitious characters, but they transfer their own behavioural patterns from the real world to the virtual reality in the game (Eladhari and Mateas 2009). It is much more beneficial for human behavioural studies because the researchers can study people's behaviour while providing them entertainment. The subjects are usually much more involved when playing a game than when participating in a regular scientific study, thus making the experimental study results more reliable.

The games that make a particularly valuable contribution to scientific research are tabletop role-playing games in which the participants enact their roles in their imagination and describe their character's actions through speech. The play is controlled by one of the participants called the game master who presents the rules of the game to other players and then describes the outcomes of their decisions. The game master is responsible for the proper course of the story in the game. Essentially, the game is an interactive story continued within a certain predetermined frame which the game master can modify depending on the players' actions. Technical problems in transferring the tabletop role-playing game onto a computer platform result in losing the storyline flexibility (Tychsen et al. 2005; Anders et al. 2007).

There are no technical contraindications against combining computer and noncomputer games. Some elements of the game can be performed on a computer, while some can be played at a table. In this way, we can introduce some elements of virtual reality to regular tabletop role-playing games. In the case of the consumer behaviour studies, only some elements of the real world can be placed in the virtual reality, e.g. the interior of a store. Some aspects of shopping, such as the shelf layout, cannot be represented in the tabletop role-playing game, but it can be easily done in the virtual world. Those elements of the game that are taking place outside the store can be played at a table with the assistance of the game master. The virtual environment for such games has been created as a part of the project Market Consumer Behaviour Simulator (MNiI No 1 H02C 013 29) (Nermend 2008).

The mock-up environment has been created with the client–server technology. The client is activated in the browser window and then links with the www server. The most important part of the client which is responsible for the store visualization has been generated as a Java applet. On the server, the database server is activated that is responsible for the storage of configuration data as well as for the data about the players' activities. When planning the research project, the researcher can create a character just like in a classical tabletop role-playing game. The essential modification is the possibility to attribute qualities to the characters. The researcher can define the qualities that are relevant for the character, e.g. gender, age, education or salary, and introduce them into the system. Even though the subject (the player) should follow the role attributed to their character, it is recommendable for the character's qualities to reflect the player's actual personality. We could hardly expect the research results to be reliable if a 20-year-old player enacted the role of an 80-year-old.

The software provides an opportunity to define numerous virtual worlds to which any number of players can be assigned. Each world is designed to one game which does not necessarily have to end after one session. Therefore, many games can be played simultaneously and stopped or resumed at any time. Every player has their own account which gives them access to the game server not only in the lab where the research project is being conducted but at any place with an Internet access. The researcher can access the server by means of the administration account where they can add or ban users, create and eliminate worlds as well as modify the virtual world parameters. The researcher can also introduce new merchandise along with their various attributes (Fig. 12.1). The goods have to be displayed on the shelves of the virtual store, so the researcher must provide their photographs and information concerning their size. The photographs enable us to test the effect of packaging on the consumers' decisions. Moreover, the researcher can define the initial product price, stocking schedules and market saturation. These parameters help force the circulation of goods on the market and find out how consumers and sellers respond to the product shortage or surplus. Also, the researcher can define the number and size of stores in the virtual world.

In every store, the researcher can decide about the shelf layout, product display and prices. This enables them to differentiate one store from another. There is also an alternative option—the researcher can appoint store owners who will play a dual role. There will be consumers who have to buy goods outside the range of products that are sold in their store. There will also be store owners whose shopping budget depends on their profits from their own store. The store owners can modify the shelf layout and decide about the prices of products, thus releasing the researchers from

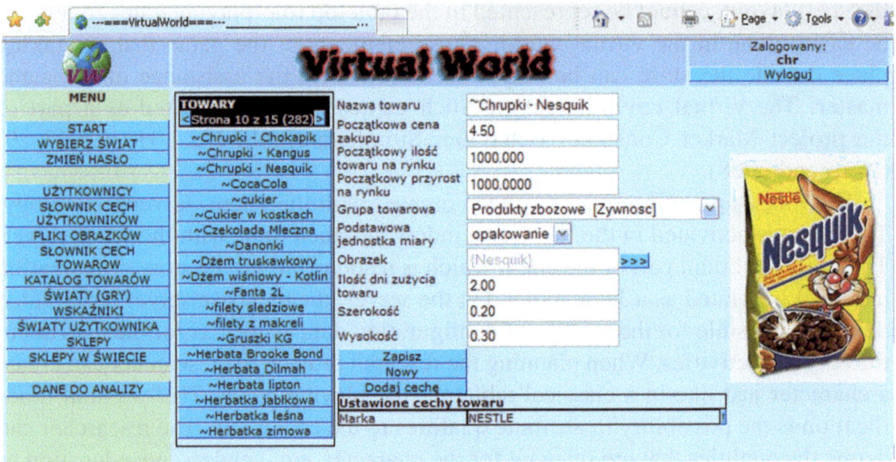

Fig. 12.1 Introduction of goods (Nermend 2008)

this task. Instead, they define the wholesale prices of products and the product sizes and provide their photos.

Entering the store, the consumer can see a 3D mock-up of the real-world store (Fig. 12.2). They move around with arrow keys. They can walk along the aisles and zoom in the shelves to see the products on display better. The shelves contain photos with product labels and price tags just like in a real store. Some shelves are marked red, which means a special offer. It is the owner who decides about discounts, but they are not obliged to lower the merchandise prices. To the contrary—they can raise them if they believe that it will enhance their profits. Additionally, the buyer can use a special key to see the product label in a separate window. The labels contain information identical to the real-world one.

The consumer can place selected merchandise in a cart. At the checkout, they receive the shopping list and the amount to be paid. They can give up the purchase if the price turns out high or if they decide that they have been cheated. The price at the checkout may be different from the one on the shelf. The store owner has the right to make them differ.

In this case, the virtual reality is just a part of the game which is simultaneously played at a table. The researcher has to write a script for the play whose essential factor is visits to the store, as it happens in almost every tabletop role-playing game. The characters in the game need food so shopping for consumer staples is necessary for these games to continue. Lack of supplies leads to the character's weakness and eventually to their failure. The most common way to provide characters with food is shopping. When creating the game storyline, we need to make sure that shops are a natural element of the virtual world in a game and must fit in the game reality. What is more, in order to ensure the research validity, the characters animated by the players should operate in the environment which is similar to the players' own real-life reality.

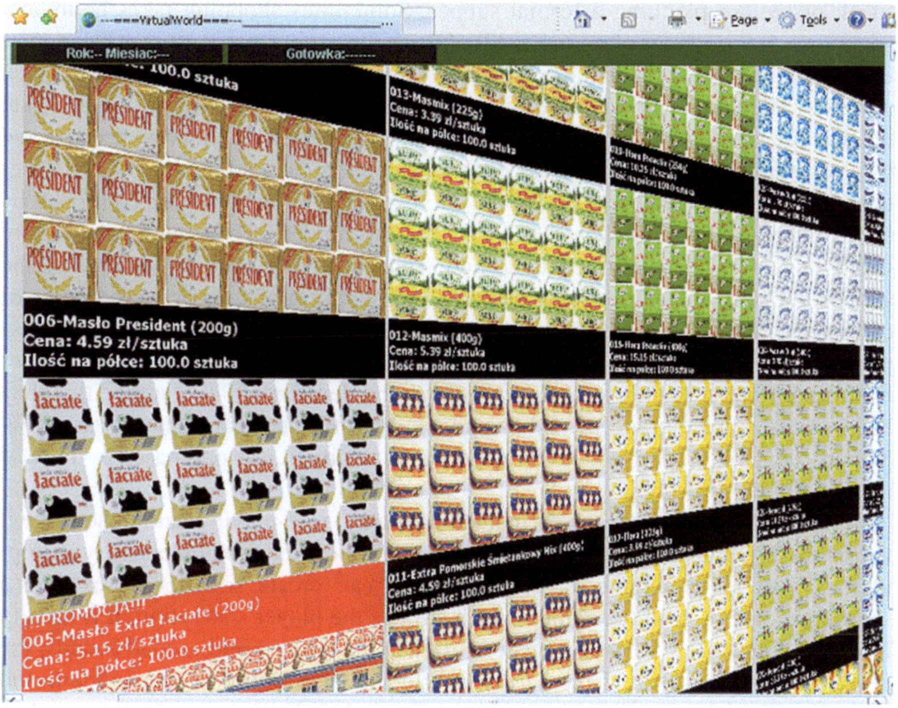

Fig. 12.2 Shelves with merchandise in a virtual store (Nermend 2008)

The researcher can create their own game or adapt the existing one (also an adventure game) to their needs. The game itself is happening in the players' imagination, yet game masters often use various accessories, such as sheets of paper, printouts and drawings. Sometimes a game master needs a calculator. And there is nothing wrong in the players using tablets to go virtual shopping when the need arises.

Combining tabletop role-playing games with virtual stores brings multiple benefits. Studies using solely virtual stores have proved to be burdened with many flaws that can be eliminated by the introduction of a tabletop role-playing game. These flaws result from three main problems faced by most researchers: the lack of the players' involvement, their excessive interest in the procedure and the research itself as well as the lack of the research context. Some players were bored with the survey and wanted to complete it as quickly as possible. Another large group showed strong interest in the virtual world and consequently indulged in testing its functions, which was far from natural consumer behaviour. Yet, the crucial difficulty emerging in the project was how to exclude these players' results from the general evaluation.

The real-world shopping always takes place in some context. For example, we buy groceries because our fridge needs restocking or we are hungry and need a snack or we are planning a formal supper. Sometimes shopping takes hours and sometimes it is a matter of minutes. All of these determine our consumer behaviour. Unfortunately, in experimental research projects, it is very difficult to simulate such contexts. The research design requires from the player to live their role or replicate the real-life shopping situation they have actually experienced. Surveys are affected by a self-perception error. They record the way people would like to behave rather than their actual behaviour. This flaw of survey methodology has been confirmed by comparative studies (Frankowska 2008). The discrepancies between questionnaire results and actually registered data were enormous. For instance, in one of the studies, 34 % of the respondents declared the purchase of four or more bottles of carbonated water. The records from the virtual store proved that only 14 % of those players had bought four or more bottles of carbonated water. Also, their preferences regarding product brands were different from the declared: 60 % claimed that they had bought Żywiec brand of carbonated water, while the real number was 37 %. Nobody declared buying Nałęczowianka, but in reality, it was purchased by 11 % of the players.

In the research projects which include a tabletop role-playing game, the context is provided by the storyline. The player is given specified assignments. By manipulating with the assignments, the researcher can create situations providing a shopping context. Also the game as such attracts the player's attention. It is usually long and takes a few several-hour-long rounds. In the first and second rounds, the players learn the rules of the virtual world, and they may be unconfident and cautious. Once they get familiar with the game, their behaviour changes and they transfer their real-world behavioural patterns to the virtual reality with more ease. Therefore, it is recommendable not to start the observation until the players have completed at least two rounds.

The elicited data can be used for consumer behaviour analyses as well as for building a consumer behaviour simulator (Borawski 2008). Prior to constructing the simulator, we need to create a reliable consumer model. Tabletop role-playing games can contribute to the simulation reliability. The simulator provides the opportunity to represent a large group of consumers (up to several millions), which makes it possible to observe consumer behaviour-related market mechanisms on a general scale.

12.3 Conclusions

Economics experiments involving human subjects require their maximum engagement, which is difficult to achieve. Games can be a useful tool to attract the subjects' attention. However, computer games are a costly option. The solution may be combining them with tabletop role-playing games with the purpose of replicating the world logics by means of some elements of virtual reality. Tabletop role-playing games offer the opportunity to manipulate these logics without the IT support so that the researchers can unaidedly and autonomously arrange the dependencies that rule the simulated reality.

References

Anders T, Ken N, Thea B, Michael H (2007) Cross-format analysis of the gaming experience in multi-player role-playing games. In: DiGRA'07 - Proceedings of the 2007 DiGRA International Conference: Situated Play. The University of Tokyo

Angehrn AA (2015) The EIS Simulation. http://www.calt.insead.edu/eis/. Accessed 8 Aug 2015

Borawski M (2008) Prototyp symulatora naśladującego zachowania konsumentów. In: Witek J, Nermend K (eds) Zachowania konsumenta w świetle badań ankietowych i symulacyjnych. ZAPOL, Szczecin, pp 58–78

Burdea G, Coiffet P (2003) Virtual reality technology, 2nd edn. Wiley, New Jersey

Buttle F (1984) Merchandising. Eur J Mark 18:104–123

DecisionWare (2015) MAGNUS. http://www.decisionwaresim.com/. Accessed 9 Aug 2015

Donovan RJ, Rossiter JR (1982) Store atmosphere: an environmental psychology approach. J Retail 58:34–57

Dovetail Games (2015) Train simulator. http://railsimulator.com/. Accessed 5 Jul 2015

EA (2015) The SimsTM 2. http://www.ea.com/pl/the-sims-2. Accessed 6 Aug 2015

Eladhari MP, Mateas M (2009) Rules for role play in virtual game worlds case study: the Pataphysic Institute. In: Digital arts and culture conference. University of California, Irvine, CA

Foxall GR, Goldsmith RE (1998) Psychologia konsumenta dla menadżera marketingu. PWN, Warszawa

Frankowska M (2008) Analiza porównawcza badań ankietowych i symulacyjnych. In: Witek J, Nermend K (eds) Zachowania konsumenta w świetle badań ankietowych i symulacyjnych. ZAPOL, Szczecin, pp 79–130

Hall Marketing (2015) Business Simulations from knowledge through simulated experience to wisdom. http://www.simulations.co.uk/. Accessed 8 Aug 2015

Jorgensen AH (2009) Context and driving forces in the development of the early computer game nimbi. IEEE Ann Hist Comput 31:44–53

Linden Research (2015) Second Life. http://secondlife.com/. Accessed 10 Aug 2015

Maxis (2015) The Sims. http://www.thesims.com/. Accessed 6 Aug 2015

May FE (1965) Buying behaviour: some research findings. J Bus 38:379–386

Microsoft (2015) Flightsim. http://www.flightsim.com/. Accessed 5 Jul 2015

Nermend K (2008) Symulator do badań zachowań konsumentów. In: Witek J, Nermend K (eds) Zachowania konsumenta w świetle badań ankietowych i symulacyjnych. ZAPOL, Szczecin, pp 38–57

Sommer R, Herrick J, Sommer TR (1981) The behavioural ecology of supermarkets and farmers' markets. J Environ Psychol 1:13–19. doi:10.1016/S0272-4944(81)80014-X

Tychsen A, Hitchens M, Brolund T, Kavakli M (2005) The game master. In: Second Australasian conference on Interactive entertainment. Creativity & Cognition Studios Press, 215–222

References

Chapter 13
Multi-criteria Preference Vector Method as Support Tool for Decision-Making in Virtual Worlds

Kesra Nermend

Abstract The chapter presents the theoretical foundations of the preference vector method (PVM). This is the development of methods used by the Polish school which can be used in the decision-making process. The ranking of objects according to decision-maker's preferences is performed on the basis of a combination of the following two methods for the construction of aggregate measures: the Hellwig method, in which the Euclidean distance is used, and the vector measure construction method (VMCM), which uses a vector projection.

Keywords Synthetic measures • Multi-criteria method • PVM • Preference vector

13.1 Introduction

As it has been shown in Chap. 11, one of numerous computer methods that support laboratory economic experiments is a computer simulation. In simulation models, we can reconstruct economic phenomena or even build whole virtual worlds (Łatuszyńska and Nermend 2008; Łatuszyńska 2010, 2012), reproducing any fragment of the economic reality by means of virtual objects such as companies, stores, banks, institutions, customers, etc. Some of these virtual objects, e.g. consumers, can function as the program agents and mock human behaviour in the real world. Therefore they can make decisions of many kinds, for instance, select goods or services. In order to implement the decision-making mechanism for this type of agents, we can choose from the variety of solutions offered by multi-criteria methods. After all, even in the real world, consumers, when facing a decision concerning the purchase of goods or services related with their everyday life (i.e. buying a car or holidays, choosing an insurance company), need some method to help them make a good choice on the basis of several criteria. In the

---

K. Nermend (✉)
Department of Computer Methods in Experimental Economics,
Faculty of Economics and Management, Institute of IT in Management,
University of Szczecin, Mickiewicza 64, 71-101 Szczecin, Poland
e-mail: kesra@wneiz.pl

K. Nermend, M. Łatuszyńska (eds.), *Selected Issues in Experimental Economics*,
Springer Proceedings in Business and Economics, DOI 10.1007/978-3-319-28419-4_13

majority of cases, consumers are manipulated by manufacturers and sellers, which significantly obstructs their well-informed purchasing decisions.

Decision-making support methods can help the consumer make their choice in a more rational way. There are different schools dealing with such methods: the French, the Belgian, the Polish and the American one. The French school developed the ELECTRE group of methods (find more in the works by (Roy 1968; Grolleau and Tergny 1971; Duckstein and Gershon 1983; Vallée and Zielniewicz 1994; Karagiannidis and Moussiopoulos 1997; Mousseau et al. 2001). The PROMETHEE method (Scharlig 1996) is being developed by the French and Belgian schools, while the AHP (Saaty 1980) and ANP (Saaty 2005) methods are being created by the American school. Another popular world-known method is TOPSIS used for object ranking and selection (Hwang and Yoon 1981; Jahanshahloo et al. 2006). This chapter is based on the experience of the Polish school and focuses on the ranking methods derived from the Hellwig method (Hellwig 1968) that were subsequently developed by many scientists.

The Hellwig method has found many applications including the construction of synthetic variables in the process of econometric modelling (Bartosiewicz 1984), product quality assessment (Borys 1984), as well as the studies on regional development (Młodak 2006; Nermend 2006; Strahl 2006; Nermend 2008a), on socioeconomic development (Kompa and Witkowska 2010), on the stock exchange financial efficiency (Kompa 2014), on the attractiveness of stock market investments (Tarczyński and Łuniewska 2006), on the effectiveness of Chinese banks (Witkowska 2010), on the demand for durable electronic consumer goods in Poland (Dittman and Pisz 1975), on the demand for qualified staff in Poland (Cieślak 1974; Cieślak 1976), on the synthetic assessment of company performance in Poland (Pluta 1977), on the socioeconomic development of countries worldwide (Grabiński et al. 1989), on the agricultural production in chosen European countries (Nowak 1990) and on the investment attractiveness of companies listed on the Warsaw Stock Exchange (Tarczyński 2004). Moreover, the Polish school has developed non-model methods induced by radar diagrams proposed by Binderman et al. (2008). These methods were also used to create synthetic indicators of the diversification of Polish agriculture (Binderman 2011). The application of the Hellwig method for building a synthetic measure reduced the requirements for a pattern which must be the object that is the best in every possible aspect. This rules out the application of real-life models and indicates sensitivity of the built synthetic measures to the emergence (in the set of examined objects) of units whose coordinate values are exceptionally large and thus likely to affect the ranking.

The application of orthogonal projection for constructing synthetic measures was proposed by Kolenda (Kolenda 2006). Her method offers two alternative options called Hellwig development paths II and III. Like the Hellwig method itself, both of them require defining the distance between two points. Kolenda's method has improved the Hellwig method by adding the option to use real-life models that do not necessarily have to be the best in the set of examined objects. The papers (Nermend 2007, 2008b) proposed taking into account the properties of vector calculus in order to build a vector synthetic measure (vector measure construction method—VMCM) basing on the definition of the scalar product without reference to the distance measure. This simplifies the procedure of calculating the measure by offering the possibility to use any vector space where the scalar product has been defined without an extra condition concerning the distance measure. The method's additional advantage is its simple form, which is important when the synthetic measure of a large number of objects has to be calculated on a computer with low processing power. Borawski (2012) defined, as a part of the increment arithmetics, the scalar product for dual-component numbers consisting of the mean value and standard deviation. Such a scalar product can be used to build a synthetic measure, which has been shown in Nermend (2012). Due to this approach, we find an additional piece of information which can prove useful for the interpretation of a result. Nermend and Tarczyńska-Łuniewska (2013) applied Borawski's scalar product to construct a synthetic measure for the purpose of the research into spatial and time homogeneity of socioeconomic objects, whereas Łatuszyńska (2014) applied it to assess the development of information society.

The proposed method to build vector measures (Nermend 2008c) can be used not only to rank socioeconomic objects, but it can be found useful in the situations where a given value has to be measured along the specified direction, the example of which is measuring a particular colour in the pixels of an image. This specific measurement is of vital importance for the procedure of removing the dominating colour.

Synthetic measures based on calculating the distance from the pattern have some limitations. The main problem is the emergence of nontypical objects (Nermend 2008d), i.e. the ones whose property values are not comparable with the same characteristics of other observed objects. In such a situation, the objectivity of the constructed synthetic measure decreases due to the strong influence of insufficiently representative objects on the position of the pattern, which consequently determines the ranking order. Another problem lies in adding a new object to the set of the observed ones. It requires a repeated research procedure since the set of the observed objects is closed. We cannot choose a real-life object for the pattern as there is a risk that there may be a better object in this set. What is more, we cannot relate the study conducted in one year to the studies completed in other years due to the differences in patterns. In such a situation, it is necessary to conduct separate studies in which the pattern is common.

The VMCM, which utilises the vector calculus, has the following characteristics that compensate for the limitations of the Hellwig method:

- The measure has neither top nor bottom limits, thus allowing for objects better than the pattern.
- It permits adding objects from outside the original set without the necessity to build a new model.
- It is more vulnerable to change dynamics.
- It allows for the studies on dynamics.

After minor alterations, the VMCM can be a tool for solving multi-criteria decision-making problems. The purpose of our chapter is to present theoretical and mathematical principles of the preference vector method which is derived from the VMCM and is designed to help choose decision-making alternatives basing on the criteria indicated by the decision-maker. I also compare the PVM with other methods of similar character and I give an empirical example of its application confronting it with ELECTRE II.

13.2 Theoretical and Mathematical Description of PVM

When solving decision-making problems by means of the PVM, the decision-maker can express their preferences in a variety of ways. Figure 13.1 shows the examples of alternative ways to solve decision-making problems:

- Variant A. The decision-maker gives the name and the character of their criteria. Then the procedure is continued automatically, without the decision-maker's intervention.
- Variant B. The decision-maker gives the name and character of their criteria as well as the acceptable range of the criterion values.

In the majority of variants, the research procedure for calculating the PVM is run in six stages: selecting the criteria, defining the criterion character, attributing weights to the criteria, standardising the criterion values, determining the preference vector and, finally, building the ranking.

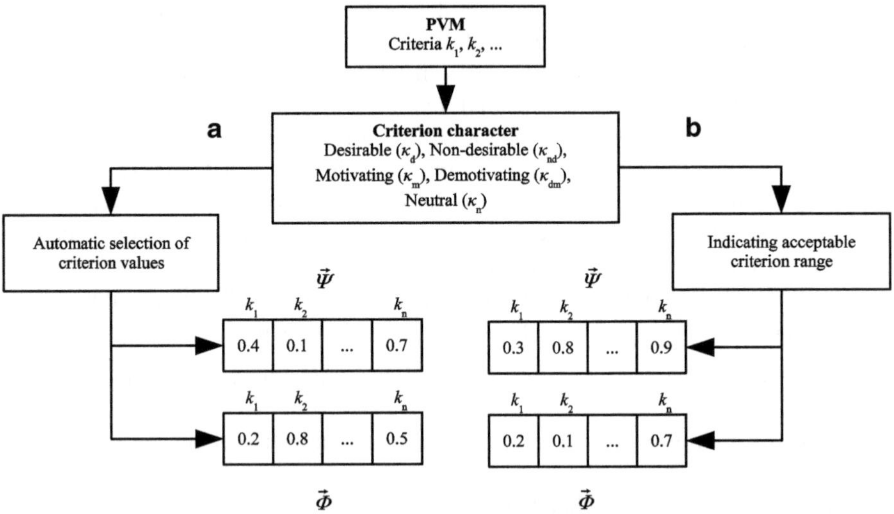

Fig. 13.1 Selected possible PVM variants designed for solving decision-making problems (ki, the i-th criterion; $\vec{\Psi}$, the motivating preference vector; $\vec{\Phi}$, the demotivating preference vector)

13.2.1 Stage I: Selecting the Criteria

The choice of criteria is determined by the decision-maker's preferences. The criteria are selected depending on the type of a decision-making situation. For many such situations, we are able to define a permanent set of criteria which can be made use of in similar cases. The criteria will further be denoted by k_i (the subscript index represents the number of a criterion). The criterion defines these characteristics of objects that can be expressed in numbers. In this chapter, the objects are denoted by $\underset{j}{\vec{X}}$, where j represents the number of an object. For instance, for the decision-maker's needs, cars can be classified according to such criteria as fuel consumption, engine power, etc. These criteria are expressed in the $\underset{j}{x_i}$ values (the value of the i-th criterion of the j-th object).

Basing on the defined criteria, we create a set of criterion values for the objects. Initially, we have to eliminate all the criteria whose span (or standard deviation) equals zero. Even though such criteria have insignificant impact on the study results, they can complicate the calculations due to division by zero which can occur when standardisation is performed by means of standard deviation or span. The criteria are eliminated with the use of the coefficient of variation V_i. The criteria with V_i less than 0.1 are eliminated. See more on the procedure of elimination with the coefficient of variation in Nermend (2008c).

However, not all the criteria can be attributed with numerical values. The qualitative criteria can be described in words, e.g. red, green or blue. In such a case, colours will be assigned values representing the decision-maker's preferences. There are various methods to do this. For instance, in the AHP method, we construct a pairwise comparison matrix. Its rows and columns correspond to the object features that are being compared. In my example, I will be comparing colours in respect of the decision-maker's preferences. The decision-maker will define how much more they prefer one colour to another. All the colours have to be juxtaposed in this way. When we have n colours, then the number of comparisons is $\frac{n^2 - n}{2}$. In our example (where $n = 3$), it is $\frac{3^2 - 3}{2} - 3$. Another, much better solution is to compare concrete objects in a given colour with one another. However, in this instance, the number of comparisons can increase significantly. For example, there may be 100 decision-making variants in four colours. Then, when comparing the colours, we have to perform six comparisons, while when we compare the objects in reference to their colours, the number of comparisons rockets to 4950. Apparently, the comparison of objects can be dull and labour intensive.

When making the comparison, we construct the $n \times n$ matrix. In our example, it is the 3×3 matrix. The main diagonal entries are all 1. Then we define how much the object entered in a row is better than the object entered in a column Fig. 13.2. The value bigger than one means that the object in a row is better than the object in a column, whereas when this value is less than one, it is worse. When the value equals one, the objects are equally important. In the AHP method, the proposed scale is Saaty's nine-step rating scale (Saaty 1980, 96):

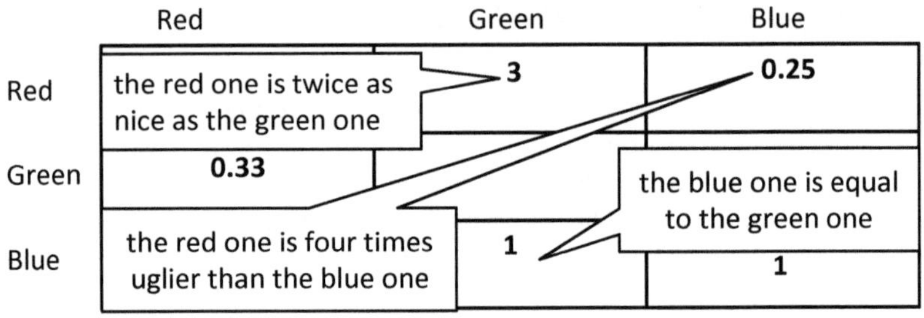

Fig. 13.2 The example of a pairwise comparison matrix for colours

1. Equal importance
2. Intermediate values
3. One object slightly favoured over the other
4. Intermediate values
5. One object strongly favoured over the other
6. Intermediate values
7. One object very strongly favoured over the other
8. Intermediate values
9. One object having the largest possible advantage over the other

Due to methodological reasons in the PVM, the value of 2 itself represents a significant advantage. This is why we assume that the value entered in the matrix provides information how much the object represented in a row is better than the one represented in a column. We can assume that the largest possible advantage starts from the value of 2.

For example, the value of 3 entered in the first row of the second column means that the red colour is rated three times nicer than the green one (according to the decision-maker's preference). If the entry in the first row of the third column is ¼, it signifies that the red colour is rated four times uglier than the blue one. When entering numbers in the matrix, it is important to remember that the values of entries are interrelated, and for each matrix entry, there is interdependence:

$$c_{i,j} = \frac{1}{c_{j,i}}, \tag{13.1}$$

It means that if the entry in the first row of the second column is 3, then the entry in the second row of the first column must be 1/3.

13.2.2 Stage II: Defining the Criterion Character

Typically, the decision-makers are not able to quantify their preferences, but they can easily indicate which objects are acceptable or unacceptable for them.

Therefore the proposed criterion character should correspond to their attitude. I suggest the following classification of their criteria (Nermend, Borawski, 2014):

- Desirable ($k_i \in \kappa_{\mathrm{d}}$), whose required values are neither too big nor too small. For example, when buying a car, the decision-maker expects a car of a certain size, neither too big nor too small (a neutral characteristic, in the Polish literature named a nominant).
- Non-desirable ($k_i \in \kappa_{\mathrm{nd}}$), whose specified value is not desirable.
- Motivating ($k_i \in \kappa_{\mathrm{m}}$), whose required values are big and motivate the decision-maker to make their mind. For example, when choosing a form of bank deposit, they will be looking for the offer with the highest interest rates (a booster, in the Polish literature named a stimulant).
- Demotivating ($k_i \in \kappa_{\mathrm{dm}}$), whose required values are small. If their attributed values are big, the decision-maker is discouraged to make up their mind (an inhibitor, in the Polish literature named a destimulant).
- Neutral ($k_i \in \kappa_{\mathrm{n}}$), whose characteristics are not relevant for this specific decision-making dilemma, so their values should not affect the decision.

In this stage, specific characteristics should be assigned to every criterion. Each of the characteristics can be described as above or by means of the terms applied in the multidimensional comparative analysis, i.e. a nominant, a stimulant or a destimulant. In my opinion, the terms I propose are more comprehensible for an average decision-maker.

13.2.3 Stage III: Attributing Weights to the Criteria

We can generally assume that all the criteria are of equal importance. Yet, there are situations when one of them can be much more appreciated than the others. An example can be the price as it is often the principal criterion on which we base our purchasing decision. Therefore, we have to attribute to it a higher weight value. For instance, we can assume that the weights of the criteria w_i are equal to 1. In a situation when it is necessary to add to the importance of certain criteria, we can increase or reduce the weights. For example, if we assign the weight of 2 to a given criterion, it will become twice as important as the remaining ones. If the assigned weight will be 0.5, the criterion will be twice less important. The weights may also adopt values ranging from 0 to 100, assuming that their total is 100. Then they become the percentage indicator of the criteria importance.

Once we have determined the weights, they should be normalised in order to eliminate the scales of values in which they have been expressed:

$$w_j' = \frac{w_j}{\sum_{i=1}^{M} w_i}, \tag{13.2}$$

where w_j is the weight value for the j-th criterion, w'_i is the value of a normalised weight for the i-th criterion and M is the number of criteria.

13.2.4 Stage IV: Normalising the Criteria

By principle, the criteria which describe objects are nonhomogenous as they represent diverse parameters of these objects which are expressed in different measurement units and have different scales of values. Consequently, the data that are recorded in this way are incomparable. Therefore, we have to be brought to a form in which they become comparable. Hence, the subsequent stage of the PVM is the normalisation of the criteria. In the course of the normalisation process, the units of measurement are eliminated and the scales of the criterion values are brought to roughly the same level. The most common method of normalisation is the following standardisation (Nermend 2008c):

$$x'_{\underset{j}{i}} = \frac{x_{\underset{j}{i}} - \overline{x}_i}{S_i}, \tag{13.3}$$

where $x_{\underset{j}{i}}$ is the value of the i-th criterion of the j-th object, $x'_{\underset{j}{i}}$ is the value of the i-th criterion of the j-th object after standardisation, $\overline{x}_i$ is the average value of the i-th criterion and S_i is the standard deviation of the value of the i-th criterion.

The normalised values will be further denoted by prim. See more on normalising in Kukuła (2000), Pawełek (2008) and Nermend and Tarczyńska-Łuniewska (2013).

In the instance when the decision-maker indicates an acceptable range of values for each criterion claiming that they are not interested in the objects outside this range, the normalisation should be performed according to the formula

$$x'_{\underset{j}{i}} = \frac{x_{\underset{j}{i}} - x_{\underset{\min}{i}}}{x_{\underset{\max}{i}} - x_{\underset{\min}{i}}}, \tag{13.4}$$

where $x_{\underset{\min}{i}}$ is a bottom limit and $x_{\underset{\max}{i}}$ is an upper limit defined by the decision-maker for the i-th criterion.

13.2.5 Stage V: Determining the Preference Vector

The preference vector represents the decision-maker's requirements concerning the analysed objects. It is a vector whose coordinates are made of the values of the criteria calculated on the basis of the difference between the motivating $\vec{\Psi}$

and the demotivating $\vec{\Phi}$ preference vector. The criterion values for the vector $\vec{\Psi}$ are indicated by the decision-maker, and they usually meet their expectations. The vector $\vec{\Phi}$ represents the values of the criteria that the decision-maker has found unwanted. How we interpret and determine the preference vectors depends on which variant to calculate the PVM we have chosen. This aspect will be further discussed in the description of the PVM variants shown in Fig. 13.1. In the calculation process, the preference vector is treated (with respect to the character of the criteria and the way of their normalising) in the same way as any other vector which is representing the object. We need to normalise the motivating and the demotivating preference vectors using the same normalisation parameters that were used for normalising the criterion values. For example, the vector $\vec{\Psi}$ can be normalised by means of the standardisation (Nermend and Borawski 2014):

$$\psi_i^{'} = \frac{\psi_i - \bar{x}_i}{S_i}, \tag{13.5}$$

where ψ_i is the value of the i-th coordinate of the vector $\vec{\Psi}$ and ψ'_i is the value of the i-th coordinate of the vector $\vec{\Psi}$ after normalisation.

13.2.6 Stage VI: Ranking Objects According to the Decision-Maker's Preferences

The ranking of objects according to the decision-maker's preferences is constructed by the combination of two methods to build aggregate measures, i.e. the Hellwig method based on the Euclidean distance and the VMCM using the vector projection. The choice of a technique to calculate the measure depends on the criterion character. For motivating and demotivating criteria, it is calculated as a coordinate of vectors/objects in a monodimensional coordinate system, while in the case of desirable and non-desirable criteria, the measure calculation is based on measuring the distance. Neutral criteria are of no relevance to the measure value.

To start building the ranking, we need to divide the criteria. The neutral criteria are discarded, while the remaining ones are divided into three groups:

- Motivating and demotivating criteria
- Desirable criteria
- Non-desirable criteria

For the motivating and demotivating criteria, the measure is calculated by determining the length of the projection of the vector representing the j-th object on the preference vector $\vec{T}_v^{'}$ being determined as the difference between the vectors $\vec{\Psi}_v^{'}$ and $\vec{\Phi}_v^{'}$:

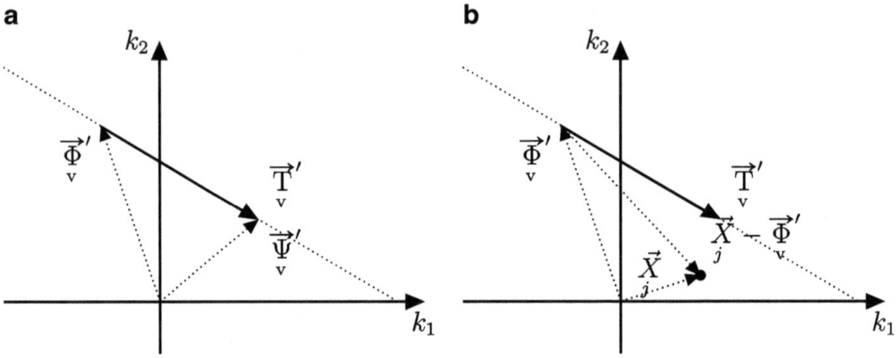

Fig. 13.3 The preference vector $\underset{v}{\vec{T}'}$: (**a**) position in the coordinate system of the criteria (k_1, criterion 1; k_2, criterion 2); (**b**) determining the position of the object against the $\underset{v}{\vec{T}'}$ origin

$$\underset{v}{\vec{T}'} = \underset{v}{\vec{\Psi}'} - \underset{v}{\vec{\Phi}'} \tag{13.6}$$

The $\underset{v}{\vec{\Psi}'}$ and $\underset{v}{\vec{\Phi}'}$ are vectors whose coordinates are the motivating and demotivating criteria of the vectors $\underset{v}{\vec{\Psi}'}$ and $\underset{v}{\vec{\Phi}'}$. Figure 13.3a shows the way the preference vector $\underset{v}{\vec{T}'}$ is determined. The origin of the vector $\underset{v}{\vec{T}'}$ is indicated by the vector $\underset{v}{\vec{\Phi}'}$.

The sign of the vector $\underset{v}{\vec{T}'}$ coordinates depends on the character of the criteria. The positive sign indicates a motivating criterion, while the negative one a demotivating criterion. It is not always consistent with the criterion character defined in Stage I because sometimes the decision-makers ignore the transitivity of their preferences and assign higher values to demotivating criteria than to the motivating ones. Therefore, we have to make adjustments to the criterion in question by changing its sign in the vector $\underset{v}{\vec{T}'}$ coordinates. The coordinates associated with a motivating criteria are given a positive sign, whereas the demotivating ones are considered negative. For each object $\underset{j}{\vec{X}'}$, we should determine its position against the origin of the vector $\underset{v}{\vec{T}'}$. For this purpose, we calculate the difference between this object and the vector $\underset{v}{\vec{T}'}$ (Fig. 13.3b). Basing on this difference, we determine the length of the object $\underset{j}{\vec{X}'}$ projection on the vector $\underset{v}{\vec{T}'}$ Fig. 13.4a. The length of the vector $\underset{v}{\vec{T}'}$ is a unit of measure to be used while projecting objects on the vector $\underset{v}{\vec{T}'}$. The length of the

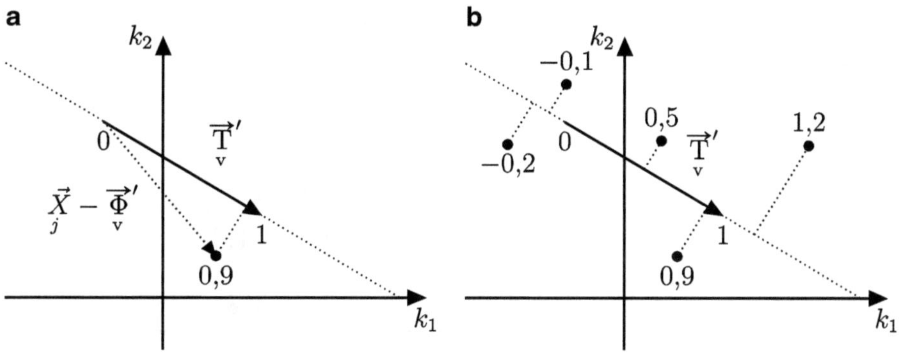

Fig. 13.4 The length of the objects $\vec{X}'_j$ projection on the vector $\vec{T}'_v$: (**a**) determination of the length of the object $\vec{X}'_j$ projection; (**b**) position of the objects and the length of their projections

object $\vec{X}'_j$ projection depends on its position against the vector $\vec{T}'_v$, as shown in Fig. 13.4b.

The fact that the length of a projection on the vector $\vec{T}'_v$ is expressed in different measurement units than the coordinate system of the criteria k_1, k_2 becomes a problem when we have to confront these lengths with the values of the distance measure calculated in k_1, k_2. Hence the vector $\vec{T}'_v$ is brought to the form of a unit vector:

$$\vec{\Theta}'_v = \frac{\vec{T}'_v}{\left\| \vec{T}'_v \right\|}, \tag{13.7}$$

whereas in the PVM we assume that

$$\left\| \vec{T}'_v \right\| = \sqrt{\sum_{i=1}^{M_v} \tau'_i 2}, \tag{13.8}$$

where M_v is the number of motivating and demotivating criteria and $\underset{v}{\tau'^2_i}$ is the i-th coordinate of the vector $\vec{T}'_v$.

The length of the projection of the j-th object on the vector $\vec{\Phi}_v$, being also the measure value, can be calculated by the formula

Fig. 13.5 Determination of the desirable criterion measure

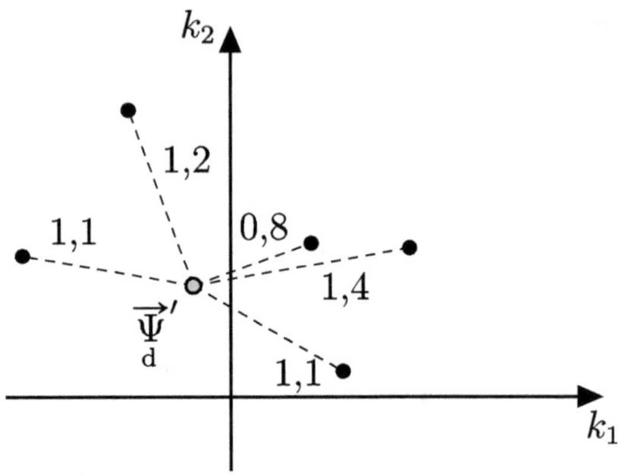

$$\underset{v}{\mu_j} = \sum_{i=1}^{M_v} (\underset{j}{x'_i} - \underset{v}{\phi'_i})\, \underset{v}{\vartheta'_i}\, \underset{v}{w'_i}, \tag{13.9}$$

where $\underset{v}{\phi'_i}$ is the i-th coordinate of the vector $\underset{v}{\phi'_i}$, $\underset{v}{\vartheta'_i}$ is the i-th coordinate of the vector $\underset{v}{\vec{\Theta}'}$ and $\underset{v}{w'_i}$ is the weight of the i-th criterion.

The bigger the value of $\underset{v}{\mu_j}$, the higher the rank of the j-th object. In the case of desirable criteria, we include in the calculations the vector $\underset{d}{\vec{\Psi}'}$ whose coordinates are the desirable criteria of the vector $\vec{\Psi}'$. The value of the measure is calculated as the distance between points (Fig. 13.5) (Nermend and Borawski 2014):

$$\underset{d}{\mu_j} = \sqrt{\sum_{i=1}^{M_d} \underset{d}{w'_i} \left(\underset{j}{x'_i} - \underset{d}{\psi'_i}\right)^2}, \tag{13.10}$$

where M_{d} is the number of desirable criteria, $\underset{d}{\psi'_i}$ is the i-th coordinate of the vector $\underset{\mathrm{d}}{\vec{\Psi}'}$ and $\underset{d}{w'_i}$ is the weight of the i-th criterion.

The smaller the value of $\underset{d}{\mu_j}$, the better the object's position in the ranking. The best objects have the measure value equal to zero.

In the case of non-desirable criteria, we include in the calculation the vector $\underset{nd}{\vec{\Phi}'}$ whose coordinates are the non-desirable criteria of the vector $\vec{\Phi}'$. Just like above, the measure value is calculated as the distance between points (Nermend and Borawski 2014):

$$\underset{nd}{\mu_j} = \sqrt{\sum_{i=1}^{M_{nd}} \underset{nd_i}{w'_i}\left(\underset{j}{x'_i} - \underset{nd}{\phi'_i}\right)^2}, \tag{13.11}$$

where M_{nd} is the number of non-desirable criteria, $\underset{nd}{\phi'_i}$ is the i-th coordinate of the vector $\underset{nd}{\vec{\Phi}'}$ and $\underset{nd}{w'_i}$ is the weight of the i-th criterion.

The bigger the value of $\underset{nd}{\mu_j}$, the higher the object's position in the ranking. The worst objects have the measure value equal to zero. The final value of the measure μ_j is counted by calculating the weighted average of the measures $\underset{v}{\mu_j}$, $\underset{d}{\mu_j}$ and $\underset{nd}{\mu_j}$:

$$\mu_\mathrm{j} = \frac{\underset{\mathrm{v}}{\mu_\mathrm{j}} M_\mathrm{v} - \underset{\mathrm{d}}{\mu_\mathrm{j}} M_\mathrm{d} + \underset{\mathrm{nd}}{\mu_\mathrm{j}} M_\mathrm{nd}}{M_\mathrm{v} + M_\mathrm{d} + M_\mathrm{nd}} \tag{13.12}$$

A minus sign at the value of μ_j is associated with its somewhat different character. As for $\underset{v}{\mu_j}$ and $\underset{nd}{\mu_j}$, the bigger the measure value, the better the object. And, conversely, in the case of $\underset{d}{\mu_j}$, the smaller the measure value, the better the object.

13.3 Mathematical Description of Variants in the Preference Vector Method

13.3.1 Variant A

The decision-maker indicates the criteria and their character. The values of the vectors $\vec{\Psi}$ and $\vec{\Phi}$ are counted on the basis of the provided data. The procedure depends on the character of the criteria. The coordinates of the vectors are determined basing on the first and third quartile while calculating $\underset{v}{\mu_j}$ and maximum and minimum while calculating $\underset{d}{\mu_j}$ and $\underset{nd}{\mu_j}$. What we take into account here are the values of criteria for all the objects of interest (Table 13.1).

Table 13.1 Calculation of the vectors $\vec{\Psi}$ and $\vec{\Phi}$ by the criterion character

Vector	Criterion				
	Motivating	Demotivating	Desirable	Non-desirable	Neutral
$\vec{\Psi}$	III quartile	I quartile	Max	–	–
$\vec{\Phi}$	I quartile	III quartile	–	Min	–

13.3.2 Variant B

The decision-maker indicates the names and character of the criteria as well as the acceptable range of the criterion values. The motivating vector $\vec{\Psi}$ and the demotivating vector $\vec{\Phi}$ are determined basing on the range of these values. When a given coordinate of the vector $\vec{\Psi}$ reflects a motivating criterion, its value is a top acceptable value indicated by the decision-maker for this particular criterion. Then, the coordinate of the vector $\vec{\Phi}$ is a bottom acceptable value indicated by the decision-maker. When a given coordinate of the vector $\vec{\Psi}$ reflects a demotivating criterion, its value is a bottom acceptable value indicated by the decision-maker for this particular criterion. Then, the coordinate of the vector $\vec{\Phi}$ is a top acceptable value indicated by the decision-maker.

13.4 Comparison of PVM with Some Multi-criteria Methods

Table 13.2 shows the characteristics of several methods supporting the decision-making process and their comparison with the PVM. According to the characteristics, the PVM is most similar to TOPSIS. The only difference lies in the one-dimensional system of coordinates applied in calculations. In contrast to the remaining methods, the PVM does not require the assessment of the relative importance of criteria, because the method can do it itself basing on indicating a positive and a negative pattern.

Table 13.3 contains the comparison of such methods as AHP, ELECTRE, PROMETHEE, TOPSIS and PVM. What is special about the PVM is its simplicity, which makes the interpretation of results easy. The method utilises the scalar product defined for the Euclidean space. However, there are no methodological contraindications as for the application of other scalar products. That offers the opportunity to easily modify the method and add new elements, e.g. multicomponent numbers describing the inaccuracy of data, which would make the PVM equivalent to those methods where fuzzy numbers are employed.

Depending on the decision-maker's needs, the PVM can be used in two variants, i.e. it can seek objects (decision-making alternatives) either as near as possible to the decision-makers' judgement or with characteristics similar or better than this judgement. The combination of these two variants is also possible, which is exceptional as none of the remaining analysed methods allows for that. The PVM calculation process is similar to TOPSIS and is one of the simplest among the methods described above. For each criterion, the number of steps is always the same and depends solely on its character. The nature of the calculations allows for writing them in a matrix form, which facilitates their parallelisation and hardware implementation. Therefore, the method can be applied wherever there is a need for an instant ranking of a large

Table 13.2 Characteristics of AHP, TOPSIS, ELECTRE and PVM (own elaboration (Özcan et al., 2011))

Characteristics	AHP	TOPSIS	ELECTRE I	ELECTRE II	ELECTRE III	PVM
Basic process	Creating a hierarchical structure and a pairwise comparison matrix	Calculating distances from a positive and a negative pattern	Determining concordance and discordance indices	Determining concordance and discordance indices	Determining indices of concordance and discordance with indifference and preference thresholds	Determining the length of a projection of a vector representing the object $\vec{X}_j$ on the vector $\vec{T}_v$ and/or the distance from $\vec{\Psi}$
Necessity to assess the relative importance of criteria	Yes	Yes	Yes	Yes	Yes	Yes
Determination of weights	Pairwise comparison matrices, scale 1–9	No specific method. Linear or vector normalisation	No specific method. Depends on the decision-maker	No specific method. Depends on the decision-maker	No specific method. Depends on the decision-maker	Double system of weights while calculating the vector $\vec{T}_v$ and basing on formula (1)
Number and type of outranking relations	N(N-1)/2	1	1	2	1 fuzzy	1
Consistency check	Yes	No	No	No	Yes	No
Problem structure	Small number of alternatives and criteria; quantitative or qualitative data	Large number of alternatives and criteria; objective and quantitative data	Large number of alternatives and criteria; objective and quantitative data	Large number of alternatives and criteria; objective and quantitative data	Objective and quantitative data; use of fuzzy logic	Large number of criteria, quantitative data
Final results	Total order	Total order	Relevant content	Partial order	Partial order	Total order

Table 13.3 Comparison of AHP, ELECTRE, PROMETHEE, TOPSIS and PVM (own elaboration on the basis of AHP, TOPSIS, ELECTRE and PROMETHEE (Velasquez, Hester, 2013))

Method	Advantages	Disadvantages	Fields of application
Analytic hierarchy process (AHP)	Easy to use, scalable; adaptable hierarchy structure so that it can be suited to problems of different size	Problems resulting from interrelations between alternatives and criteria; there is a risk of inconsistency between the decision and the ranked criteria; reversed ranking	Problems concerning efficiency, resource allocation, corporate policy and strategy, public policies, policy strategies and planning
ELECTRE	Takes uncertainty into account	The process and results can be hardly comprehensible to a lay person; outranking relations make the strengths and weaknesses of individual solutions difficult to be directly identified	Energy, economy, environment, water management, transportation
PROMETHEE	Easy to use; does not require the assumption that criteria are expressed as the percentage (i.e. that they are proportional)	Does not provide a clearly defined method of attributing weights	Environment, hydrology, water management, business and finance, chemistry, transport and logistics, production and assembly, energy, agriculture
TOPSIS	Simple process, easy to use and programmable; always the same number of steps, disregarding the number of attributes	The use of Euclidean distance does not take into consideration the correlations among attributes; weights hard to determine, the consistency of decisions hard to maintain	Supply chain management, logistics, engineering, production systems, business and marketing, environment, human resources, water resources management
PVM	Very simple process, easy to use and programmable; always the same number of steps, disregarding the number of attributes and objects; the option to use any scalar product allows for potentially allows for further development of the method, e.g. by adding the element of uncertainty	The use of Euclidean distance for desirable and non-desirable criteria does not take into consideration the correlations among criteria	Environmental protection, economy, consumer decision-making

number of data (such as the ranking of web pages in a given language or of all visitors to a given website).

13.5 Example of the Use of the PVM for Choosing a Car

The PVM usefulness is shown on the example of choosing a car that is best suited to the consumer's expectations. We have assumed that the consumer is interested in the following criteria:

k_1—engine power in kW
k_2—engine capacity in cm^3
k_3—price in PLN
k_4—type of bodywork
k_5—type of transmission
k_6—type of fuel

The data come from the authorised dealers' web pages and catalogues. The survey covers 149 models of 10 makes. Two rankings of cars on offer have been made. The first one has been designed for a rich consumer who is looking for a fast car, while the second one for a consumer who needs a relatively cheap city car.

The criteria k_1, k_2 and k_3 are quantitative. For each of them, we need to define the range of values acceptable for the consumer. In the first ranking, the values for k_1 range between the minimum of 200 kW and the maximum of 470 kW, for k_2 between 3000 cm^3 and 6000 cm^3 and for k_3 between PLN 120 and 560 thousand.

The criteria k_4, k_5 and k_6 are qualitative. They are attributed with numeric values according to the consumer's preferences. These numeric values are determined by pairwise comparison. With respect to k_4 in the case at hand, there are four types of bodywork: station wagon, hatchback, sedan and SUV. The consumer has to compare them in pairs and decide which they prefer better. Subsequently, we construct a pairwise comparison matrix. For the first ranking, we have a matrix:

$$C_4 = \begin{bmatrix} 1 & \frac{1}{3} & \frac{1}{6} & \frac{1}{7} \\ 3 & 1 & \frac{1}{8} & \frac{1}{9} \\ 6 & 8 & 1 & \frac{1}{4} \\ 7 & 9 & 4 & 1 \end{bmatrix}. \quad (13.13)$$

On its basis the numeric values for individual bodywork types have been specified: station wagon (0.0677), hatchback (0.1032), sedan (0.4227) and SUV (0.8978).

With respect to the criterion k_5, there are two types of gear boxes: manual and automatic. In this case, the comparison matrix is

$$C_5 = \begin{bmatrix} 1 & \frac{1}{8} \\ 8 & 1 \end{bmatrix}. \quad (13.14)$$

The numeric value for a manual gear box is 0.124, while for the automatic one it is 0.9923.

With respect to the criterion k_6, there are two types of fuel: petrol and diesel. The comparison matrix for this criterion is

$$C_5 = \begin{bmatrix} 1 & \frac{1}{5} \\ 5 & 1 \end{bmatrix}. \quad (13.15)$$

and the numeric value for petrol is 0.1961 and for diesel it is 0.9806.

119 car models do not satisfy the consumer's requirements. Therefore, the ranking has been limited to 30 models. The consumer has described the criteria k_1, k_2, k_4, k_5 and k_6 as motivating and the criterion k_3 as demotivating. Six best and two worst variants are shown in Table 13.4. The top positions in the ranking belong to SUVs and sedans with high engine power and capacity and with automatic transmission, which is consistent with the consumer's preferences. They preferred diesel engines, but in the set at hand, such engines are less powerful and have smaller capacity.

In the second ranking, the values adopted for k_1 range between the minimum of 40 kW and the maximum of 120 kW, for k_2 between 1000 cm^3 and 3000 cm^3 and for k_3 between PLN 30 thousand and 90 thousand. For k_4 the comparison matrix is

Table 13.4 Six best and two worst variants in the first ranking

Item	Model	Measure value	Power	Engine capacity	Type of bodywork	Transmission	Fuel type	Price (thou)
1	Mercedes E 500	0.72	450	6	SUV	Automatic	Petrol	416.5
2	Audi A8 L W12	0.67	463	6	Sedan	Automatic	Petrol	371.5
3	Mercedes E 400	0.66	400	5.5	SUV	Automatic	Petrol	416.5
4	Audi A8	0.62	390	6	Sedan	Automatic	Petrol	371.5
5	Mercedes E 200 Blue TEC	0.61	300	4.7	SUV	Automatic	Petrol	279.5
6	Mercedes E 250	0.59	285	5.5	SUV	Automatic	Petrol	416.5
29	Audi A6 Limousine	0.37	350	4	Station wagon	Manual	Petrol	134.2
30	Audi A4 Limousine	0.32	200	3	Station wagon	Automatic	Petrol	263

$$C_4 = \begin{bmatrix} 1 & \frac{1}{2} & \frac{1}{4} & \frac{1}{3} \\ 2 & 1 & \frac{1}{3} & \frac{1}{2} \\ 4 & 3 & 1 & \frac{1}{2} \\ 3 & 2 & 2 & 1 \end{bmatrix}. \tag{13.16}$$

On its basis the numeric values have been determined for individual bodywork types: station wagon (0.1636), hatchback (0.3079), sedan (0.8055) and SUV (0.4793). The comparison matrix for k_5 is

$$C_5 = \begin{bmatrix} 1 & \frac{1}{3} \\ 3 & 1 \end{bmatrix}. \tag{13.17}$$

The numeric value for the manual gear box is 0.3162, while for the automatic one it is 0.9487.

With respect to the criterion k_6, there are two types of fuel: petrol and diesel. The pairwise comparison matrix for this criterion is

$$C_5 = \begin{bmatrix} 1 & \frac{1}{2} \\ 2 & 1 \end{bmatrix}. \tag{13.18}$$

and the numeric values for petrol and diesel are 0.4472 and 0.8944, respectively.

100 car models do not meet the customer's requirements. Therefore the ranking has been limited to 49 models. The consumer described the criteria k_4, k_5 and k_6 as motivating and the criteria k_1, k_2 and k_3 as demotivating. Six best and two worst variants are shown in Table 13.5. The best ranked are cheap sedans with low engine

Table 13.5 Six best and two worst variants in the second ranking

Item	Model	Measure value	Power	Engine capacity	Type of bodywork	Transmission	Fuel type	Price (thou)
1	Volkswagen Passat	0.70	68	1.6	Sedan	Manual	Diesel	38.9
2	Volkswagen Passat Variant	0.69	55	1.2	Sedan	Manual	Petrol	38.9
3	Volkswagen Golf Variant	0.68	55	1.2	Sedan	Manual	Petrol	40.9
4	Opel ADAM	0.66	66	1.2	Hatchback	Automatic	Petrol	48.5
5	Nissan Note	0.66	44	1	Hatchback	Manual	Petrol	35.2
6	Nissan Juke	0.65	44	1	Hatchback	Manual	Petrol	36.72
48	Audi Q7	0.28	108	1.8	Station wgn	Manual	Petrol	89.9
49	Audi Q5	0.27	118	1.8	Station wgn	Manual	Petrol	86.55

power and small engine capacity. They are also mostly equipped with petrol engines and manual transmission, as such cars are cheaper.

13.6 Summary

The preference vector method presented in this chapter makes use of the preference vector to rank objects. This approach helps decision-makers make right choices. They can express their preferences and rate the importance of individual criteria by defining the desirable object and, if such be the case, the non-desirable one. It is also possible to specify preferences just basing on the criterion character.

This chapter also gives the example of the PVM applied for helping a consumer make the right choice when buying a car. The data come from the authorised dealers' web pages and catalogues. For comparison, a similar test has been conducted with ELECTRE II. On its basis a conclusion has been drawn that the preference vector method is simpler to use due to a more obvious relationship between the parameters necessary for the method to succeed and the obtained effect. Moreover, as it applies a graph, ELECTRE II is much more algorithmically complex, which obstructs its implementation and prolongs the calculation process and makes it dependent on the character of data. The PVM is much easier to translate to programming languages, especially to the ones that support matrix operations. The duration of a calculation process relies solely on the quantity of data, not on their character. The duration of calculation should not be important even if there were a thousand of criteria and a thousand of decision-making variants. As the studies have shown, due to the application of graphs, ELECTRE II may prove problematic when we have as few as 5 criteria and 24 decision-making variants. Since all the ELECTRE methods are similar to one another, we can extend these conclusions over all the methods belonging to the ELECTRE group. What is more, the objections concerning the use of graphs can apply to all the methods using them (e.g. PROMETHEE).

The proposed method can find a broad range of applications in the decision-making support. For instance, it can be used to aid consumers when choosing products. The PVM can be implemented in the smartphone software recognising products on the basis of their barcodes. The method will then help rank some products in relation to others. Another example of the PVM application is ranking social and business organisations in order to find out what is the position of a given county, province or country in relation to other similar administrative units. Such information is of crucial importance for investors. The PVM can be used when we are facing the decision to choose one out of many decision-making alternatives. It can also prove useful in computer simulation for modelling the consumer's decision-making process. Thanks to its simplicity, it employs the power of a processing unit to a small extent, which allows for a simultaneous simulation of decision-making for a very large number of consumers.

References

Bartosiewicz S (1984) Zmienne syntetyczne w modelowaniu ekonometrycznym. In: Prace naukowe Akademii Ekonomicznej we Wrocławiu. Wydawnictwo Uczelniane Akademii Ekonomicznej we Wrocławiu, Wrocław, pp 5–8

Binderman A (2011) Wielokryterialne metody analizy zróżnicowania polskiego rolnictwa w 2009 roku. Metody Ilościowe w Badaniach Ekonomicznych 12:58–68

Binderman Z, Borkowski B, Szczęsny W (2008) O pewnej metodzie porządkowania obiektów na przykładzie regionalnego zróżnicowania rolnictwa. In: Binderman Z (ed) Metody ilościowe w badaniach ekonomicznych: Wielowymiarowa analiza danych. Wydawnictwo Szkoły Głównej Gospodarstwa Wiejskiego, Warszawa

Borawski M (2012) Rachunek wektorowy z arytmetyką przyrostów w przetwarzaniu obrazów. Wydawnictwo Naukowe PWN, Warszawa

Borys T (1984) Kategoria jakości w statystycznej analizie porównawczej. Wydawnictwo Uczelniane Akademii Ekonomicznej we Wrocławiu, Wrocław

Cieślak M (1976) Modele zapotrzebowania na kadry kwalifikowane. Państwowe Wydawnictwo Naukowe, Warszawa

Cieślak M (1974) Taksonomiczna procedura programowania rozwoju i określania zapotrzebowania na kadry kwalifikowane. Przegląd Statystyczny 21:29–39

Dittman P, Pisz Z (1975) Metoda dynamicznego badania zróżnicowania przestrzennego zjawisk społeczno-ekonomicznych. Wiadomości Statystyczne 20:27–28

Duckstein L, Gershon M (1983) Multicriterion analysis of a vegetation management problem using ELECTRE II. Appl Math Model 4:254–261

Grabiński T, Wydymus S, Zeliaś A (1989) Metody taksonomii numerycznej w modelowaniu zjawisk społeczno-gospodarczych. Państwowe Wydawnictwo Naukowe, Warszawa

Grolleau J, Tergny J (1971) Manuel de reference du programme ELECTRE II. Document de travail 24, SEMA-METRA International

Hellwig Z (1968) Zastosowanie metody taksonomicznej do typologicznego podziału krajów ze względu na poziom ich rozwoju oraz zasoby i strukturę wykwalifikowanych kadr. Przegląd Statystyczny 15:307–326

Hwang CL, Yoon K (1981) Multiple attribute decision making: methods and applications. Springer-Verlag

Jahanshahloo GR, Lotfi FH, Izadikhah M (2006) An algorithmic method to extend {TOPSIS} for decision-making problems with interval data. Appl Math Comput 175:1375–1384. doi:10.1016/j.amc.2005.08.048

Karagiannidis A, Moussiopoulos N (1997) Application of ELECTRE III for the integrated management of municipal solid wastes in the greater Athens area. Eur J Oper Res 97:439–449

Kolenda M (2006) Taksonomia numeryczna. Klasyfikacja, porządkowanie i analiza obiektów wielocechowych. Wydawnictwo Akademii Ekonomicznej im. Oskara Langego we Wrocławiu, Wrocław

Kompa K (2014) Zastosowanie mierników taksonomicznych do oceny efek-tywności finansowej giełd europejskich w latach 2002–2011. Metody Ilościowe W Badaniach Ekon 15:52–61

Kompa K, Witkowska D (2010) Zastosowanie wybranych mierników synte-tycznych do porównań poziomu rozwoju społeczno-gospodarczego w krajach Unii Europejskiej. In: Jajuga K, Walesiak M (eds) Klasyfikacja i analiza danych - teoria i zastosowania. Wydawnictwo Uniwersytetu Ekonomicznego we Wrocławiu, Wrocław, pp 71–80

Łatuszyńska A (2010) Symulacja wieloagentowa w zastosowaniach biznesowych. Stud Mater Pol Stowarzyszenia Zarządzania Wiedzą 160–170

Łatuszyńska A (2014) Miary agregatowe w ocenie stopnia rozwoju społeczeństwa informacyjnego. PPH Zapol, Szczecin

Łatuszyńska M (2012) Computer simulation methods in economics and management. Actual Probl Econ 131:170–179

Łatuszyńska M, Nermend K (2008) Badania marketingowe w Internecie przy użyciu symulatora. In: Szewczyk A, Krok E (eds) Fenomen Internetu. Wydawnictwo Naukowe Uniwersytetu Szczecińskiego, Szczecin, pp 515–521

Młodak A (2006) Analiza taksonomiczna w statystyce regionalnej. Difin, Warszawa

Mousseau V, Figueira J, Naux J-P (2001) Using assignment examples to infer weights for ELECTRE TRI method: some experimental results. Eur J Oper Res 130:263–275

Nermend K (2006) A synthetic measure of sea environment pollution. Pol J Environ Stud 15:127–130

Nermend K (2008a) Employing similarity measures to examine the development of technical infrastructure in Polish counties. Folia Oeconomica Stetin 15:87–97

Nermend K (2007) Taxonomic vector measure of region development (TWMRR). Pol J Environ Stud 16:195–198

Nermend K (2008b) Zastosowanie rzutu wektora do budowy miernika syntetycznego. Przegląd Stat 55:10–21

Nermend K (2012) Method for examining the variability of socio-economic objects quoting the example of Baltic Sea countries. Actual Probl Econ Sci Econ J 2:201–211

Nermend K (2008c) Rachunek wektorowy w analizie rozwoju regionalnego. Wydawnictwo Naukowe Uniwersytetu Szczecińskiego, Szczecin

Nermend K (2008d) Problem obiektów nietypowych w badaniach taksonomicznych. Metody Inform Stosow 13:105–112

Nermend K, Tarczyńska-Łuniewska M (2013) Badanie jednorodności przestrzennej i czasowej rozwoju obiektów społeczno-gospodarczych. Przegląd Stat 60:85–100

Nowak E (1990) Metody taksonomiczne w klasyfikacji obiektów społeczno-gospodarczych. Państwowe Wydawnictwo Ekonomiczne

Pluta W (1977) Wielowymiarowa analiza porównawcza w badaniach ekonomicznych: metody taksonomiczne i analizy czynnikowej. Państwowe Wydawnictwo Ekonomiczne, Warszawa

Roy B (1968) Classement et choix en pr´esence de points de vue multiples (la methode ELECTRE). In: La Revue d'Informatique et de Recherche Opérationelle. pp 57–75

Saaty T (1980) The analytical hierarchy process. McGraw-Hill, New York

Saaty T (2005) Theory and applications of the analytic network process: decision making with benefits, opportunities, costs and risks. RWS Publications, Pittsburgh, PA

Scharlig A (1996) Pratiquer ELECTRE et PROMETHEE: Un Complement'a Decider sur Plusieurs Crit'eres. Polytechniques et Universitaires Romandes, Lau-sanne

Strahl D (ed) (2006) Metody oceny rozwoju regionalnego. Wydawnictwo Akademii Ekonomicznej im. Oskara Langego we Wrocławiu, Wrocław

Tarczyński W (2004) Dynamiczne ujęcie taksonomicznej miary atrakcyjności inwestycji na przykładzie wybranych spółek notowanych na giełdzie papierów wartościowych w Warszawie. Zesz Nauk Uniw Szczec 394:299–322

Tarczyński W, Łuniewska M (2006) Metody wielowymiarowej analizy porównawczej. Wydawnictwo Naukowe PWN

Vallée D, Zielniewicz P (1994) Electre III-IV, version 3. x. Guide d'utilisation (tome 2). Université de Paris Dauphine, France

Witkowska D (2010) Zastosowanie syntetycznych mierników taksonomicznych do pomiaru efektywności Chińskich banków. Metody Ilościowe w Badaniach Ekonomicznych 11:281–292

Chapter 14
Selected Issues of Rank Reversal Problem in ANP Method

Paweł Ziemba and Jarosław Wątróbski

Abstract The ANP method is used to solve decision problems and to construct forecast models, among others, in the field of economics. It is related to the fact that the method extends a decision process with essential, in current research experiments, psychological aspects of decision making. The ANP is a generalization of the AHP and, similarly, it is at risk of occurring the rank reversal problem. In the chapter the occurrence of the problem in practical applications of the ANP, related to economic experiments and forecast model, is examined.

Keywords ANP method • Economic experiment

14.1 Introduction

The ANP method plays an essential part in the decision theory and is also one of fundamental method of so called an "America school" of Multicriteria Decision Making. The method is based on the AHP (Saaty 2004a) and it is based on pair-wise comparison matrices from which preference vectors are aggregated. How-ever, it extends the AHP with additional perspectives on decision alternatives and the whole decision process as well as essential, in valid experimental research, psychological aspects of decision-making (Sałabun 2012). The ANP method makes it possible to solve decision problems from many walks of life. However, Saaty, the creator of the method, in his works provides examples of its application in economic experiments, such as: estimating market share, the analysis of benefits, costs, opportunities and risks, and forecasting an economic resurgence or a financial

P. Ziemba (✉)
Department of Technology, Jacob of Paradyż University of Applied Sciences in Gorzów Wielkopolski, Teatralna 25, Gorzów Wielkopolski 66-400, Poland
e-mail: pziemba@pwsz.pl

J. Wątróbski
Department of Information Systems Engineering, Faculty of Computer Science and Information Technology, West Pomeranian University of Technology Szczecin, Żołnierska 49, Szczecin 71-210, Poland
e-mail: jwatrobski@wi.zut.edu.pl

K. Nermend, M. Łatuszyńska (eds.), *Selected Issues in Experimental Economics*, Springer Proceedings in Business and Economics, DOI 10.1007/978-3-319-28419-4_14

crisis (Saaty and Vargas 2013a; Saaty 2005a). Moreover, when making a decision in other fields, economical criteria are often taken into consideration (Piegat and Sałabun 2014; Wątróbski et al. 2015).

Since the ANP stems directly from the AHP, it also inherits theoretical weaknesses of the assumptions of the AHP which, above all, are: the rank reversal problem, the priorities derivation method and the comparison scale (Ishizaka and Lusti 2006). The rank reversal problem (Sałabun 2015) and priorities derivation method are closely related to each other, for they refer to the preferences aggregation method from pairwise comparison matrices used in the AHP and ANP. The rank reversal problem assumes that there is a set alternative ranking determined for a decision problem task with the use of the preferences aggregation method (as a computational algorithm in the AHP and ANP a right eigenvector method is used). Solving a reversal problem and performing a preferences aggregation with the use of a left eigenvector method should, as a result, produce a reverse sequence of elements which were pairwise-compared in a matrix. However, it is not always like that (Ishizaka and Labib 2009). In the literature one can find a great deal of publications concerning the analysis of the phenomena and a general analysis of preferences aggregation methods for the AHP, e.g. (Ishizaka and Lusti 2006; Choo and Wedley 2004; Lin 2007). Yet, even a partial analysis of the problem for the ANP has not been found in the literature. A direct reference of the results of the papers concerning the AHP method is illegitimate because of the differences in computational algorithms between the methods.

The aim of this chapter is to examine and verify economic experiments carried out with the use of the ANP. The subject of the research is the resistance of the solutions obtained in the experiments to the use of preferences aggregation methods other than the right eigenvector. The alternative methods used were the left eigenvector and logarithmic least squares. In the chapter a survey of the literature, in which economic experiments had been carried out with the use of the ANP method, was conducted. The chapter also discusses the issue of the ANP and chosen preferences aggregation methods. Next, the economic experiments, in which the ANP had been applied using also alternative preferences aggregation methods, presented in the literature were repeated. Finally, the chapter presents research conclusions.

14.2 Literature Review

The ANP method is more and more often employed to support decision making in many walks of life including economy and marketing. It can be applied in decision problems related to, for example, economic forecast, analysis of market and economy, finance and banking, organization management, production or logistics. They are mostly areas where originally research was conducted with the use of the AHP method. The growing popularity of the ANP results from current economic research trends, where issues related to behavioural economy, neuroeconomics and particularly experimental economy are of great importance. In the case of the ANP method more emphasis was put, compared to the AHP, to reproduce a model of a generalized complex structure of a problem (a network model instead of a hierarchical one) or to take into consideration emotional factors in a model. The legacy of the AHP and the abovementioned features make the ANP become a useful research tool in modelling macroeconomic and microeconomic decision problems.

As for macroeconomic forecast, by means of the ANP method of the forecast of the date for the resumption of growth of the US economy in 1992 (Saaty and Vargas 2001, 2012a; Blair et al. 2002; 2010) was made, using expert opinions for this purpose. Similarly, with the use of the ANP method, a model of forecasting a financial and bank crisis was constructed (Niemira and Saaty 2004). It was later reversely verified by setting the probability of the occurrence of the financial and bank crisis in the USA in the early 1990s of the last century.

In publications concerning the AHP and ANP, there are also examples of applying the ANP to assessing the value of market share: individual supermarkets, (Saaty 2003a, b, 2005b), footwear manufactures (Saaty 2005b), airlines (Saaty 2003a, b; Whitaker 2007) or ready-to-eat breakfast cereal industry (Saaty 2005a; Whitaker 2007). The research was carried out on the basis of expert assessment without quantitative economic data. Similarly, market shares and channels for selling child disposable nappies with regard to individual market shares (Neira et al. 2009) were determined. Moreover, a forecast model for selling a new car model was constructed (Mimovic 2012). Also, by means of the ANP method an economic analysis of economy on the basis of Leontief's Input-Output Model (Saaty 2005a; Whitaker 2007) was conducted and an analytical model, whose aim is to determine resources and actions, leading to overcoming the financial crisis (Andreichicova and Andreichicov 2009). The ANP method was also used to evaluate efficiency of expense items of state budget (Andreichicova and Andreichicov 2013).

In the field of decisions related to finance and banking the Analytical Network Process was applied in order to, for example, evaluate the creditability of emerging industries (Chen et al. 2011), evaluate banking performance (Pakdin Amiri et al. 2012), evaluate banks with reference to their finance services (Wu et al. 2009), evaluate financial results of commercial banks (Ozdemir 2013) and support investment decisions on the stock market (Lee et al. 2009). By means of the ANP method a comprehensive evaluation model for enterprise financial position was constructed (Li and Tang 2012), the influence of key factors on financial achievements of companies was examined (Lee 2014) as well as an evaluation of assets, such as, for instance, arable lands (Garcia-Melon et al. 2008) or industrial areas (Aragones-Beltran et al. 2008) was carried out.

With reference to the applications of the ANP in organization management, the method, in combination with the classic SWOT analysis, was applied to select a company functioning strategy (Yuksel and Dagdeviren 2007). Among other examples of employing the ANP in an organization one can list, among other things, an evaluation of a company's business strategy (Kuo and Chang 2013), project portfolio management for organizational sustainability (Turan et al. 2009), and a management evaluation of human resources in a company (Zhao 2013). The ANP can also be used in manager decision making, such as, an analysis of e-business decisions in organizations, based on management heuristics and e-commerce strategies, as well as business-level strategies (Raisinghani et al. 2007). The method can also be applied in order to choose a company's information system, such as an enterprise resource planning system (ERP) (Percin 2008), or a manufacturing executive system (MES) (Liang and Li 2008).

In production management the ANP was used, among other things, for the selection of a product mix for efficient manufacturing to maximize the manufacturing efficiency in considering the aspects of product, equipment efficiency and finance (Chung et al. 2005). The method is applicable to new product development (NPD), as a tool to evaluate a set of conceptual design alternatives (Ayag and Ozdemir 2007). The ANP is also widely used to support logistic decisions, such as, for example, vendor selection (Palanisamy and Abdul Zubar 2013), location selection (Tuzkaya et al. 2008), supply chain management (Agarwal et al. 2006), or reverse logistics (Ravi et al. 2005). Many other applications of the ANP method in the business environment were presented in (Jayant et al. 2014). Furthermore, the ANP is also used to solve other decision problems in which often appear economic criteria, such as, for instance, risk evaluation (Chen and Khumpaisal 2009), technical decisions (Aragones-Beltran et al. 2010), or socioeconomic analyses (Cortes-Aldana et al. 2009).

14.3 State of the Art

The Analytic Network Process (ANP) is the generalization of the Analytic Hierarchy Process (AHP) (Saaty 2004a). Both techniques employ pairwise comparison matrices and the Saaty rating scale, and matrix preferences are aggregated by means of a principal right eigenvector. The AHP enables to solve a decision problem on the basis of a hierarchical model. However, many decision problems cannot be organized hierarchically, since there are interactions and dependencies, which cannot be described by means of a hierarchy (Saaty and Sodenkamp 2010). In such decision problems the ANP technique is applied, for it allows to enlarge constructed decision models with feedbacks and additional dependences (inner dependences and outer dependences) among elements of the model (Saaty 2004b). Therefore, the ANP, in comparison with the AHP, allows to construct much more complex decision models (Cortes-Aldana et al. 2009). It should be emphasized, that a hierarchical model constructed on the AHP technique is a special case of a network model constructed in the ANP (Saaty 2005b). In that case all hierarchical models (AHP) are also network models (ANP). In the hierarchical model there are: an aim, criteria, subcritera and alternatives, whereas in the network model all these components are represented by clusters containing elements, which could be criteria or alternatives (Saaty 2004b).

In the ANP technique, global priorities are obtained with the use of a supermatrix assuming successive forms. Firstly, it is an interfactorial dominance matrix (Cortes-Aldana et al. 2009) containing information about which elements of individual clusters are comparable and with relation to which elements in determined clusters such comparisons are conducted. Next, an unweighted supermatrix (Saaty 2005b) is constructed which contains eigenvectors of pairwise comparison matrices. By normalizing the totals of a column supermatrix to 1 a scholastic matrix comes into existence which is described as a weighted supermatrix (Saaty 2004b). In the next step it is exponentiated until no changes take place in it any more. In this way a limit supermatrix is obtained which contains global priorities of elements in individual clusters (of criteria and alternatives) (Saaty 2004b; Adams 2011). When going from a weighted supermatrix to a limit supermatrix the Markov chain process (Ishizaka and Nemery 2013) is employed.

Contained in the unweighted supermatrix, eigenvectors of pairwise comparison matrices are obtained by means of the right eigenvector (REV) method, according to instructions of Saaty, creator of the AHP and ANP (Saaty 1998, 2003a, b). The right eigenvector is calculated by solving the Eq. (14.1):

$$Aw = \lambda_{\max} w \tag{14.1}$$

If a pairwise comparison matrix A is consistent, then there is only one non-zero eigenvalue $\lambda_{\max}$ and it equals the size of the matrix. Next, a vector w is a preference vector related to the value $\lambda_{\max}$ (Saaty and Vargas 2012b). When there are relatively slight inconsistencies in the matrix, the preference vector is a vector related to the highest eigenvalue (other λs have values close to 0). Saaty suggests solving the Eq. (14.1) according to a formula (14.2) (Saaty 1998, 2004b):

$$w = \lim_{k\to\infty} \left(\frac{A^k e^T}{eA^k e^T} \right) \tag{14.2}$$

where $e = [1,1,\ldots,1]$.

The right eigenvector is orthogonal towards a left eigenvector (LEV) (Saaty 2005b) what means that the left eigenvector is a solution to a reversely formulated problem. When searching is the best solution, in the left eigenvector the worst solution has the highest value. In the left eigenvector method an Eq. (14.3) is solved (Langer 2001):

$$wA = \lambda_{\max} w \tag{14.3}$$

The Eq. (14.3) can be solved in accordance with a formula (14.4):

$$u = \lim_{k\to\infty} \left(\frac{eA^k}{eA^k e^T} \right) \tag{14.4}$$

One can easily notice that for a matrix raised to the near-infinity, row totals are calculated, not column totals. Therefore, as it has been written earlier, a vector u constitutes a solution to a reversely formulated problem. After reversing the vector u, the solution should be identical to the solution obtained by means of the right eigenvector. In the case of greater-than-3 pairwise comparison inconsistent matrices (even if they are nearly consistent), sometimes there is an inconsistency that ranking received by means of right eigenvector and left eigenvector are not opposite, and after reversing the left vector they are inconsistent (Johnson et al. 1979; Tung and Tang 1998; Ishizaka and Lusti 2006). The eigenvector method thereby is accused of not complying with an independence-of-scale-inversion property (Dijkstra 2013). Saaty explains the phenomena that in practice the issue of "how much A1 dominates A2" is completely different from the issue of "how much A2 is dominated by A1" (Saaty 1990). Nonetheless, a great deal of researchers are of the opinion that using the left vector is as well justified as employing the right vector (Johnson et al. 1979; Tung and Tang 1998; Gass and Rapcsak 2004).

Free from an inconsistency, which occurs in the eigenvector method when generating an original ranking (REV) and a reversed ranking (LEV) from an inconsistent matrix, is a logarithmic least squares (simple geometric mean (SGM)) method. In the method both using a column mean and a row the same results are obtained (Ishizaka and Lusti 2006; Dijkstra 2013). Furthermore, for $n = 3$ matrices it produces the same preference vector as the right eigenvector and left eigenvector (after reversing the vector) methods (Dijkstra 2013). Nevertheless, Saaty in his numerous works criticizes using the geometric mean as a method for obtaining a preference vector (Saaty 1987, 1990, 1998, 2004a). The logarithmic least squares method uses the logarithmized values of pairwise comparison matrices and the logarithmized values of the preference vector, according to a formula (14.5) (Ishizaka and Labib 2011):

$$\min \sum_{i=1}^{n} \sum_{j=1}^{n} \left(\ln(a_{ij}) - \ln\left(\frac{w_i}{w_j}\right) \right)^2 \tag{14.5}$$

The logarithmic least squares method produces one unique solution which is a geometric mean of individual rows (Ishizaka and Labib 2011) Eq. (14.6):

$$w_i = \left(\prod_{j=1}^{n} a_{ij} \right)^{\frac{1}{n}} \tag{14.6}$$

Further research takes into consideration three methods, which are characterized above, of a preference aggregation from pairwise comparison matrices. The preferences obtained by means of every method were used to construct unweighted supermatrices in the ANP technique applied to solve economic problems.

14.4 Research Procedure

In the adopted research procedure the preferences aggregation methods: right eigenvector, left eigenvector and logarithmic least squares, characterized earlier, were taken into consideration. The research was based on scientific publications, in which, by means of the ANP, economic problems were solved. In order that a scientific publication could be used in the research, the publication had to include all constructed pairwise comparison matrices. This allowed to reconstruct a complete decision problem and to examine the influence of applying individual preferences aggregation methods on obtained results. In the research, the authors' ANP implementation, made in the Octave program (Eaton 2012), was employed. Three different unweighted supermatrices based on individual preferences aggregation methods were built in the implementation. Next, global priorities from every supermatrix was calculated according the principles of the ANP.

Having chosen a literature position containing an economic problem solved with the use of the ANP, the problem was modelled in Octave and in a SuperDecisions application. The model constructed in SuperDecisions was used to verify that the implementation in Octave was carried correctly and the results obtained in the REV method in both cases are the same. To verify the correctness of the model the results of the decision process contained in this publication were also used. Having received global priorities for individual elements of the model, their values for supermatrices obtained with the use of individual preferences aggregation methods were compared. Moreover, if a different kind of result verification was possible, it was also applied. Similarly, when a decision model was to forecast a value, then the forecasts were compared for subsequent supermatrices and a forecast, which was nearest to the real results, was determined. The sequence of the research procedure was graphically presented in Fig. 14.1.

14.5 Research Results

In the research five literature items, in which economic problems had been solved, were examined. Moreover, in all of them pairwise comparison matrices were presented. On the basis of the considered publications, seven decision models were examined. Unfortunately, other analyzed literature items did not contain sets of pairwise comparison matrices and consequently they did not allow to reconstruct a decision process.

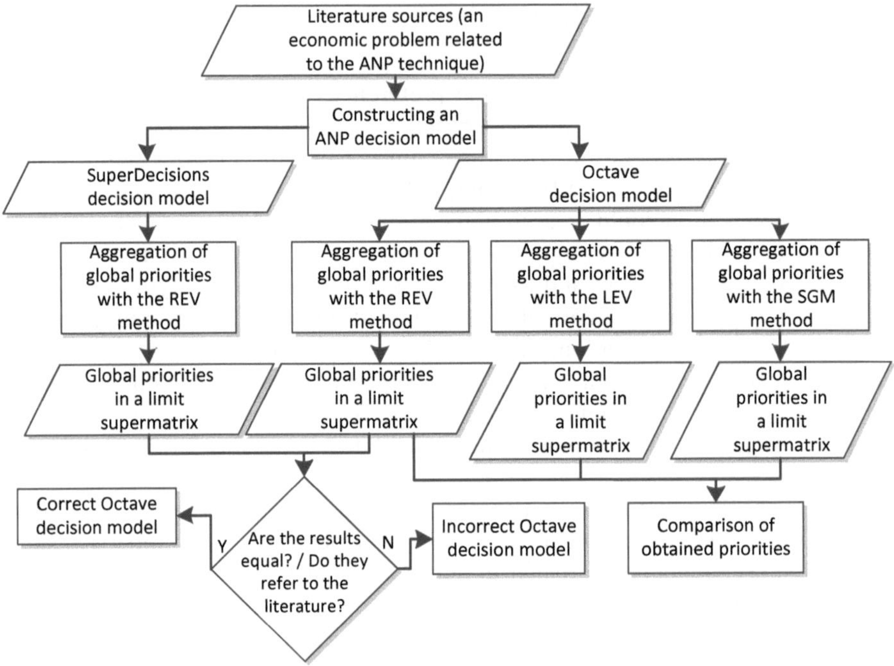

Fig. 14.1 The course of the research procedure

14.5.1 Case 1: The US Economic Forecast in 1992

The example comes from Saaty and Vargas' monograph on the AHP method (Saaty and Vargas 2012a). By means of the ANP a forecast of the date of a turnaround in economic stagnation in the USA was determined. the decision model nine economic factors (subcriteria) belonging to two groups (criteria) as well as four considered dates of turnaround occurrence (alternatives) were taken into consideration. Furthermore, there is feedback between alternatives and criteria in the model. The decision model is presented in Fig. 14.2.

As a result of the ANP computational procedure conducted by means of three preferences aggregation methods, the values of: weights of criteria, subcriteria and evaluations of alternatives were obtained, which are presented in Table 14.1. Also, Table 14.1 contains the positions of individual criteria and alternatives in a local ranking describing the position of a given element in its group (criteria, subcriteria and alternatives). For example, a local ranking of criteria determines which criteria, among these taken into consideration, are most important and which are less important.

While analyzing Table 14.1 one can notice that different preferences aggregation methods allowed to obtain a bit different values of weights of criteria and subcriteria and evaluations of alternatives. Nevertheless, employing individual methods did not influence the sequence of alternatives or criteria.

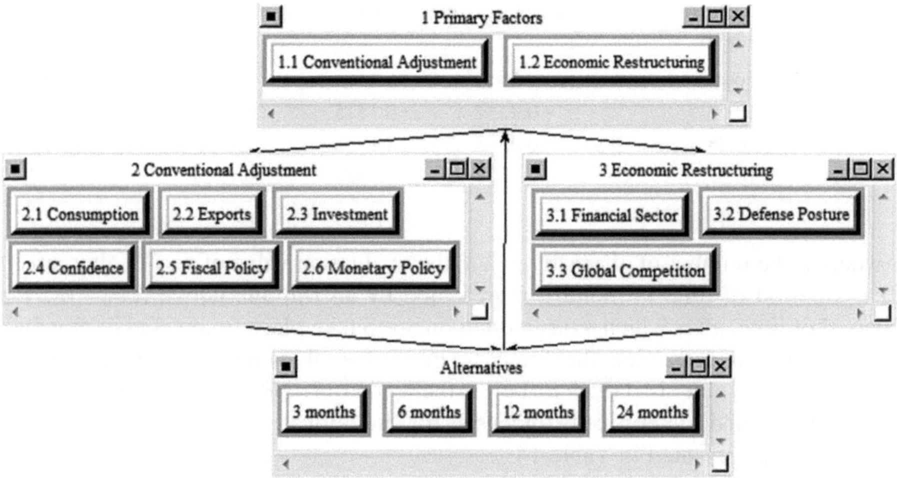

Fig. 14.2 Decision model in Case 1

Table 14.1 Values of individual elements obtained in the ANP and their positions in rankings (LR—position in a local ranking)

		REV		LEV		SGM	
Cluster	Element	Value	LR	Value	LR	Value	LR
Criteria	1.1 Conventional adjustment	0.1613	2	0.1638	2	0.1632	2
	1.2 Economic restructuring	0.1721	1	0.1695	1	0.1702	1
Subcriteria	2.1 Consumption	0.0190	7	0.0175	7	0.0177	7
	2.2 Exports	0.0046	9	0.0041	9	0.0044	9
	2.3 Investment	0.0094	8	0.0088	8	0.0091	8
	2.4 Confidence	0.0539	3	0.0534	3	0.0548	3
	2.5 Fiscal policy	0.0190	6	0.0200	6	0.0193	6
	2.6 Monetary policy	0.0553	2	0.0599	2	0.0579	2
	3.1 Financial sector	0.1005	1	0.0990	1	0.0994	1
	3.2 Defence posture	0.0483	4	0.0476	4	0.0478	4
	3.3 Global competition	0.0232	5	0.0229	5	0.0230	5
Alternatives	3 Months	0.0746	2	0.0784	2	0.0776	2
	6 Months	0.0505	4	0.0512	4	0.0508	4
	12 Months	0.0670	3	0.0654	3	0.0662	3
	24 Months	0.1413	1	0.1383	1	0.1388	1

In the analyzed case of the ANP application, the forecast of the turnaround date in economy was determined on the basis of the following formula (14.7):

$$T = \sum_{i=1}^{n} Va_i {*} \left(Ta_{i-1} + \frac{1}{2} (Ta_i - Ta_{i-1}) \right) \tag{14.7}$$

Table 14.2 Forecasts determined by means of the ANP with the use of different preferences aggregation methods

Method	Forecast (months)	3 Months	6 Months	12 Months	24 Months
REV	10.45	0.2237	0.1515	0.2011	0.4238
LEV	10.28	0.2353	0.1536	0.1963	0.4148
SGM	10.32	0.2327	0.1523	0.1986	0.4164

where n the number of alternatives, Va_i the evaluation value of an i-th alternative, Ta_i a period of time in months, represented by an i-th alternative ($Ta_0 = 0$), T a period of time, after which a turnaround ought to take place (expressed in months).

In order to determine the forecast, the value of evaluations of alternatives presented in Table 14.1 had to be normalized to 1. Normalized evaluations of alternatives and determined forecasts for individual preferences aggregation methods are presented in Table 14.2.

On the basis of Table 14.2 one can state that in the researched case the application of various preferences aggregation methods with pairwise comparison matrices does not significantly influence the value of the forecast. Both using the right eigenvector method, as Saaty and Vargas did, and employing other methods (Left Eigenvector, Simple Geometric Mean) indicates that the turnaround in the economy will happen in 10–10.5 months.

14.5.2 Case 2: Forecasting the Resurgence of the US Economy in 2001

In this case, prepared in 2001, a forecast of the resurgence of the US economy was prepared (Blair et al. 2002). A decision model, which was used for this purpose, consisted of three criteria and twelve subcriteria. Four decision alternatives, same as in the previous example (3, 6, 12 and 24 months), were considered. Also, in this case feedback between clusters of alternatives and criteria was used. The decision model is presented in Fig. 14.3.

By calculating the model according to the ANP procedure the results were obtained and presented in Table 14.3.

In the researched case the use of the individual preferences aggregation methods influenced the sequence of subcriteria in the ranking. Using, recommended by Saaty, the REV method makes “Natural Resource Costs” the most important criterion influencing the economic evaluation. The use of the LEV and SGM methods gives the subcriterion “Monetary Policy” the highest weight. Moreover, as a result of employing the REV method for preferences aggregation, the subcriteria “Major Economic Relations” and “Fiscal Policy” are considered equally essential. However, using the LEV and SGM methods allows to differentiate the gravity of these criteria, acknowledging “Fiscal Policy” as a bit more important criterion.

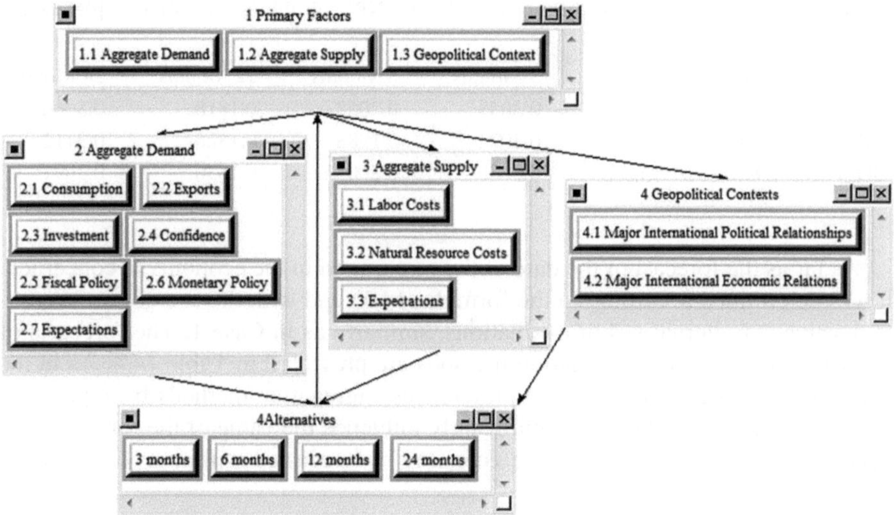

Fig. 14.3 Decision model of Case 2

Table 14.3 Values of individual elements obtained in the ANP and their positions in rankings

Cluster	Element	REV Value	LR	LEV Value	LR	SGM Value	LR
Criteria	1.1 Aggregate demand	0.2079	1	0.2073	1	0.2075	1
	1.2 Aggregate supply	0.0994	2	0.0999	2	0.0998	2
	1.3 Geopolitical context	0.0260	3	0.0261	3	0.0261	3
Subcriteria	2.1 Consumption	0.0204	5	0.0209	5	0.0206	5
	2.2 Exports	0.0044	12	0.0052	12	0.0047	12
	2.3 Investment	0.0117	10	0.0118	10	0.0117	10
	2.4 Confidence	0.0462	3	0.0397	3	0.0465	3
	2.5 Fiscal policy	0.0174	6	0.0200	6	0.0190	6
	2.6 Monetary policy	0.0736	2	0.0815	1	0.0753	1
	2.7 Expectations	0.0344	4	0.0283	4	0.0297	4
	3.1 Labour costs	0.0119	9	0.0119	9	0.0119	9
	3.2 Natural resource costs	0.0742	1	0.0747	2	0.0745	2
	3.3 Expectations	0.0133	8	0.0134	8	0.0133	8
	4.1 Major political relations	0.0087	11	0.0087	11	0.0087	11
	4.2 Major economic relations	0.0174	6	0.0174	7	0.0174	7
Alternatives	3 Months	0.1019	2	0.1025	2	0.1023	2
	6 Months	0.0686	3	0.0663	3	0.0669	3
	12 Months	0.0606	4	0.0609	4	0.0610	4
	24 Months	0.1022	1	0.1037	1	0.1030	1

Table 14.4 Forecasts determined by means of the ANP with the use of different preferences aggregation methods

Method	Forecast (months)	3 Months	6 Months	12 Months	24 Months
REV	8.54	0.3058	0.2058	0.1818	0.3066
LEV	8.60	0.3074	0.1988	0.1826	0.3112
SGM	8.57	0.3070	0.2008	0.1830	0.3091

As far as the forecast of the date of the turnaround in the economy is concerned, it was determined according to the formula (14.1) and with the use of normalized-to-1 values of alternatives of evaluations, similarly as in Case 1. The forecasts of individual preferences aggregation methods are presented in Table 14.4. As in the previous case, the use of different preferences aggregation methods from pairwise comparison matrices does not significantly influence the value of the forecast. The occurrence of the turnabout in the economy is forecasted within a period of 8.5 months.

14.5.3 Case 3: Forecasting the Resurgence of the US Economy in 2010

Case 3 is very similar to the previous ones. Also, the date of a turnabout in economy is determined, but it refers to 2010 (Blair et al. 2010, 2015; Saaty and Vargas 2013b). In this case the decision model employed in 2001 was used. The model was extended with additional subcriteria and clusters. Moreover, examined periods of time, represented by decision alternatives, were extended. The model is presented in Fig. 14.4. The results of the conducted computational ANP procedure is presented in Table 14.5.

As in previous examples, in this case using different preferences aggregation methods also influenced the sequence of subcriteria in the ranking. As far as the subcriteria “Confidence” and “Labour Costs” are concerned, preferences aggregation with the use of the LEV and SGM methods reverses their sequence with relation to the sequence obtained with the use of the REV. However, in the case of the subcriteria “Future Value of the Dollar” and “Role of Credit-Default Swaps” employing the SGM method allows to obtain the same sequence as the use of the REV. The change of positions of these subcriteria in the ranking takes place with the use of the LEV.

The forecasted economic resurgence time was determined analogically to Cases 1 and 2. The results of the forecast is shown in Table 14.6. Similarly to previous cases, the value of the forecast is not significantly different for individual preferences aggregation methods.

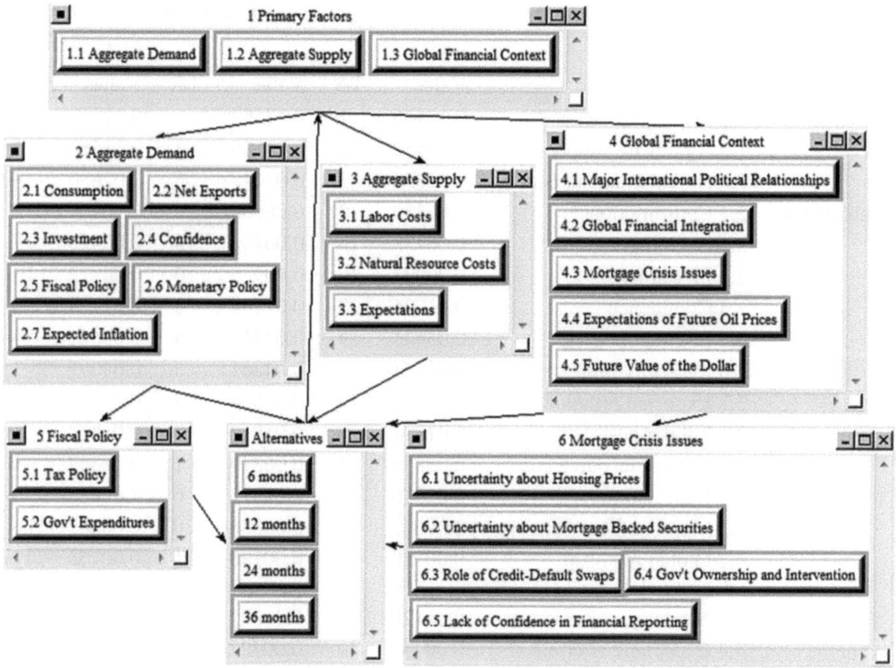

Fig. 14.4 Decision model of Case 3

14.5.4 *Case 4: Valuation of Urban Industrial Land*

The examined case deals with the problem of valuating a plot in an industrial park (Aragones-Beltran et al. 2008). The case comprises three decision models, in which feedback between decision criteria and decision alternatives was used. In each model five alternatives were examined. In Model 1 only two criteria were taken into consideration, whereas in Models 2 and 3 another cluster containing four additional criteria was added. Individual decision models are presented in Figs. 14.5 and 14.6.

Models 2 and 3 differed only in weights attributed to the criteria of clusters. In Model 2 both clusters containing criteria had different weights, whereas in Model 3 the cluster "Plot characteristics" had a weight of 0.9 and "Plot location in industrial park" had a weight of 0.1.

The ANP calculation results of Model 1 are shown in Table 14.7, the priorities of alternatives and weights of criteria for Model 2 are presented in Table 14.8, whereas the results for Model 3 are depicted in Table 14.9. What is worth noting is the fact that the use of both the REV and LEV produces the same weights of criteria. However, the use of the SGM method for preferences aggregation gives different weights of criteria in the cluster "Plot location in industrial park", in comparison with the REV and LEV methods. Slight differences between the operation of each

Table 14.5 Values of individual elements obtained in the ANP and their positions in rankings

Cluster	Element	REV Value	LR	LEV Value	LR	SGM Value	LR
Criteria	1.1 Aggregate demand	0.17545	1	0.17553	1	0.17550	1
	1.2 Aggregate supply	0.11552	2	0.11538	2	0.11550	2
	1.3 Global financial context	0.02650	3	0.02648	3	0.02650	3
Subcriteria	2.1 Consumption	0.06230	2	0.06008	2	0.06169	2
	2.2 Net exports	0.00435	15	0.00404	15	0.00423	15
	2.3 Investment	0.00923	10	0.00928	10	0.00912	10
	2.4 Confidence	0.01826	7	0.01704	8	0.01759	8
	2.5 Fiscal policy	0.03641	4	0.03711	4	0.03661	4
	2.6 Monetary policy	0.03977	3	0.04261	3	0.04099	3
	2.7 Expected inflation	0.00513	13	0.00536	13	0.00527	13
	3.1 Labour costs	0.01814	8	0.01812	7	0.01814	7
	3.2 Natural resource costs	0.06858	1	0.06849	1	0.06857	1
	3.3 Expectations	0.02880	6	0.02877	6	0.02880	6
	4.1 Major political relations	0.00087	20	0.00086	20	0.00087	20
	4.2 Global financial integration	0.00719	11	0.00790	11	0.00755	11
	4.3 Mortgage crisis issues	0.01120	9	0.01071	9	0.01090	9
	4.4 Expectations of oil prices	0.00442	14	0.00427	14	0.00436	14
	4.5 Future value of the dollar	0.00283	17	0.00273	18	0.00281	17
	5.1 Tax policy	0.00607	12	0.00618	12	0.00610	12
	5.2 Gov't expenditures	0.03034	5	0.03092	5	0.03051	5
	6.1 Uncert. Housing prices	0.00426	16	0.00397	16	0.00412	16
	6.2 Uncert. Mortgage backed securities	0.00278	19	0.00270	19	0.00272	19
	6.3 Role of credit-default swaps	0.00281	18	0.00280	17	0.00278	18
	6.4 Gov't ownership and intervention	0.00050	22	0.00045	22	0.00047	22
	6.5 Lack of conf. in financial report	0.00086	21	0.00080	21	0.00081	21
Alternatives	6 Months	0.0307	4	0.0305	4	0.0306	4
	12 Months	0.0634	3	0.0640	3	0.0637	3
	24 Months	0.0953	2	0.0952	2	0.0951	2
	36 Months	0.1281	1	0.1277	1	0.1282	1

Table 14.6 Forecasts determined by means of the ANP with the use of different preferences aggregation methods

Method	Forecast (months)	6 Months	12 Months	24 Months	36 Months
REV	19.590	0.0968	0.1997	0.3001	0.4034
LEV	19.572	0.0959	0.2018	0.3000	0.4023
SGM	19.594	0.0963	0.2005	0.2995	0.4037

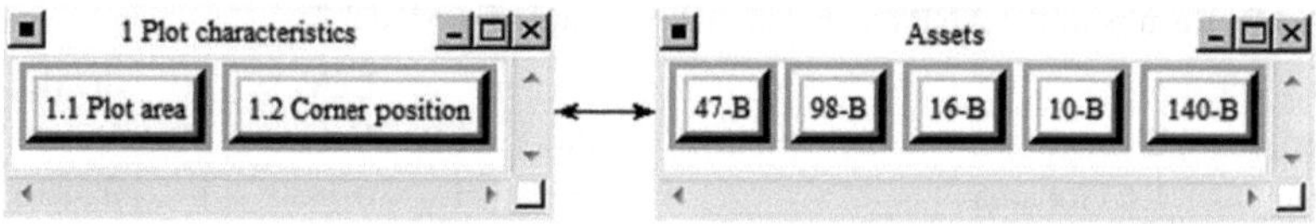

Fig. 14.5 First decision model of Case 4

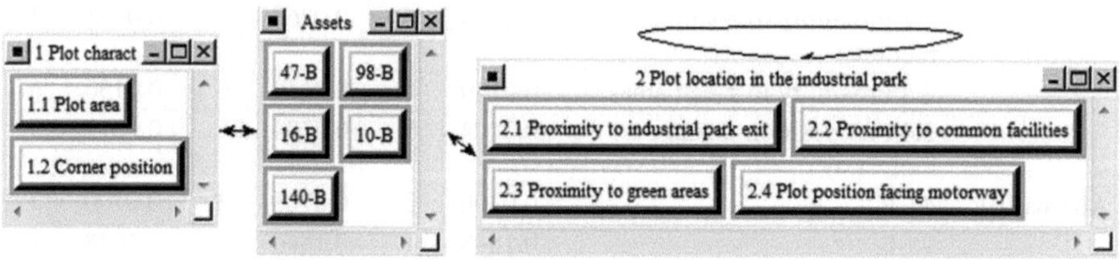

Fig. 14.6 Second and third decision model of Case 4

Table 14.7 Results of the ANP computational procedure for Model 1

		REV		LEV		SGM	
Cluster	Element	Value	LR	Value	LR	Value	LR
Criteria	1.1 Plot area	0.4467	1	0.4467	1	0.4467	1
	1.2 Corner position	0.0533	2	0.0533	2	0.0533	2
Alternatives	47-B	0.0691	3	0.0694	3	0.0693	3
	98-B	0.2010	1	0.2006	1	0.2007	1
	16-B	0.0290	4	0.0291	4	0.0290	4
	10-B	0.1318	2	0.1316	2	0.1318	2
	140-B	0.0691	3	0.0694	3	0.0693	3

Table 14.8 Results of the ANP computational procedure for Model 2

		REV		LEV		SGM	
Cluster	Element	Value	LR	Value	LR	Value	LR
Criteria	1.1 Plot area	0.1789	1	0.1789	1	0.1789	1
	1.2 Corner position	0.0211	6	0.0211	6	0.0211	6
	2.1 Proximity to industrial park exit	0.1424	2	0.1424	2	0.1400	2
	2.2 Proximity to common facilities	0.1091	3	0.1091	3	0.1055	3
	2.3 Proximity to green areas	0.0627	5	0.0627	5	0.0653	5
	2.4 Plot position facing motorway	0.0858	4	0.0858	4	0.0892	4
Alternatives	47-B	0.0729	3	0.0730	3	0.0725	3
	98-B	0.1328	1	0.1327	1	0.1337	1
	16-B	0.0548	4	0.0549	4	0.0543	4
	10-B	0.0882	2	0.0881	2	0.0881	2
	140-B	0.0512	5	0.0513	5	0.0514	5

Table 14.9 Results of the ANP computational procedure for Model 3

		REV		LEV		SGM	
Cluster	Element	Value	LR	Value	LR	Value	LR
Criteria	1.1 Plot area	0.3830	1	0.3830	1	0.3830	1
	1.2 Corner position	0.0456	2	0.0456	2	0.0456	2
	2.1 Proximity to industrial park exit	0.0339	3	0.0339	3	0.0333	3
	2.2 Proximity to common facilities	0.0260	4	0.0260	4	0.0251	4
	2.3 Proximity to green areas	0.0149	6	0.0149	6	0.0156	6
	2.4 Plot position facing motorway	0.0204	5	0.0204	5	0.0212	5
Alternatives	47-B	0.0700	3	0.0703	3	0.0700	3
	98-B	0.1848	1	0.1844	1	0.1848	1
	16-B	0.0351	5	0.0352	5	0.0350	5
	10-B	0.1215	2	0.1213	2	0.1214	2
	140-B	0.0649	4	0.0651	4	0.0650	4

preferences aggregation method can be observed in the case of the obtained evaluations of alternatives. Nevertheless, there were no changes in the sequence of rankings, prepared with the use of individual preferences aggregation methods, of criteria or alternatives.

In the analyzed case the value of a plot, marked as 140-B, was determined. For this purpose a formula (14.8) was used:

$$Pa_5 = Va_5 * \frac{\sum_{i=1}^{4} Pa_i}{\sum_{i=1}^{4} Va_i} \tag{14.8}$$

where Pa_5 the value of the fifth alternative in € (plot 140-B), Va_5 the value of the fifth alternative obtained in the ANP computational procedure. In order to determine the forecast of the value of the plot, the values, obtained in the ANP, of the evaluations of the alternatives had to be normalized to 1. The value of other plots, which were used in the valuation were as follows: 47-B—187 160.45€; 98-B—605 512.18€; 16-B—63 439.95€; 10-B—329 807.28€. Table 14.10 presents forecasted values of Plot 140-B, determined by means of the ANP with the use of different preferences aggregation methods. Also, Table 14.10 contains a forecast error with relation to the real value of plot 140-B amounting to 193 668.90€.

The analysis of Table 14.10 indicates that in each model the use of the REV suffers from the highest forecast error. In the cases of Models 1 and 3 the value of the plot, closest to the real one, is obtained with the use of the LEV. In Model 2 the best forecast is obtained thanks to the SGM methods.

Table 14.10 The value of plot 140-B determined with the use of different preferences aggregation methods

	Decision model 1		Decision model 2		Decision model 3	
Method	Value (€)	Deviation (€)	Value (€)	Deviation (€)	Value (€)	Deviation (€)
REV	190235.60	3433.30	174081.98	19586.92	186971.09	6697.81
LEV	191103.27	2565.63	174518.82	19150.08	187734.83	5934.07
SGM	190655.72	3013.18	175012.39	18656.51	187505.31	6163.59

14.5.5 Case 5: Using the ANP in a SWOT Analysis

The last case refers to the quantitative SWOT analysis on a strategic level for a textile company (Yuksel and Dagdeviren 2007). In this case four possible strategies, represented as decision alternatives, of the company's operation were defined. Four criteria reflected the SWOT aspects, i.e. strengths, weaknesses, opportunities and threats. Within the criteria, in total, fourteen subcriteria were distinguished. The decision model used in the discussed analysis is presented in Fig. 14.7.

The calculation results with the use of the ANP method are depicted in Table 14.11. The analysis of the results showed in Table 14.11 allows to notice that in this case the REV and LEV methods enable to obtain very similar evaluations of the alternatives as well as the weights of criteria and subcriteria. Nonetheless, they differ from the results of using the SGM method. In the case of the SGM method, changes of the weights of subcriteria and their rankings also bring about changes in the final ranking of alternatives. Although the change does not refer to the most preferable alternative, it points to the problem of a ranking change when using different preferences aggregation methods.

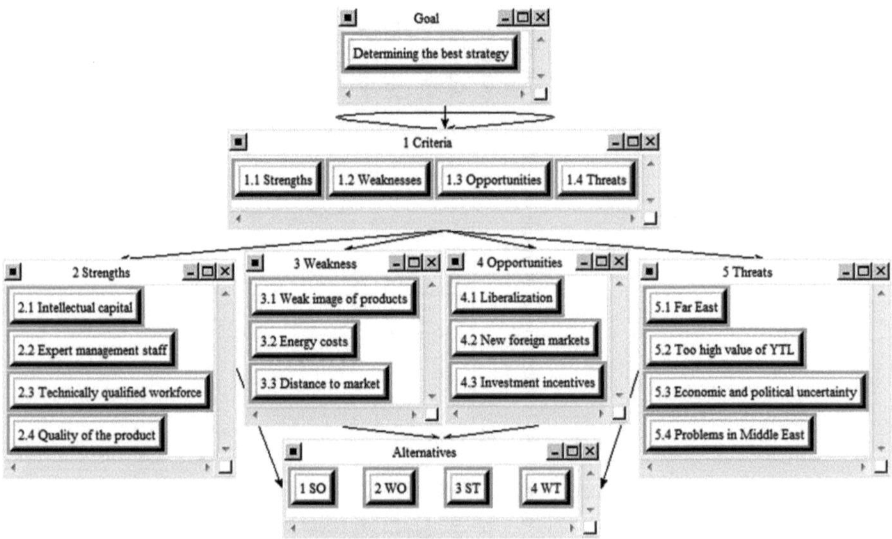

Fig. 14.7 Decision model of Case 5

Table 14.11 Values of individual elements obtained in the ANP and their positions in rankings

		REV		LEV		SGM	
Cluster	Element	Value	LR	Value	LR	Value	LR
Criteria	1.1 Strengths	0.2126	1	0.2125	1	0.1996	1
	1.2 Weaknesses	0.0731	3	0.0738	3	0.0808	3
	1.3 Opportunities	0.1041	2	0.1039	2	0.0966	2
	1.4 Threats	0.0547	4	0.0543	4	0.0675	4
Subcriteria	2.1 Intellectual capital	0.0438	1	0.0431	1	0.0407	1
	2.2 Expert management staff	0.0329	3	0.0326	3	0.0309	3
	2.3 Technically qualified workforce	0.0105	7	0.0106	7	0.0099	7
	2.4 Quality of the product	0.0191	5	0.0200	5	0.0184	5
	3.1 Weak image of products	0.0228	4	0.0231	4	0.0253	4
	3.2 Energy costs	0.0087	9	0.0088	9	0.0096	8
	3.3 Distance to market	0.0050	11	0.0050	11	0.0055	12
	4.1 Liberalization	0.0093	8	0.0093	8	0.0086	10
	4.2 New foreign markets	0.0037	13	0.0037	13	0.0034	14
	4.3 Investment incentives	0.0391	2	0.0390	2	0.0363	2
	5.1 Far East	0.0077	10	0.0078	10	0.0096	9
	5.2 Too high value of YTL	0.0045	12	0.0045	12	0.0056	11
	5.3 Economic and political uncertainty	0.0122	6	0.0120	6	0.0150	6
	5.4 Problems in Middle East	0.0029	14	0.0028	14	0.0035	13
Alternatives	1 SO	0.1220	1	0.1218	1	0.1202	1
	2 WO	0.0920	2	0.0919	2	0.0901	3
	3 ST	0.0906	3	0.0907	3	0.0941	2
	4 WT	0.0287	4	0.0289	4	0.0289	4

14.6 Summary

In the last years we can see that the ANP method is gaining more and more popularity. The decision models with the use of the method are employed in many scientific disciplines including economy. The popularity results from the simplicity of the method and the fact that the ANP allows to create complex decision models in which psychological and emotional aspects are taken into consideration.

Nevertheless, similarly to the AHP, it is not resistant to the rank reversal problem and thereby it does not fulfil the independence-of-scale inversion property. Consequently, using the right and left eigenvector methods for preferences aggregation from pairwise comparison matrices may render different global priorities of alternatives and criteria as well as a different sequence of the alternatives and criteria in rankings.

The conducted research was to examine the existence of the rank reversal problem in practical applications of the ANP method. To date the existence of the problem in the AHP has been demonstrated, however, the authors of the chapter were unable to find in the literature any research concerning a theoretical, and especially, practical aspect related to the occurrence of the problem in the ANP. It may result from the fact that the ANP is relatively new and, apart from SuperDecision, its software implementations are not used.

As it is demonstrated, in this chapter, in the analysis of the decision problems presented in the literature that the rank reversal is not only a theoretical problem. It appears in practical applications of the ANP method and influences decision problem solutions and results of economic experiments. In the case of the decision models, presented in the chapter, the application of the right and left eigenvectors sometimes caused changes in the sequence of rankings of criteria or it also influenced the results of forecast model operation, implemented in the ANP. The logarithmic least squares method is, however, resistant to the rank reversal problem. That means that in this method using both a row geometric mean and a column geometric mean does not cause changes in rankings and priority values. An interesting direction of future work is the development of an ontology (Ziemba et al. 2015a, b; Wątróbski and Jankowski 2015) about the preferences aggregation procedures and to build and maintain a repository of AHP and ANP methods.

References

Adams B (2011) SuperDecisions limit matrix calculations. Proc Int Symp Analyt Hierarchy Process. http://isahp.lascomedia.com/dati/pdf/4_0164_Adams.pdf. Accessed 15 Jan 2016

Agarwal A, Shankar R, Tiwari MK (2006) Modeling the metrics of lean, agile and leagile supply chain: an ANP-based approach. Eur J Oper Res 173(1):211–225

Andreichicova O, Andreichicov A (2009) Analytic network process as qualitative simulating tool: researching of financial crisis. Proc Int Symp Analyt Hierarchy Process. http://www.isahp.org/2009Proceedings/Final_Papers/3_Andreichicova_ANP_Financial_Crisis_REV_FIN.pdf. Accessed 15 Jan 2016

Andreichicova O, Andreichicov A (2013) About some features of AHP/ANP applications. Proc Int Symp Analyt Hierarchy Process. http://www.isahp.org/uploads/15.pdf. Accessed 15 Jan 2016

Aragones-Beltran P, Aznar J, Ferris-Onate J, Garcia-Melon M (2008) Valuation of urban industrial land: an analytic network process approach. Eur J Oper Res 185(1):322–339

Aragones-Beltran P, Chaparro-Gonzales F, Pastor-Ferrando JP, Rodriguez-Pozo F (2010) An ANP-based approach for the selection of photovoltaic solar power plant investment projects. Renew Sustain Energy Rev 14(1):249–264

Ayag Z, Ozdemir RG (2007) An analytic network process-based approach to concept evaluation in a new product development environment. J Eng Des 18(3):209–226

Blair AR, Mandelker G, Saaty TL, Whitaker R (2015) Forecasting the resurgence of the U.S. economy in 2010: an expert judgment approach. Rev Econ Finance 5(2):1–18

Blair AR, Mandelker GN, Saaty TL, Whitaker R (2010) Forecasting the resurgence of the U.S. economy in 2010: an expert judgment approach. Socioecon Plann Sci 44(3):114–121

Blair AR, Nachtmann R, Saaty TL, Whitaker R (2002) Forecasting the resurgence of the US economy in 2001: an expert judgment approach. Socioecon Plann Sci 36(2):77–91

Chen YS, Lin CT, Lu JH (2011) The analytic network process for the banking sector: an approach to evaluate the creditability of emerging industries. Afr J Bus Manag 5(4):1343–1352

Chen Z, Khumpaisal S (2009) An analytic network process for risks assessment in commercial real estate development. J Property Invest Finance 27(3):238–258
Choo EU, Wedley WC (2004) A common framework for deriving preference values from pairwise comparison matrices. Comput Oper Res 31(6):893–908
Chung SH, Lee AHI, Pearn WL (2005) Analytic network process (ANP) approach for product mix planning in semiconductor fabricator. Int J Prod Econ 96(1):15–36
Cortes-Aldana FA, Garcia-Melon M, Fernandez-de-Lucio I, Aragones-Beltran P, Poveda-Bautista R (2009) University objectives and socioeconomic results: a multicriteria measuring of alignment. Eur J Oper Res 199(3):811–822
Dijkstra TK (2013) On the extraction of weights from pairwise comparison matrices. Cent Eur J Oper Res 21(1):103–123
Eaton JW (2012) GNU Octave and reproducible research. J Process Contr 22(8):1433–1438
Garcia-Melon M, Ferris-Onate J, Aznar-Bellver J, Aragones-Beltran P, Poveda-Bautista R (2008) Farmland appraisal based on the analytic network process. J Global Optim 42(2):143–155
Gass SI, Rapcsak T (2004) Singular value decomposition in AHP. Eur J Oper Res 154(3):573–584
Ishizaka A, Labib A (2009) Analytic hierarchy process and expert choice: benefits and limitations. OR Insight 22(4):201–220
Ishizaka A, Labib A (2011) Review of the main developments of the analytic hierarchy process. Expert Syst Appl 38(11):14336–14345
Ishizaka A, Lusti M (2006) How to derive priorities in AHP: a comparative study. Cent Eur J Oper Res 14(4):387–400
Ishizaka A, Nemery P (2013) Multi-criteria decision analysis, Methods and software. Wiley, Chichester
Jayant A, Paul V, Kumar U (2014) Application of analytic network process (ANP) in business environment: a comprehensive literature review. Int J Res Mech Eng Tech 5(1):29–37
Johnson CR, Beine WB, Wang TJ (1979) Right-left asymmetry in an eigenvector ranking procedure. J Math Psychol 19(1):61–64
Kuo CW, Chang SC (2013) An evaluation of firms' best strategies with the ANP, AHP and sensitivity test approaches. Adv Info Sci Serv Sci 5(1):316–325
Langer H (2001) Matrices with a strictly dominant eigenvalue. Elemente der Mathematik 56 (2):55–61
Lee WS, Tzeng GH, Guan JL, Chien KT, Huang JM (2009) Combined MCDM techniques for exploring stock selection based on Gordon model. Expert Syst Appl 36(3):6421–6430
Lee YJ (2014) Evaluated weights affecting financial performances' key factors: as exemplified with listed IC design corporations in Taiwan. Asian J Empir Res 4(1):18–40
Li Z, Tang C (2012) Study on evaluation of enterprise financial position based on ANP. Int J Adv Comput Technol 4(14):196–202
Liang C, Li Q (2008) Enterprise information system project selection with regard to BOCR. Int J Proj Manage 26(8):810–820
Lin C (2007) A revised framework for deriving preference values from pairwise comparison matrices. Eur J Oper Res 176(2):1145–1150
Mimovic P (2012) Application of analytical network process in forecasting automobile sales of fiat 500 l. Econ Horiz 14(3):169–179
Neira E, Castillo M, Lesmes D (2009) Analytic network process (ANP): an approach to estimate the Colombian baby diapers market share. Proc Int Symp Analyt Hierarchy Process. http://www.isahp.org/2009Proceedings/Final_Papers/15_Castillo_Neira_ANPinColombianDiaperMarketShare_REV_FIN.pdf. Accessed 15 Jan 2016
Niemira MP, Saaty TL (2004) An analytic network process model for financial-crisis forecasting. Int J Forecast 20(4):573–587
Ozdemir A (2013) Integrating analytic network process and data envelopment analysis for efficiency measurement of Turkish commercial banks. Banks Bank Syst 8(2):86–103
Pakdin Amiri M, Pakdin Amiri A, Pakdin Amiri M (2012) An analytical network process approach for evaluating banking performance based on balanced scorecard. Trends Appl Sci Res 7 (6):456–466

Palanisamy P, Abdul Zubar H (2013) Hybrid MCDM approach for vendor ranking. J Manuf Tech Manag 24(6):905–928

Percin S (2008) Using the ANP approach in selecting and benchmarking ERP systems. Bench-Marking Int J 15(5):630–649

Piegat A, Sałabun W (2014) Identification of a multicriteria decision-making model using the characteristic objects method. Appl Comput Intell Soft Comput 536492:1-536492:14

Raisinghani MS, Meade L, Schkade LL (2007) Strategic e-business decision analysis using the analytic network process. IEEE Trans Eng Manag 54(4):673–686

Ravi V, Shankar R, Tiwari MK (2005) Analyzing alternatives in reverse logistics for end-of-life computers: ANP and balanced scorecard approach. Comput Ind Eng 48(2):327–356

Saaty RW (2003) Validating the analytic hierarchy process and the analytic network process with applications having known and measurable outcomes. Proc Int Symp Analyt Hierarchy Process. http://www.isahp.org/2003Proceedings/paper/p04.pdf. Accessed 15 Jan 2016

Saaty TL (1987) Rank according to Perron: a new insight. Math Mag 60(4):211–213

Saaty TL (1990) Eigenvector and logarithmic least squares. Eur J Oper Res 48(1):156–160

Saaty TL (1998) Ranking by eigenvector versus other methods in the analytic hierarchy process. Appl Math Lett 11(4):121–125

Saaty TL (2003b) Decision-making with the AHP: why is the principal eigenvector necessary. Eur J Oper Res 145(1):85–91

Saaty TL (2004a) Decision making – the analytic hierarchy and network processes (AHP/ANP). J Syst Sci Syst Eng 13(1):1–35

Saaty TL (2004b) Fundamentals of the analytic network process – dependence and feedback in decision-making with a single network. J Syst Sci Syst Eng 13(2):129–157

Saaty TL (2005a) Making and validating complex decisions with the AHP/ANP. J Syst Sci Syst Eng 14(1):1–36

Saaty TL (2005b) The analytic hierarchy and analytic network process for the measurement of intangible criteria and for decision-making. In: Figueira J, Greco S, Ehrgott M (eds) Multiple criteria decision analysis: state of the art surveys. Springer, Boston, pp 345–407

Saaty TL, Sodenkamp M (2010) The analytic hierarchy and analytic network measurement processes: the measurement of intangibles. Decision making under benefits, opportunities, costs and risk. In: Zopounidis C, Pardalos PM (eds) Handbook of multicriteria analysis. Springer, Heidelberg, Berlin, pp 91–166

Saaty TL, Vargas LG (2012a) Incorporating expert judgment in economic forecasts: the case of the U.S. economy in 1992. In: Saaty TL, Vargas LG (eds) Models, methods, concepts & applications of the analytic hierarchy process, 2nd edn. Springer, New York, pp 171–186

Saaty TL, Vargas LG (2012b) The seven pillars of the analytic hierarchy process. In: Saaty TL, Vargas LG (eds) Models, methods, concepts & applications of the analytic hierarchy process, 2nd edn. Springer, New York, pp 23–40

Saaty TL, Vargas LG (2013a) Decision making with the analytic network process. Economic, political, social and technological applications with benefits, opportunities, costs and risks, 2nd edn. Springer, New York

Saaty TL, Vargas LG (2013b) Forecasting the resurgence of the U.S. economy in 2001: an expert judgment approach. In: Saaty TL, Vargas LG (eds) Decision making with the analytic network process. Economic, political, social and technological applications with benefits, opportunities, costs and risks, 2nd edn. Springer, New York, pp 41–74

Sałabun W (2015) The characteristic objects method: a new distance-based approach to multicriteria decision-making problems. J Multi-Criteria Decision Anal 22(1–2):37–50

Sałabun W (2012) The use of fuzzy logic to evaluate the nonlinearity of human multi-criteria used in decision making. Electr Rev 88(10b):235–238

Tung SL, Tang SL (1998) A comparison of the Saaty's AHP and modified AHP for right and left eigenvector inconsistency. Eur J Oper Res 106(1):123–128

Turan FK, Scala NM, Besterfield-Sacre M, Needy KL (2009) An analytic network process (ANP) Approach to the project portfolio management for organizational sustainability. Proceedings of the 2009 industrial engineering research conference

Tuzkaya G, Onut S, Tuzkaya UR, Gulsun B (2008) An analytic network process approach for locating undesirable facilities: an example from Istanbul, Turkey. J Environ Manage 88(4):970–983
Wątróbski J, Jankowski J (2015) Knowledge management in MCDA domain. In: Proceedings of the federated conference on computer science and information systems, pp. 1455–1460. IEEE Digital Library, doi: 10.15439/2015F295
Wątróbski J, Ziemba P, Wolski W (2015) Methodological aspects of decision support system for the location of renewable energy sources. In: Proceedings of the federated conference on computer science and information systems, pp. 1461–1469. IEEE Digital Library, doi: 10.15439/2015F294
Whitaker R (2007) Validation examples of the analytic hierarchy process and analytic network process. Math Comput Model 46(7–8):840–859
Wu CR, Lin CT, Tsai PH (2009) Analysing alternatives in financial services for wealth management banks: the analytic network process and the balanced scorecard approach. J Manag Math 20(3):303–321
Yuksel I, Dagdeviren M (2007) Using the analytic network process (ANP) in a SWOT analysis – a case study for a textile firm. Inform Sci 177(16):3364–3382
Zhao YM (2013) Power supply enterprise human resources management ability fuzzy comprehensive evaluation based on ANP. The 19th international conference on industrial engineering and engineering management, pp. 929–938
Ziemba P, Jankowski J, Wątróbski J, Becker J (2015a) Knowledge management in website quality evaluation domain. In: Nunez M et al (eds) ICCCI 2015, part II, lecture notes in computer science (lecture notes in artificial intelligence), vol 9330. Springer, Heidelberg, pp 75–85
Ziemba P, Jankowski J, Wątróbski J, Wolski W, Becker J (2015b) Integration of domain ontologies in the repository of website evaluation methods. In: Proceedings of the federated conference on computer science and information systems, pp. 1601–1610. IEEE Digital Library, doi: 10.15439/2015F29

Chapter 15
Research on the Properties of the AHP in the Environment of Inaccurate Expert Evaluations

Paweł Ziemba, Jarosław Wątróbski, Jarosław Jankowski, and Mateusz Piwowarski

Abstract The chapter deals with the issue of preference aggregation from pairwise comparison matrices in the AHP. The technique is widely used in economic research as a tool supporting decision making in finance, management and experimental economics. When inaccurate expert evaluations are made, it is essential to employ a procedure, in the technique, which correctly aggregates a decision-maker's preferences and makes it possible to find a proper solution to a decision problem. In this chapter, with the use of simulations, fourteen aggregation procedures with different degrees of expert evaluation inaccuracies and for different sizes of decision problems are examined. Among the researched procedures there were: classical ones, based on column sums and a eigenvector of a matrix; ones based on the method of least squares using error minimization; as well as the method of a data envelope. As a result, procedures are indicated which aggregate a decision-maker's assessment in the most precise manner and which find solutions closest to a reference.

Keywords AHP method • Economic experiment

P. Ziemba (✉)
Department of Technology, Jacob of Paradyż University of Applied Sciences in Gorzów Wielkopolski, Teatralna 25, Gorzów Wielkopolski 66-400, Poland
e-mail: pziemba@pwsz.pl

J. Wątróbski • J. Jankowski • M. Piwowarski
Department of Information Systems Engineering, Faculty of Computer Science and Information Technology, West Pomeranian University of Technology Szczecin, Żołnierska 49, Szczecin 71-210, Poland
e-mail: jwatrobski@wi.zut.edu.pl; jjankowski.pl@gmail.com; mpiwowarski@wi.zut.edu.pl

K. Nermend, M. Łatuszyńska (eds.), *Selected Issues in Experimental Economics*, Springer Proceedings in Business and Economics, DOI 10.1007/978-3-319-28419-4_15

15.1 Introduction

The Analytic Hierarchy Process (AHP) technique is a detailed procedure for solving a multicriteria decision problem developed by Thomas L. Saaty at the turn of the 1970s and 1980s of the twentieth century (Saaty 1980). It is based on pairwise comparison matrices from which preference vectors are aggregated. The technique, similarly to Multicriteria Decision Aid/Making methods, is used to solve discreet decision problems in many walks of life. It is universally employed to make diverse economic (Saaty 2010), financial (Hulle et al. 2011), banking (Bhattarai and Yadav 2009) as well as broadly understood management (Sum 2013; Al-Subhi Al-Harbi 2001; Wątróbski and Jankowski 2016) decisions. Moreover, when making a decision in other fields, economical criteria are often taken into consideration (Piegat and Sałabun 2014; Wątróbski et al. 2015). On the other hand, decision making theory and decision support methods constitute basic research instruments in the field of experimental economics and, more commonly, behavioural economics (Jankowski et al. 2011; Jankowski et al. 2015). It is related with the change of a paradigm and a strong trend in economic research where the notion of a rational choice was strongly completed with emotional factors (Sałabun 2012).

Practical decision making with the use of the AHP can be a nuisance because a proper reproduction of its assessment scale. It is a 9-point ratio (Saaty and Ozdemir 2003) in which one cannot express all possible preferences between the pairs of variants. Furthermore, experts' evaluations can be inconsistent and imprecise, especially in decision problems which contain many debated alternatives or criteria (Ziemba et al. 2014; Laininen and Hamalainen 2003). Because of decision-makers' imprecise evaluations, the AHP may not provide a correct solution (Agha 2011; Szczypińska and Piotrowski 2009).

There are different procedures which are used to determine a preference vector W (Lin 2007). Every procedure, in the case of a consistent matrix, gives a true preference vector V (Choo and Wedley 2004). Depending on the size of a decision problem and the inaccuracy of expert evaluations and thus the incoherence degree of pairwise comparison matrices, individual procedures allow to determine a different approximation of the vector V. The aim of the chapter is to examine, in the environment of inaccurate expert evaluations, individual preferences aggregation procedures used in the AHP and to find out procedures which give an approximation of the true preference vector in the most effective way. The chapter surveys the publications in which economic decision problems were solved by means of the AHP and which discuss the matter of the AHP as well as the literature dealing with the problem of aggregation preferences in the AHP. Next, simulation research of individual preferences aggregation procedures with different degrees of expert evaluation inaccuracies and different sizes of decision problems has been carried out. Finally, the chapter presents the research results.

15.2 Literature Review

The AHP is used to solve various decision problems (Wątróbski et al. 2014). Also, it is employed to make economic decisions and marketing. Saaty, author of the technique, provides examples of its diverse applications in experimental and behavioural economics. He uses the AHP to solve complex microeconomic as well as macroeconomic problems,, for instance, to determine a forecast exchange rate of the dollar to the yen on the basis of foreign exchange rate forecasting factors, to generate input–output coefficients for the econometric model of a country's economy or to determine the period and force of an economic recovery in the USA (Saaty 2010). In his works, Saaty gives examples of applying the AHP to support binary complicated economic decisions (Yes/No) on the basis of the BOCR model (Benefits, Opportunities, Costs and Risks), for instance, examining a decision on imposing sanctions on China for breaking intellectual property rights (Saaty 2004), or a decision on the admission of China to the World Trade Organisation (Saaty 2005b). As far as other applications of the AHP in macroeconomics are concerned, one can list, for example, the comparison of economic stabilization models in Latvia (Rivza et al. 2009), the evaluation of economic development achieved by local governments in China (Lin et al. 2011), the comparison of individual countries' economic situations and the evaluation of their Gross National Product (Saaty 2005a), or prioritizing of development targets in low-income developing countries (Ehie et al. 1990). Apart from macroeconomic decisions, the AHP can also be applied to financial decisions: the choice of an investment strategy minimizing a risk (Wu et al. 2012), an evaluation of non-material investments (Kivijarvi and Tuominen 1992), an analysis of a company's portfolio (Saaty et al. 1980), forecasting exchange rates (Ulengin and Ulengin 1994), or a decision on credit granting in nonfinancial firms (Srinivasan and Ruparel 1990). As to management decisions, examples of applying the AHP are: an assessment of corporate performance (Lee et al. 1995; Babic and Plazibat 1998), an evaluation of bank Mergers and Acquisitions (M&A) strategy (Arbel and Orgler 1990), virtual organization management (Kim 1998), distribution network optimization (Sharma et al. 2008), a decision support in merging companies (Saaty et al. 2003), launching a new product for production and on the market (Ishizaka and Labib 2011b; Chin et al. 2008), choosing a project for improving an information system of an organization (Abu-Sarhan 2011), or choosing the Enterprise Resource Planning (ERP) information system (Wei et al. 2005), a choice of a company's management model (Chen and Wanh 2010) and different dimensions of human resources management (Onder and Dogan 2013; Saaty et al. 2007). These are just several possible applications of the AHP, since it is also used in other areas and to solve other decision problems. A wide survey of AHP applications can be found, for example, in (Vaidya and Kumar 2006).

15.3 State of the Art

The Analytic Hierarchy Process is a multicriteria decision support technique stemming from the expected utility hypothesis (Piegat and Sałabun 2015). One can distinguish four stages:

1. Defining a decision problem and a kind of knowledge one is looking for.
2. Preparing a hierarchical structure containing the main goal, intermediate goals (criteria) and alternatives.
3. A pairwise comparison of alternatives in relation to each of the criteria and a pairwise comparison of importance of individual criteria.
4. Using vectors of priorities obtained in comparisons to receive a solution to the decision problem (Saaty 2008).

Variant comparisons are conducted with the use of pairwise comparison matrices. Each matrix ought to be reciprocal and positive (Saaty 2004). When specifying the positivity of matrices one needs to point out that it should contain the Saaty rating scale, i.e. from the range of 1–9 and their opposite values, where 1 indicates equality of compared alternatives or criteria and 9 indicates an extreme advantage of an alternative or criterion i over j (Saaty 2008). For every pairwise comparison matrix a preference vector $W = [w_1, w_2 \ldots w_n]^T$ is defined, which demonstrates the force of alternatives or criteria compared in matrices. Components of the vector are included in the pairwise comparison matrix, which is presented in the formula (15.1) (Saaty 1990):

$$M = \begin{pmatrix} \frac{w_1}{w_1} & \frac{w_1}{w_2} & \cdots & \frac{w_1}{w_n} \\ \frac{w_2}{w_1} & \frac{w_2}{w_2} & \cdots & \frac{w_2}{w_n} \\ \vdots & \vdots & \ddots & \vdots \\ \frac{w_n}{w_1} & \frac{w_n}{w_2} & \cdots & \frac{w_n}{w_n} \end{pmatrix} \tag{15.1}$$

When the matrix is consistent, a preference vector W corresponds to a true preference vector V. Consistency of matrices takes place if: $a_{ij} \times a_{jk} = a_{ik}$ for each i,j,k (Saaty and Vargas 2011), when elements of a preference vector are their own multiples (e.g. $[1\ 3\ 6]^T$ or $[4\ 2\ 1\ 8]^T$). Therefore, preference consistency is identical to transitivity of evaluations, for instance, if in a decision-maker's opinion a variant a_i is two times better than a variant a_j and four times better than a_k, then the variant a_j should be two times better than the variant a_k. However, most often the true preference vector V does not contain only and exclusively values which are mutually their multiples, therefore, the vector W is only its approximation (Lin 2007). The phenomenon brings about the occurrence of minor inconsistencies in the pairwise comparison matrix, which results from rounding of true preferences to the values from a set {1/9, 1/8, …, 1,…, 8, 9}. More significant inconsistencies in the pairwise comparison matrix are most often caused by a decision-maker's mistakes which lie in not keeping, by him or her, the rule of full transitivity of evaluations between compared variants (Laininen and Hamalainen 2003). In the literature there are many procedures for determining the preference vector W, such as: Simple Column Sum (Tsyganok 2010), Simple Normalized Column Sum (Ishizaka and Labib 2011a), Right Eigenvector (Saaty 1998), Normalized Right Eigenvector (Choo and Wedley 2004), Left Eigenvector (Ishizaka and Labib 2009), Least Square (Bozóki and Lewis 2005), Logarithmic Least Square (Simple Geometric Mean) (Ishizaka and Labib 2011a), Preference Weighted Least Square (Blankmeyer 1987), Preference Weighted Geometric Mean (Choo and Wedley 2004), Preference Weighted Least Absolute Error (Garcia et al. 2010), Preference Weighted Least Worst Absolute Error (Bertolini and Bevilacqua 2006), Logarithmic Least Absolute Error (Zakaria et al. 2010), Logarithmic Least Worst Absolute Error (Muata and Bryson 2006), Data Envelopment Analysis (Wang and Chin 2009).

In the literature one can come across a publication whose authors compare different preferences aggregation procedures of a pairwise comparison matrix. In the paper (Golany and Kress 1993) six procedures, in relation to seven criteria in matrices 7×7, were compared. Tsyganok (2010) compared five procedures on matrices 5×5. In this case the comparison criterion was the ratio of a relative error to an initial error. He used four vectors initiating the construction of four different types of matrices, which then were modified by means of a genetic algorithm. The publication (Zakaria et al. 2010) compares how seven procedures work on eleven matrices and the criterion of procedure evaluation was total deviation of determined preference vectors with relation to a reference vector. Ishizaka and Lusti (2006) compared four procedures for matrices from 3×3 to 7×7 and consistency ratios from the range of (0–0.1]. In this research the comparison criterion was a correlation of rankings which were determined with the use of individual procedures. In this paper (Bajwa et al. 2008) seven procedures using matrices 4×4, 5×5 and 7×7 were compared with relations to four criteria. In this case four test scenarios were used. The scenarios differed in standard deviation of errors inserted in matrices and a preference vector used for constructing matrices. Another paper (Choo and Wedley 2004) researched eighteen procedures (Lin (2007) proved that some of the researched procedures are identical, therefore, one can say that there were fifteen procedures). Here, a comparison criterion was the mean absolute deviation of a determined preference vector in relation to a true preference vector. The procedures were examined with the use of two test scenarios. In the first scenario there were many insignificant errors inserted in consistent matrices, whereas in the second procedure one significant error was inserted in a consistent matrix. All tested matrices were generated by means of the same six-element vector. Lin (2007) developed a research procedure of Choo and Wedley (2004) by adding two additional test scenarios in which many minor errors and one major error as well as many major errors were inserted in matrixes. To generate matrices he used a preference vector of Choo and Wedley (2004) and researched fifteen procedures examined by them.

15.4 Research Procedure

In our research the operation of fourteen preferences aggregation procedures has been examined on $n = 3,5,7,9$ matrices. Pairwise comparison matrices in subsequent iterations were generated on the basis of random true preference vectors (reference vectors) with a size n. Other reference vectors were used to verify the operational effects of each procedure. Elements of every vector contained random values from 1 to 10 with the provision that generated vectors cannot allow to construct fully consistent matrices (e.g. they cannot take the form of $[2\ 8\ 1\ 4]^T$). The research was supposed to reflect to the greatest extent the course of the AHP. Therefore, in pairwise comparison matrices other values than 1/9, 1/8, ..., 1/2, 1, 2, ..., 8, 9 were not used. One needs to emphasize that in the aforementioned works the rule was not always kept (e.g. in (Choo and Wedley 2004; Lin 2007)) a vector $[1,2.5,4,5.5,7,8.5]^T$ was used what resulted in occurring a value 4/7 in a comparison matrix). Using only seventeen values from 1/9 to 9 in comparison matrices required a proper rounding of a value in the matrices generated on the basis of a reference vector. In order to take the inaccuracy of expert evaluation to the highest degree, additional errors were inserted in the matrix containing deviations resulting from the rounding of a value. They consisted in increasing the values of matrices' cells by integers. In the research four test scenarios were used.

1. An n-element reference vector was generated which contained two same values. Next, on the basis of a vector a pairwise comparison matrix was generated. In the generated matrices there were always rounded-off errors of dominance of one variant over the other one to the Saaty's scale, i.e. for example, 2/9 was rounded 1/5, 4/9 to 1/2, 5/4 to 1 etc. The scenario was to simulate the behaviour of an experienced expert who made insignificant errors in assessment resulting from, in most cases, limitations of the assessment scale. The research was to determine which procedures could be used for preference aggregation when several variants are equally good.
2. The second scenario was similar to the first one, however, in this case in a reference vector there could not be two variants of the same value. The research was to determine which procedures allow to achieve the best results when there are differently preferred variants.
3. In a matrix constructed according to Scenario 1 $n/2-1$ (with rounding down to an integer) errors were inserted. The errors consisted in enhancing a randomly selected variant with relation to another one. It was achieved by increasing the value of a proper matric cell $1 \leq a_{ij} \leq 7$ by 1 or 2 as well as proper decreasing the value of an element a_{ji} (if a cell $a_{ij} < 1$, was drawn, then the value of a cell a_{ji} was decreased by 1 or 2 and the value of a_{ij} was appropriately increased). The research was to simulate decision-makers' behaviour who make various assessment errors. It was to give an answer to the question which preferences aggregation procedures are applicable to matrices with a considerable number of insignificant errors (resulting from rounding the value of a reference vector) and a small number of significant errors.

4. Scenario 4 was very similar to Scenario 3, however, errors related to enhancing a random variant could not be inserted in the verse of a dominant variant over all other variants.

In Scenarios 1 and 2 one hundred $n = 3,5,7,9$ matrices were used (altogether 800 matrices). Scenarios 3 and 4 were based on $n = 5,7,9$ matrices (altogether 600 matrices). In the case of every iteration (every generated pairwise comparison matrix) a preference vector determined on the basis of a pairwise comparison matrix was compared to a reference vector, on the basis of which the pairwise comparison matrix was generated. Here, three features were examined.

1. Does the sequence of variants in the ranking, received by a given procedure, differ from the sequence in the reference vector?
2. How many variants in the ranking, received by a given procedure, took different positions than in the reference ranking?
3. What is the mean absolute deviation (Pham-Gia and Hung 2001) of the preference vector, received by a given procedure, with relation to the reference vector?

15.5 Research Results

The conducted research was to determine which procedure, despite imprecise expert evaluations in pairwise comparison matrices, allows to determine the preference vector which is to the greatest degree similar to the reference vector, which can be obtained from a fully consistent matrix. In other words, the aim of the research was to determine which procedures can minimize the influence of errors, made by decision-makers, on the evaluation of aggregated variants.

Table 15.1 shows a real characteristic of a consistency ratio (CR) for individual research cases. The ratio was calculated by means of a generated matrix and reference vector. In almost all tests a part of generated matrices exceeded the value of a coefficient 0,1 recommended by Saaty. Nevertheless, the values of CR calculated with the use of vectors generated by individual aggregation preferences procedures in every case were close to 0. The values of CR, however, must be only treated as information revealing what the degree of differences between generated matrices and reference vectors was.

The results of the research conducted in accordance with Scenario 1 is presented in Table 15.2. When analyzing Table 15.2 one can easily notice that for $n = 3$ matrices almost all procedures produce the same results. The exception here is the PWLS procedure. In this case an auxiliary matrix C (Blankmeyer 1987) for this size of the matrix was often a singular matrix. For $n = 5$, $n = 7$ and $n = 9$ matrices, with regard to changes in rankings, the results achieved by the PWLAE, LLWAE, DEA and partly by the PWLWAE differ from the results obtained by the majority of procedures. Except for the DEA there are procedures using, for the construction of a preference vector, the absolute values of errors occurring in matrices. Nevertheless, among the best procedures is the LLAE using a logarithmized distance function and

Table 15.1 Values of a consistency ratio CR for subsequent test scenario

Scenario		Max CR	Min CR	Mean CR	Median CR	Dominant CR
1	$n=3$	0.8242	0.1068	0.3245	0.2747	0.3205
	$n=5$	0.2574	0.0225	0.118	0.1126	0.1502
	$n=7$	0.1605	0.0309	0.0874	0.0844	0.0617
	$n=9$	0.1108	0.0335	0.0714	0.0739	0.0862
2	$n=3$	0.6868	0.0534	0.2812	0.2404	0.1923
	$n=5$	0.2252	0.045	0.113	0.1126	0.1126
	$n=7$	0.1411	0.0309	0.0757	0.0723	0.0617
	$n=9$	0.0739	0.0369	0.0577	0.0603	0.0616
3	$n=5$	0.7132	0.0375	0.2538	0.2252	0.2252
	$n=7$	0.6104	0.0391	0.1939	0.1617	0.1235
	$n=9$	0.4023	0.0575	0.1656	0.1530	0.0739
4	$n=5$	0.6569	0.0375	0.2176	0.1752	0.2252
	$n=7$	0.7747	0.0549	0.1971	0.1576	0.1235
	$n=9$	0.5194	0.0479	0.1849	0.1652	0.1006

absolute values of errors. As far as the DEA procedure is concerned, it gives worst results because of the fact it tries to insert a preference of one of the variants with regard to another one even in a situation when the variants are equal. Next, the PWLAE introduces a great deal of changes in the rankings although it produces low values of the mean absolute deviation. In this test scenario, in general, the best procedures are the SCS, SNCS, REV, LEV, SGM and LLAE, which introduce the fewest changes in the rankings and at the same time have low values of the mean absolute deviation.

In Scenario 2 for an $n=3$ matrix from the results obtained by other procedures differs only the result of the PWLAE procedure, which also in this case produces very good results of the mean absolute deviation. For $n=5$ and $n=7$ matrices the best results, with regard to the changes introduced in the ranking, gives the DEA. The worst results happen to be (similarly to Scenario 1) in the following procedures: PWLAE, LLWAE and—in the case of an $n=5$ matrix—PWLWAE. As far as $n=9$ matrices are concerned, all procedures except for the DEA produce equally good results. As for the DEA it has been found out that for $n=9$ matrices it generates incorrect rankings when the ratio CR was 0.060345 and the reference vector contained a value $w_i \in \{1{:}10\backslash 4\}$. Also, in this research scenario the PWLAE procedure, in spite of a high number of number changes in the rankings with reference to the best procedures, has had very good values of the mean absolute deviation. The best procedures in this scenario, similarly to Research 1, are the SCS, SNCS, REV, LEV, SGM and LLAE. As to the DEA, the errors generated by it for $n=9$ matrices require further research. Table 15.3 shows the results obtained in the research in accordance with Scenario 2.

The research in Scenarios 3 and 4 were conducted with the use of $n=5$, $n=7$ and $n=9$ matrices because the formula used, for the number of inserted errors $n/2-1$, does not take into consideration introducing errors for $n=3$ matrices.

Table 15.2 Results of the experiment according to Scenario 1

	No. of changed rankings								No. of changes in the rankings							
	$n=3$		$n=5$		$n=7$		$n=9$		$n=3$		$n=5$		$n=7$		$n=9$	
Procedure	δ	R	δ	R	δ	R	δ	R	δ	R	δ	R	δ	R	δ	R
SCS	40	1	28	1	12	1	5	1	56	1	42	1	16	1	6	1
SNCS	40	1	28	1	12	1	5	1	56	1	42	1	16	1	6	1
REV	40	1	28	1	12	1	5	1	56	1	42	1	16	1	6	1
NREV	40	1	28	1	12	1	5	1	56	1	42	1	16	1	6	1
LEV	40	1	28	1	12	1	5	1	56	1	42	1	16	1	6	1
SGM	40	1	28	1	12	1	5	1	56	1	42	1	16	1	6	1
PWGM	40	1	28	1	12	1	5	1	56	1	42	1	16	1	6	1
LS	40	1	28	1	12	1	5	1	56	1	42	1	16	1	6	1
PWLS	40	1	28	1	12	1	5	1	56	1	42	1	16	1	6	1
PWLAE	40	1	30	2	17	3	6	2	56	1	45	2	25	3	8	2
LLAE	40	1	28	1	12	1	5	1	56	1	42	1	16	1	6	1
PWLWAE	40	1	33	3	13	2	5	1	56	1	57	3	20	2	6	1
LLWAE	40	1	36	4	24	4	17	3	56	1	62	4	54	4	31	3
DEA	40	1	75	5	69	5	69	4	56	1	103	5	81	5	78	4

	Mean absolute deviation (*100)							
	$n=3$		$n=5$		$n=7$		$n=9$	
	δ	R	δ	R	δ	R	δ	R
SCS	2.7255	1	0.8800	2	0.4914	2	0.3198	3
SNCS	2.7255	1	1.1414	8	0.6788	9	0.4403	9
REV	2.7255	1	1.1418	9	0.6766	8	0.4349	7
NREV	2.7255	1	1.3249	11	0.8299	13	0.5577	13
LEV	2.7255	1	1.1386	6	0.6723	4	0.4241	4
SGM	2.7255	1	1.1411	7	0.6748	5	0.4288	5
PWGM	2.7255	1	1.3288	12	0.8288	12	0.5540	12
LS	2.7255	1	1.3311	13	0.8238	11	0.5461	11
PWLS	3.1306	2	1.2555	10	0.7574	10	0.5046	10
PWLAE	2.7255	1	0.8141	1	0.4544	1	0.2956	1
LLAE	2.7255	1	1.1384	5	0.6762	7	0.4375	8
PWLWAE	2.7255	1	0.9562	3	0.5271	3	0.3065	2
LLWAE	2.7255	1	1.3572	14	0.8880	14	0.6564	14
DEA	2.7255	1	1.1362	4	0.6749	6	0.4296	6

* denotes multiplication

Therefore, the results of these matrices were identical to the results produced in Scenario 2. The results of research conducted in accordance with Scenario 3 are presented in Table 15.4.

In Research 3 for $n=5$ matrices every procedure in alternated rankings introduces only one error in relation to a reference vector. The error consisted in equal preference of two variants with different values in the reference vector. It is a typical error stemming from rounding a preference value to the AHP scale. As to

Table 15.3 Research results according to Scenario 2

	No. of changed rankings								No. of changes in the rankings							
	$n=3$		$n=5$		$n=7$		$n=9$		$n=3$		$n=5$		$n=7$		$n=9$	
Procedure	δ	R	δ	R	δ	R	δ	R	δ	R	δ	R	δ	R	δ	R
SCS	32	1	15	2	9	2	0	1	40	1	20	2	9	1	0	1
SNCS	32	1	15	2	9	2	0	1	40	1	20	2	9	1	0	1
REV	32	1	15	2	9	2	0	1	40	1	20	2	9	1	0	1
NREV	32	1	15	2	9	2	0	1	40	1	20	2	9	1	0	1
LEV	32	1	15	2	9	2	0	1	40	1	20	2	9	1	0	1
SGM	32	1	15	2	9	2	0	1	40	1	20	2	9	1	0	1
PWGM	32	1	15	2	9	2	0	1	40	1	20	2	9	1	0	1
LS	32	1	15	2	9	2	0	1	40	1	20	2	9	1	0	1
PWLS	32	1	15	2	9	2	0	1	40	1	20	2	9	1	0	1
PWLAE	34	2	18	4	11	3	0	1	42	2	26	4	11	2	0	1
LLAE	32	1	15	2	9	2	0	1	40	1	20	2	9	1	0	1
PWLWAE	32	1	16	3	9	2	0	1	40	1	23	3	9	1	0	1
LLWAE	32	1	24	5	16	4	0	1	40	1	43	5	26	3	0	1
DEA	32	1	8	1	6	1	11	2	40	1	16	1	9	1	22	2

	Mean absolute deviation (*100)							
	$n=3$		$n=5$		$n=7$		$n=9$	
	δ	R	δ	R	δ	R	δ	R
SCS	1.8763	2	0.7648	2	0.4171	3	0.2628	3
SNCS	2.1826	5	0.9992	8	0.5787	9	0.3752	9
REV	2.1872	6	0.9995	9	0.5749	7	0.3694	7
NREV	2.4430	9	1.1942	13	0.7386	13	0.4958	13
LEV	2.1872	6	0.9840	4	0.5527	4	0.3408	4
SGM	2.1872	6	0.9933	6	0.5631	6	0.3543	5
PWGM	2.4490	10	1.1895	12	0.7285	12	0.4816	12
LS	2.4510	11	1.1810	11	0.7193	11	0.4741	11
PWLS	2.5325	12	1.1129	10	0.6686	10	0.4481	10
PWLAE	1.8881	3	0.7333	1	0.3964	1	0.2432	2
LLAE	2.1817	4	0.9961	7	0.5760	8	0.3730	8
PWLWAE	1.8432	1	0.7879	3	0.4114	2	0.2248	1
LLWAE	2.3712	8	1.2625	14	0.8506	14	0.6064	14
DEA	2.1886	7	0.9843	5	0.5641	5	0.3638	6

* denotes multiplication

the quality of the results obtained by individual procedures, in the case of $n=5$ matrices, the PWLS and LS procedures using the norm of the least squares acquit themselves badly. The PWLWAE and PWLAE procedures, similarly to other sizes of matrices, acquit themselves well. For $n=9$ matrices, along with the PWLWAE and PWLAE, also the SCS procedure produces very good results. In general, in this research the best results are by the PWLWAE and PWLAE. Also, the SCS, SNCS and LLWAE work without fault.

Table 15.4 Research results according to Scenario 3

	No. of changed rankings						No. of changes in the rankings					
	$n=5$		$n=7$		$n=9$		$n=5$		$n=7$		$n=9$	
Procedure	δ	R	δ	R	δ	R	δ	R	δ	R	δ	R
SCS	46	4	50	5	51	2	46	4	89	2	92	1
SNCS	48	6	48	4	55	3	48	6	112	4	140	5
REV	48	6	54	8	56	4	48	6	124	11	144	7
NREV	47	5	48	4	56	4	47	5	120	8	163	11
LEV	48	6	47	3	58	6	48	6	115	6	152	8
SGM	49	7	53	7	56	4	49	7	114	5	135	4
PWGM	49	7	47	3	55	3	49	7	121	9	157	9
LS	50	8	50	5	56	4	50	8	123	10	164	12
PWLS	51	9	55	9	65	8	51	9	136	14	196	14
PWLAE	40	2	45	2	45	1	40	2	96	3	98	2
LLAE	49	7	50	5	56	4	49	7	116	7	142	6
PWLWAE	36	1	38	1	51	2	36	1	74	1	118	3
LLWAE	48	6	56	10	57	5	48	6	130	13	160	10
DEA	45	3	51	6	63	7	45	3	127	12	175	13

	Mean absolute deviation (*100)					
	$n=5$		$n=7$		$n=9$	
	δ	R	δ	R	δ	R
SCS	1.5091	2	0.8202	1	0.5539	2
SNCS	1.6821	5	0.9887	5	0.6811	5
REV	1.7406	8	1.0320	8	0.7123	8
NREV	1.8469	11	1.1646	11	0.8240	11
LEV	1.7072	6	1.0137	6	0.7054	6
SGM	1.6767	4	0.9760	4	0.6591	4
PWGM	1.8349	10	1.1430	10	0.7962	10
LS	1.8952	13	1.1862	12	0.8472	13
PWLS	1.9008	14	1.2078	13	0.9016	14
PWLAE	1.5737	3	0.8793	3	0.5533	1
LLAE	1.7171	7	1.0160	7	0.7061	7
PWLWAE	1.5063	1	0.8597	2	0.6062	3
LLWAE	1.8774	12	1.1862	12	0.8443	12
DEA	1.7646	9	1.0601	9	0.7644	9

* denotes multiplication

The results of the last research are presented in Table 15.5. With the use of an $n=5$ matrix the best results are from the DEA. The results from the SCS, PWLAE and PWLWAE fall behind from those of other ones. The best results are from the PWGM for $n=7$ matrices. The worst procedures are again the SCS, PWLAE and PWLWAE. One can see here dependence of the obtained results on the use of a logarithmized function of a distance in procedures using the norm of absolute errors. In the case of the procedures based on the norm of absolute errors, which

Table 15.5 Research results according to Scenario 4

	No. of changed rankings						No. of changes in the rankings					
	$n=5$		$n=7$		$n=9$		$n=5$		$n=7$		$n=9$	
Procedure	δ	R	δ	R	δ	R	δ	R	δ	R	δ	R
SCS	35	5	52	10	54	10	70	7	105	12	103	5
SNCS	32	3	39	5	48	6	64	5	84	6	112	7
REV	32	3	42	7	49	7	64	5	95	9	120	9
NREV	31	2	34	2	42	3	62	3	71	2	100	3
LEV	33	4	42	7	53	9	67	6	99	11	128	10
SGM	33	4	38	4	45	4	67	6	81	3	101	4
PWGM	31	2	29	1	33	1	61	2	65	1	79	1
LS	31	2	36	3	41	2	60	1	82	4	96	2
PWLS	32	3	40	6	45	4	63	4	91	7	107	6
PWLAE	45	7	60	11	54	10	96	9	146	14	139	11
LLAE	32	3	43	8	50	8	64	5	97	10	119	8
PWLWAE	38	6	49	9	60	12	80	8	121	13	147	13
LLWAE	33	4	38	4	46	5	67	6	83	5	107	6
DEA	29	1	38	4	57	11	63	4	94	8	143	12

	Mean absolute deviation (*100)					
	$n=5$		$n=7$		$n=9$	
	δ	R	δ	R	δ	R
SCS	1.4668	4	0.8919	1	0.6083	2
SNCS	1.4542	2	0.9253	3	0.6289	3
REV	1.4666	3	0.9439	5	0.6382	4
NREV	1.5717	11	0.9914	11	0.6857	12
LEV	1.4763	6	0.9669	9	0.6452	7
SGM	1.4389	1	0.8970	2	0.6004	1
PWGM	1.5364	9	0.9307	4	0.6442	6
LS	1.5594	10	0.9731	10	0.6704	11
PWLS	1.4979	8	0.9615	8	0.6673	9
PWLAE	1.7821	14	1.0289	12	0.6994	13
LLAE	1.4748	5	0.9539	6	0.6436	5
PWLWAE	1.6269	12	1.0615	13	0.6676	10
LLWAE	1.6396	13	1.1046	14	0.7841	14
DEA	1.4871	7	0.9584	7	0.6553	8

* denotes multiplication

do not rely on the logarithmized function of a distance, one can see worse and worse results compared to the procedures with the logarithmized function of a distance. Applying an $n=9$ matrix in the research it was confirmed once again that the best results are obtained by the PWGM. However, the PWLWAE, DEA, PWLAE and LEV performed poorly in the research. Also, the SCS, with regard to the number of changed rankings, produces unsatisfactory effects, although the number of changes introduced in the rankings is in this case relatively small. In the research in

Table 15.6 Experiment results from the perspective of scenarios and matrix sizes

	Research scenario				Matrix size				
Procedure	1	2	3	4	$n=3$	$n=5$	$n=7$	$n=9$	General ranking
SCS	1	1	3	12	2	9	11	7	10
SNCS	6	6	4	7	4	3	4	6	4
REV	5	5	11	8	5	4	10	8	8
NREV	9	10	6	2	8	1	2	3	2
LEV	2	2	7	11	5	8	6	12	9
SGM	3	3	10	4	5	10	7	5	5
PWGM	8	9	5	1	9	2	1	1	1
LS	7	8	9	3	10	6	3	2	3
PWLS	10	7	14	6	11	11	9	10	11
PWLAE	12	13	2	14	12	12	12	4	12
LLAE	4	4	8	10	3	7	8	9	7
PWLWAE	11	11	1	13	1	5	5	11	6
LLWAE	13	14	13	5	7	13	13	13	13
DEA	14	12	12	9	6	14	14	14	14

accordance with Scenario 4, in general, the best effects were obtained for the PWGM. The operation of the DEA, which for some matrices produces very good results and for other values n it does not perform well, is debatable. The worst in this research are the PWLAE, PWLWAE and SCS, which, however, have very good values of the mean absolute deviation.

The results obtained for different scenarios and different sizes of matrices are presented in Table 15.6. There are rankings reflecting the sequence of results obtained by each procedure from the best to the worst in relation to a given scenario and a defined size of a matrix. In these rankings the most essential factor in comparing the preferences aggregation procedures was the number of rankings changed by them. The second important criterion was the number of changes introduced to the rankings by the researched procedures. The least important characteristic was the mean absolute deviation. The rankings, which concern the perspective of research scenarios and the perspective of matrix sizes, based on the criteria are presented in Table 15.6. One needs to emphasize that the results for $n=3$ matrices aggregate only two first test scenarios, since for Scenarios 3 and 4 $n=3$ matrices were not examined. Table 15.6 also shows a general ranking of variants obtained by summing up separate quantities of the changed rankings, the number of changes in the rankings and the mean absolute deviations of all matrix sizes and all test scenarios. Next, the positions in the general ranking was determined analogically to other rankings in Table 15.6.

15.6 Summary

In this Chap. 14 preferences aggregation procedures of pairwise comparison matrices in the AHP have been examined. That is why, four test scenarios were used. The scenarios reflected the decision-making process by means of the AHP in the environment of imprecise expert evaluations. In the chapter some imperfections of the researched procedures were mentioned. The imperfections are: frequent occurrence of oddness in the auxiliary matrix for the PWLS when the procedure works on $n = 3$ matrices, generating incorrect preference vectors by the DEA in Scenario 2 or generating, by the procedure, incorrect rankings when two variants in the matrix should have the same preference. When analyzing the general ranking of preferences aggregation procedures it was found out that the sequence of procedures in (Bajwa et al. 2008) with regard to the number of changes in the rankings, where the SGM, SNCS, REV, SCS, PWLS and LLAE were examined, refers to, to a great extent, the sequence of these procedures determined in this research. The ranking of researched procedures only partially overlaps with the rankings determined in (Lin 2007) and (Choo and Wedley 2004), but in the papers the reference criterion was only the mean absolute deviation. Moreover, they were conducted on $n = 6$ matrices which were always generated on the basis of the same reference vector. The conclusion of this research is that the mean absolute deviation is not closely related to the number of errors in a preference vector determined by a given procedure. What is more, on the basis of Scenario 2 and the PWLAE one can state that even a procedure which could be characterized in the research as the best value of the mean absolute deviation can generate in the research much worse preference vectors compared to other procedures. An interesting direction of future work is the development of an ontology (Ziemba et al. 2015a, b; Wątróbski and Jankowski 2015) about the preferences aggregation procedures and to build and maintain a repository of AHP and ANP methods.

References

Abu-Sarhan Z (2011) Application of analytic hierarchy process (AHP) in the evaluation and selection of an information system reengineering projects. Int J Comput Sci Netw Secur 11 (1):172–177

Agha SR (2011) Multi-stakeholder industrial projects selection: an analytic hierarchy process and zero-one goal programming approach. Proceedings of the 41st international conference on computers and industrial engineering

Al-Subhi Al-Harbi KM (2001) Application of the AHP in project management. Int J Proj Manag 19(1):19–27

Arbel A, Orgler YE (1990) An application of the AHP to bank strategic planning: the mergers and acquisitions process. Eur J Oper Res 48(1):27–37

Babic Z, Plazibat N (1998) Ranking of enterprisees based on multicriteria analysis. Int J Prod Econ 56(7):29–35

Bajwa G, Choo EU, Wedley WC (2008) Effectiveness analysis of deriving priority vectors from reciprocal pairwise comparison matrices. Asia Pac J Oper Res 25(3):279–299

Bertolini M, Bevilacqua M (2006) A combined goal programming – AHP approach to maintenance selection problem. Reliab Eng Syst Saf 91:839–848

Bhattarai S, Yadav SR (2009) AHP Application in banking: unfolding utility in a situation of financial crisis. Proceedings of the international symposium on the analytic hierarchy process, ISAHP2013

Blankmeyer E (1987) Approaches to consistency adjustment. J Optim Theor Appl 54(3):479–488

Bozóki S, Lewis RH (2005) Solving the least squares method problem in the AHP for 3×3 and 4×4 matrices. Cent Eur J Oper Res 13(3):255–270

Chen MK, Wanh SC (2010) The critical factors of success for information service industry in developing international market: using analytic hierarchy process (AHP) approach. Expert Syst Appl 37(1):694–704

Chin KS, Xu DL, Yang JB, Lam JPK (2008) Group-based ER-AHP system for product project screening. Expert Syst Appl 35(4):1909–1929

Choo EU, Wedley WC (2004) A common framework for deriving preference values from pairwise comparison matrices. Comput Oper Res 31(6):893–908

Ehie I, Benjamin C, Omurtag Y, Clarke L (1990) Prioritizing development goals in low-income developing countries. Omega 18(2):185–194

Garcia F, Guijarro F, Moya I (2010) A goal programming approach to estimating performance weights for ranking firms. Comput Oper Res 37:1597–1609

Golany B, Kress M (1993) A multicriteria evaluation of methods for obtaining weights from ratio-scale matrices. Eur J Oper Res 69(2):210–220

Hulle J, Kaspar R, Moller K (2011) Multiple criteria decision-making in management accounting and control – state of the art and research perspectives based on a bibliometric study. J Multi-Criteria Decis Anal 18(5-6):253–265

Ishizaka A, Labib A (2009) Analytic hierarchy process and expert choice: benefits and limitations. OR Insight 22(4):201–220

Ishizaka A, Labib A (2011a) Review of the main developments in the analytic hierarchy process. Expert Syst Appl 38(11):14336–14345

Ishizaka A, Labib A (2011b) Selection of new production facilities with the group analytic hierarchy process ordering method. Expert Syst Appl 38(6):7317–7325

Ishizaka A, Lusti M (2006) How to derive priorities in AHP: a comparative study. Cent Eur J Oper Res 14(4):387–400

Jankowski J, Watrobski J, Piwowarski M (2011) Fuzzy modeling of digital products pricing in the virtual marketplace. In: Proceedings of 6th international conference on hybrid artificial intelligent systems. Lecture notes in computer science, vol. 6678, Springer, Heidelberg, pp. 338–346

Jankowski J, Wątróbski J, Ziemba P (2015) Modeling the impact of visual components on verbal communication in online advertising. Lect Notes Comput Sci 9330:44–53

Kim J (1998) Hierarchical structure of intranet functions and their relative importance: using the analytic hierarchy process for virtual organizations. Decis Support Syst 23(1):59–74

Kivijarvi H, Tuominen M (1992) A decision support system for semistructured strategic decisions: a multi – tool method for evaluating intangible investments. J Decis Syst 1(4):353–376

Laininen P, Hamalainen RP (2003) Analyzing AHP-martices by regression. Eur J Oper Res 148 (3):514–524

Lee H, Kwak W, Han I (1995) Developing a business performance evaluation system: an analytic hierarchical model. Eng Economist 30(4):343–357

Lin C (2007) A revised framework for deriving preference values from pairwise comparison matrices. Eur J Oper Res 176(2):1145–1150

Lin MI, Lee YD, Ho TN (2011) Applying integrated DEA/AHP to evaluate the economic performance of local governments in China. Eur J Oper Res 209(2):129–140

Muata K, Bryson O (2006) An action learning approach for assessing the consistency of pairwise comparison data. Eur J Oper Res 174:234–244

Onder E, Dogan A (2013) Ranking the strategies of human resource management during economic crisis period using analytic hierarchy process. Adv Manag Appl Econ 3(5):57–72
Pham-Gia T, Hung TL (2001) The mean and median absolute deviations. Math Comput Model 34 (7-8):921–936
Piegat A, Sałabun W (2014) Identification of a multicriteria decision-making model using the characteristic objects method. Appl Comput Intell Soft Comput 2014:536492:1–536492:14
Piegat A, Sałabun W (2015) Comparative analysis of MCDM methods for assessing the severity of chronic liver disease. Lect Notes Comput Sci 9119:228–238
Rivza P, Rivza B, Rivza J, Bikse V (2009) Using AHP for the evaluation of the economic stabilization program in Latvia. Proceedings of the international symposium on the analytic hierarchy process, ISAHP2009
Saaty TL (1980) The analytic hierarchy process: planning, priority setting, resource allocation. McGraw-Hill International Book Co., New York
Saaty TL (1990) How to make a decision: the analytic hierarchy process. Eur J Oper Res 48:9–26
Saaty TL (1998) Ranking by eigenvector versus other methods in the analytic hierarchy process. Appl Math Lett 11(4):121–125
Saaty TL (2004) Decision making – the analytic hierarchy and network processes (AHP/ANP). J Syst Sci Syst Eng 13(1):1–35
Saaty TL (2005a) Making and validating complex decisions with the AHP/ANP. J Syst Sci Syst Eng 14(1):1–36
Saaty TL (2005b) The analytic hierarchy and analytic network process for the measurement of intangible criteria and for decision-making. In: Figueira J, Greco S, Ehrgott M (eds) Multiple criteria decision analysis: state of the art surveys. Springer, Boston, pp 345–407
Saaty TL (2008) Decision making with the analytic hierarchy process. Int J Serv Sci 1(1):83–98
Saaty TL (2010) Economic forecasting with tangible and intangible criteria: the analytic hierarchy process of measurement and its validation. Ekonomski Horizonti 12(1):5–45
Saaty TL, Ozdemir MS (2003) Why the magic number seven plus or minus two. Math Comput Model 38(3-4):233–244
Saaty TL, Peniwati K, Shang JS (2007) The analytic hierarchy process and human resource allocation: half the story. Math Comput Model 46(7–8):1041–1053
Saaty TL, Rogers PC, Pell R (1980) Portfolio selection through hierarchies. J Portfolio Manage 6 (3):16–21
Saaty TL, Vargas LG (2011) The possibility of group choice: pairwise comparisons and merging functions. Soc Choice Welfare 38(3):481–496
Saaty TL, Vargas LG, Dellmann K (2003) The allocation of intangible resources: the analytic hierarchy process and linear programming. Socioecon Plann Sci 37(3):169–184
Sałabun W (2012) The use of fuzzy logic to evaluate the nonlinearity of human multi-criteria used in decision making. Electr Rev 88(10b):235–238
Sharma MJ, Moon I, Bae H (2008) Analytic hierarchy process to assess and optimize distribution network. Appl Math Comput 202(1):256–265
Srinivasan V, Ruparel B (1990) CGX: an expert support system for credit granting. Eur J Oper Res 45(2–3):293–308
Sum RM (2013) Risk management decision making. Proceedings of the international symposium on the analytic hierarchy process, ISAHP2013
Szczypińska A, Piotrowski EW (2009) Inconsistency of the judgment matrix in the AHP method and the decision maker's knowledge. Phys A Stat Mech Appl 388(6):907–915
Tsyganok V (2010) Investigation of the aggregation effectiveness of expert estimates obtained by the pairwise comparison method. Math Comput Model 52:538–544
Ulengin F, Ulengin B (1994) Forecasting foreign exchange rates: a comparative evaluation of AHP. Omega 22(5):505–519
Vaidya OS, Kumar S (2006) Analytic hierarchy process: an overviews of applications. Eur J Oper Res 169(1):1–29

Wang Y, Chin K (2009) A new data envelopment analysis method for priority determination and group decision making in the analytic hierarchy process. Eur J Oper Res 195:239–250

Wątróbski J, Jankowski J, Piotrowski Z (2014) The selection of multicriteria method based on unstructured decision problem description. In: ICCCI 2014. Lecture notes in artificial intelligence, vol. 8733, Springer, Heidelberg, pp. 454–465

Wątróbski J, Jankowski J (2016) Guideline for MCDA method selection in production management area. In: Różewski P, Novikov D, Bakhtadze N, Zaikin O (eds) New frontiers in information and production systems modelling and analysis, vol 98, Intelligent systems reference library. Springer, Heidelberg, doi: 978-3-319-23337-6

Wątróbski J, Jankowski J (2015) Knowledge management in MCDA domain. In: Proceedings of the federated conference on computer science and information systems, pp. 1455–1460. IEEE Digital Library, doi: 10.15439/2015F295

Wątróbski J, Ziemba P, Wolski W (2015) Methodological aspects of decision support system for the location of renewable energy sources. In: Proceedings of the federated conference on computer science and information systems, pp. 1461–1469. IEEE Digital Library, doi: 10.15439/2015F294

Wei CC, Chien CF, Wang MJJ (2005) An AHP-based approach to ERP system selection. Int J Prod Econ 96(1):47–62

Wu W, Kou G, Peng Y, Ergu D (2012) Improved AHP-group decision making for investment strategy selection. Technol Econ Dev Econ 18(2):299–316

Zakaria NF, Dahlan HM, Hussin AR (2010) Deriving priority in AHP using evolutionary computing approach. WSEAS Trans Inform Sci Appl 7(5):714–724

Ziemba P, Piwowarski M, Jankowski J, Wątróbski J (2014) Method of criteria selection and weights calculation in the process of web projects evaluation. In: ICCCI 2014. Lecture notes in computer science (lecture notes in artificial intelligence), vol. 8733, Springer, Heidelberg, pp. 684–693

Ziemba P, Jankowski J, Wątróbski J, Becker J (2015a) Knowledge management in website quality evaluation domain. In: Nunez M et al (eds) ICCCI 2015, part II, lecture notes in computer science (lecture notes in artificial intelligence), vol 9330. Springer, Heidelberg, pp 75–85

Ziemba P, Jankowski J, Wątróbski J, Wolski W, Becker J (2015b) Integration of domain ontologies in the repository of website evaluation methods. In: Proceedings of the federated conference on computer science and information systems, pp. 1601–1610. IEEE Digital Library, doi: 10.15439/2015F297

Chapter 16
Neural Networks in Economic Problems

Wojciech Sałabun and Marcin Pietrzykowski

Abstract In most of experimental research, we generally need to solve a problem of classification, regression or time-series forecasting. On the other hand, artificial neural networks are universal and highly flexible function approximators. Neural networks are primarily used in the fields of cognitive science and engineering. In recent years, the use of neural network applications in economics has dramatically increased. Today, neural networks are a basic tool in experimental economics. However, the large number of parameters that must be selected to develop a neural network model has meant that the design process still involves much effort. The objective of this chapter is to provide a practical introductory guide in the design of a neural network for solving problems in experimental economics. Our proposed procedure to design a neural network to solve economic experiments uses Matlab® environment. The approach is explained, and the chapter includes a discussion of trade-offs in parameter selection, as well as some common pitfalls.

Keywords Neural networks • Economics

16.1 Introduction

Artificial neural networks are key features of a significant family of techniques for numerical learning. They are used to support a experimental research, i.e. in solving classification, regression and time-series forecasting problems. Neural networks consist of many computational elements (neurons) that form the network nodes, linked by weighted interconnections. This structure is analogous to neurological systems in animals, though artificial neural networks are much simpler than biological ones (Hopgood 2011; Rojas 2013). However, artificial neural networks can approximate any non-linear function so long as their structure is properly specified

W. Sałabun (✉) • M. Pietrzykowski
Department of Artificial Intelligence Methods and Applied Mathematics, Faculty of Computer Science and Information Technology, West Pomeranian University of Technology Szczecin, Żołnierska 49, Szczecin 71-210, Poland
e-mail: wsalabun@wi.zut.edu.pl; mpietrzykowski@wi.zut.edu.pl

K. Nermend, M. Łatuszyńska (eds.), *Selected Issues in Experimental Economics*, Springer Proceedings in Business and Economics, DOI 10.1007/978-3-319-28419-4_16

(Tkacz and Hu 1999). Therefore, it is necessary to develop a method of designing a properly specified artificial neural network for use in experimental economics.

Artificial neural networks can be used to solve a wide variety of tasks that are hard to solve using classical methods, e.g. the design of conversion oriented websites problem (Jankowski 2013, 2015; Ziemba et al. 2014, 2015a, b). Nowadays, regression, classification and time-series forecasting are the most important and typical tasks that use artificial neural network in experimental economics (Aminian et al. 2006; Bahrammirzaee 2010; Chen and Wang 2004; Nguyen and Cripps 2001). In this area, artificial neural networks are used for bankruptcy or crisis prediction (Alfaro et al. 2008; Charalambous et al. 2000; Kim et al. 2004), credit rating analysis (Angelini et al. 2008; Hajek 2011; Huang et al. 2004; Lee and Chen 2005), optimization (Azadeh et al. 2015; Ghiassi et al. 2006; Kalogirou 2004; Rafiei et al. 2011), sales forecasting (Thomassey and Happiette 2007), price or cost estimation (Parisi et al. 2008; Selim 2009; Verlinden et al. 2008) and forecasting different time series (Ghiassi et al. 2005; Hamzacebi 2008; Hamzacebi et al. 2009; Huarng and Yu 2006; Khashei and Bijari 2011, 2010; Khashei et al. 2008; Kim 2003; Palmer et al. 2006; Zhang and Qi 2005; Zhang et al. 2001).

In this chapter, the authors present a practical introductory guide to the design of a neural network for solving the tasks mentioned above. Of the available types of artificial neural networks, the perceptron algorithm for classification tasks, feed forward neural network for regression, and the recurrent artificial neural network for forecasting time series are used. Of course, there are other artificial networks and methods for learning them, e.g. self-organizing maps, the Hopfield network, and others. These specific networks are developed for specific problems.

The rest of the chapter is organized as follows. Section 16.2 provides a brief introduction on classification, regression and forecasting time series task with a simple example of using artificial neural networks. Section 16.3 describes three economic case studies. Finally, Sect. 16.4 presents concluding remarks.

16.2 Theory Preliminaries of Neural Networks

In this section, we describe the three most common tasks that can be solved by neural networks: classification, regression and time series.

16.2.1 Classification Task

In statistics and machine learning, classification is the task of identifying to which set of classes (categories) a new observation (sample) belongs. We classify new data on the basis of a training set of data that contains samples whose class (category) membership is known. An example would be patient classification into "healthy" or "ill" classes by observed characteristics of the patient (temperature, blood pressure, erythrocyte sedimentation rate etc.). In economics, we can use classifications such as the task of credit approval, where we assign the customer to the "low credit risk", "medium credit risk" or "high credit risk" class. The single sample can be described by several different data types:

- Categorical (e.g. "A", "B", "AB" or "O" for blood type),
- Ordinal (e.g. "large", "medium" or "small"),
- Integer-valued; or
- Real-values.

For simple data classification, we can use perceptron, which is an algorithm for the supervised learning of binary classifiers. In the context of neural networks, a perceptron is a single artificial neuron with a step activation function. Figure 16.1 shows a perceptron diagram. Perceptron can be described by the following equation:

$$
\begin{aligned}
y &= f(s) \\
s &= \sum_{i=1}^{n} w_i x_i + w_0 \\
f(s) &= \begin{cases} 1, & \text{if } s > 0 \\ -1, & \text{if } s \le 0 \end{cases}
\end{aligned}
\tag{16.1}
$$

Perceptron can take only two different output values. It is determined by the activation function. It means that the perceptron can assign input data to only two different classes. This algorithm is simple and can only classify the data that is linearly separable (i.e. there is a linear border between two classes). This situation is caused by the fact that perceptron is able to find the plane (hyperplane in multidimensional space) that divides the whole input space into two half-spaces. This plane is called *the decision border*. In situations when we have only two inputs x_1, x_2 the decision border is described by the straight line:

$$w_0 + w_1 x_1 + w_2 x_2 = 0 \tag{16.2}$$

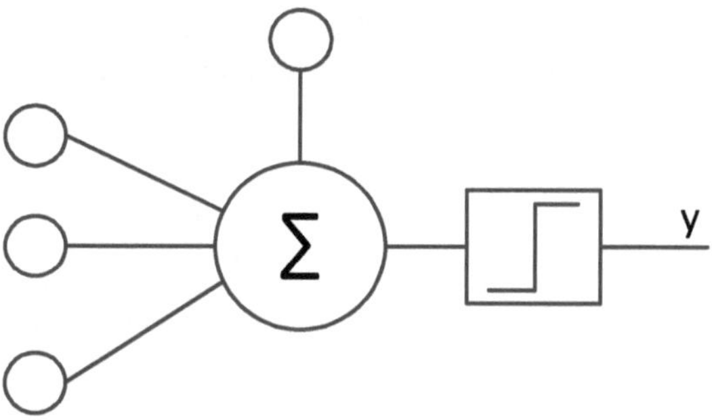

Fig. 16.1 Perceptron diagram

Which we can write as:

$$x_2 = -\frac{w_1}{w_2} \times x_1 - \frac{w_0}{w_2} \tag{16.3}$$

The perceptron is able to learn. In this process, its weights (w_i) are modified. Its learning method belongs to the group of supervised learning methods. This means that the training data consists of a set of training examples. In supervised learning, each example is a pair consisting of an input value and the desired output value. The learning algorithm modifies the weights in to minimize the error between the desired and the obtained output value. The perceptron learning algorithm is as follows:

1. Initialize weights with random values.
2. Apply the vector $x = [x_1, \ldots, x_n]$ to the neuron and compute the answer of the neuron.
3. Compare the desired value y_i with the neuron answer $f(x)$.
4. Change the weights if the neuron answer is different from the expected value according to the formula $w_i(t+1) = w_i(t) + y_i(x_i(t))$.
5. Return to step 2.

This algorithm is repeated until the error for all input vectors is less than a user-specified error threshold (or a predetermined number of iterations have been completed).

Table 16.1 shows a very simple example in Matlab® code using the Neural Network Toolbox™. The code creates learning data containing 100 samples divided into two classes. These two classes are clearly linearly separable. Then the perceptron is used to find the decision border between classes. Of course this is a very simple example but it gives us a view as to how the single artificial neuron works and the general idea of classification. More complex problems of classification must be solved with multilayer artificial neural networks. A real-world example is shown in the next section of this chapter.

16.2.2 Regression

In statistics, regression analysis is a process for estimating relationships among variables. It tries to find the relationship between a dependent variable (output) and one or more independent variables (inputs). In other words, regression analysis is

Table 16.1 Perceptron code

```
x=[rand(100,1); 0.45*rand(50,1), 0.55+0.45*rand(50,1)];
t=[−1 * ones(50, 1), ones(50, 1)];
net=perceptron;
net=train(net,x,t);
view(net);
y=net(x);
```

used to understand how the value of the dependent variable changes when any one of the independent variables varies. An example would be relationship between the unemployment rate in Poland (dependent variable) and independent variables: inflation rate, minimum wage, and a number of pensioners. To estimate this kind of relationship, we have at our disposal a finite number of learning samples that we use to try to identify (to approximate) the real dependence $y = f(x_1, \ldots, x_n)$ existing in the system. When we know this kind of dependency we can try to answer a simple question such as "What does the unemployment rate in Poland amount to when the inflation rate amounts to 3 % minimum wage to 1500 zł, and number of pensioners to 7.9 million people?"

For a simple example of function approximation and data regression we use a simple neural network with one hidden layer. Multilayer neural networks are built with neurons placed in two or more layers, and connected in specified way. A diagram representing a multilayer neural network is shown in Fig. 16.2.

Usually, input and hidden layers contain sigmoid neurons. It works similar to a perceptron but the activation function is different. It can be an unipolar function which takes a value from the range [0; 1]:

$$f(x) = \frac{1}{1 + e^{-\beta x}} \tag{16.4}$$

Or it can be bipolar which takes a value from the range [−1; 1]

$$f(x) = \frac{1 - e^{\beta x}}{1 + e^{-\beta x}} \tag{16.5}$$

A sigmoid neuron is shown in Fig. 16.3. Usually an output layer neural network has neurons with linear activation functions. If the network contains only two layers then the input layer is considered the hidden layer. In this kind of structure, a signal is only pushed forward between particular layers. Neurons that belong to the same layer do not have connections between each other. The signal is simply transmitted from input to output. In the literature, this type of network is commonly known as *a feed forward neural network*.

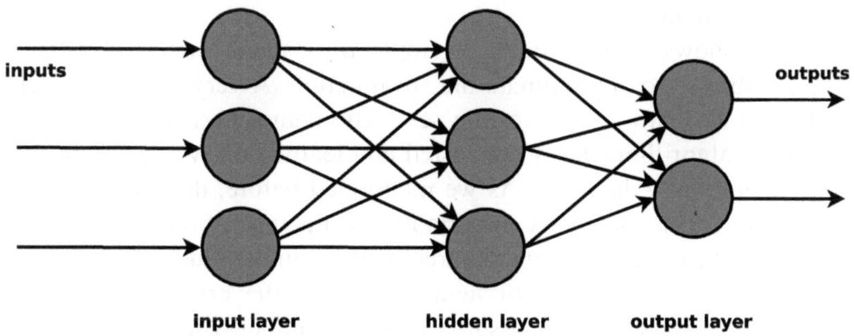

Fig. 16.2 Feed forward neural network diagram

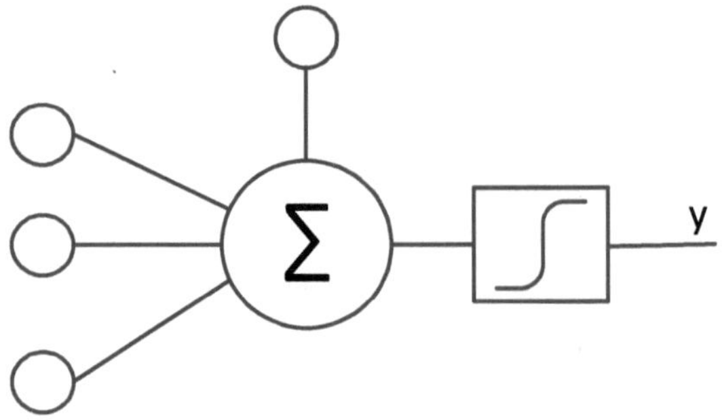

Fig. 16.3 Sigmoid neuron diagram

Backpropagation algorithm is the most common method of training artificial neural networks. It is an abbreviation for "backward propagation of errors". There are several modification of this algorithm: backpropagation with momentum (Leung et al. 2003; Zhang et al. 2014), Levenberg–Marquardt algorithm (Chan et al. 2012; Dahoe et al. 2013; Shawash and Selviah 2013), resilient backpropagation (Pattanayak and Nandi 2013; Prasad et al. 2013), quick-propagation (Banerjee et al. 2011) etc. This method belongs to the supervised learning methods. Some of these variations, like backpropagation in the basic version, are *online training* algorithms. This means that we learn the network by correcting neuron weights for every single sample that becomes available. The second type of learning is *batch learning*. Changes are not applied immediately after every training example, but instead aggregated over all training examples. Only at the end of a learning epoch (i.e. after all training samples have been traversed), the aggregated changes are applied. Then the training examples are traversed again until the error vanishes or reaches an acceptable level. An example of this type of methods is the resilient backpropagation algorithm.

The number of neurons in particular layers is very important. This value depends on the problem we would like to solve. If the number of neurons is too high, this extends the amount of time required for the learning process. Moreover, if the number of samples is too small in comparison to the number of neurons, the network can be over-learned (over-fitted). This kind of network fits the training data very well but it loses its ability to generalize its knowledge, and thus performs poorly with new data.

Table 16.2 shows a very simple example in Matlab® code using the Neural Network Toolbox™ to approximate the sin function. A very important step is the data division into learning and testing sets. The neural network, similar to other approximation algorithms, has to be tested and learned on two different data sets. Thus we generate two data sets. As we mentioned before, the number of neurons inside the neural network is very important. For this type of data network, the best results are achieved when it contains three neurons in the hidden layer. Table 16.3 demonstrates how the number of neurons affects the error committed by the network. Figure 16.4 shows the result when the number of neurons is too low or too high.

Table 16.2 Matlab code of sin function approximation

```
x_learn=linspace(0,2*pi,10);
y_learn=sin(x_learn);
x_test=2*pi*rand(1, 10);
y_test=sin(x_test);
net=feedforwardnet(3);
net=train(net,x_learn,y_learn);
net.divideFcn='';
net.trainParam.epochs=5;
view(net)
y=net(x_test);
perf=perform(net, y, y_test); %print neural network response
x=0:0.05:2*pi;
y=net(x);
plot(x,y);
```

Table 16.3 Error of networks with different numbers of neurons in hidden layer

No. of neurons	1	2	3	4	5	6	7
Error	0.086	0.076	0.000	0.017	0.001	0.005	0.009

16.2.3 Time-Series Forecasting

A time series is a sequence of data points that comes from successive measurements made over a time interval. Time series are used in many scientific areas: statistics, signal processing, mathematical finance, econometrics and many other areas. Time-series forecasting tries to predict future values based on previously observed values. A strictly economic example is stock price forecasting. In this example, we try to model the future price of a particular stock based on the price history and other factors like economic indicators, other stocks values, and stock market indices. This example is extended in the next section of this chapter. This kind of example is very complex and very difficult to implement. We start from a simpler task with one input and one output. As an example we use the data collected from the magnetic levitation system. The system consists of an electromagnet and a permanent magnet. If the electromagnet is supplied by electrical power the permanent magnet is repelled. The level of the voltage indicates the repulse force, and thus the location. If the repulse force is too weak, then the permanent magnet will fall on the electromagnet. The input data is a voltage applied to the electromagnet, and the output is the position of the permanent magnet. The data was collected at a sampling interval of 0.01 s to form two time series.

For a time-series task we use nonlinear autoregressive neural network with external input (NARX). This is a recurrent dynamic network with feedback connections enclosing several layers of the network. The equation for the NARX model is defined as: $y(t) = f(y(t-1),\ldots,y(t-n_y),u(t-1),\ldots,u(t-n))$. We can see that the next value of the dependent output signal $y(t)$ is regressed on previous values of the output signal and previous values of an independent

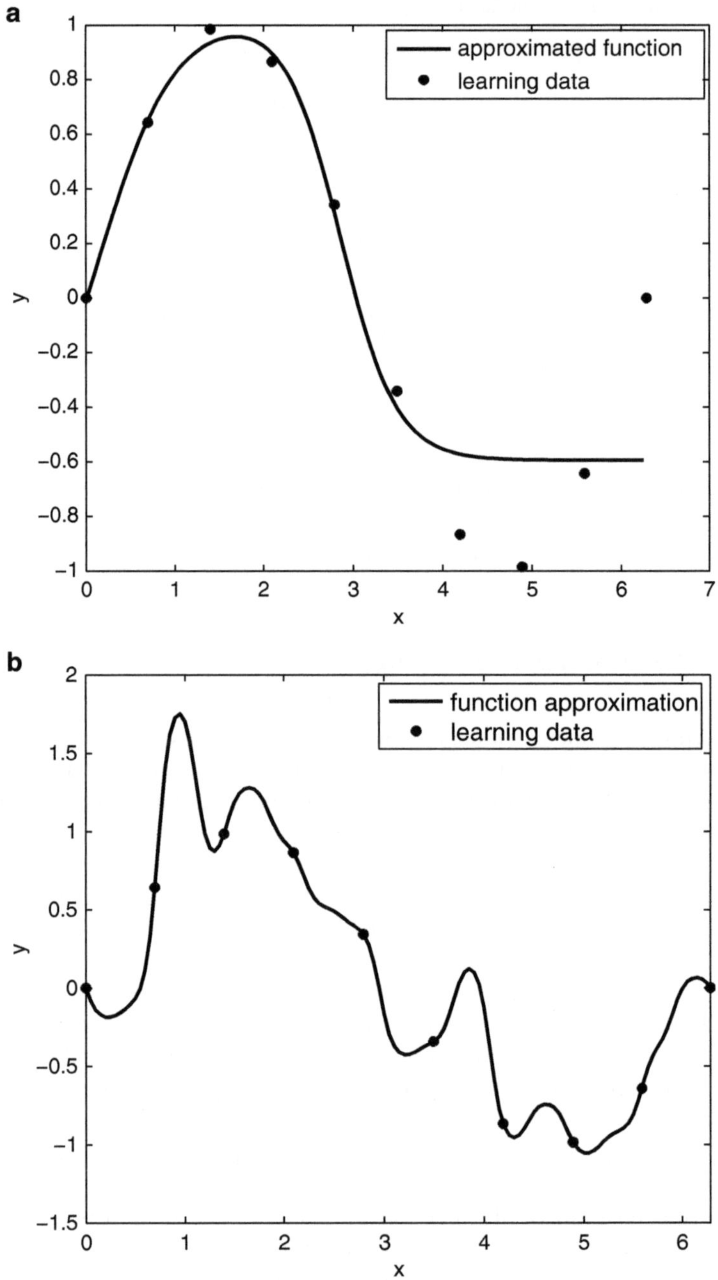

Fig. 16.4 Effect of too few neurons (*left*) and too many neurons (*right*) in the neural network

input signal. This type of architecture we can call Series-Parallel Architecture. We can use this architecture because the true output is available during the training of the network. It has two advantages: the input to the feedforward network is more accurate, and a network with feedforward architecture can be trained with a backpropagation algorithm. We have also a second type of architecture, Parallel Architecture. We use it in a situation in which we would like to forecast the data that is many-steps ahead but we simply do not have future data and thus we have to use an estimated output. Figure 16.5 shows the differences between these two architecture types.

Table 16.4 shows the Matlab code of learning NARX network. Figure 16.6 shows the network response and error. In line 20 we "close the loop", which

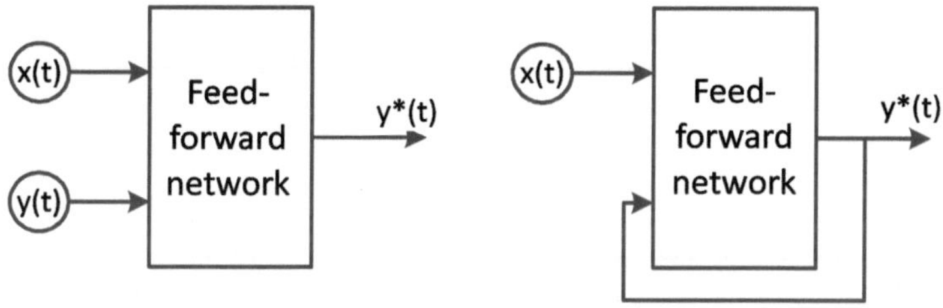

Fig. 16.5 Differences between series-parallel architecture (*left*) and parallel architecture (*right*)

Table 16.4 Matlab code of learning NARX network

```
1:  load magdata
2:  y=con2seq(y);
3:  u=con2seq(u);
4:  %Create the series-parallel NARX network;
5:  narx_net=narxnet([1:2],[1:2],10);
6:  narx_net.divideFcn='';
7:  narx_net.trainParam.min_grad=1e-10;
8:  [p,Pi,Ai,t]=preparets(narx_net,u,{},y);
9:  narx_net=train(narx_net,p,t,Pi); % training
10: %simulate the network and plot the resulting errors for the series-parallel implementation.
11: yp=sim(narx_net,p,Pi);
12: e=cell2mat(yp)-cell2mat(t);
13: plot(e)
14: %converting networks from the series-parallel configuration (open loop), to the parallel
15: configuration (closed loop)
16: narx_net_closed=closeloop(narx_net);
17: view(narx_net)
18: view(narx_net_closed)
19: y1=y(1700:2600);
20: u1=u(1700:2600);
21: [p1,Pi1,Ai1,t1]=preparets(narx_net_closed,u1,{},y1);
22: yp1=narx_net_closed(p1,Pi1,Ai1);
23: TS=size(t1,2);
24: plot(1:TS,cell2mat(t1),'b',1:TS,cell2mat(yp1),'r')
25:
```

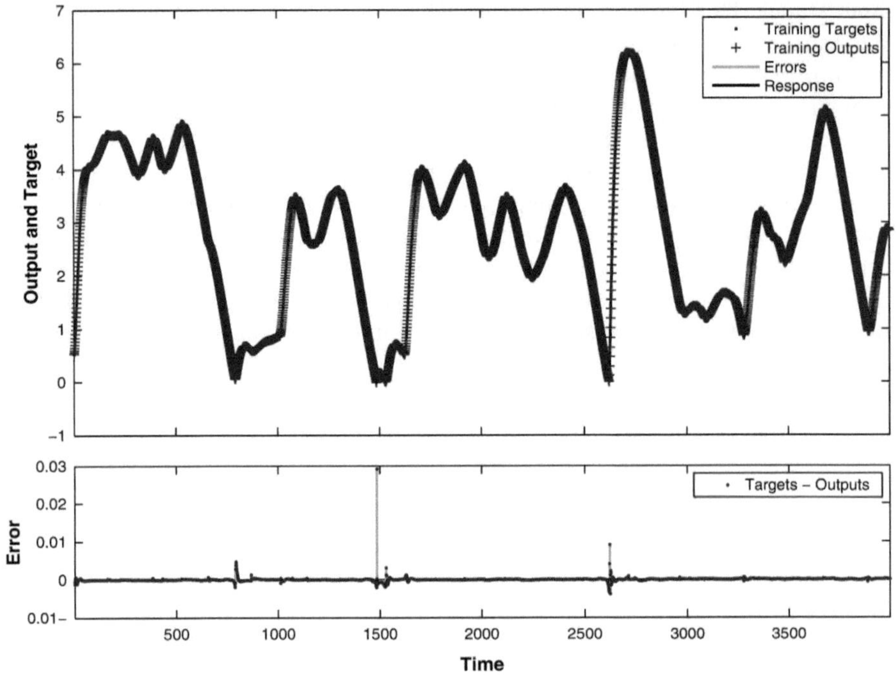

Fig. 16.6 Network response for time-series data

means that we change the architecture from series-parallel into parallel. In Fig. 16.7 we can see the estimated output of the system. As we can see, the network response is quite accurate. This system is quite simple, as we have only one input and one output. The dependency between input and output can be pretty well described with physical laws and mathematical equations. Unfortunately, for more complex tasks like stock price forecasting the response of the network would not be so ideal. This is caused by the fact that we have more inputs and we do not critical information about these factors (e.g. because they are unavailable). In our code, the function *preparets* is very important. It prepares the dataset according to the neural net structure. For example, if our neural network uses output data from three previous time moments as an input, then we have to prepare our input datasets by adding to them the output information. Moreover, we have to perform a "time-shifting" of a three time unit in our data because we are unable learn our network with the inputs from first three time moments. We simply do not have information about the earlier outputs of the system (i.e. those that occurred before the starting point).

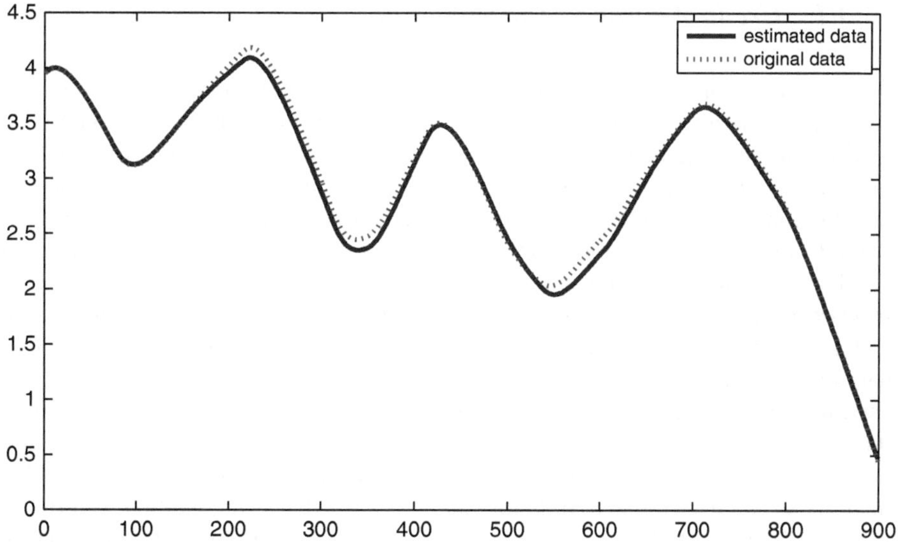

Fig. 16.7 Estimated output of the system in "close-loop"

16.3 Economic Case Studies

In this section we provide three examples of using neural networks on real world datasets. All datasets were taken from the *UCI Machine Learning repository*. Similar to the previous simple examples, we use Matlab® and Neural Network Toolbox™. After taking the dataset from the repository, we have to remember to perform preliminary preparations of the data. We need to encode categorical attributes in the data. Sometimes, normalization of the numeric data into the range [0, 1] or [−1, 1] is also necessary. In theory, it is not necessary to normalize numeric input data. However, practice has shown that when numeric values are normalized, neural network training is often more efficient, which leads to better predictions. Because neural networks natively process numeric data, categorical data like sex or location type must be encoded as numeric values. For example, one possibility for sex is to encode male as 0 and female as 1. A more difficult situation is when data has three or more possible values, as happens with a variable like location which we can have three different values: city, suburban, countryside. In this case, we can use dummy encoding by creating three new attributes: city (1, 0, 0), suburban (0, 1, 0), countryside (0, 0, 1). In our scripts, we use proceeded data. Using Matlab, the user can work with graphical tools like *nnstart, nprtool* etc., but in our examples we show the Matlab code.

16.3.1 Credit Approval: Classification

We have data from credit card applications. We would like to design a network that can classify the bank client's solvency, given 15 pieces of client information. In this data set, all attribute names and values have been changed to meaningless symbols in order to protect the confidentiality of the data. In our example, this lack of information is of secondary importance. This dataset is interesting because there is a good mix of attributes: continuous, nominal with small numbers of values, and nominal with larger numbers of values. For a classification we use a two-layer feed-forward network, with sigmoid hidden and output neurons (*patternet* in Matlab code). The network is trained with scaled conjugate gradient propagation. Our dataset is divided into three groups. First, there is a training set, or a set of examples used for learning (i.e. to fit the neural network to the specified problem). Second, there is validation set, namely a set of examples used to tune the parameters of a neural network. We use the validation set to find the "optimal" number of hidden neurons or to determine a stopping point for the back-propagation algorithm. Finally, there is a test set, or a set of examples used only to assess the performance of a fully-trained neural network. We use the test set to estimate the error rate after we have chosen the final model (i.e. network size and actual weights).

After the learning process we can see two interesting plots that represent how the network works. In Fig. 16.8, we can see the network performance over the learning

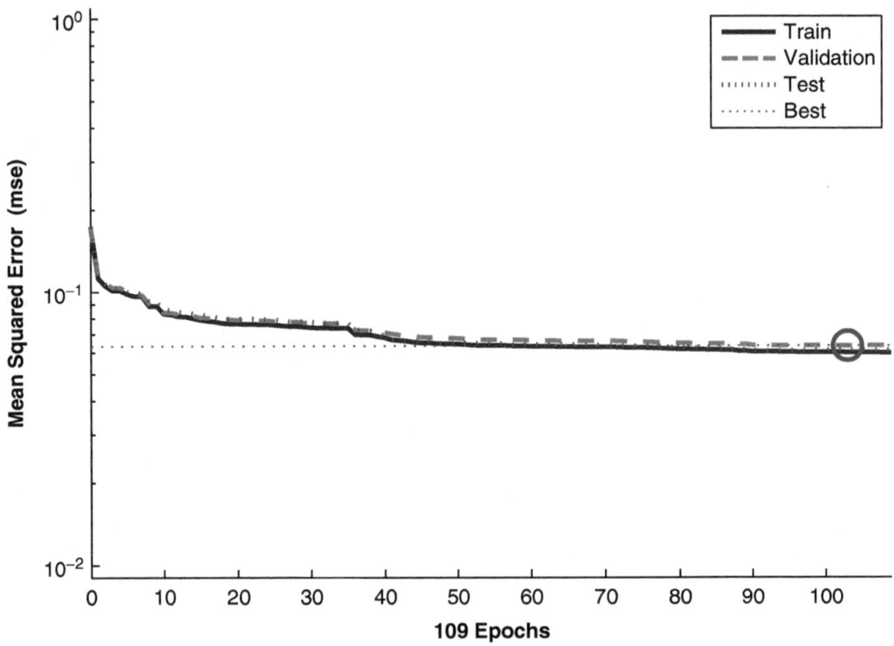

Fig. 16.8 Network performance over learning epoch

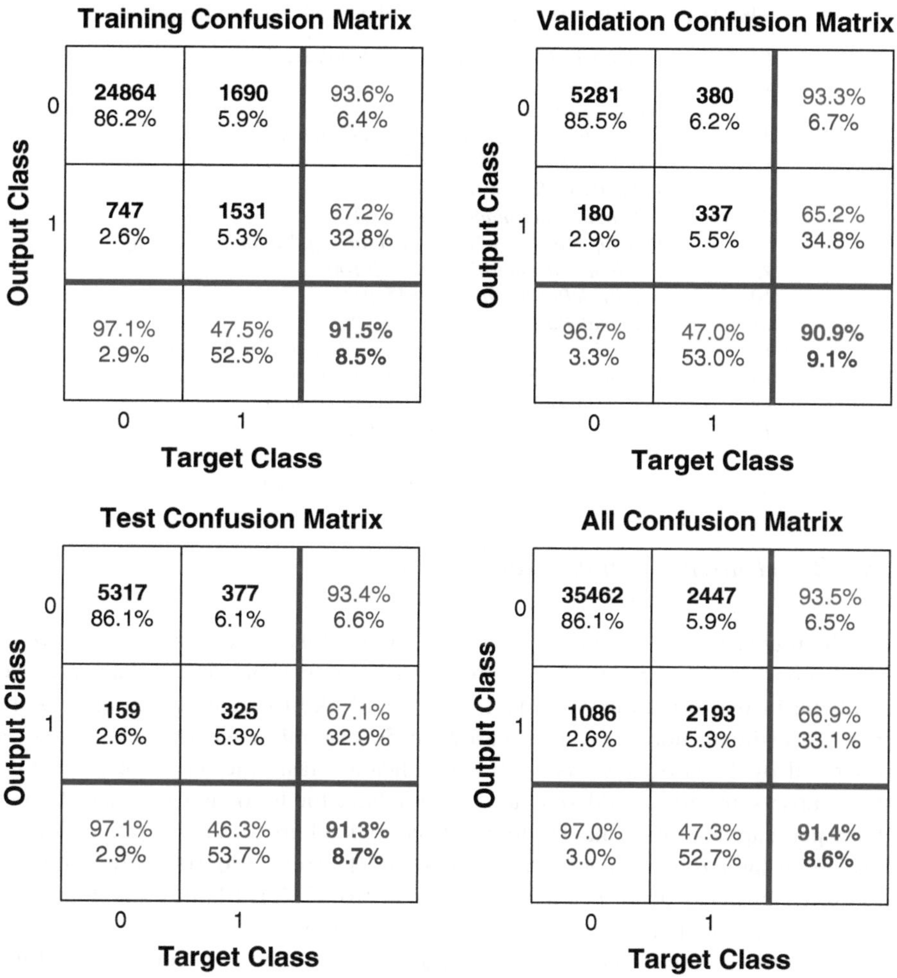

Fig. 16.9 Confusion matrix

epochs. The learning line constantly tends to zero, because the neural network has been trying to learn the learning samples. We have to find the moment in which the network begins to over-learn (over-fit the data). We can find this moment by analyzing the validation trend line. In the moment when the validation trend line starts to constantly increase, this means that the neural network has lost its ability to generalize and has started to memorize only the learning samples. The second very important figure (Fig. 16.9) shows us the confusion matrix for all three sets. It presents to us how many samples were properly classified. We can see that in test dataset 89.8 % of samples were properly classified. We have to remember that training multiple times will generate different results due to different initial conditions and sampling (Table 16.5).

Table 16.5 Matlab code of learning neural network for credit approval

```
load bank_data; % load file with dataset
inputs=data(:, 1:end-1)';
outputs=data(:, end)';
% Create a Pattern Recognition Network
% for hiddenLayerSize=5:1:25
hiddenLayerSize=10;
net=patternnet(hiddenLayerSize);
% setup Division of Data for Training, Validation, Testing
net.divideParam.trainRatio=70/100;
net.divideParam.valRatio=15/100;-
net.divideParam.testRatio=15/100;
[net,tr]=train(net,inputs,targets); % train the Network
outputs=net(inputs); % test the Network
performance=perform(net,targets,outputs)
view(net) % view the Network Diagram
figure, plotperform(tr) %plot
figure, plotconfusion(targets,outputs) %plot
```

16.3.2 Housing Values: Regression

For the regression task, we have data from the *UCI machine learning repository*, which concerns housing values in the suburbs of Boston. These data are also available in the Matlab environment. We would like to create a neural network that can estimate housing values based on 506 samples, where each sample is described by 14 attributes. As in the classification task, the data is divided into three subsets: training, validation and test. We have the following 13 types of input data: per capita crime rate by town (from 0.0063 to 88.9762), proportion of residential land zoned for lots over 25,000 sq. ft. (from 0 to 100), proportion of non-retail business acres per town (from 0.46 to 27.74), Charles River dummy variable (1 if tract bounds river; 0 otherwise), nitric oxides concentration (in parts per 10 million; from 0.3850 to 0.8710), average number of rooms per dwelling (from 3.5610 to 8.7800), proportion of owner-occupied units built prior to 1940 (from 2.9 to 100), weighted distances to five Boston employment centres (from 1.1296 to 12.1265), index of accessibility to radial highways (from 1 to 24), full-value property-tax rate per \$10,000 (from 187 to 711), pupil-teacher ratio by town (from 12.60 to 22.00), 1000 $(Bk—0.63)^2$ where Bk is the proportion of blacks by town (from 0.32 to 396.9), lower status of the population (from 1.73 to 37.97). As we can see these input variables have a wide variety of range values. The output means the median value of owner-occupied homes in the \$1000s (from 5 to 50).

The Matlab code, which creates and learns a fitting neural network, is presented in Table 16.6. As the result of running this code, we obtain a regression model and two figures. Figure 16.10 presents the network performance over the learning epoch, where the best validation performance is 7.6513 at epoch 4. The error histogram is presented in Fig. 16.11, which shows the dispersion of errors for all the data. Our results are dependent on the initial conditions and sampling, therefore we obtain different results for different training sessions.

Table 16.6 Matlab code of learning neural network for housing value

```
load house_dataset;
inputs=houseInputs;
targets=houseTargets;
% Create a Fitting Network
hiddenLayerSize=10;
net=fitnet(hiddenLayerSize);
% Setup Division of Data for Training, Validation, Testing
net.divideParam.trainRatio=70/100;
net.divideParam.valRatio=15/100;
net.divideParam.testRatio=15/100;
[net,tr]=train(net,inputs,targets);% Train the Network
outputs=net(inputs); % Test the Network
performance=perform(net,targets,outputs)
view(net) % View the Network
errors=targets - outputs;
figure, plotperform(tr); % Plot Best Validation
figure, ploterrhist(errors); % Plot Error Histogram
```

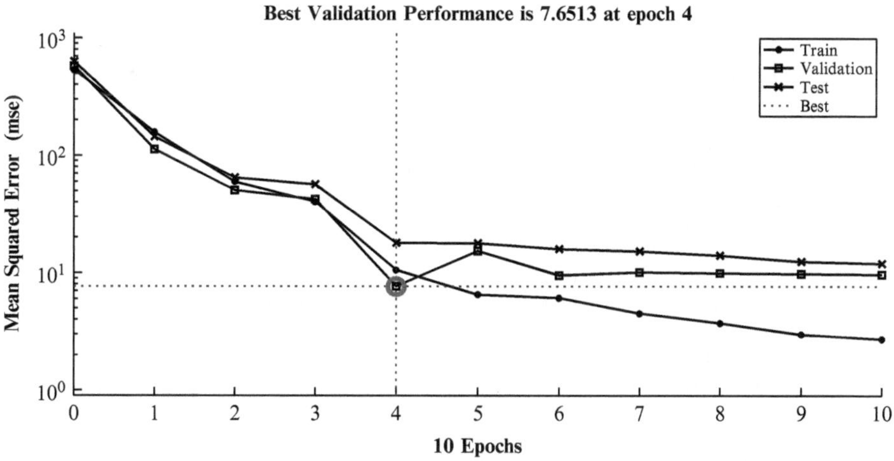

Fig. 16.10 Network performance over the learning epoch

16.3.3 *Stock Time-Series Forecasting*

The last case study is on time-series forecasting. We analyze Istanbul Stock Exchange data with respect to eight attributes. The data is organized with regards to the working days in the Istanbul Stock Exchange. It is an autoregression problem with external inputs. To solve this task, a NARX Neural Network is used. The Matlab code for this neural network is presented in Table 16.7. First, we prepare the data for training and simulation. The function *preparets* prepares time-series data for a particular network, shifting time by the minimum amount to fill input states

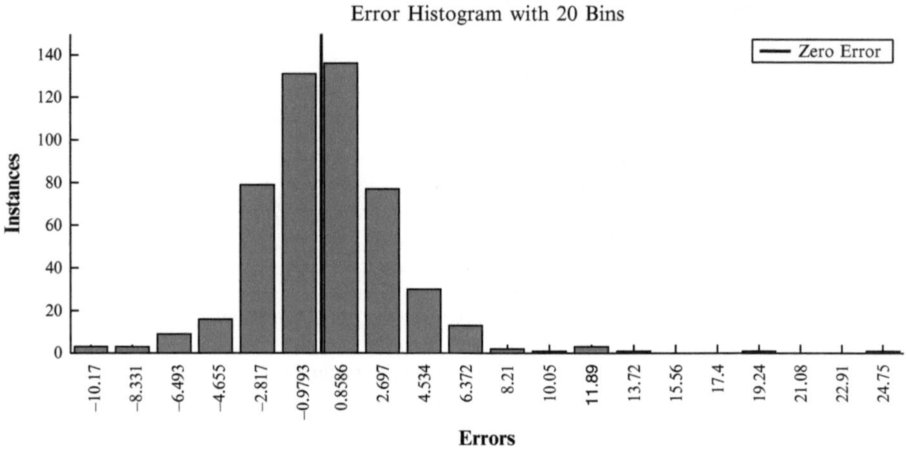

Fig. 16.11 Error histogram with 20 binds

Table 16.7 Matlab code of learning neural network for stock exchange

```
Stock;
inputSeries=con2seq(data(1:400, 3:end)');
targetSeries=con2seq(data(1:400, 2)');
% Create a Nonlinear Autoregressive Network with External Input
inputDelays=1:2;
feedbackDelays=1:2;
hiddenLayerSize=10;
net=narxnet(inputDelays,feedbackDelays,hiddenLayerSize);
% Prepare the Data for Training and Simulation
[inputs,inputStates,layerStates,targets]=...
preparets(net,inputSeries,{},targetSeries);
% Setup Division of Data for Training, Validation, Testing
net.divideParam.trainRatio=70/100;
net.divideParam.valRatio=15/100;
net.divideParam.testRatio=15/100;
% Train the Network
[net,tr]=train(net,inputs,targets,inputStates,layerStates);
% Test the Network
outputs=net(inputs,inputStates,layerStates);
errors=gsubtract(targets,outputs);
performance=perform(net,targets,outputs)
view(net) % view the Network
figure, plotperform(tr) % plot
figure, plotresponse(targets,outputs) % plot
```

Table 16.8 Matlab code of learning neural network for closed loop and early prediction network

```
inputSeries=con2seq(data(401:end, 3:end)');
targetSeries=con2seq(data(401:end, 2)');
[xc,xic,aic,tc]=preparets(net,inputSeries,{},targetSeries);
yc=net(xc,xic,aic);
openLoopPerformance=perform(net,tc,yc)
figure, plotresponse(tc,yc)
% Closed Loop Network
netc=closeloop(net);
netc.name=[net.name ' - Closed Loop'];
view(netc)
[xc,xic,aic,tc]=preparets(netc,inputSeries,{},targetSeries);
yc=netc(xc,xic,aic);
closedLoopPerformance=perform(netc,tc,yc)
figure, plotresponse(tc,yc)
% Early Prediction Network
nets=removedelay(net);
nets.name=[net.name ' - Predict One Step Ahead'];
view(nets)
[xs,xis,ais,ts]=preparets(nets,inputSeries,{},targetSeries);
ys=nets(xs,xis,ais);
earlyPredictPerformance=perform(nets,ts,ys)
figure, plotresponse(ts,ys)
```

and layer states. Therefore, we can keep our original time-series data unchanged, while easily customizing it to networks with differing numbers of delays, and with open loop or closed loop feedback modes. The code for a closed loop network and for an early prediction network is showed in Table 16.8. We should use closed loop network for multi-step predictions. The function *closeloop* replaces the feedback input with a direct connection from the output layer. For some applications, it helps to get the prediction of a time step early (i.e. early prediction network). The original network returns the predicted $y(t+1)$ at the time it is given $y(t+1)$. For some applications such as decision making (Jankowski et al. 2011; Wątróbski et al. 2014, 2015; Wątróbski and Jankowski 2016, Wątróbski and Jankowski 2015), it would be more useful to have the predicted $y(t+1)$ once $y(t)$ is available, but before the actual $y(t+1)$ occurs. The network can be made to return its output a time step early by removing one delay so that its minimal tap delay is now 0 instead of 1. In this case, the new network returns the same outputs as the original network, but the outputs are instead shifted left one time step.

In Fig. 16.12, we observe the best validation performance over the learning epoch of our network, which is equal to 0.000454 at epoch 4. The response of our network for the Istanbul Stock Exchange is showed in Fig. 16.13. Figure 16.14 presents the results of the multi-step prediction by using a closed loop network. Finally, Fig. 16.15 shows the results for an early prediction network.

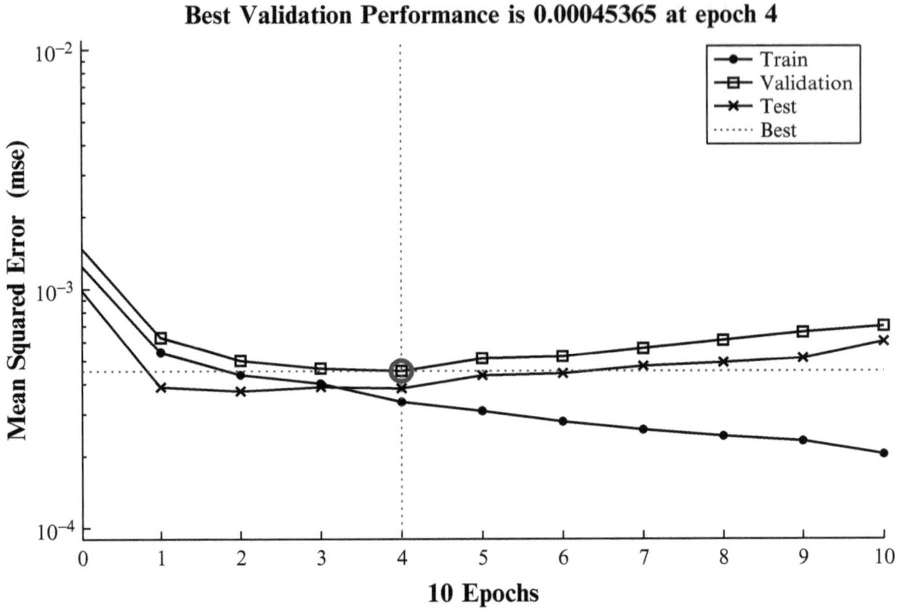

Fig. 16.12 Network performance over the learning epoch

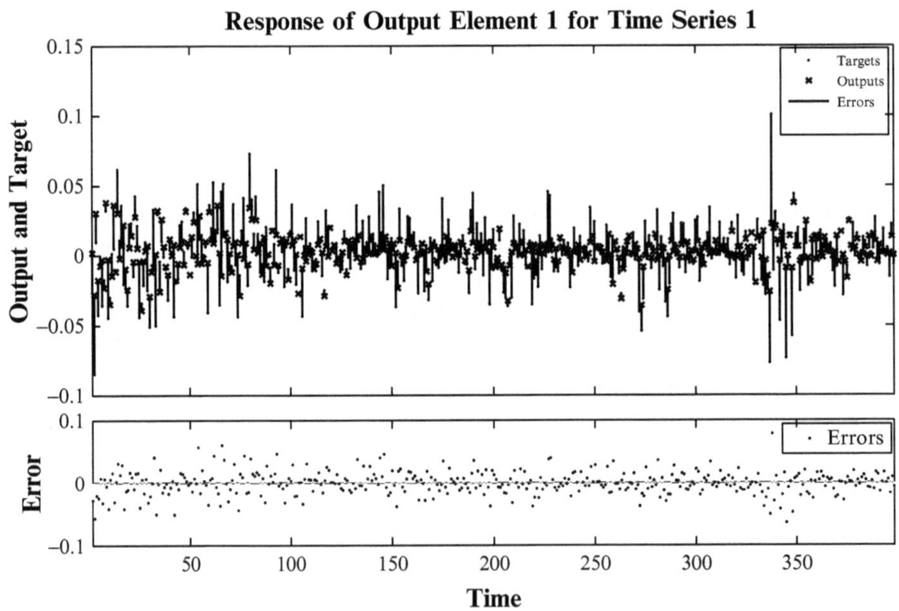

Fig. 16.13 Network response for time series data

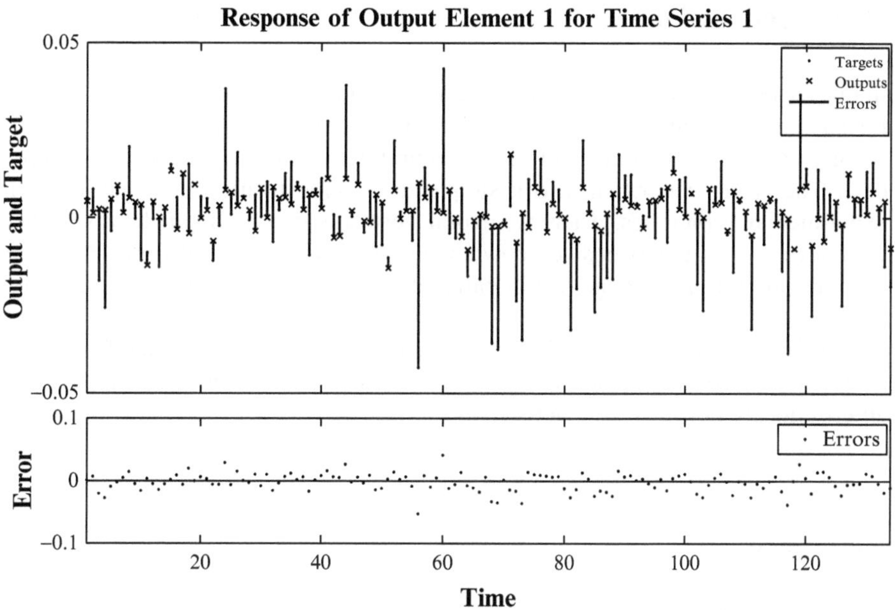

Fig. 16.14 Network response for time series data with closed loop

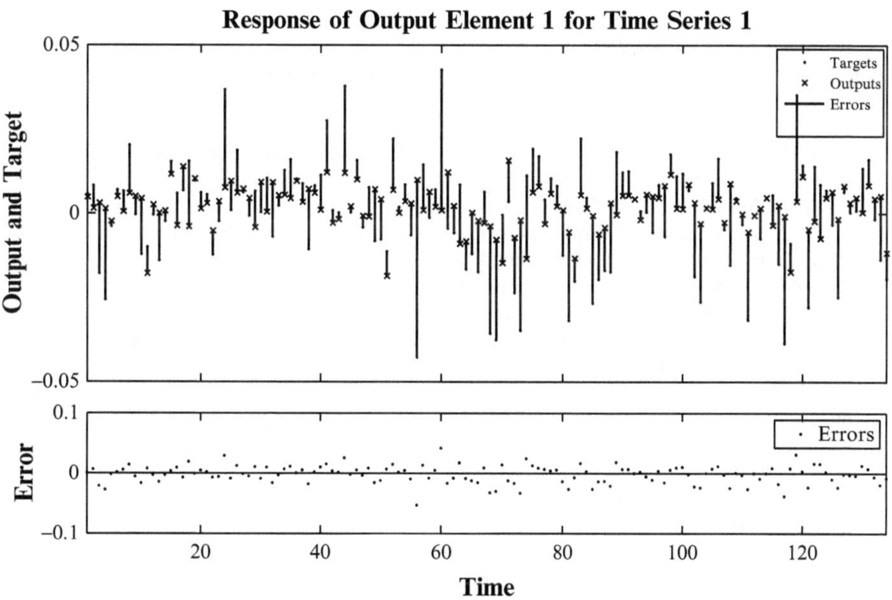

Fig. 16.15 Network response for time-series data with earlier prediction

16.4 Conclusion

In this chapter, we present a practical framework for the design of a neural network for solving problems in economic regression, classification and time-series forecasting. We present examples of the use neural networks using theoretical and real data. Therefore, we obtain also a simple user guide to use neural networks in experimental economics. Thereby, neural networks can be applied by scientists who have not got the extensive knowledge of artificial neural networks. Additionally, we present practical advice in parameter selection, as well as some common pitfalls.

For future works, we would like to concentrate on the time-series forecasting problem because it is the most complicated problem in neural networks application, and results are not fully satisfactory.

References

Alfaro E, Garcia N, Gamez M, Elizondo D (2008) Bankruptcy forecasting: an empirical comparison of adaboost and neural networks. Decis Support Syst 45(1):110–122

Aminian F, Suarez ED, Aminian M, Walz DT (2006) Forecasting economic data with neural networks. Comput Econ 28(1):71–88

Angelini E, di Tollo G, Roli A (2008) A neural network approach for credit risk evaluation. Q Rev Econ Finance 48(4):733–755

Azadeh A, Zarrin M, Rahdar Beik H, Aliheidari Bioki T (2015) A neuro-fuzzy algorithm for improved gas consumption forecasting with economic, environmental and IT/IS indicators. J Petrol Sci Eng 133:716–739

Bahrammirzaee A (2010) A comparative survey of artificial intelligence applications in finance: artificial neural networks, expert system and hybrid intelligent systems. Neural Comput Appl 19(8):1165–1195

Banerjee P, Singh VS, Chattopadhyay K, Chandra PC, Singh B (2011) Artificial neural network model as a potential alternative for groundwater salinity forecasting. J Hydrol 398(3):212–220

Chan KY, Dillon TS, Singh J, Chang E (2012) Neural-network-based models for short-term traffic flow forecasting using a hybrid exponential smoothing and Levenberg–Marquardt algorithm. IEEE Trans Intell Transp Syst 13(2):644–654

Charalambous C, Charitou A, Kaourou F (2000) Comparative analysis of artificial neural network models: application in bankruptcy prediction. Ann Oper Res 99(1–4):403–425

Chen SH, Wang PP (2004) Computational intelligence in economics and finance, Advanced information processing. Springer, Heidelberg, pp 3–55

Dahoe AE, Skjold T, Roekaerts DJEM, Pasman HJ, Eckhoff RK, Hanjalic K, Donze M (2013) On the application of the Levenberg–Marquardt method in conjunction with an explicit Runge–Kutta and an implicit Rosenbrock method to assess burning velocities from confined deflagrations. Flow Turbul Combust 91(2):281–317

Ghiassi M, Saidane H, Zimbra DK (2005) A dynamic artificial neural network model for forecasting time series events. Int J Forecasting 21(2):341–362

Ghiassi M, Zimbra DK, Saidane H (2006) Medium term system load forecasting with a dynamic artificial neural network model. Elec Power Syst Res 76(5):302–316

Hajek P (2011) Municipal credit rating modelling by neural networks. Decis Support Syst 51 (1):108–118

Hamzacebi C (2008) Improving artificial neural networks performance in seasonal time series forecasting. Inform Sci 178(23):4550–4559
Hamzacebi C, Akay D, Kutay F (2009) Comparison of direct and iterative artificial neural network forecast approaches in multi-periodic time series forecasting. Expert Syst Appl 36 (2):3839–3844
Hopgood AA (2011) Intelligent systems for engineers and scientists. CRC Press/Taylor & Francis Group, Boca Raton, FL
Huang Z, Chen H, Hsu CJ, Chen WH, Wu S (2004) Credit rating analysis with support vector machines and neural networks: a market comparative study. Decis Support Syst 37(4):543–558
Huarng K, Yu THK (2006) The application of neural networks to forecast fuzzy time series. Phys A Stat Mech Appl 363(2):481–491
Jankowski J. (2013) Balanced approach to the design of conversion oriented websites with limited negative impact on the users. In: Proceedings of 5-th international conference on computational collective intelligence technologies and applications, LNCS 7803, Springer, Heidelberg, pp. 527–536
Jankowski J, Wątróbski J, Piwowarski M (2011) Fuzzy modeling of digital products pricing in the virtual marketplace. In: Proceedings of 6th international conference on hybrid artificial intelligent systems, LNCS 6678, Springer, Heidelberg, pp 338–346
Jankowski J, Wątróbski J, Ziemba P (2015) Modeling the impact of visual components on verbal communication in online advertising. ICCCI 2015, part II, LNCS 9330, Springer, Heidelberg, pp. 44–53
Kalogirou SA (2004) Optimization of solar systems using artificial neural-networks and genetic algorithms. Appl Energ 77(4):383–405
Khashei M, Bijari M (2011) A novel hybridization of artificial neural networks and ARIMA models for time series forecasting. Appl Soft Comput 11(2):2664–2675
Khashei M, Bijari M (2010) An artificial neural network (p, d, q) model for time series forecasting. Expert Syst Appl 37(1):479–489
Khashei M, Hejazi SR, Bijari M (2008) A new hybrid artificial neural networks and fuzzy regression model for time series forecasting. Fuzzy Set Syst 159(7):769–786
Kim K (2003) Financial time series forecasting using support vector machines. Neurcomputing 55 (1):307–319
Kim TY, Oh KJ, Sohn I, Hwang C (2004) Usefulness of artificial neural networks for early warning system of economic crisis. Expert Syst Appl 26(4):583–590
Lee TS, Chen IF (2005) A two-stage hybrid credit scoring model using artificial neural networks and multivariate adaptive regression splines. Expert Syst Appl 28(4):743–752
Leung FH, Lam HK, Ling SH, Tam PK (2003) Tuning of the structure and parameters of a neural network using an improved genetic algorithm. IEEE Trans Neural Netw 14(1):79–88
Nguyen N, Cripps A (2001) Predicting housing value: a comparison of multiple regression analysis and artificial neural networks. J Real Estate Res 22(3):313–336
Palmer A, Montano JJ, Sese A (2006) Designing an artificial neural network for forecasting tourism time series. Tour Manage 27(5):781–790
Parisi A, Parisi F, Diaz D (2008) Forecasting gold price changes: rolling and recursive neural network models. J Multinational Financial Manage 18(5):477–487
Pattanayak S, Nandi R (2013) Identification of spectrum holes using ANN model for cognitive radio applications. In EUROCON IEEE, pp. 133–137
Prasad N, Singh R, Lal SP (2013) Comparison of back propagation and resilient propagation algorithm for spam classification. In: Computational intelligence, fifth international conference on modelling and simulation (CIMSim), pp. 29–34
Rafiei FM, Manzari SM, Bostanian S (2011) Financial health prediction models using artificial neural networks, genetic algorithm and multivariate discriminant analysis: Iranian evidence. Expert Syst Appl 38(8):10210–10217
Rojas R (2013) Neural networks: A Systematic Introduction. Springer Science and Business Media, Berlin Heidelberg
Selim H (2009) Determinants of house prices in turkey: hedonic regression versus artificial neural network. Expert Syst Appl 36(2):2843–2852

Shawash J, Selviah DR (2013) Real-time nonlinear parameter estimation using the Levenberg–Marquardt algorithm on field programmable gate arrays. IEEE Trans Ind Electron 60 (1):170–176

Thomassey S, Happiette M (2007) A neural clustering and classification system for sales forecasting of new apparel items. Appl Soft Comput 7(4):1177–1187

Tkacz G, Hu S (1999) Forecasting GDP growth using artificial neural networks. Bank of Canada

Verlinden B, Duflou JR, Collin P, Cattrysse D (2008) Cost estimation for sheet metal parts using multiple regression and artificial neural networks: a case study. Int J Prod Econ 111 (2):484–492

Wątróbski J, Jankowski J (2016) Guideline for MCDA method selection in production management area. New Frontiers in information and production systems modelling and analysis. Intelligent systems reference library, vol. 98(6), Springer, Heidelberg

Wątróbski J, Jankowski J (2015) Knowledge management in MCDA domain. In: Proceedings of the federated conference on computer science and information systems, pp. 1455–1460. IEEE Digital Library, doi: 10.15439/2015F295

Wątróbski J, Jankowski J, Piotrowski Z (2014) The selection of multicriteria method based on unstructured decision problem description. Lect Notes Artif Intell 8733:454–465

Wątróbski J, Ziemba P, Wolski W (2015) Methodological aspects of decision support system for the location of renewable energy sources. In: Proceedings of the federated conference on computer science and information systems, pp. 1461–1469. IEEE Digital Library, doi: 10.15439/2015F294

Zhang GP, Qi M (2005) Neural network forecasting for seasonal and trend time series. Eur J Oper Res 160(2):501–514

Zhang GP, Patuwo BE, Hu MY (2001) A simulation study of artificial neural networks for nonlinear time-series forecasting. Comput Oper Res 28(4):381–396

Zhang H, Xu D, Zhang Y (2014) Boundedness and convergence of split-complex back-propagation algorithm with momentum and penalty. Neural Process Lett 39(3):297–307

Ziemba P, Jankowski J, Wątróbski J, Becker J (2015a) Knowledge management in website quality evaluation domain. ICCCI 2015, part II, LNCS 9330, Springer, Heidelberg, pp. 75–85

Ziemba P, Jankowski J, Wątróbski J, Wolski W, Becker J (2015b) Integration of domain ontologies in the repository of website evaluation methods. In: Proceedings of the federated conference on computer science and information systems, pp. 1601–1610. IEEE Digital Library, doi: 10.15439/2015F29

Ziemba P, Piwowarski M, Jankowski J, Wątróbski J (2014) Method of criteria selection and weights calculation in the process of web projects evaluation. ICCCI 2014. LNAI 8733, Springer, Heidelberg, pp. 684–693

Part III
Practical Issues: Case Studies

Introduction

Anna Borawska

The last part of the volume presents examples of broadly understood experiments in economics. They refer to different areas and utilize various methods, which are described in methodological chapters of the book. As for the areas that are covered, they are shown in more detail in the first part and described in Chaps. 2 and 4. According to these contributions, in experimental economics research, four major areas can be mentioned and these are:

- individual decision-making and preferences,
- functioning of the market and its regulations,
- game theory,
- social dilemmas.

Experiments concerning the macroeconomics (more details can be found in Chap. 5) have also become quite popular. These topics set the framework for application of experiments in economics. However, it can be expected that in future the range of their applicability will widen a lot. The first signs of this can be already observed.

The third part of the book includes chapters, in which some examples of actually designed and performed experiments can be found. The first three of them stick to the list of primary uses of experimental method in economics, which was mentioned before (individual choices and preferences, and functioning of the market). The following four refer to another application, that is becoming recently very popular—it is marketing research.

A. Borawska
Faculty of Economics and Management, University of Szczecin, Szczecin, Poland
e-mail: anborawska@gmail.com

Individual decision-making is tested in two different settings. In Chap. 17 the main interest of the researchers is focused on attitudes to risk, consume, invest and save, with the respect to personality features of participants. Experiment described in this chapter emphasizes the importance of psychological features in economic research. In the experimental set-up presented these elements are expressed as personality types. It is hypothesized that personality types determine propensities to risk, consume, invest and save. An attempt to confirm this hypothesis is undertaken by researchers with the use of questionnaire that measures: features of the character (according to two different theories by Rotter and Fromm) and propensities of interest. The results obtained from the experiment allow to conclude that personality features are important factors determining behaviours and are also correlated with sex and human propensities.

A very interesting insight into individual choices and preferences is presented also in the Chap. 18. It concentrates on valuation of privacy by respondents and their willingness to share their data in exchange for financial benefits. The objective set by the author was to verify a hypothesis concerning the valuation of privacy by respondents and whether it has value for them that can be expressed in financial terms. The research used an experiment conducted at one of Polish shopping centres. According to the research conducted, privacy has its price for people and they are willing to sell it, but the appraisal of this good is non-linear.

Chapter 19 presents remarkable natural experiment that shows the functioning of the online auctions market. The research was conducted with the use of the leading online auctions platform in Poland (Allegro) and it investigates online auctions buyers' behaviour. The authors suggest that, due to key features of online environment, there are some signals that the sellers could implement to influence online auction buyers' behaviour to obtain higher profits. The results of the experiment show that there is substantial impact of online auction design parameters on the number of entries/hits per page and the sales volume of the product. The chapter presents also some forecasts of online auction market's future in Poland as more and more online auction buyers gain experience.

The rest of the third part presents some insights into marketing research. The four remaining chapters have one major element in common. In all of them some novel approaches and techniques of experiments are used. These are tools of cognitive neuroscience. In following contributions authors applied eye tracking, electroencephalography (EEG), galvanic skin response measurement (GSR) and heart rate measurement (HR). Introduction of neurophysiological signals recorded from the participants of experiments allowed to draw some interesting conclusions that would be inaccessible otherwise.

Chapter 20 contains research related to the online systems and behaviours of their users. In addition to the traditional survey based methods, measuring systems associated with eye tracking, that allow precise determination of visual paths and areas of websites or ads that absorb the attention of the recipient, are used. In this chapter, the main assumptions of the use of eye tracking in experimental economics and the results of an experiment are presented. The designed experiment was aimed at the detection of relation between the characteristics of interactive advertising units, its location within the site and the level of interest of the recipient based on absorption and attention. Conducted research allowed to determine the layout of website that would be the most appropriate for presenting the advertising content.

The topic of advertisement is in the spotlight also in the next chapter. It is focused on the appropriate preparation of advertising spots and all promotional materials. Properly prepared commercial significantly increases the chances of its positive reception and arouse consumer interest in a product or service. The study of advertising content and its influence can be carried out with using different research methods. Chapter 21 presents one of the modern approaches to analysis of advertising content, i.e. with application of the electroencephalography (EEG). The primary objective of the study was to identify features which should be characteristic of an advertisement answering the current situation on the market and meeting the expectations of the customer. The application of EEG provided a lot of new information about irrational choices, the role of taste, smell or touch in deciding to purchase a product, the choice of background music or the timbre of voice in a commercial. This data not only allows the commercial be perceived positively but also to be remembered for a long time.

A similar topic is dealt with in the next chapter. In this work, authors present the findings of an experiment aimed to investigate cognitive and emotional changes of cerebral activity during the observation of TV commercials. In particular, the electroencephalographic (EEG), galvanic skin response (GSR) and heart rate (HR) from a group of 24 healthy subjects during the observation of a series of TV advertisements was recorded. The group was equally divided also by gender (male, female) and age (young, old). Comparisons of cerebral and emotional indices previously defined have been performed to highlight gender differences between TV commercial and scenes of interest of specific commercials. Findings of this study show how EEG methodologies, along with the measurements of autonomic variables, could be used to obtain information not obtainable otherwise with verbal interviews. These cerebral and emotional indexes could help to analyze the perception of TV advertisements according to the consumer's gender and age.

A novel approach to marketing research is shown in Chap. 23. Authors present an innovative study aimed to prove, in a systematic way, that brain approach–withdrawal index, estimated from EEG signal, is correlated with the "pleasant" or "no-pleasant" perception of olfactory stimuli, conveniently produced by standardized methods in the sensory specific scientific literature. Findings show that it is possible to evaluate the pleasantness or no-pleasantness of odorous substances by means of the analysis of EEG signals collected during the presentation of such substances, making way for new applications of such measure kind in experimental environments more and more ecological, as the typical ones of the marketing research areas, especially when it comes to food choices made by consumers.

The third part of this book with its chapters presents only selected experiments and approaches to experimental economics. It shows, however, the wide range of topics and methods that can be used within this field of study. Recent advancements in technology allow for designing more and more advanced and interesting experiments; it can be assumed, therefore, that experimental economics will develop dynamically in the future.

Chapter 17
Is There Enough Psychology in Behavioural Economics? Personality Types and Human Propensities

Mariusz Doszyń and Sebastian Majewski

Abstract An attempt to add a psychological background into an analysis of human behaviour is made in the chapter. Behaviours are viewed in the context of human propensities. Problems connected with dependencies between personality types and chosen propensities are discussed. The main focus is put on differences in propensities with respect to personality orientations. To identify personality types, Rotter's locus of control concept as well as Fromm's personality theory is applied. Some methodological issues related to propensities are presented. In an empirical example the differences in propensity to risk, consume, invest and save with respect to personality features are analysed. The results obtained in the research are compared with the observations of Barber and Odean.

Keywords Rotter's locus of control • Fromm's personality theory • Personality types • Human propensities • Propensity to risk • Propensity to consume • Propensity to invest • Propensity to save • Overconfidence

17.1 Introduction

Nowadays there is a lot of research confirming the importance of psychological features' impact on decision making processes, see for example (Rabin 1996; Doszyń 2012). Most of these outcomes come from behavioural economics, in which psychological factors are treated as being decisive. In this chapter it is stated that personality type is an important factor determining human decisions and

---

M. Doszyń (✉)
Department of Econometrics, Faculty of Economics and Management,
Institute of Econometrics and Statistics, University of Szczecin, Mickiewicza 64,
Szczecin 71-101, Poland
e-mail: mariusz.doszyn@gmail.com

S. Majewski
Department of Insurance and Capital Markets, Faculty of Economics and Management,
Institute of Finance, University of Szczecin, Mickiewicza 64, Szczecin 71-101, Poland
e-mail: masaj@wneiz.pl

K. Nermend, M. Łatuszyńska (eds.), *Selected Issues in Experimental Economics*,
Springer Proceedings in Business and Economics, DOI 10.1007/978-3-319-28419-4_17

actions. In economics, but also in behavioural economics, those kinds of factors are rarely taken into account. Instead of personality features, other proxy variables are added into decision making models. According to the presented hypothesis, more psychology should be put into behavioural economics, by adding into an analysis more psychological variables, such as, for instance, personality features. On the other hand, taking into account psychological factors should not be done without the recognition of conditions of the appearance of these factors. If it were true, it would become in contradiction with the theory that personality is shaped by the environment of life (Fromm 1941). Such variables as being male, age and marital status have a very strong impact on individual reactions on a stimulus (Barber and Odean 2001).

To sum up, the main hypothesis of this chapter is that personality types determine human propensities. To identify personality type, Rotter's locus of control concept and Fromm's character orientation theory are used. These psychological features are analysed in context of such propensities as the propensity to risk, consume, invest and save.

17.2 Personality Types

In psychology there are many theories of personality (Eysenck 2013). In this chapter two concepts are discussed:

1. Rotter's locus of control theory,
2. Fromm's theory of character orientations.

Locus of control refers to an individual's perception about the underlying causes of events in life. According to Rotter, individuals hold beliefs about what causes life occurrences. These beliefs, in turn, affect attitudes and behaviours. It could be stated that locus of control orientation is a belief about whether the results of our actions depend on what we do (internal control orientation) or on factors outside our personal control (external control orientation). Locus of control could be understood as a continuum, ranging from external to internal. Individuals with external locus of control believe that their life is guided by fate, luck or other external circumstances. On the other hand, individuals with an internal locus of control believe that life is guided by their personal decisions and efforts. The question is whether locus of control determines such human propensities as the propensity to risk, consume, invest or save.

According to Fromm, personality could be described as a set of innate and acquired psychical properties that characterise a given person (Fromm 1990; Doszyń 2013). Temper is constituted by innate properties but character—by acquired features. Fromm stated that character could be shaped (to some degree). He also thought that character influences not only behaviour, but also feelings and thoughts.

Table 17.1 Positive and negative aspects of characterological orientations according to Fromm (Fromm 1990; Doszyń 2013)

Positive aspects	Negative aspects
Receptive orientation	
Acceptable, sensitive, sacrificing, modest, engaging, elastic, adapted, idealistic, polite, optimistic, trustful	Passive, without opinion, subordinate, without pride, parasitical, without rules, servile, unrealistic, cowardly, wishful, naive
Exploitative orientation	
Active, able to be initiative, demanding, proud, impulsive, self-confident, winsome	Exploitative, aggressive, egocentric, conceited, impetuous, arrogant, seductive
Hoarding orientation	
Practical, economical, cautious, with reserve, patient, careful, conservative, calm, not stressful, systematic, loyal	Without imagination, stingy, suspicious, cold, lethargic, anxious, stubborn, pedantic, obsessive, greedy
Marketing orientation	
Purposeful, changeable, youthful, thinking about future, open minded, sociable, experimenter, not dogmatic, effective, curious, intelligent, adaptive, tolerant, brilliant, generous	Opportunistic, inconsequent, infantile, without a past and a future, without values, without goals, relativistic, too active, tactless, indifferent, stupid, wasteful

It is worth noticing that Fromm's concept of character is an evolvement of Freud's theory, according to which character is a system of endeavours that are the basis of human behaviour but are not always identical with it. Fromm accepted Freud's claim that character traits form the basis of behaviour and should be deduced from it. Character qualities could be understood as strong, often unconscious, forces and should be treated not as single traits but as a whole characterological orientation that determines specific personal features (Fromm 1990). E. Fromm defined character as a relatively stable form of energy distribution in processes of assimilation (of things) and socialisation. Fromm identified five types of characterological orientations:

- Receptive,
- Exploitative,
- Hoarding,
- Marketing,
- Productive.

Every individual consists of elements of all the mentioned orientations but usually one of them prevails. The first four orientations are classified as being unproductive. They could have both positive and negative aspects which depend on the level of personal vitality. Typical traits related with these orientations are presented in Table 17.1.

An individual with productive orientation could be described as a mature, independent, conscious, active, creative and spontaneous person. This is an ideal type of character (and personality). Everybody is productive but to a different extent.

17.3 Behavioural Effects and Gender Differences in Economic Literature

The one of most explored effects in behavioural finance is the overconfidence effect. It is a behavioural phenomenon where an investor has excessive confidence in his internal ability to overcome problems. On the stock exchange this effect is closely tied with the belief that investor's experience and his knowledge allow him to defeat the market. This is not so difficult to find many scientific dissertations in the economic literature about the overconfidence effect and its dependence on gender. The first scientific work about this subject was written in 1974 by Deaux and Emswiller and it concludes that overconfidence is a domain of the masculine gender (Barber and Odean 2001). Gender is also connected with personality types. Table 17.2 presents the most important findings on analysed field until the paper of Barber and Odean.

The research of Barber and Odean raised two hypotheses. The first assumes that men trade more than women and the second—men hurt their performance more than women by trading more. A test provided by the authors allows concluding that (Barber and Odean 2001):

- Human deviations from rationality are often systematic,
- Overconfident investors trade too much,
- Overconfident investors overestimate the precision of their information and thereby the expected gains of trading,
- Men trade more than women and thereby reduce their returns more than women—this difference is stronger in the case of single men and women.

According to another work of Barber and Odean (2000) one of the factors which could make differences between investors is the hazard. They describe the existence of the hazard as the need of risk seeking or as entertainment. If the assumption that the stock exchange is dedicated for men is true, therefore the market could be treated as a place of the ensuring investor's needs. Such a market plays the role of the place where the emotional needs could be fulfilled. Needs just like rivalry, overcoming an enemy or fear and succumbing to the temptation of greed are mostly assigned to men. Women investors are better than men in long-time horizons (Barber and Odean 2001) because of such features as: patience, calmness, composure and risk aversion. One of the last Polish research in this matter was provided by Majewski (2013) and his results are generally convergent to the conclusions of Barber and Odean.

17.4 What Is Propensity?

It seems that human behaviour could be described in the context of propensities. Propensity is defined as a "slope of posture" towards something (or somebody) that makes the probability of a certain event higher (Doszyń and Hozer 2004).

Table 17.2 The most important findings in the field of gender and overconfidence (Barber and Odean 2001)

Findings	Author(s)	Work	Year
Differences in confidence are greatest for tasks perceived to be in the masculine domain	K. Deaux T. Emswiller	Explanations of successful performance on sex-linked tasks: what is skill for the male is luck for the female	1974
	E. Lenney	Women's self-confidence in achievement settings	1977
	S. Beyer E.M. Bowden	Gender differences in self-perceptions: Convergent evidence from three measures of accuracy and bias	1997
The perception of differences in the ability to taking different types of tasks is different in group of men and women, but men are strongly overconfident	K. Deaux E. Farris	Attributing causes for one's own performance: the effects of sex, norms, and outcome	1977
Men are generally more overconfident than women	M.A. Lundeberg, P.W. Fox, J. Puncochar	Highly confident but wrong: gender differences and similarities in confidence judgments	1994
Gender differences in overconfidence are highly task dependent			
Men are inclined to feel more competent than women in financial matters	M. Prince	Women, men, and money styles	1993
Investors have the tendency to take too much credit for their success, they become overconfident	S. Gervais, T. Odean	Learning to be overconfident	1998
The self-serving attribution bias is greater for men than for women	K. Deaux, E. Farris	Attributing causes for one's own performance: the effects of sex, norms, and outcome	1977
	A.M. Meehan, W.F. Overton	Gender differences in expectancies for success and performance on Piagetian spatial tasks	1986
	S. Beyer	Gender differences in the accuracy of self-evaluations of performance	1990
Men spend more time and money on security analysis, rely less on their brokers, make more transactions, believe that returns are more highly predictable and anticipate higher possible returns than do women	W.G. Lewellen, R.C. Lease, G.G. Schlarbaum	Patterns of investment strategy and behaviour among individual investors	1977

Propensities impact human decisions and make the probabilities of many events different. There are many kinds of propensities important in economic life. The very important ones are the propensity to risk, consume, save and invest.

It is worth noticing that, in philosophical literature, two groups of propensity theories could be identified. In the first group propensity is understood as *a characteristic of a whole situation*. In this case propensity depends both on objective and subjective factors. *Human (psychological) propensities* are just one of the conditions that determine the *propensity of a whole situation*. These theories are mostly based on Popper's works (Doszyń 2012).

The second group contains theories in which propensity depends on the *internal characteristics of a given object* (for example a human being). Individual propensities depend mainly on the type of personality. In this context, propensity describes the internal (psychological) structure of an individual. That kind of attitude to propensities was presented by C. Peirce (Gillies 2000).

In this chapter propensities are understood as factors describing the psychological aspects of human behaviour that make the probabilities of certain events higher. Propensities are therefore treated as generalised *psychological* causes of events. Generally, propensity could be measured by means of frequency and trigonometric methods (Doszyń 2013). In the frequency method the intensity of a given propensity is obtained as a:

$$s = \frac{m}{n}, \tag{17.1}$$

where s (frequency) measure of propensity, m number of cases in which propensity appears, n number of all possible cases.

Dependency (17.1) is very general. It could be applied in many different cases. For instance, while measuring propensity to save, in the nominator (m) we could have an amount of money that was saved by a given individual in an appropriate period and in the denominator—amount of money that was possible to save (n). The same formulations are true in the case of other propensities such as the propensity to consume or invest. Propensity might also be presented in degrees, by means of a trigonometric measure (Doszyń 2013).

17.5 Empirical Example

The main aim of the undertaken research was to verify if psychological factors are correlated with the chosen economic propensities. The survey was conducted mainly among students, 48 respondents were asked to complete the questionnaire. Most of the participants were female (75 %). The majority of respondents were 21–22 years old but most of the men were at least 23 years old. The structure of the respondents with respect to sex and age is presented in the graph (Fig. 17.1).

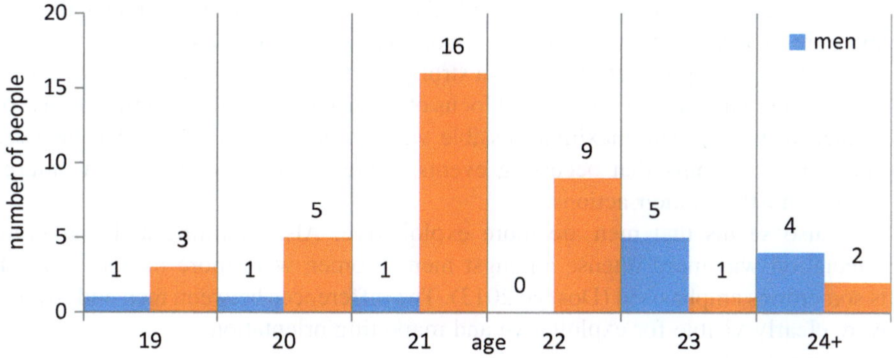

Fig. 17.1 Distribution of respondents according to sex and age (source: own calculations)

Table 17.3 Characteristics of respondents (median) due to age, sex and psychological features (own calculations)

Sex	Women	Men	Total
Age	21.00	23.00	21.00
Locus of control	5.00	6.50	5.00
Receptive orientation	20.00	19.50	20.00
Exploitative orientation	17.00	20.00	18.00
Hoarding orientation	19.00	19.50	19.00
Marketing orientation	20.00	21.50	21.00
Propensity to risk	0.25	0.50	0.25
Propensity to risk (nominal scale)	0.00	0.00	0.00
Propensity to consume	0.50	0.40	0.50
Propensity to invest	0.20	0.50	0.40
Propensity to save	0.50	0.65	0.50

In the first part of the questionnaire respondents were analysed for the locus of control (see Appendix). The higher the number of points, the higher the intensity of internal locus of control (maximal value in this part was 10). In the next part, character orientation was identified. In the case of all orientations the maximum number of points was 30 (minimum was equal to 10). In the last section of the questionnaire, propensities were measured, such as propensity to risk, consume, invest and save. Propensity measures belong to the interval from zero to one (the higher the propensity, the higher the value). If propensity was the lowest, measure of propensity was equal to zero. If propensity was at its maximum, propensity was equal to one. There was one exception. Propensity to risk was estimated also on the nominal scale. In this case propensity was equal to one if there was a propensity to risk and zero otherwise. The used questionnaire is presented in Appendix.

In the first stage differences in psychological types with respect to sex were analysed (see Table 17.3). To verify the intensity of the analysed psychological features median values were calculated. The reason was that beyond age, all variables are qualitative so an ordinal (and nominal) scale was used.

The first finding is that men have a stronger internal locus of control. In case of men the median value of the internal locus of control was equal to 6.5 (in the case of women it was 5). The maximal possible value was 10. This means that men are more prone to think that occurring events, achievements, successes and failures depend mostly on their actions.

It also seems that men are more exploitative. Also hoarding and marketing orientation was more intense amongst men. Women were more receptive which is sometimes emphasised (Doszyń 2013). The differences between men and women were clearly visible for exploitative and marketing orientation.

Men have also a higher propensity to risk, invest and save. Only the propensity to consume has higher intensity in the case of women. This could mean that women are to a higher extent consumers and men investors with a more intense propensity to risk and save.

In the next stage of the survey dependencies between psychological traits as well as propensities were analysed (see Table 17.4). As it was mentioned, ordinal scale was mostly used, so Spearman's rank correlation coefficient was applied (R). All statistically significant coefficients were bolded. Because of the rather low number of respondents, the significance level was set to 0.2. As many as 11 of Spearman's rank correlation coefficients turned out to be statistically significant (Table 17.4).

As we can see, the propensity to risk was positively correlated with the internal locus of control ($R = 0.438$). This means that people who think that their actions have a strong impact on their lives are more inclined to risk. That kind of individual probably thinks that it will be possible for them to achieve positive results by taking risky actions.

Receptive orientation was negatively correlated with exploitative orientation ($R = -0.388$) which is reasonable, because each of these orientations consists of different and often excluding traits. Receptive orientation was also negatively correlated with the propensity to risk ($R = -0.233$). Individuals with this orientation often rely on others. They have difficulties with making independent decisions, so the propensity to risk of such people is rather low.

Exploitative orientation turned out to be positively correlated with marketing orientation ($R = 0.433$). This seems to be justified because psychological traits for these orientations are to a high degree consistent.

Hoarding orientation was positively correlated with the propensity to save ($R = 0.222$) and propensity to risk ($R = 0.205$). The propensity to save is a very specific trait of hoarding orientation so this result is meaningful. Hoarding orientation is also connected with some other economic traits so this could be the reason why the propensity to risk was also important for those kinds of individuals.

The propensities to risk and invest were positively correlated with marketing orientation which is consistent with those traits that form this type of personality.

As it was mentioned, the propensity to risk was measured in two ways. In the first case the propensity to risk belongs to the interval from zero to one. The propensity to risk was also measured on a nominal scale. As we can see, these

Table 17.4 Spearman's correlation coefficient between the psychological traits of respondents

	Locus of control	Receptive orientation	Exploitative orientation	Hoarding orientation	Marketing orientation	Propensity to risk	Propensity to risk (nominal scale)	Propensity to consume	Propensity to invest	Propensity to save
Locus of control	1									
Receptive orientation	−0.093	1								
Exploitative orientation	0.014	**−0.388**	1							
Hoarding orientation	0.025	−0.025	0.023	1						
Marketing orientation	0.027	−0.044	**0.433**	−0.081	1					
Propensity to risk	**0.438**	**−0.233**	0.109	**0.205**	**0.234**	1				
Propensity to risk (nominal scale)	−0.088	−0.005	−0.122	0.154	0.135	**0.220**	1			
Propensity to consume	−0.089	−0.132	0.088	0.027	0.085	0.122	**−0.216**	1		
Propensity to invest	−0.006	−0.122	0.156	−0.040	**0.374**	**0.314**	0.156	0.050	1	
Propensity to save	0.179	−0.052	0.009	**0.222**	−0.165	0.059	0. 28	0.001	−0.126	1

*Coefficients with statistical significance are in *bold* (significance level 0.2)

two measures were positively correlated ($R = 0.220$). It is also worth noticing that the propensity to risk was positively correlated with the propensity to invest ($R = 0.314$). These propensities are complementary, so this result seems to be interesting. The propensity to risk (measured on a nominal scale) was negatively correlated with the propensity to consume ($R = -0.216$). It could be due to the fact that the propensity to risk is higher in the case of investors which are not always very prone to consume.

17.6 Concluding Remarks

According to the results obtained by Barber and Odean (2001) some of the differences in the results in the female and male groups in this experiment could be explained by the overconfidence effect. Despite the fact that there were not any significant differences in the characteristics of the respondents due to sex and psychological orientation (Figs. 17.2 and 17.3), there were very interesting differences in the characteristics of the respondents due to sex and economic propensities. Only one type of economic propensity is assigned to women—the propensity to consume but the difference is not so distinct. The most distinct differences between men and women respondents were obtained in the case of the propensities to risk and to invest. As it might be expected, these two cases were practically dominated by men—men indicate a two times higher propensity than women. Taking into account the propensity to save, the difference was not significant but it was the men's domain again. Concluding the main characteristics of the respondents, it is justified to maintain that our experiment confirms the previous results cited in this chapter.

The highest correlation coefficient was obtained for the propensity to risk and internal locus of control ($R = 0.438$). The positive value of the correlation coefficient for these factors might be interpreted as wishful thinking that taking a risky

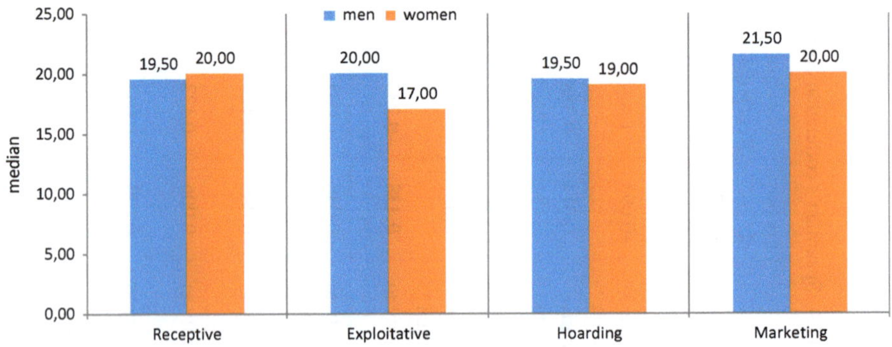

Fig. 17.2 Characteristics of the respondents (median) due to sex and psychological orientation (source: own calculations)

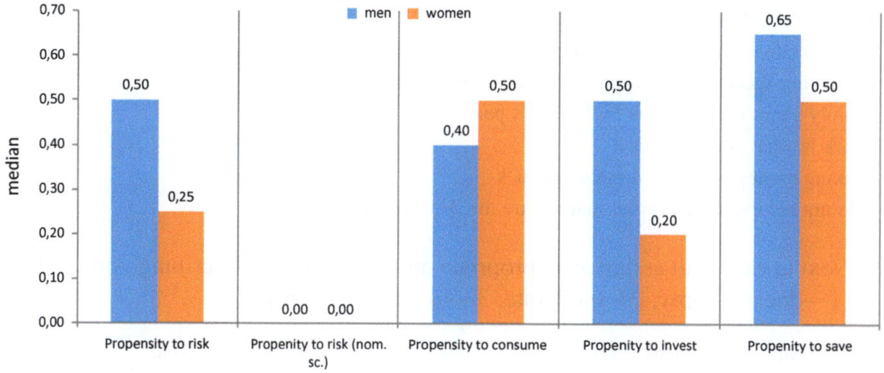

Fig. 17.3 Characteristics of the respondents (median) due to sex and propensity (source: own calculations)

investment gives the highly probable possibility to achieve financial goals. The lack of the possibility of dividing the respondents into two homogenous (depending on the sex—only 25 % of whole sample were men) groups because of their small number, may be a reason for obtaining such a correlation. On the other hand the research conducted on the group of single men and women suggest that in both groups individuals could behave similarly.

Another important correlation coefficient was obtained for exploitative and marketing orientation ($R = 0.433$). It should be justified because of the psychological traits for these orientations. It also possible to notice that the propensity to risk and invest was positively correlated with marketing orientation. It seems that this may mean that in such a young group of respondents the need of gain plays a very important role.

Concluding, such a small experiment has given a very interesting contribution to conduct deeper research on other groups of potential economic agents (investors, etc.). It seems that personality features are important factors determining behaviours and are also correlated with sex and human propensities. Thanks to these results the direction of further research has been obtained.

Appendix

Age: ....
Sex: .....

A. Next to each question choose an appropriate number expressing your opinion (1—I don't agree, 2—hard to say, 3—I agree)

Only with luck you can be an efficient leader	1–2–3
When I have plans I'm sure that I can realize them	1–2–3
People with high incomes usually have more luck	1–2–3

(continued)

I believe that fortune and luck could matter	1–2–3
Unfortunate events often arise from the fact that people have bad luck	1–2–3
Achieving success is a matter of hard work, not luck	1–2–3
Mainly genes determine an individual's personality	1–2–3
Work is what you make of it	1–2–3
Making money is mostly a matter of luck	1–2–3
I do not believe in fate, what matters are the decisions I make	1–2–3

B. Next to each trait assign an appropriate number of points describing your attitude (1—doesn't apply, 2—moderate, 3—to a large extent)

No.	Trait	Points	Trait	Points	Trait	Points	Trait	Points
1	Accepting		Active		Practical		Purposeful	
2	Passive		Exploitative		Unimaginative		Searching for opportunities	
3	Sensitive		Capable of initiative		Economical		Fond of change	
4	Often without opinion		Aggressive		Rather stingy		Little consistent	
5	Sacrificing		Able to make demands		Careful		Youthful	
6	Like to execute commands		Egocentric		Suspicious		Infantile	
7	Modest		Proud		With reserve		Planning	
8	Does not pay much attention to pride		Rather conceited		Not emotional		Don't care about the past and the future	
9	Winsome		Impulsive		Patient		With an open mind	
10	Relying on others		Short-tempered		Lethargic		Attaching no attention to the rules	

C1. You participate in a lottery in which two results may appear: K or L (Tab. C1). For example, if you choose strategy A you might win 2000 PLN, if you choose strategy B you might win 1800 or 2800 PLN, if you choose strategy C you might win 1600 or 3200 PLN, and so on.

Which option you choose, if you do not know whether K or L will appear (check the appropriate box in Table C1)?

Table C1. Lottery results depending on the selected option (payment in PLN)

	K	L
A	2000	2000
B	1800	2800
C	1600	3200
D	1200	3400
E	400	3600

C2. You can get for sure 950 PLN or take part in a lottery where you can win 1000 PLN with a probability of 90 % and 500 PLN with a probability of 10 %. Would you take part in the lottery?

(a) Yes.
(b) No.
(c) I don't care.

C3. You have an additional 1000 PLN which you can spend as you wish. For consumption you will spend:

(a) Not more than 200–300 PLN,
(b) Not more than 500 PLN,
(c) At most 700–800 PLN,
(d) The whole amount.

C4. Suppose that after meeting your typical needs you have an additional 1000 PLN, which you can spend on savings (bank deposit) and/or investments (purchase of shares). A bank deposit gives a certain profit in the amount of 3 % per year. The acquisition of shares may provide a greater profit, but there is also a risk of losing at least part of the capital. Which of the following options best suits your preferences?

	Savings (bank deposit)	Investments (purchase of shares)
A	0	1000
B	200	800
C	400	600
D	600	400
E	800	200
F	1000	0

C5. If you have an additional 500 PLN usually you save:

(a) Nothing,
(b) Not more than 100–150 zł,
(c) Not more than 250 zł,
(d) Not more than 350–400 zł,
(e) The whole amount.

References

Barber B, Odean T (2001) Boys will be boys. Gender, overconfidence and common stock investment. Q J Econ 116(1):261–292

Barber B, Odean T (2000) Trading is hazardous to your wealth: the common stock investment performance of individual investors. J Finance 55(2):773–806

Beyer S (1990) Gender differences in the accuracy of self-evaluations of performance. J Pers Soc Psychol 59:960–970
Beyer S, Bowden EM (1997) Gender differences in self-perceptions: convergent evidence from three measures of accuracy and bias. Pers Soc Psychol Bull 23:157–172
Deaux K, Emswiller T (1974) Explanations of successful performance on sex-linked tasks: what is skill for the male is luck for the female. J Pers Soc Psychol 29:80–85
Deaux K, Farris E (1977) Attributing causes for one's own performance: the effects of sex, norms, and outcome. J Res Pers 11:59–72
Doszyń M (2012) Econometric analysis of the impact of propensities on economic occurrences – a macroeconomic perspective. Folia Oeconomica Stetinensia 10(18)/2011(12):138–154
Doszyń M (2013) Women and men propensities to smoke and drink alcohol. Folia Oeconomica Stetinensia 13(21)/2013(1):108–120
Doszyń M, Hozer J (2008) Econometric models of propensities. Folia Oeconomica Stetinensia 6 (14):15–25
Eysenck HJ (2013) The structure of human personality. Routledge, New York
Fromm E (1990) Man for himself. Henry Holt and Company, New York
Fromm E (1941) Escape from freedom. Rinehart, New York
Gervais S, Odean T (1998) Learning to be overconfident. University of Pennsylvania, Wharton School
Gillies D (2000) Varieties of propensity. Br J Philos Sci 51(2000):807–835
Lenney E (1977) Women's self-confidence in achievement settings. Psychol Bull 84:1–13
Lewellen WG, Lease RC, Schlarbaum GG (1977) Patterns of investment strategy and behavior among individual investors. J Bus 50:296–333
Lundeberg MA, Fox PW, Punccohar J (1994) Highly confident but wrong: gender differences and similarities in confidence judgments. J Educ Psychol 86:114–121
Majewski S (2013) The influence of behavioural factors on the market value of shares quantitative approach [in Polish]. WNUS, Szczecin
Meehan AM, Overton WF (1986) Gender differences in expectancies for success and performance on Piagetian spatial tasks. Merrill-Palmer Q 32:427–441
Prince M (1993) Women, men, and money styles. J Econ Psychol 14:175–182
Rabin M (1996) Psychology and economics. University of California, Berkeley

Chapter 18
I Will Sell My Private Data: The Results of an Experimental Study on the Valuation of Privacy

Andrzej Poszewiecki

Abstract The presented chapter contributes to the experimental current of research on privacy. The objective set by the author was to verify a hypothesis concerning the valuation of privacy by respondents and whether it has value for them that can be expressed in financial terms. The research used an experiment conducted at one of Polish shopping centres. According to the research, privacy has its price for people and they are willing to sell it, but the appraisal of this good is non-linear (you can even see the relationship that higher pay for the data causes a greater caution of respondents).

Keywords Privacy • Experimental design • Valuation of personal information

18.1 Introduction

The issue of privacy represent a subject of interest not only to lawyers, ethicists or philosophers but also to the economists, who point out to its major role in and impact on the economy. Further, privacy is becoming an issue that is more and more present in contemporary scientific and political studies. The question of privacy is entering the scientific discourse as well. There are two opposite approaches in these discussions. One stresses the potential benefits related to renouncing one's privacy, the other pointing to related risks (this voice is most clearly heard).

The value of information has been a subject of economic analyses since the work by Hayek (1945). Privacy is related to information about us and our behaviour. However, privacy may have various meanings to different people (Solove 2006).

The proposed and conducted research stems from other research conducted in recent years, including by Acquisti et al. (2013a, b)); however, it takes account of certain conditionings related to e.g. the method of privacy control.

* This study was funded by the National Science Centre (Poland), by the funds assigned on the base of decision number DEC-2012/07/D/HS4/02014

A. Poszewiecki (✉)
Faculty of Economics, University of Gdańsk, Armii Krajowej 119/121, Sopot, 81-824, Poland
e-mail: pos@panda.bg.univ.gda.pl

K. Nermend, M. Łatuszyńska (eds.), *Selected Issues in Experimental Economics*, Springer Proceedings in Business and Economics, DOI 10.1007/978-3-319-28419-4_18

18.2 State of the Art (Privacy as an Economic Good)

Questions about privacy are becoming more and more popular (to an extent prompted by scandals like the one over PRISM). Collecting and analysing huge volumes of personal data is becoming easier and easier, giving a powerful tool that may be used by companies to achieve competitive advantages. This shows how important the privacy issues are not just in the macro scale but also from the point of view of individual businesses. There are new papers (Greenstein et al. 2013) indicating that the dynamic changes concerning the digitalization of our privacy create new sources of competitive advantage and build new business models.

From an economic point of view, it becomes important to find answers to the following questions: is too much privacy something bad for the society, or should we aim at "zero privacy", what are the costs of privacy, should privacy be protected (and who should do it), are people actually concerned with privacy issues, or perhaps the constitutional protection of privacy is not necessary.

As in any other science, in economics the models are the basic tool for analysis. We take from Maslow (1943) that people are motivated to action by their needs (from satisfying hunger to self-realisation). The satisfaction of higher-order needs (e.g. a dignity) follows after satisfaction of basic needs (e.g. satiety). Consumption directly satisfies the needs. All that serves for needs satisfaction of the people, is called in economics a good. Privacy is also a good. Which needs does it satisfy? We consume our privacy by revealing information about ourselves to the interested parties whether it is for financial, or for information reasons, for example in the case of a recommendation or advice. Customers can receive discounts for sharing their privacy (loyalty cards of various types). We can also feel appreciated when we receive a personalised offer, prepared "especially for us".

On the other hand, non-disclosure could result in some problems for a consumer. This is related to the fact that more and more products and services are dependent on disclosure of personal data (for example, social meeting or the concert for which the invitations will be sent only via the social network: the more somebody's friends (and other consumers) reveals without their data online, the greater are the costs for those people who would not join the social network to protect their data).

In economic theory, the concept of privacy has been analysed since 1970s (Posner 1978; Stigler 1980). Nowadays, due to the popularity of IT and the Internet, it is becoming more and more important.

Following the neoclassical economic theories of perfectly competitive markets, the "complete" information (availability of proper information to all market participants) leads to the higher economic efficiency. For example, if all consumers know prices for which a business sells its products, such competition reduces the prices to the lowest level possible, thus increasing the consumers' welfare. According to Posner, the privacy protection creates the inefficiency in the market, as it conceals the potentially important information from other economic agents.

The results of such research have been confirmed among others by Calzolari and Pavan (2006), who discovered that the unlimited exchange of consumer information between two firms can in fact reduce market deviations and improve the situation of the whole population, including the consumers. Varian (1996) concluded that a consumer may want some information about him/her to be known to other persons. For example, a consumer may want call centre operators to be familiar with his/her holiday preferences, to receive offers that may be actually interesting for him/her.

The importance of privacy led to the formulation of the concept of privacy economics (Acquisti 2014), which has examined the costs and benefits associated with access to private data. The main source of data for analysis is the internet. Access to large amount of data (big data) creates numerous analytical possibilities. But there are few research studies, which have been carried out in the real world (field studies). On the other hand, part of the experiments carried out in the laboratory conditions are carried out only on a group of students (Beresford et al. 2012).

In the case of virtually any good we are dealing with a market that in various forms sets the price of a given good. However, in the case of privacy, this type of market is not functioning, and the valuation of privacy is difficult. One form of attempt to evaluate the privacy may be application of experimental economics tools. This involves, among others, the more and more often questioning the assumptions about rationality of *homo oeconomicus*. Experimental economics science provides more and more confirmation that people are guided in their activities (including economic activities) by their emotions, they are subject to delusions and blatantly incorrectly assess of a situation, in which they make their decisions.

18.3 Measurement of Privacy by Using an Experiment

A corollary issue is the problem of the valuation of privacy. A reasonable consumer evaluates the same goods on a similar level, regardless of being their owner or not. However, some studies indicate the existence of a disproportion between the limit sale price (a minimum price for which a consumer is ready to sell his goods—WTA) and the limit purchase price (a maximum price a consumer is ready to pay for the goods—WTP). Such differences are often interpreted in terms of the income effect, although this approach does not explain such large disparities in appraisals.

The "endowment effect" proposed by Thaler (1980) is an attempt to justify the WTA–WTP disparity from a perspective of behavioural economics. Its core assumption is that consumers prefer things they actually own, ceteris paribus.

Some studies (among others Czajkowski (2004)) indicated that the WTA–WTP disparity more affects the consumer goods than abstract concepts (values).

In this study we want demonstrate that in the case of non-consumer goods, we have to deal with a significant disparity.

Experimental methods become more popular only after the Nobel Prize in economics was granted to Kahneman and Smith (2002), who have been rewarded for applying the economic experiments to scientific research and for launching experimental economics in this way. Valuation of privacy, by virtue of its different from most of the goods, may be the subject of research but using the experimental methods.

An empirical examination of the privacy valuation can be classified into two groups. The first and larger group includes research that directly or indirectly measures the amount or benefits, that the customer deems as sufficient to pass on the personal data, or willingness to accept (WTA—willingness to accept) to give away their data (examples in: Spiekermann et al. (2001), Chellapa and Sin (2005), Wathieu and Friedman (2005), Huberman et al. (2006), Cvrcek et al. (2006), Hui et al. (2007)). A second, smaller group, includes the research on actual prices or intangible costs that customers are willing to pay (WTP—willingness to pay), to protect their privacy (Acquisti and Grossklags (2005), Varian et al. (2005), Png (2007), Tsai et al. (2011).

Most of the research studies, which have been carried out till now, are the laboratory experiments. The results obtained usually indicate a quite low valuation of privacy. Tsai et al. (2011) came to the conclusion that participants of the experiment paid in addition small amounts (about 50 cents) in exchange for purchases with a better protection of privacy. Varian et al. (2005), explored how much American consumers are willing to spend on protection against telemarketers, the values ranged from a few cents to $30.2. Tedeschi (2002) proved that 82 % of the online shoppers were willing to share their personal data for a new shopping centre in return for a chance to win $100. Spiekermann et al. (2001) check the readiness of tested persons to answer personal questions in exchange for discounts or recommendations. It was also checked whether the consumers are willing to pay to have their privacy preserved, the percentage of such persons was 47 %.

An example of a field experiment can be presented the research, which was carried out in Pittsburgh (Acquisti et al. 2013a, b). Customers the mall were asked to fill the survey, which was the bait for real test. As a reward for participation in this study the respondents receive gift cards.

- Subjects received ownership of:
  - Anonymous gift card for $10. On the card there was note “your name will not be associated with transactions performed by using this card and its use will not be tracked by the researchers.”
  - Personal gift card for $12. On this card there was note “your name will be associated with transactions performed by using this card and its use will be tracked by the researchers.”

- Interviewees were asked whether they wish to exchange the cards:
  - The anonymous card of $10 for the personal card of $12 (WTA).
  - The personal card of $12 for the anonymous card of $10 (WTP).

The key difference between the offered cards, despite their different values, was related to whether the performed purchases may be subject to monitoring (that is, the investigator could check what the person bought).

18.4 Description of the Experiment

On the basis of above study it was designed a new study in which the subject of a sale-purchase transaction was access to the social security number (PESEL) (ID number). That is, at this point, the investigator has received in return for increased remuneration, an access to sensitive information relating to a particular person. The respondent was also informed that the social security number will be associated with the need to show a personal ID document to the interviewer.

Prior to the start of the test there were set three hypothesis:

H1 People assign different values to their private information (personal) depending on whether they focus on protecting it or disclosure of it.
H2 Privacy valuations by individuals are not consistent.
H3 Group of consumers who accept the offered money in exchange for reduced privacy (WTA), is larger than the group of consumers who accept economically equivalent offer to pay money in exchange for increased privacy (WTP).

The study was carried out during 1 day (Saturday) in the biggest shopping mall in Gdansk (Poland), the Baltic Gallery (approximately 45 thousand square metres).

Interviewers (female and male) stopped every 15th person passing through the stand (Fig. 18.1) with the logo of the University of Gdańsk (the largest University in Northern Poland, about 30,000 students), and offered to fill a short survey on the subject related to personal finance, in exchange for Sodexo gift voucher with a value of 10 PLN (Polish zloty) (without any additional conditions) or voucher of PLN 20 or 30 PLN (with the need to provide a social security number (PESEL) which was verified he was showing an ID document to the interviewer). In the last two cases, this requirement was given during the presentation of the proposal to participate in the poll.

Four decision-making situations occurred in the survey:

- [WTA/Δ10] Keep voucher of 10 PLN (2.5 EUR), which is anonymous, or the convert it to the voucher of 20 PLN (5 EUR), which is linked to the social security number (PESEL),
- [WTA/Δ10] Keep voucher of 20 PLN (5 EUR), which is linked to presenting the social security number (PESEL), or the convert it to the voucher of 10 PLN (2.5 EUR), which is anonymous,

Fig. 18.1 Interviewers' stand at the mall (own materials)

- [WTA/Δ20] Keep voucher of 10 PLN (2.5 EUR), which is anonymous, or the convert it to the voucher of 30 PLN (7.5 EUR), which is linked to presenting the social security number (PESEL),
- [WTA/Δ20] Keep voucher of 30 PLN (7.5 EUR), which is linked to presenting the social security number (PESEL), or the convert it to the voucher of 10 PLN (2.5 EUR), which is anonymous.

Schematic diagram of experiment is presented in Fig. 18.2.

In the study took part 120 people who decided to fill out a survey. The number of people who were proposed to participate in the study was greater. Refusal of participation took place only in the case when the first proposal concerned the participation in the survey, in which the person had to enter the personal data (interviewers talked with total of 154 people).

The distribution of respondents and their decisions is contained in Table 18.1 and in Fig. 18.3.

None of the people, who were proposed 10 PLN for completing the survey has not refused to participate in the study. Respondents were proposed PLN 20 or 30 PLN and were required, in return, to enter their data (social security number (PESEL). It was noted that in the case, when the proposed amount was higher (that is, disclosure of their privacy), there was a larger percentage of denials among of total surveyed persons and it was the same in a group of men. Differences were

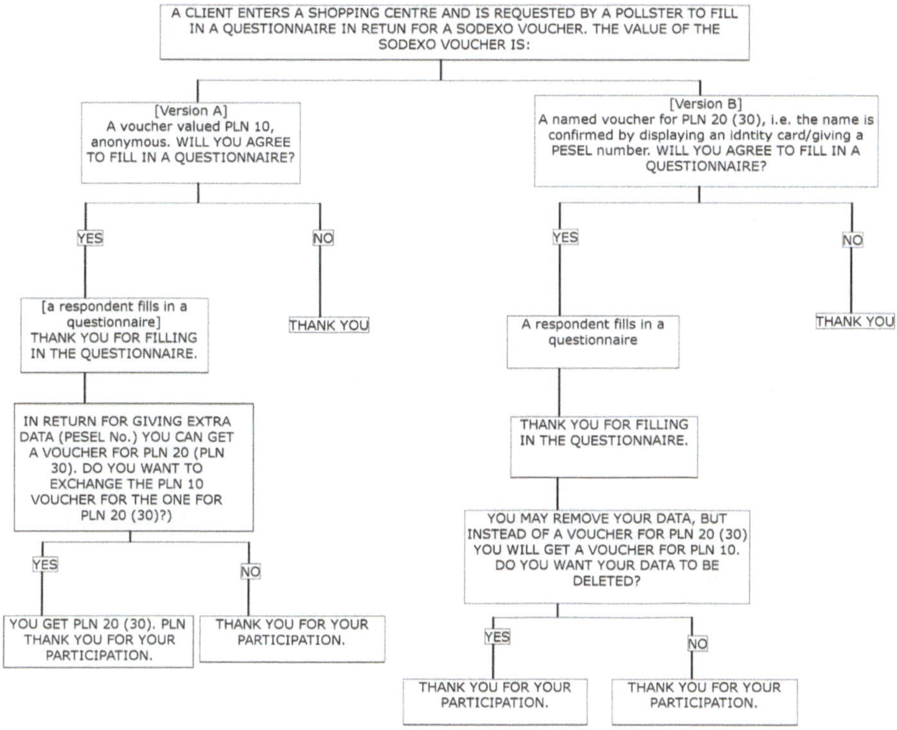

Fig. 18.2 Diagram of experiment (own study)

Table 18.1 Proposed amount and the decision of the (quantitative distribution)

	Total	Women	Men						
Decision	Amount								
	10	20	30	10	20	30	10	20	30
Participation in the study	60	30	30	29	18	18	31	12	12
Refusal	0	16	18	0	9	8	0	7	10
Total	60	46	48	29	27	26	31	19	22

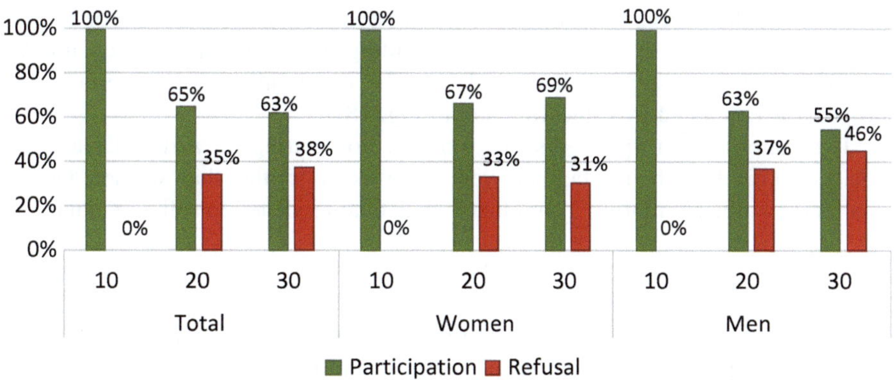

Fig. 18.3 The amount of proposal and a decision (percentage distribution) (own study)

Table 18.2 Data sales proposal ($\Delta \geq 0$), and respondents' reactions

Decision	Total	Women	Men
Non-disclosure of the data ($\Delta = 0$)	15	10	5
Sale of the data ($\Delta = 0$)	45	19	26
Total	60	29	31

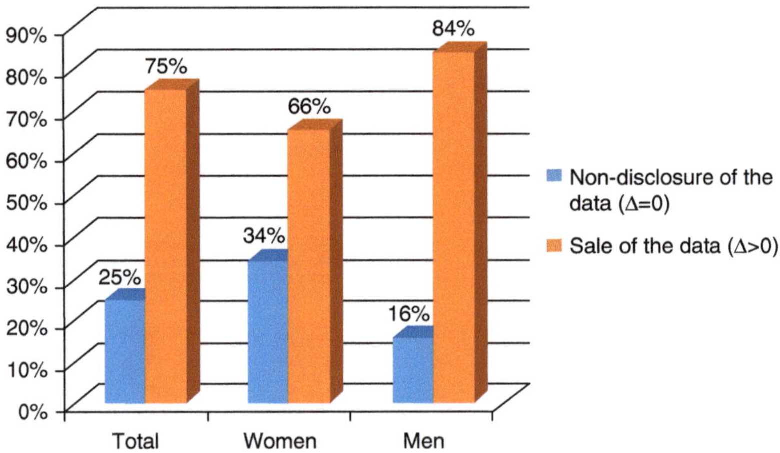

Fig. 18.4 Response of customer for proposal to sell their data (WTA) (own study)

statistically insignificant (total of tested persons: $\chi^2(1) = 0.075$, $p = 0.392$, men: $\chi^2(1) = 0.312$, $p = 0.289$, $p = 0.289$, women: $\chi^2(1) = 0.40$, $p = 0.421$).

Verifying the first hypothesis (H1 People assign different values to their private (personal) information depending on whether they focus on protecting it (WTP) or its disclosure (WTA)), it was compared the responses in the situation of proposal for their data sale (that is, from an anonymous 10 PLN to bid with a higher value in exchange for personal information) to the situation of a proposal for paying for their data (i.e. from offer 20/30 PLN to offer without providing their data on the voucher for 10 PLN).

Those who agreed to fill out a survey and receive a $10 after filling it, were proposed by the interviewer to receive the additional amount of 10 PLN or 20 PLN (random proposal) in exchange for providing their social security number (i.e. received proposal to sell their data). The distribution of responses to this proposal is contained in Table 18.2 and in Fig. 18.4.

The majority of respondents, in exchange for getting an additional amount, decided to disclose their data, men were more likely for that than women. Gender is a factor in differentiating a significant statistical tendency to sell own data

$$\chi^2(1) = 2.692,\ p = 0.0505 \tag{18.1}$$

In the case of the mall customers, who first heard the offer of receiving 20/30 PLN, associated with submitting their social security number and who agreed for it, after

Table 18.3 Proposal of buyback of own data (privacy recovery) ($\Delta \geq 0$), and respondents' reactions

Decision	Total	Women	Men
Privacy has no value ($\Delta = 0$)	56	35	21
I buy the privacy ($\Delta < 0$)	4	1	3
Total	60	36	24

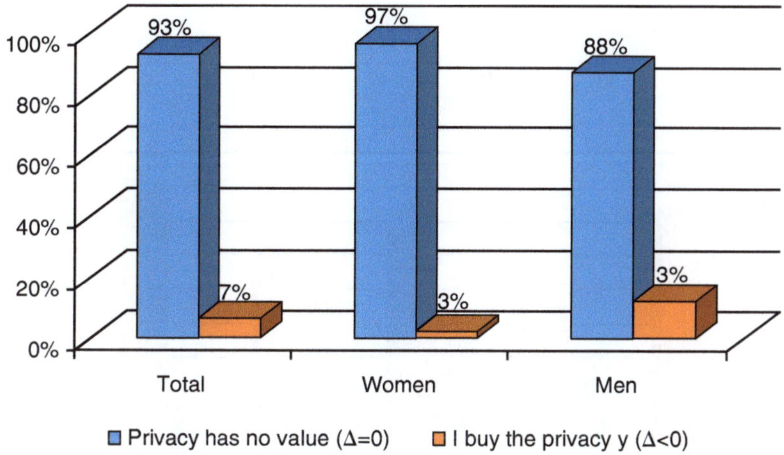

Fig. 18.5 Response of customer for proposal to buy back their data (WTA) (own study)

they filled in survey questionnaire, the interviewer suggested that might give away the social security number of the questionnaire, however, then the respondent would receive a voucher with a value of only PLN 10 (that is, whether person would be willing to pay for own privacy (WTP). The distribution of responses to this proposal is contained in Table 18.3 and Fig. 18.5.

Most of the respondents were not willing to change their decision about selling their data. They did not accept the proposal to recover their privacy in exchange for reducing the originally proposed amount by 10 or 20 PLN. From statistical point of view the gender was not a significant factor differentiating the tendency to buy privacy.

$$\chi^2(1) = 2.188, \ p = 0.171 \tag{18.2}$$

Hypothesis 1 was verified positively.

Within the verification of the second hypothesis (H2 privacy valuations by individuals are not consistent) it was examined whether the proposed remuneration (in the case of WTA) and charges (WTP) has an impact on decisions. It was assumed that this should take place, but the relationship should not be linear.

The distribution of the respondents' behaviour in the case of data sales (WTA) is contained in Table 18.4 and Fig. 18.6.

Table 18.4 Decisions of the respondents in the case of a proposal for the sale of their privacy depending on the proposed amount

Decision	Total amount	Women	Men			
	20 PLN ($\Delta+10$)	30 PLN ($\Delta+20$)	20 PLN ($\Delta+10$)	30 PLN ($\Delta+20$)	20 PLN ($\Delta+10$)	30 PLN ($\Delta+20$)
Non-disclosure of the data ($\Delta=0$)	7	8	5	5	2	3
Sale of the data	23	22	12	7	11	15
Total	30	30	17	12	13	18

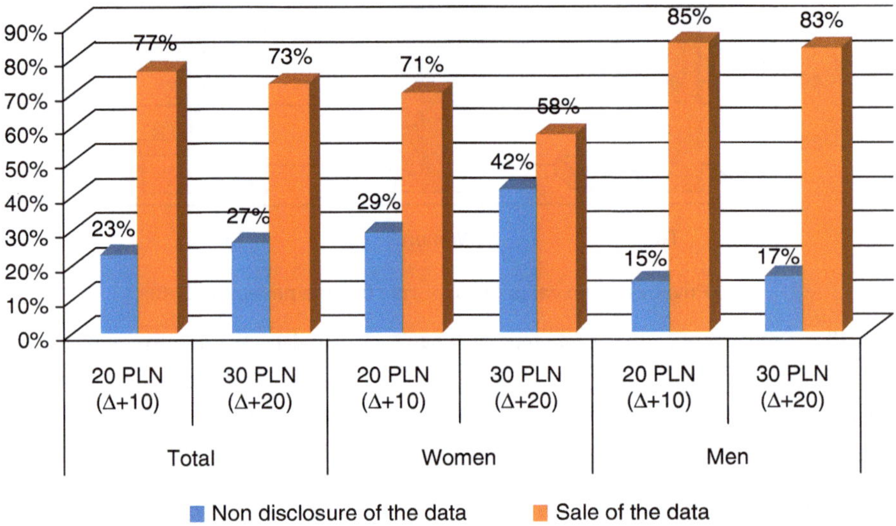

Fig. 18.6 Distribution of respondents' decision depending on the proposal amount (WTA) (own study)

There was no statistically significant relationship between the proposed amount and decision to sell the data ($\chi^2(1)=0.089$, $p=0.383$). This regularity is characteristic both for women

$$\left(\chi^2(1) = 0.468,\ p = 0.385\right) \text{ and men } \left(\chi^2(1) = 0.009,\ p = 0.659\right). \tag{18.3}$$

There were also analysed the reactions of surveyed people on the situation related to the proposal to protect their privacy or how to respond to the offer of buyback of their social security number, and whether there was any relationship related to the amount of the fee.

The distribution of the respondents' behaviour in the case of proposal of data buyback (WTA) is contained in Table 18.5 and Fig. 18.7.

Table 18.5 Decisions of the respondents in the case of a proposal for the sale of their privacy depending on the proposed amount

	Total amount (Δ)		Women		Men	
Decision	10 PLN (Δ-10)	20 PLN (Δ-20)	10 PLN (Δ-10)	20 PLN (Δ-20)	10 PLN (Δ-10)	20 PLN (Δ-20)
Privacy has no value	27	29	17	18	10	11
I buy privacy (anonymity)	3	1	1	0	2	1
Total	30	30	18	18	12	12

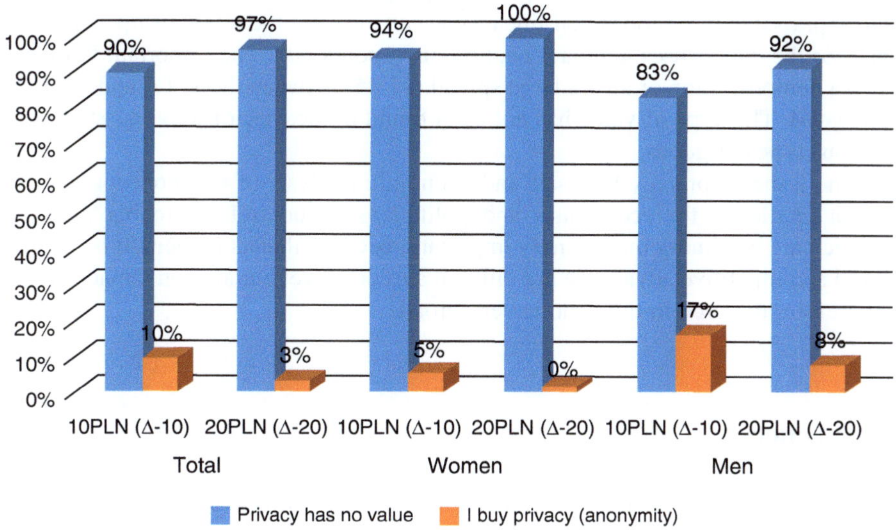

Fig. 18.7 Distribution of respondents' decision depending on the proposal amount (WTP) (own study)

Almost all respondents have not changed their earlier decision and at the expense of resignation from the amount of 10 or 20 PLN, this way they did not decide to purchase of anonymity (privacy). The decision was not affect by the proposed amount ($\chi^2(1) = 1.071$, $p = 0.303$). This regularity is characteristic both for women ($\chi^2(1) = 0.1021$, $p = 0.500$) and men ($\chi^2(1) = 0.381$, $p = 0.500$).

The second hypothesis was verified positively. The amount of proposed remuneration / fee did not affect the decisions of participants in the experiment.

In the case of third hypothesis (H3 group of consumers who accepted the offered money in exchange for reduced privacy (WTA), is larger than the group of consumers, who accept economically equivalent offer to pay money in exchange for increased privacy (WTP)), the very simple analysis is enough to prove its validity. 45 people (75 %) take advantage of the exchange 10–>20/30, 4 people

(6.7 %) take advantage of the exchange 20/30–>10. The ratio between the WTA and WTP is 11.25. Test of proportion (fraction) rejects the hypothesis of identical tendency to convert in both groups ($p < 0.0001$). Then there is statistically significant difference in behaviour.

18.5 Summary

The performed experiment allowed us to conclude that privacy is a specific type of good, which is characterised by other characteristics than most goods. The key conclusion is that privacy has its price for people and they are willing to sell it, but the appraisal of this good is non-linear (you can even see the relationship that higher pay for the data causes a greater caution of respondents). The important finding is also a demonstration of a very large spread (11.25) between the WTA and WTP for this good. This type of value has not been found in the case of previous studies on various types of goods.

The issue of privacy by itself and economic analysis of this concept is still a major challenge for economists and politicians. Issues related to big data and privacy are becoming increasingly important, because thanks to them, it is possible build a competitive advantage not only on a micro-level but also on a macro-level. Therefore, research in this field is very broad.

References

Acquisti A (2014) The economics and behavioral economics of privacy. In: Lane J et al (eds) Privacy, big data and the public good. University Press, Cambridge
Acquisti A, John LK, Loewenstein G (2013a) What is privacy worth? J Leg Stud 42(2):249–274
Acquisti A, Grossklags J (2005) Privacy and rationality in decision making. IEEE Secur Priv (1): 24–30
Acquisti A, John LK, Loewenstein G (2013b) What is privacy worth? J Leg Stud 42(2):249–274
Beresford AR, Kübler D, Preibusch S (2012) Unwillingness to pay for privacy: a field experiment. Econo Lett 117(1):25–27
Calzolari G, Pavan A (2006) On the optimality of privacy in sequential contracting. J Econ Theor 130(1):168–204
Chellapa R, Sin RG (2005) Personalization versus privacy: an empirical examination of the online consumers' dilemma. Inform Technol Manag 6(2–3):181–202
Cvrcek D, Kumpost M, Matyas V, and Danezis G (2006) A study on the value of location privacy. Proceedings of workshop on privacy in the electronic society (WPES'06), pp. 109–118
Czajkowski M (2004) Przyczyny powstania dysparytetu WTA-WTP dla dóbr konsumpcyjnych. Ekonomia 11(2004):197–211
Greenstein S, Lerner J, Stern S (2013) Digitization, innovation, and copyright: what is the agenda? Strat Organ 11(1):110–121
Hayek F (1945) The use of knowledge in society. Am Econ Rev 35(4):519–530
Huberman B, Adar E and Fine L (2006) Valuating privacy. Proceedings of the workshop on the economics of information security (WEIS'06), pp. 22–25

Hui KL, Teo HH, Lee TSY (2007) The value of privacy assurance: an exploratory field experiment. MIS Quart 31(1):19–33

Kahneman D, Smith V (2002) Foundations of Behavioral and Experimental Economics. Nobel Prize in Economics Documents, 1.

Malheiros M, Brostoff S, Jennett C, Sasse MA (2013) Would you sell your mother's data? personal data disclosure in a simulated credit card application. In The Economics of Information Security and Privacy (pp. 237–261). Springer Berlin Heidelberg.

Maslow AH (1943) A theory of human motivation. Psychol Rev 50:370–396

Png IPL (2007) On the value of privacy from telemarketing: evidence from the "Do Not Call" registry. http://ssrn.com/abstract=1000533

Posner RA (1978) The right of privacy. Georgia Law Rev 12(3):393–422

Preibusch S, Kübler D, Beresford AR (2013) Price versus privacy: an experiment into the competitive advantage of collecting less personal information. Electron Commerce Res 13:423–455

Solove DJ (2006) A taxonomy of privacy. Univ Penn Law Rev 154(3):477–564

Spiekermann S, Grossklags J, Berendt B (2001) E-privacy. In: 2nd generation ECommerce: privacy preferences versus actual behavior. Proceedings of the ACM conference on electronic commerce, pp. 38–47

Stigler GJ (1980) An introduction to privacy in economics and politics. J Leg Stud 9:623–44

Tedeschi B (2002) Everybody talks about online privacy, but few do anything about it. New York Times, June 3, Section C, Page 6, Column 1

Thaler R (1980) Toward a positive theory of consumer choice. J Econ Behav Organ 1(1):39–60

Tsai J, Egelman S, Cranor LF, Acquisti A (2011) The effect of online privacy information on purchasing behavior: an experimental study. Inform Syst Res 22(2):254–268

Varian HR (1996) Economic aspects of personal privacy. In: Privacy and self-regulation in the information age, National Telecommunications and Information Administration

Varian HR, Wallenberg F, Woroch G (2005) The demographics of the do-not-call list. IEEE Secur Priv 3(1):34–39

Wathieu L, Friedman A (2005) An empirical approach to understanding privacy valuation. Proceedings of the fourth workshop on the economics of information security (WEIS'05), Cambridge, MA

Chapter 19
The Behaviour of Inexperienced Buyers in Buy-It-Now Online Auctions

Jacek Cypryjański, Aleksandra Grzesiuk, and Edyta Rudawska

Abstract Online auctions combine the conventional auction model with information technology. The research investigates online auctions buyers' behaviour. The authors suggest that due to key features of online environment there are some signals that the sellers could implement to influence online auction buyers' behaviour. The chapter is in the context of experimental economy. The research project was conducted by natural experiment through Allegro.pl, the leading online auctions platform in Poland. The online transactions were conducted in compliance with all statutory requirements of Allegro by a professional company focused on online business. The basic transaction was the sale of mobile phone pouch during buy-it-now online auction. Observations were carried out for 30 days. The whole project covers 370 transactions in total. There are two main groups of recommendations from the project. The first relates to the impact of online auction design parameters on the number of entries/hits per page and the sales volume of the product. The other group of recommendations allows forecasting the future of online auction market in Poland as more and more online auction buyers gain experience and passes from inexperienced to experienced group.

Keywords Buyers' experience • Sellers' reputation • Online auctions • Field experiment

---

J. Cypryjański (✉)
Department of Computational Methods in Experimental Economics, Faculty of Economics and Management, Institute of IT in Management, University of Szczecin, Mickiewicza 64, 71-101 Szczecin, Poland
e-mail: cypra@wneiz.pl

A. Grzesiuk
The West Pomeranian Business School, ul. Żołnierska 53, 71-210 Szczecin, Poland
e-mail: agrzesiuk@zpsb.pl

E. Rudawska
Department of Marketing, Institute of Management and Marketing, Faculty of Economics and Management, University of Szczecin, Mickiewicza 64, 71-101 Szczecin, Poland
e-mail: edyta@rudawska.pl

K. Nermend, M. Łatuszyńska (eds.), *Selected Issues in Experimental Economics*, Springer Proceedings in Business and Economics, DOI 10.1007/978-3-319-28419-4_19

19.1 Introduction

Within the last decade, the growth of online auctions as a distribution channel has been enormous. According to Statistics Portal, the world leading online auction platform eBay, in the second quarter of 2015 reached 157 million active users compared to 140 million active users at the end of 2013. In 2012, eBay net revenue amounted to almost 14.07 billion US dollars and reached 16.05 billion US dollars in 2013. The most important market for eBay is US online market. In 2014, eBay generated regional (US) net revenue of close to 8.5 billion US dollars, up from 7.71 billion US dollars in 2013 (Statistics Portal 2015).

This chapter is devoted to the analysis of online auction market in Poland. Therefore, some key statistics regarding regional market are presented. According to Aukcjostat.pl in June 2015 the average number of all online auctions in Poland per day was over 47 million. However, the structure of the market in Poland differs from other markets. Polish-origin Allegro.pl is the online auction market leader with market share over 82 %. It has more than 7 million active users in Poland and ca. 40 million auctions per day. For comparison, the market share of eBay Poland is only ca. 1 % with 0.5 million online auctions per day (Aukcjostat 2015). Data prepared by Gemius shows that 76 % of Polish Internet users evoked Allegro brand as the first, when they were asked about shopping on the Web (Gemius 2014).

Despite all competitive pressure, online auction market in Poland is growing rapidly. If worldwide eBay brand became synonymous to online auctions, in Poland this is synonymous with Allegro. Despite business interest and the increasing role of online market, the domestic (Polish) economic literature has done little to address the questions concerning online auctions' buyers' behaviour. Are there differences in the experienced and inexperienced buyers' behaviour? Are there any differences in behaviour in relation to gender? What can online auction sellers do strategically to make use of buyers' experience and generate more revenue?

Insights from the buyer behaviour are critical to the design of auction design parameters, which directly affect the seller's revenue. Therefore, are there any particular online auction parameters, which significantly affect buyers' behaviour?

The chapter begins to answer some of these questions by demonstrating the results of natural experiment conducted through Allegro platform. The main goal of the chapter is to assess buyer behaviour across buy-it-now online auctions versus buyers' experience. The added value of the project is derived from the benefits of field experiment as the investigative empirical method. It allowed us to observe the buyers' behaviour in natural environment, in the form of actually executed transactions. The buyers were not aware of the fact that they are participating in the research study. Additionally some remarks concerning field experiments conducted through online auction platform will be presented.

19.2 Allegro Platform as an Environment for Field Experiments

The Internet environment creates unprecedented opportunities for researchers' to conduct field experiments. A field experiment has major benefits over laboratory experiment or other research methods. It is because it takes place in a naturally occurring setting, in contrast to the artificiality of a laboratory (Suh et al. 2013). It is run in normal conditions, which are well-known and familiar places for participants—their place of residence, education or work. Whether influencing factors are used or not in this type of experiments may not be noticed by the participant at all. Since the participant may not even know that the experiment is being conducted, his unnatural behaviour is eliminated. The participant does not act as expected by the researcher and the society, but he acts spontaneously. In a natural experiment it is possible to induce a particular phenomenon and to control determining factors. Repeatability is also very important, i.e. the fact that the phenomenon may be induced many times in order to verify the obtained results of the experiment.

The Internet offers, nowadays, favourable conditions to conduct this type of experiments. It makes that form of research more realistic. There are four basic experimental technologies for intervention within an online community. They include: e-mail and SMS/texting, modified web interfaces, bots (program or script that makes automated edits or suggestions), and add-ons—software to monitor a participant's behaviour across multiple site (Yan Chen and Konstan 2015). The Internet provides the opportunity for retailers to conduct experiments as marketing tests to observe customers' behaviour. The form of these experiments is observation conducted through online platforms.

In the field experiment conducted through online auction platform we are not dealing with simulated phenomenon. Neither sellers nor buyers are participants in the actual transaction. And depending on the research goals, a bidder in this environment or a seller is not aware that they participate in research project. In the reported study the bidders just bought mobile phone pouch.

Such a design of experiment allows us to eliminate all factors that could modify the natural buyers' behaviour. However, the use of auction platform makes it necessary to comply with the rules of the platform. Therefore, the design of the experiments is limited by the statutory regulations. The main obstacle that the researchers encounter on Allegro is certain cost of delivery. Allegro platform administrator removes listings from inflated costs of delivery. The fact that the price for an item must be in accordance with the price lists of the Polish Post or other couriers says Allegro Regulations. Apart from the price set in the sales offer, seller may charge only the cost of delivery in the actual amount.

It is not allowed overcharging for shipping. This is only permitted rounding or to reduce these costs in order to simplify the rules for buyers.

For the price in the final Allegro commission or fee for credit card payments cannot be counted. To the final price the seller cannot include the costs associated with preparing the course for shipment (packaging, service). These costs should be included in the price of an item. Prices of items must be gross prices given in PLN. Personal collection should be free. In the description of the offer the seller is obliged to provide the actual cost of delivery.

These facts significantly reduce running experiments in which variable is the cost of delivery. For Allegro there is a group of goods that cannot be offered for sale (in any form: also add free of charge to other products). There are also such items, the production of which involves additional requirements.

Despite the limitations indicated, Allegro platform is widely available and provides very favourable conditions for both sellers and bidders. It therefore constitutes appropriate environment to conduct field experiments.

19.3 Experience vs. Online Buyers' Behaviour

As mentioned earlier, the rapid growth of online auction market in Poland affects the research interest. The impressive growth and the crucial role of auction market in e-commerce in Poland have occurred despite the fact that bidders face substantial risks because of the nature of the market and e-transactions.

Additionally, practitioners stress the need for solutions to improve efficiency of online business. In the centre of the authors' interest are the online auction parameters, key features and signals to influence buyers' behaviour. However, the modification of buyers' behaviour may be different depending on their experience.

The role of experience in economic decision making is not well understood. Specifically, it is difficult to observe repeated decision making of particular buyer because it could really extend the research process. Additionally, even repeated buying decisions of particular buyer are taken under different conditions or there are other additional factors affecting decisions that did not exist previously.

Several recent empirical studies have found that inexperienced and experienced buyers exhibit different bidding behaviours but the arguments for varied behaviour are different. However, there are some interesting studies on online buyers' experience that enrich our knowledge and stimulate further projects.

Srinivasan and Wang (2010) compared the effect of experience based on bidders' complete bidding history with conventional experience measures that use feedback ratings. They tracked the whole bidding history of novice bidders on eBay over a period of 6 months and analysed auction and product characteristics, bidders' behaviour (i.e. bids, number of bids, bid amount and bidding timing), and the auction outcome. The analysis offers three key implications: (1) inexperienced bidders learn from their experiences and become more sophisticated in bidding, (2) their learning speed is not as slow as suggested by an analysis based on feedback ratings and (3) to gauge experience and learning effects properly, it is imperative to use the complete bidding history, because selecting winning experiences or losing experiences alone is likely to cause major biases in the conclusions.

Pownall and Wolk (2013) investigated the role of experience in the online art auctions and they supported the evidence of a learning effect. Their findings suggest that more experienced buyers not only bid earlier in auctions but also revise their bids less often. Borle et al. (2006) show that more experienced buyers time their bids differently than inexperienced buyers and revise their bids less. Bidder's experience with online buying modifies also the way and time of purchase (Livingston 2010). The study investigated bidders' behaviour in relation to seller's reputation. He concludes that buyers alter their strategies as they gain market experience. While inexperienced buyers bid the same high amounts regardless of the seller's reputation, experienced buyers bid substantially less if the seller's reputation is lower. Livingston's study also supports our knowledge in strategic timing of bid placement. Experienced buyers place their bids much closer to the end of the auction, although it takes very little experience to learn that waiting to submit a bid is a superior strategy. Goes et al. (2012) observations show that buyers learn from experience and adapt their choices of strategies to possibly maximise their surplus. They find that buyers demand, participation experience and auction design parameters affect the choice of purchasing strategies. Buyers with unit demand are likely to choose early buying strategies, while those with multiple demand adopt late bidding strategies.

Hence, considering the above, for the purpose of the chapter the authors propose the following research hypotheses:

Hypothesis 1. There is a relation between buyers' experience and the type of online auction design parameters.

The other research stream denies relationship between experience and buyers' behaviour. Such conclusions are based on Lee and Malmendier (2011) studies. They do not find effects of experience by analysing feedback scores from eBay.

As concluded from the theory of customers' behaviour, buyers' behaviour can vary over geographical regions, cultural groups etc. Therefore, some research results from studies conducted in Poland should be presented. However, the authors found the subject unexplored in Polish literature. Therefore, the authors conclude that the reported study can enhance our knowledge about the online buyers' behaviour in Poland.

For the purpose of the recent study, to infer buyers' experience, the amount of feedback a buyer has received was used as a variable defining experience.

19.4 Sellers' Reputation in Online Auction Market

According to different reports, main reasons for not buying online in Poland are security and privacy concern (Gemius 2014; Internet Standard 2014). According to Gemius reports, the desire to see the product before buying is the main argument for not buying online, followed by nondelivery fraud, concerns with a product guarantee and safety of delivery.

The above mentioned results imply the research interest in the factors that can reduce customers concerns and encourage them to buy online. These concerns are more important in case of online auctions because there is a perception that the online auctioneers are temporary entities, which can disappear or close their business at any moment. Therefore, potential online buyers can perceive greater purchase risk.

When dealing with unknown web vendors, online buyers are more concerned about privacy and are less likely to trust the vendors (Walczuch and Lundgren 2004). Zhao and Huang (2008) indicated that seller reputation is an important factor that influences buyer decisions, due to uncertainty and risk of online transactions.

Perceived risk in online auctions affects the role of reputation systems in electronic markets. The critical role of reputation is well understood and investigated from different perspectives. In the context of behavioural economy, significant information asymmetry between sellers and buyers is observed and therefore the role of reputation is underlined (Ba and Pavlou 2002; Dellarocas 2003). Buyers usually depend on online reputation systems to check the seller's reputation, because such systems can record and report a seller's reputation according to other buyers' feedback (Finch 2007). Additionally, perceived risk negatively influences consumer attitude toward the website and online purchase intention, while consumer attitude toward the website positively influences purchase intention (Wann-Yih Wu et al. 2011).

It seems that despite the development of e-commerce, the question of the online seller' reputation is still important for buyers. Low-quality online sellers manipulate their reputations and masquerade as high-quality sellers. That is the result of research on eBay conducted by Ye et al. (2014). They found that these sellers reacted strongly to eBay's announcement of a proposed ban on revoking. Interestingly, after the power of these strategic sellers is curtailed, there is an evidence that they exert more efforts to improve their reputation scores.

As mentioned, nondelivery fraud is well-known problem. The study conducted by Almendra (2012) tested the effect of reputation, product price, and buyer experience on the outcome of nondelivery fraud attempts. Furthermore, the study supports the hypothesis that less experienced buyers get swindled more often than more experienced ones. The results were similar to those of Gregg and Scott (2006); however, the difference between the rate obtained by Almendra and Gregg and Scott could be attributed to the different methodologies used.

Hence, considering the above, for the purpose of the chapter the authors propose the following research hypotheses:

Hypothesis 2a. There is a relation between online sellers' reputation and the online auction parameter—number of hits per page.

Hypothesis 2b. There is a relation between online sellers' reputation and the online auction volume of sales.

19.5 Experimental Procedure

The study was carried out by natural experiment through Allegro.pl, the leading online auctions platform in Poland. The transactions were conducted in compliance with all statutory requirements from online selling on Allegro.

Auctions were held by a professional company specialising in the online auctions between 9 April and 8 May 2014. Observations were conducted for 30 days. The basic transaction was the sale of mobile phone pouch during buy-it-now online auction. The total number of transactions made during the experiment amounted to 370. For further analysis it was assumed that 370 observed transactions meant 370 customers buying a mobile phone pouch. The assumption was made on the basis of the specificity of the product (a mobile phone pouch—a temporary purchase product) and the time frame of the experiment (30 days), thus eliminating customer loyalty in a behavioural dimension.

During the experiment there was no single purchase of a greater batch of goods. No other seller offered exactly the same mobile phone pouches.

The number of hits on the auction site and the number of items sold were observed.

As part of each experiment mobile phone pouches were sold at two simultaneous auctions, out of which one was an ordinary auction and the other was a highlighted auction (together four auctions were followed for each of the analysed feature). Highlighting enabled better offer positioning on the listing of searched auctions. Each of the mentioned methods of increasing attractiveness of the online auction was a separate experiment, i.e. four natural experiments were conducted.

The project covered six variables: (1) modified product description, (2) auction title written by capital letters, (3) modified cost of delivery (within the scope of regulation of online platform), (4) the quality of photo, (5) sellers' reputation, (6) the effect of herd cues (Cypryjański et al. 2015). For the purpose of the chapter, two variables were selected and verified: buyers' experience and sellers' reputation.

19.6 Research Results

As mentioned earlier, the buyers' experience is measured by the number of comments, which the buyers placed on the platform. For results' analyses, the buyers were divided into two groups according to their experience measured by the number of posted comments: 0–23 posted comments—inexperienced buyers, >24 posted comments—experienced buyers. The number of comments (24) divided the research sample in half. Including sample structure by gender, 54 % of all women belonged to inexperienced group vs. 42 % of men defined as inexperienced.

Although the buyers' behaviour vs. gender is not the main focus of the chapter, it is worth mentioning, that the research results can support the general belief that men are more experienced in online auctions.

To verify hypotheses stated above Chi square test was used. Null hypotheses were stated, which indicated the lack of relation between analysed factors for $\alpha = 0.05$. With the use of statistical tools for data analysis in Excel program, the value of the chi square test was calculated for H1 and the result is: 3.841.

In case of the hypothesis regarding the relation of experience in online auctions and the type of online auction design parameters (H1), there is no justification for rejecting null hypothesis, indicating the inexperienced and experienced buyers represent similar buying behaviours. It means that the relation between buyers experience and type of online auction is not statistically significant. Thus Hypothesis 1 cannot be supported.

As stated above, the project covered six variables and in depth analysis of relations between modified variables and buyers' experience was tested.

The first analysed experiment referred to the way the product was described to the buyer. Two auctions were conducted simultaneously: one with description including technical parameters of the product and some elements of the marketing description indicating some benefits of the product to the purchaser, the other auction—description with only technical parameters of the product. We suppose that the form of product description—more or less friendly for customer should influence buyers' behaviour. To be more precise, we suppose that inexperienced buyers are more influenced by friendly form of product description then experienced buyers.

Therefore, we decided to test supplementary hypothesis (H1a) regarding the relation between buyers' experience and type of product description.

Hypothesis 1a. There is a significant relation between the experience and the type of product description. We assume that inexperienced buyers are more inclined to purchase products with more friendly description.

To verify hypotheses stated above Chi square test with Yeats' correction was used. On the significance level 0.05 the relation between experience and type of product description is statistically significant. The value of the Chi square test (6.490) indicates that the null hypothesis cannot be accepted. On the significance level 0.05 the relation between experience and the type of product description is statistically significant. The study shows that inexperienced buyers are more inclined to purchase products with more friendly description.

No inexperienced buyers bought at auction with only technical product description; every inexperienced bought at auction with more friendly, marketing description. Therefore, the results support the general belief that inexperienced buyers are influenced by form of product description. In the contrary, experienced buyers are less influenced by the form of product description.

In order to test research hypotheses: H2a and H2b, the data obtained from the experiments were analysed with the dependent samples *t*-test ($p < 0.05$).

The results of the experiments (see Table 19.1) indicate that the reputation of the seller, measured by the number of positive comments from online auction bidders on a particular vendor, significantly determines the number of hits per page ($p = 0.0$). Dependence has been confirmed for both the ordinary auctions as well as for the highlighted auctions. Thus, the Hypothesis 2a was supported.

Table 19.1 Estimation results

Hypothesis	The value of the Chi square test	Hypothesis verification
Hypothesis 1	0.102	Hypothesis not supported
Hypothesis 1a	6.490 The value of dependent samples *T*-test ($p < 0.05$)	Hypothesis supported
Hypothesis 2a	0.0	Hypothesis supported
Hypothesis 2b	0.04 for highlighted auctions 0.02 for ordinary auctions	Hypothesis supported

Furthermore, the results confirm that the reputation of the online seller determines the number of units sold, with p-value $= 0.04$ for highlighted auctions and $p = 0.02$ for ordinary auctions. Thus, the Hypothesis 2b was supported.

19.7 Conclusions and Recommendations

The rapid growth of online auction market in Poland and its role in e-commerce justify the research interest in that area.

The current research has indicated the need for a strong commitment of online auction sellers in creating a positive image and its own credibility. Analysis of online auction bidding behaviour, measured by the number of page views and the number-sales units, clearly indicates that buyers are sensitive to visual cues/auction design parameters. It should be noted, however, that this proposal may result from the nature of the product used in the experiments. Mobile phone punch is a relatively simple product, with probably little significance for the customer, and thus is associated with low customer involvement in the buying process. However, the most interesting conclusions come from the analysis of customers' experience.

According to the authors it is valuable for business practice to observe how the future will change the auction market as more and more buyers gain experience and switch from inexperienced to experienced group.

Although the general hypothesis about the relationship between buyer experience and their bidding behaviour has not been supported, the research results provide valuable lessons. The research results draw to the conclusion that males are more experienced purchasers than females.

The study shows strong support for the role of reputation in auction market. The results indicate that seller reputation, measured by the number of positive comments from online auction buyers on a particular vendor, significantly determines the number of hits per page and number of units sold. The importance of reputation seller is independent from the buyers' experience. In each investigated buyers' group reputation is an important argument for the buyer.

19.8 Limitations and Further Research

The reported research covered the observation of online buying process of mobile phone pouch. A mobile phone pouch is rather simple product of low value for customers. It results in relatively low-risk purchase, and thus, a low degree of involvement of the buyer in the purchase process. We hypothesised that the value and character of the product could affect and modify both experienced and inexperienced buyers' behaviour. Therefore, the further research should focus on products of different values. However, the authors also consider carrying out a similar experiment on other categories of products with low involvement of a buyer in the sales process to investigate gender differences in buying behaviour.

The next element for further research is the possible seasonality of sales. The study was conducted over a period of 30 days, at the time, according to the researchers, rather neutral. It is possible that the bidders' behaviour differs in the period of peak seasonal sales (e.g. before Christmas). The statement above would require observation over a longer period of time.

The study shows that inexperienced buyers are more inclined to purchase products with more friendly description.

As presented in the text, the results support the general belief that inexperienced buyers are influenced by form of product description. In the contrary, experienced buyers are less influenced by the form of product description. In our opinion, the arguments for this relation can be presented and tested in the further research. We believe that in the case of products with low importance for the purchaser, experienced buyers pay attention to the cost of purchase and not the way the product is described. On the contrary, inexperienced draw attention to the product description to make sure that making the right choice. For those buyers price is not critical.

And finally, the presented field experiments examine one type of auction—BIN. Further research may relate to other types of auction (e.g. BID—buy-in-auction) and analyse potential similarities and differences in buyers/bidders' behaviour vs. different types of auction.

Acknowledgements The authors wish to thank Mr. Jakub Kopacki for assistance in conducting the field experiments and valuable support for the implementation of research.

References

Almendra V (2012) A comprehensive analysis of nondelivery fraud at a major online auction site. J Internet Commer 11:309–328

Ba S, Pavlou PA (2002) Evidence of the effect of trust building technology in electronic markets: price premiums and buyer behavior. MIS Q 26(3):243–268

Borle S, Boatwright P, Kadane JR (2006) The timing of bid placement and extent of multiple bidding: an empirical investigation using eBay online auctions. Stat Sci 21(2):194–205

Cypryjański J, Grzesiuk A, Rudawska E (2015) Cechy aukcji internetowych a wielkość generowanej sprzedaży – wyniki eksperymentu naturalnego. Logistyka 2:1166–1174

Dellarocas C (2003) The digitization of word of mouth: promise and challenges of online feedback mechanisms. Manag Sci 49(10):1404–1424

E-commerce Standard (2014) www.internetstandard.pl. Accessed 3 Jun 2015

E-commerce w Polsce (2014) Gemius dla E-commerce Polska. www.infomonitor.pl/download/e-commerce-w-polsce-2014.pdf. Accessed 3 Apr 2015

Finch BJ (2007) Customer expectations in online auction environments: an exploratory study of customer feedback and risk. J Oper Manag 25(5):985–997

Goes PB, Karuga GG, Tripathi AK (2012) Bidding behavior evolution in sequential auction: characterization and analysis. MIS Q 36(4):1021–2042

Gregg D, Scott J (2006) The role of reputation systems in reducing online auction Freud. International Journal of Electronic Commerce 10(3):97–122

http://aukcjostat.pl/id1_pl/statystyki_serwisow_polskich.html. Accessed 4 Jul 2015

Lee YH, Malmendier U (2011) The bidders curse. Am Econ Rev 101(2):749–787

Livingston JA (2010) The behavior of inexperienced bidders in internet auctions. Econ Inq 48 (2):37–253

Pownall RAJ, Wolk L (2013) Bidding behavior and experience in internet auctions. Eur Econ Rev 61:14–27

Ye S, Gao G, Viswanathan S (2014) Strategic behavior in online reputation systems: evidence from revoking on eBay. MIS Q 38(4):1033–1056

Srinivasan K, Wang X (2010) Bidders' experience and learning in online auctions: issues and implications. Mark Sci 29(6):988–993

Suh K-S, Benbasat I, Suh E-K (2013) The impact of listing location on visits, bids, and final prices in online auctions: a field experiment. Int J Electron Commer 17(3):87–108

Walczuch R, Lundgren H (2004) Psychological antecedents of institution-based consumer trust in e-retailing. Inf Manag 42(1):159–177

Wu W-Y, Po-Ching H, Chen-Su F (2011) The influence of an online auction's product price and e-retailer reputation on consumers' perception, attitude, and behavioral intention. Scand J Psychol 52:290–302

www.statista.com/topics/2181/ebay/. Accessed 30 Jun 2015

Yan C, Konstan J (2015) Online field experiments: a selective survey of methods. http://yanchen.people.si.umich.edu/papers/online_field_exp_2015_03.pdf

Zhao J, Huang JH (2008) An empirical research on tobacco: seller reputation's impact on auction price premium. Proceedings of 2008 I.E. symposium on advanced management of information for globalized enterprises, pp 219–223

Chapter 20
Eye Tracking Based Experimental Evaluation of the Parameters of Online Content Affecting the Web User Behaviour

Jarosław Jankowski, Jarosław Wątróbski, Katarzyna Witkowska, and Paweł Ziemba

Abstract Research related to the online systems and behaviours of their users could be implemented with the participation of online systems and measurement oriented on the final recipient. In addition to the traditional survey based methods, measuring systems associated with eye tracking that allow precise determination of visual paths and areas of websites or ads that absorb the attention of the recipient are used. In this chapter, the main assumptions of the use of eye tracking in experimental economics and the results of the experiment are presented. Designed experiment was aimed to the detection of relation between the characteristics of interactive advertising units, its location within the site and the level of interest of the recipient based on absorption and attention.

Keywords Eye tracking • Website evaluation • Advertising content

20.1 Introduction

The evolution of electronic marketing affects the need to develop systems and technologies for support of increasing the efficiency of operations. Management systems, advertising servers and online optimization mechanisms associated with them are used for this purpose. Optimization activities may relate to the whole complex advertising campaigns as well as individual advertising objects that are carriers of marketing messages (Jankowski et al. 2015). Modern marketing is increasingly based on the achievements of neuroscience. Several areas can be

---

J. Jankowski (✉) • J. Wątróbski • K. Witkowska
Department of Information Systems Engineering, Faculty of Computer Science and Information Technology, West Pomeranian University of Technology Szczecin, Żołnierska 49, 71-210 Szczecin, Poland
e-mail: jjankowski.pl@gmail.com; jwatrobski@wi.zut.edu.pl

P. Ziemba
Department of Technology, Jacob of Paradyż University of Applied Sciences in Gorzów Wielkopolski, Teatralna 25, 66-400 Gorzów Wielkopolski, Poland

K. Nermend, M. Łatuszyńska (eds.), *Selected Issues in Experimental Economics*, Springer Proceedings in Business and Economics, DOI 10.1007/978-3-319-28419-4_20

specified such as neuroeconomics, neurotic, neuromarketing or cognitive science. Changes in the trends indicate that by analyzing economic phenomena emotional factors must be taken into account. Therefore, the direction of research has developed a new branch of economics called behavioural economics. The publication of research by Neumann and Morgenstern represented a high impact on the field. The proposed combination of traditional and behavioural economics allowed to take into account the psychological aspect of the behaviour of decision makers. Neuromarketing is a source of information about the psychological aspect of the economy and is often based on experiments. Its use is associated with experimental economics, which allows hypotheses in many areas of research. The main tool of experimental economics research are experimental environments under realistic conditions. Proper preparation of assumptions and experiment construction provides a better understanding of decisions taken in individual behaviour and correlations between elements of the phenomenon studied.

An important approach to the problem of experimental economics took place between 1990s (Roth et al. 2013). It defines the application areas of experimental economics, including an experiment testing the hypothesis utility, which has been raised in that work. Currently, one of the areas of research is the use of measurement systems based on eye tracking and precise monitoring of visual paths in conjunction with the presented material. Today, this technique is used in many research projects that examine the usability of the solutions used, among others, in e-commerce (Horsley 2014). The experiment described in this chapter concerns the investigation into the levels of absorption of attention recipient of commercials located within the website. To carry out this kind of experiment, the goal was to indicate experimental factors and the direction of their changes. In the case of advertising, the indicators were colour, location and size. Each of the three factors could occur with varying intensity. On this basis, the direction of user attentions and other relations were detected. The aim of the experiment was to identify the relationship between independent variables and the dependent related to user attention. Among the observed dependent variables, was defined the average time for which the advertising was catching user attention, the amount of a return visit and time after which it has been noticed for the first time. This approach allowed the researcher to observe the extent to which the variables influence each other. The whole experiment is based on the use of an eye tracker that allows the observation of the eye movement behaviour of the test subject. Information on eye tracking, and the same test procedure is described in the following sections of work. With data obtained during the test it was possible to establish a correlation between the studied independent variables X and Y. Dependent precondition of the study was choosing the appropriate research sample, and the same experiment consisted in presenting elements of websites with editorial content, where additional advertising occurred. The aim was to observe the interest aroused in particular advertisements, and to link the level of interest with the parameters of communication. Therefore, the presented advertisement was composed of three main elements {E1, E2, E3}, each of which could be found in three variants, to give the set of design options {E11, E12, E13}, {E21, E22, E33}, {E31, E32, E33} with total 27 possible combinations. As assumed in the study, each achieved different results for a variable Y. The performed analyses made it possible to observe how the value of variable X on the user behaviour and the final Y value on this basis have been applied to indicate the direction in which should be advertising designed to maximize their effectiveness associated with the level of absorption of attention of the recipient.

20.2 Eye Tracking in Experimental Economics

The basis for interactive communication within web pages are the most common objects based on the hypertext, graphics, or multimedia allocated dynamically within the editorial content delivered by online publishers for advertising purposes. Trends in the development of electronic marketing point to a wider use of available sources of information and integration of the various components of the communication process. For complex conditions online, various measurement methods are carried out on the server side of web systems are recently increasingly used measurement targeted to behaviours and reactions of customers using external systems. Research carried out and targeted to the user is often based on the measurements using eye tracking. The use of experimental economics allows verification of hypothesis in the experimental environment, which precedes the implementation of practical and costly impact on reducing costs and increasing efficiency. These technologies allow proper selection of parameters of marketing communication and research testing to ensure a certain level of efficiency with a view to maximizing results in many dimensions. Eye tracking research is determining a set of research techniques which allow the researcher to obtain information on eye movement in a given period of time and the fixation points. The obtained data allows the researcher to characterize the activity of visual attention and check how it is processed in relation to the pictorial and textual content.

The first non-invasive method of tracking eye movement was presented by Dodge and Cline (1901). It was based on the observation of light reflected from the cornea of the eye. The first research in the field of marketing based on tracking eye movement was conducted by Nixon, who was watching eye movements during reading. In the 1940s, the first helmet was developed for eye tracking by Hartridge and Thompson (1948). The increased interest in eye tracking took place in the 1970s. Advances were driven by progress in the field of tracking eye movement and cognitive processes of perception (Monty and Senders 1976; Sanders et al. 1978). The 1980s focused mainly on the link between traffic data eyeball collected in real time with traditional modes of communication between the user of the computer (Just and Carpenter 1980; Bolt 1981, 1982; Levine 1981; Glenn et al. 1986; Ware and Mikaelian 1987). In the next decade there was an increased interest in eye tracking techniques for investigating the usefulness of computer interfaces and human computer interactions (Benel et al. 1991; Ellis et al. 1998; Cowen 2001).

Table 20.1 The evolution of eye tracking methods

Year	References	Areas of applications
1900s	Dodge and Cline (1901), Judd et al. (1905)	The first non-invasive method of tracking eye movement. Observation of eye movement based on the substance introduced into the eye.
1930s	Tinker (1931)	The use of photographic techniques to study eye movement
1940s	Fitts et al. (1950), Hartridge and Thompson (1948)	The use of cameras for monitoring eye movements while observing pilot cockpit. The first eye tracking helmet.
1950s	Mackworth and Mackworth (1958)	The development of an electronic system for eye movements measurement.
1960s	Mackworth and Thomas (1962)	Work to improve the helmet to study eye movement.
1970s	Cornsweet and Crane (1973), Monty and Senders (1976), Anliker (1976), Sanders et al. (1978)	The increase precision of observation. Cognitive science in relation to eye tracking studies. The use of eye tracking in real time to the study of human-computer interaction.
1980s	Bolt (1981, 1982), Levine (1981), Glenn et al. (1986), Ware and Mikaelian (1987)	Analysis of eye movement used in human-computer communication.
1990s	Starker and Bolt (1990), Vertegaal (1999), Jacob (1991), Zhai et al. (1999)	Study the usability and effectiveness of computer interfaces.
2000s	Rösler et al. (2004), Maughan et al. (2007)	Increasing the use of an eye tracker studies in various fields. The use of commercial research.

Lohse (1997) showed that colour graphics, size and location of advertising on the website have a significant impact on its effectiveness. The study showed, among others things, that colourful advertising had an advantage over black and white, and that advertising often attracted a great amount of attention from the user. The 2000s showed how broad the scope of application of eye tracking is in a variety of areas including e-commerce (Tzanidou 2003), medicine (Arolt et al. 1996; Thaker et al. 2004) economics (Reutskaja et al. 2011). Development of technologies for observing the movement of the eyeballs is presented in Table 20.1.

Eye tracking is often used to test the designs of websites. This tests allow to observe how internet users perceive the particular details on the website. These observations made it possible, among other things, the observation of a phenomenon called banner blindness, which is based on ignoring advertising content (Benway 1998; Lapa 2007). In the e-commerce application of eye tracking researchers presented many academic studies and experiments. The devices have been used among other in a study aimed at correlation between advertising on the page and the expectations of users (Roth 1993). Eye tracking can also be used to predict user preferences (Currim et al. 2015). Due to the ease of adaptation, it is used in various fields of e-commerce, for example tourism (Hernández-Méndez and Muñoz-Leiva 2015) and banking (Yuan et al. 2014). One of the most popular methods of eye tracking is a video recording of visual activity using equipment mounted on the head (mobile eye tracking). Mobile eye tracking works by enabling the movement of the test or placed remotely presented to a test material is used in the subsequent analysis of visual and recording activity combined with the obtained results. Currently, this method is most often used together with infrared cameras to facilitate identification of the location of the corneal reflection, which allows to determine the vector of view.

The results obtained from the measurements can be presented in four main formats: fixation maps, heat maps, opacity maps and bee swarm. The main metrics used in eye tracking are the fixations and saccades. In clinical use, indicators are also derivatives of these measures. It is also possible to observe the size of the movement and blink frequency. Fixation as determined by pointing the phenomenon of the central part of the retinas of both eyes on the viewed object and runs from 0.15 to 1.5 s. A measure of fixation can be interpreted according to the context in which it is considered and 2 (Poole and Ball 2006), duration (Just and Carpenter 1978), repeatability fixation (Goldberg and Kotval 1999), the percentage fixation and areas of interest (Albert 2002) or spatial density (Cowen et al. 2002). This approach is used in many areas of the research. In the case of web design frequency of fixation may indicate the location where should be given particular attention during design. A similar approach can be used in advertising sector (Jacob and Karn 2003). Saccade is known as a very fast movement of the eye between the two fixations. They are approximately 4–6 times a second and last in the range of 0.03–0.06 s. Like the fixation saccades, they can be interpreted depending on the context. They can be measured by the number of saccades (Goldberg and Kotval 1999), the amplitude (Goldberg et al. 2002), reverse saccades presenting minor elements (Sibert et al. 2000) and saccades revealing directional changes (Cowen et al. 2002). The combined sequence of saccades and fixation is called scanpaths, and they are often used in the evaluation of web systems and marketing content.

20.3 Assumptions for Experimental Research

This section presents the assumptions of experimental studies conducted with the participation of eye tracking focused on the relation between the effectiveness of the marketing message, its invasiveness, and the size and allocation within the website. The proposed solution is based on the decomposition of interactive objects on components, and can reduce the dimensionality of decision-making problems as well as increase the effectiveness of the participation factor analysis methods and is an extension of our earlier studies related to the recommending interfaces (Jankowski 2013a), web conversions (Jankowski 2013b) and repeated contacts with the marketing content (Jankowski 2013c). The test performed and the results indicate no justification for the high intensity of communication, and the need to promote better integration of communication with the editorial part of

Table 20.2 Parameters of advertising content and it's variants

Level	Intensity (P)	Localization (L)	Size (S)
1	Low	Top	Big
2	Medium	Middle	Medium
3	High	Down	Small

the site. The experiment has agreed to take part 16 participants, whose average age did not exceed 30 years. None of the members showed no visual defects that could distort the results.

In addition, each of the respondents confirmed that regularly use search engines and has contact with online advertisements. Content that has been used in the experiment was designed to their needs and none of the subjects had not seen them prior to the experiment. The website is made up of several components. One of them may be internet advertising, the construction of which also can be based on several components. Proper selection of components provides the ability to generate the desired interactions. For the purpose of the experiment, researchers created 27 websites. Each of the parties contained four elements. Three of them presented a text bearing the heading, and content related to current events related to e-commerce. The fourth element presented advertising built on the basis of three elements: colour intensity, size and location on the page. Each feature may have occurred in the three variants, to give a total of 27 possible combinations to obtain advertisements. Acceptable values of each of the characteristics are show in Table 20.2.

20.4 Empirical Results and Data Analysis

During the study, the group measured was used to detect how much time was spent on advertising and whether or not it was noticed by a user. In Table 20.3 are results for 10 of the 27 ads shown in the experimental process. The first column presents the specification of design variant. The numbers in brackets refer to the characteristics presented in Table 20.2, wherein the categorical values mean location, size and intensity of colour, respectively.

Given the presence of three variants of each of the elements of advertising, the following hypotheses were posed:

1. Intensive colour of the advertising on the website effectively attracts the attention of the user (Ramalingam and Palaniappan 2006). This hypothesis was partially confirmed. Most attention was gained from content where the colour intensity was average. Ads with an intensity of colour at level 2 and 3 attracted the attention of 44 % of people. Advertising on level 1 attracted the attention of 37.5 % of people. The least colourful advertising was also noticed the latest (after approx. 6 s) and the average time for which it attracted attention was 2.5 s.

Table 20.3 Values obtained for selected design variants

Design variant	Number of viewers	First view (s)	Viewed times (s)	Viewed times (%)	Number of revisitors	Revisits
1 (1-1-1)	7.00	5.2	0.56	3.76	5	1.4
3 (2-3-2)	9	7.27	0.46	3.09	1	1
8 (2-2-2)	9	7.39	0.67	4.49	5	1.8
12 (1-1-3)	8	3.2	0.68	4.51	6	2.7
14 (3-3-1)	5	8.14	0.41	2.71	1	1
17 (3-2-1)	2	6.75	0.06	0.37	1	1
18 (2-1-2)	6	8.68	0.21	1.4	2	1.5
21 (2-3-3)	5	8.48	0.66	4.37	2	1.5
25 (1-3-2)	5	4.71	1.21	8.06	3	1.7
27 (1-3-3)	8	5.72	0.2	1.32	4	1.3

The differences in average times for ads on level 2 and 3 were respectively 3.74 and 2.76 s.

2. Absorption of the attention of the recipient depends on the location within the site (Calisir and Karaali 2008). The assumption proved to be true. Advertising situated at the top of the page was looked at by 44 % of the 16 respondents. At other locations these values were 12.5 and 18.75 %. Location is also reflected in the average time a user spent on advertising—amounted to 3.5 s for the first location. The values obtained for ads located on the middle and the bottom of the page were similar.
3. Ad size affects the absorption of user attention (Robinson et al. 2007). The results obtained showed that the advertising consisting of larger sizes attracted more users—44 % of respondents. Advertising of any size caught the eye of 37.5 %, and was noticed the latest (after approx. 6 s), however, it was characterized by the highest efficiency. The average time on what attracted attention was 0.49 s which accounted for 3.25 % of the total time spent on the site. This value for the largest advertising spending amounted to 2.86 %.

In Table 20.3 are shown the least and most efficient advertising a cording to the measured factors.

Using the analytical methods and data processing, heat maps and gaze paths were received. Figures 20.1, 20.2, 20.3 and 20.4 show the heat map for the selected ads. For comparison, each of the selected maps is presented using one user behaviour and five participants. Variant 13 for a single user may be noted that the ad was noticed by him. Particular attention is attracted, and the form placed on the graphics. After applying the heat map to five users, it can be seen that the average interest in advertising was lower than the selected user. It is clear however that, as in the case of Fig. 20.1 button area and form a lighter. In the case of variant 17, the result in both cases shows that attention in advertising linger button. The reason for this may be that it is placed at the edge, which directly adjacent to the presented content.

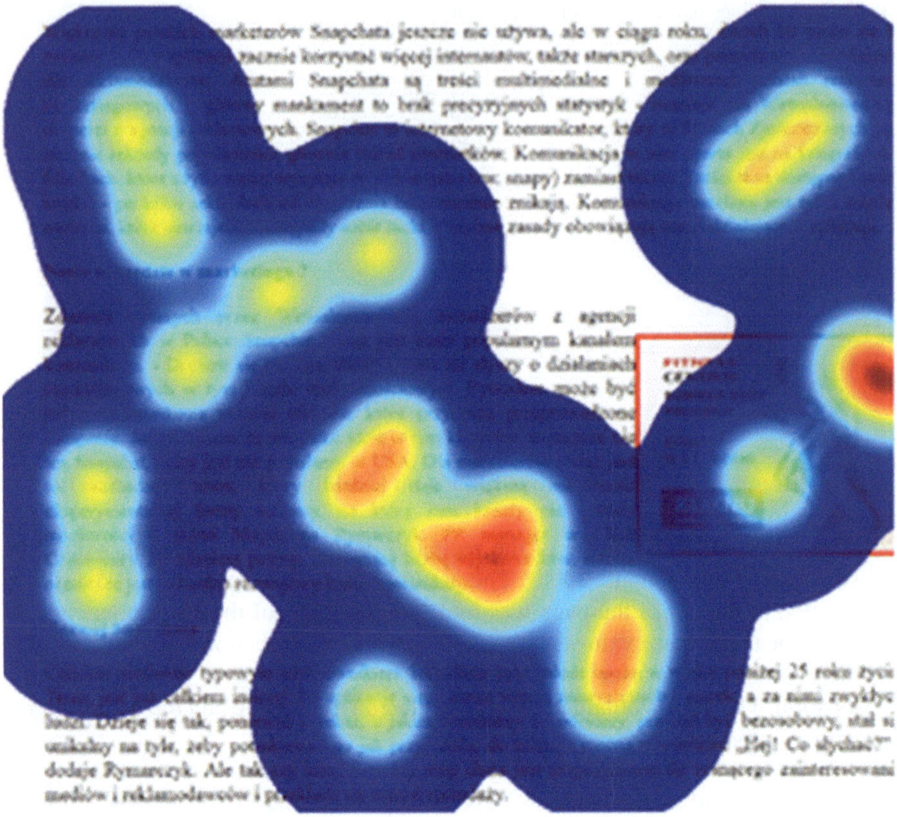

Fig. 20.1 Heat map for variant 13—1 user

A similar analysis was conducted for the tracks of vision, a visualization of the selected options shown in Figs. 20.5, 20.6, 20.7 and 20.8. In the example Fig. 20.5, the user focused on the main page elements which were headers. The same advertisement with two gazes attracted a comparatively long period of time as indicated by the fixations. After applying a few tracks, it can be seen that the behaviour of this person differed from that of other subjects. Other users did not pay attention to the advertising. This phenomenon is associated with banner blindness. For variant 4 shows a high number of return visits. Interpreting the length users find that this ad is a quick way to select users gaze despite the fact that the ad was at the bottom of the page.

On the basis of data received, a number of statistical analyses was performed in order to identify links between factors of P, L, S. The first step was a conducted analysis of the correlation between test components and test results obtained. At a significance level of 0.05, the strongest correlations were observed between the number and location of advertising Revisited (−0.49). The other element proved to

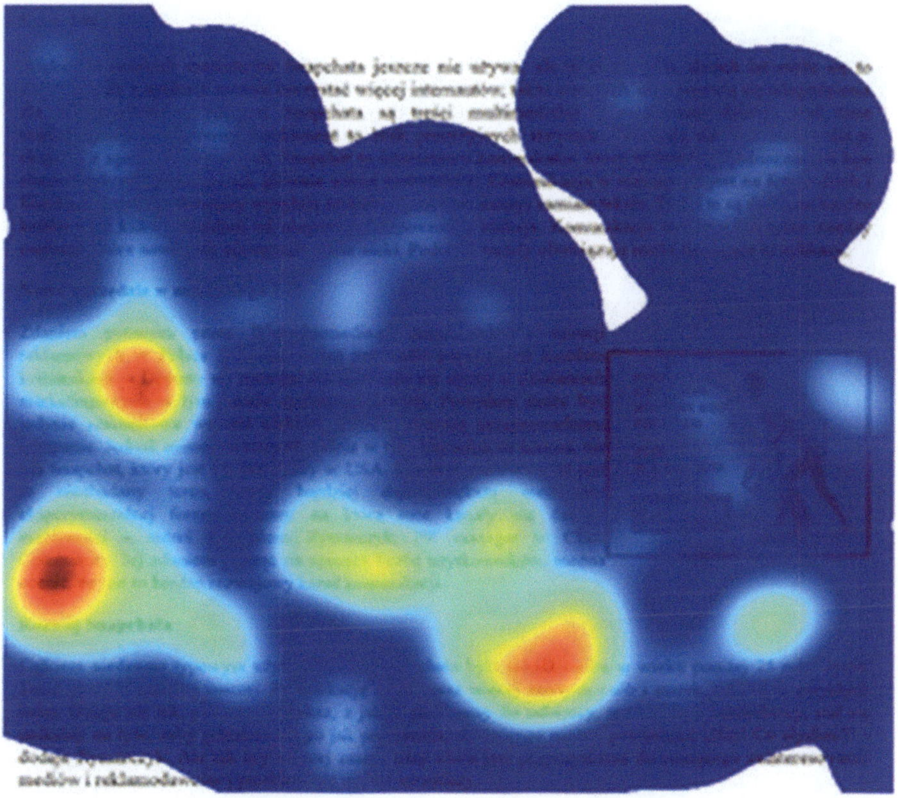

Fig. 20.2 Heat map for variant 13—5 users

be poorly correlated. Cluster analysis based on the method of Ward with a measure of Euclidean distance was used. Based on the Mojeny rule, it is suggested that level of division occurs at stage 2. Based on the resulting graph, it can be determined by ad groups, which have received similar results as the number of users who noticed the ad. The best were advertising the group in which repeated factor was the size of the ad (s) at level 2, i.e. 250×200. To find out whether a number is linked to a return visit with elements of advertising, the obtained data was subjected to analysis of variance main factors (ANOVA). The conducted analysis showed that the greatest impact on the amount of a return where advertising was in its upper part, the amount revisited averaged 5. This means that the ads that are on top are often perceived by users faster and attracts the eye several times. This may translate to better recognition of the promoted product. The number of visits ad also affects its size (F (2,20) = 4.32, $p = 0.028$). The analysis showed that the ads, which are medium in size have a greater impact on the return visit than ads with larger dimensions. Their effectiveness is about 23 % higher. Colour intensity of

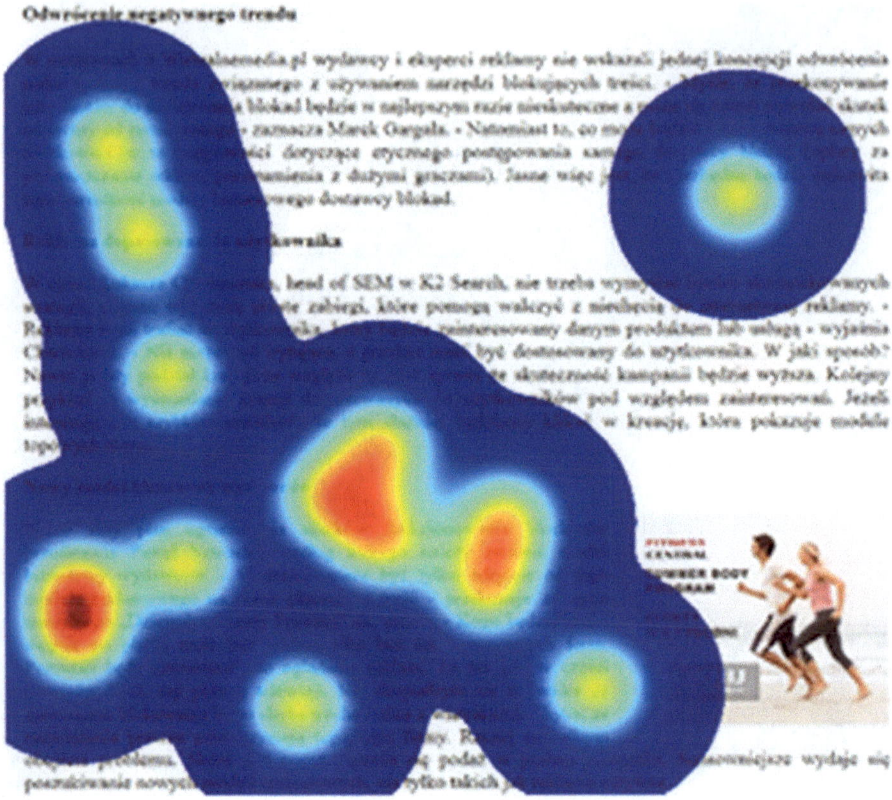

Fig. 20.3 Heat map for variant 17—1 user

advertising has proved to be the least important factor differentiating the level Revisited (F (2,20) $= 1.07, p = 0.36$). The effect of the important factors is shown in Fig. 20.9.

The rest of the ANOVA was used with the design of experiments methods and the central compositional plans. The results are presented in Table 20.4.

Based on these results, important factors proved to be the location ($p = 0.003$) and ad size ($p = 0.014$). The intensity of the colour turned out not to be significant ($p = 0.313$). The location and size of the ad to the greatest extent explain the variation amount revisit advertising. Between them there is also the biggest dependency. The least are interrelated location and intensity of colour. On the basis of charts fitting surfaces between the individual elements of the ad can be observed variability in the effectiveness of individual combinations with respect to the intensity of each of the features. Figure 20.10 shows that the effects of differences in size and colour intensity is not varied. Next, Fig. 20.11 shows the relationship between the location and intensity of colour. It shows that the best results are

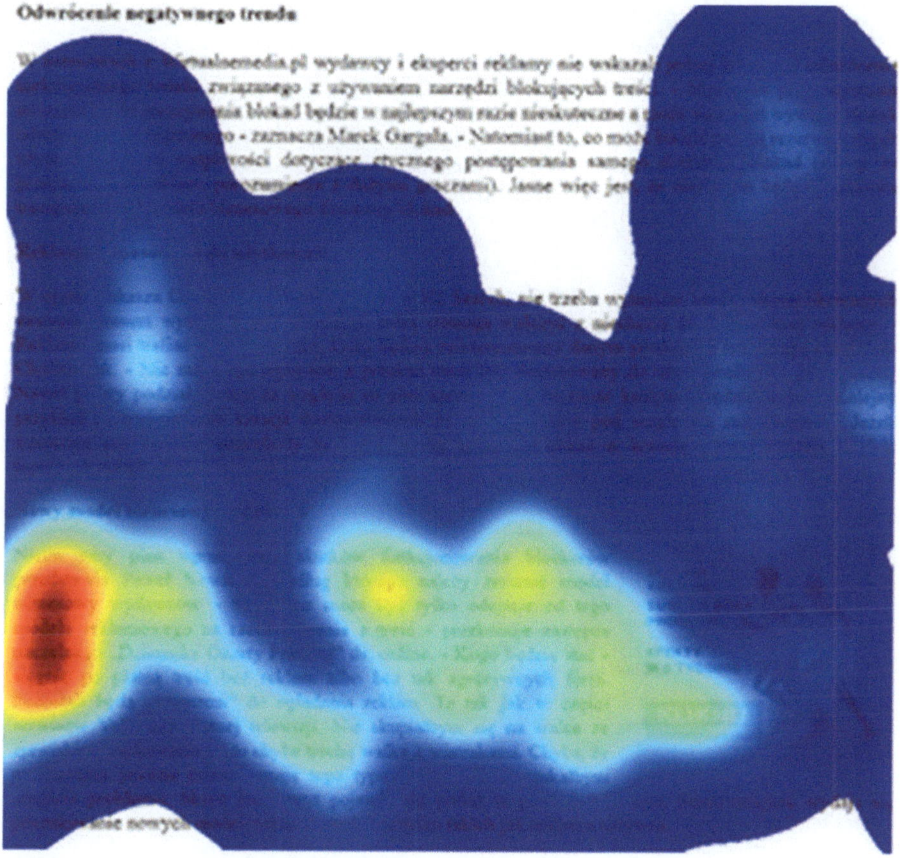

Fig. 20.4 Heat map for variant 17—5 users

achieved for advertising localized at the highest point on the site and for colour at P2. The change in the amount revisited affected by the location where the change causes a drop in renewed interest of users.

Figures 20.12 and 20.13 shows three dimensions surface plots. In Fig. 20.12, as in the case of area charts, the results obtained are poorly differentiated. Figure 20.13 shows that the highest level is achieved for revisited are with the location L1. The value of P is not in a mean way to differentiate the results. On the 3D view, a decline in interest in advertising is observed with a variable advertising space. This shows that the user often looks at advertising, which is on the top of the page. Another relationship to the size VS localization confirms that affect the amount revisited also has a location. Loss of interest, however, is not as large as in the case of the relationship P-L. It follows that the manipulation of advertising placement with an appropriate size will not bring big changes in performance.

Figure 20.14 shows the Pareto chart showing the significance of the effects of each of the elements. As in previous analyses, essential elements proved to be the

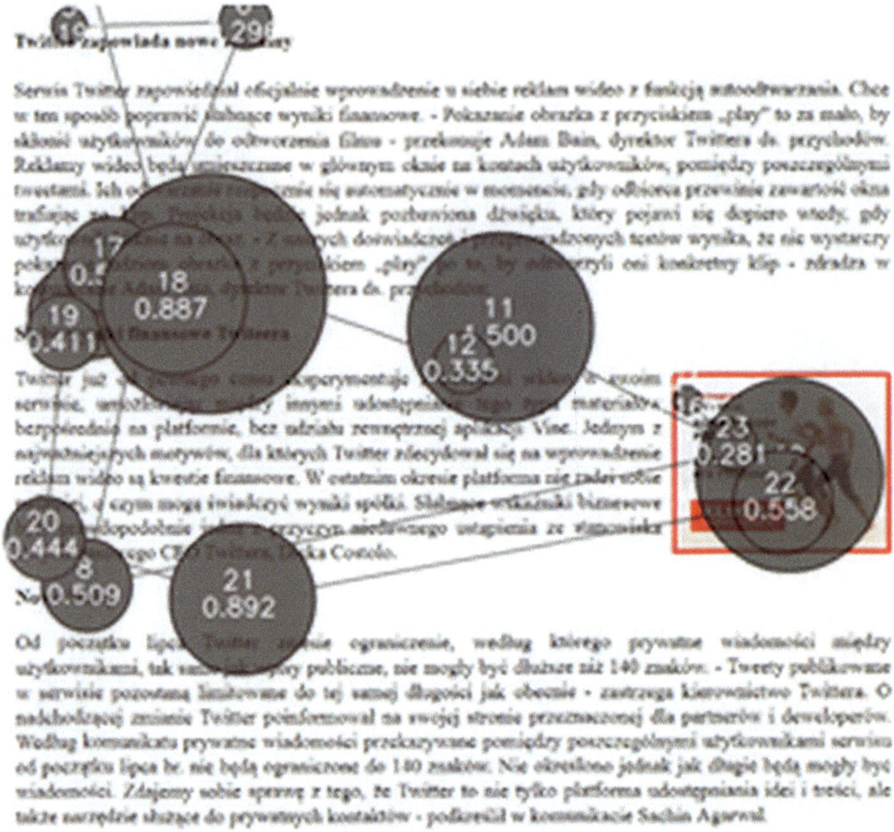

Fig. 20.5 Scan path for the variant 21—1 user

location and size. The smallest impact on the number of reciprocal visits was the relationship between the location and the applied colour.

The results show that increasing the intensity of the interactive content may result in greater absorption of the recipient's attention. However, the overall assessment, also through the prism of satisfaction, the recipient tends to take account also of other parameters of assessment related to website usability and user experience (Ziemba et al. 2014, 2015a, b).

20.5 Summary

Elements of marketing communication are an important component of the constituent websites. They are integrated with internet portals and platforms, social networking, entertainment subsystems and e-commerce systems. Their main objective can be both strengthening and building the company's awareness as well as the immediate effects in the form of interaction generated or increasing sales.

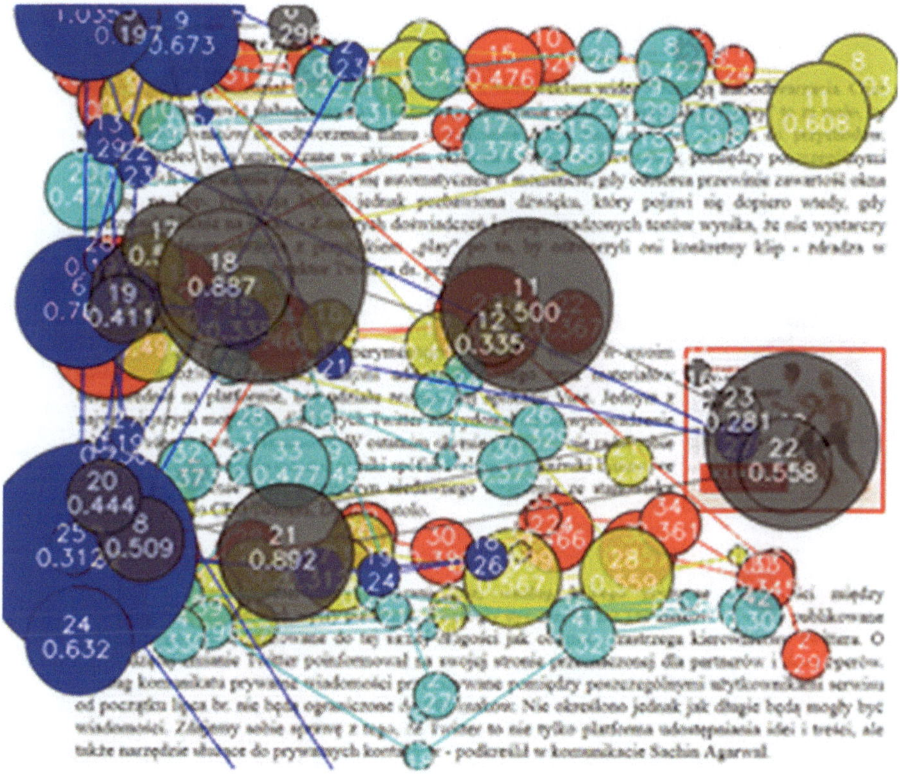

Fig. 20.6 Scan path for the variant 21—5 users

Results indicate studies on the relationship between the level of influence of the interface elements and the absorption of the recipient to do measured within a system involving eye tracking. The impact of the issue of selection levels is treated as a compromise, where the objective was to find a design options for increasing absorption levels of attention, while avoiding the negative impact on the users. The proposed method of visual design of interactive objects can be used in analytical processes and in the search for optimal design options. The nature of the parameters which are difficult to precisely characterize constitute an incentive to use varying levels of impact and the results confirm the desirability of such a solution.

The approach can be used to select design options and help to avoid situations in which elements of high-impact decisions have a negative impact for the wider user experience. Excessively intrusive elements attract attention, but cause a decline in customer satisfaction. As a result, it may contribute to the emergence of negative side effects, while priority should be placed on building positive relationships with customers. In this chapter, an example of application of experimental economics with the use of eye tracking is presented. The planned and performed experiment allowed to determine the relationship between the visual elements of advertising, their severity, and the results achieved by advertising usability. For independent

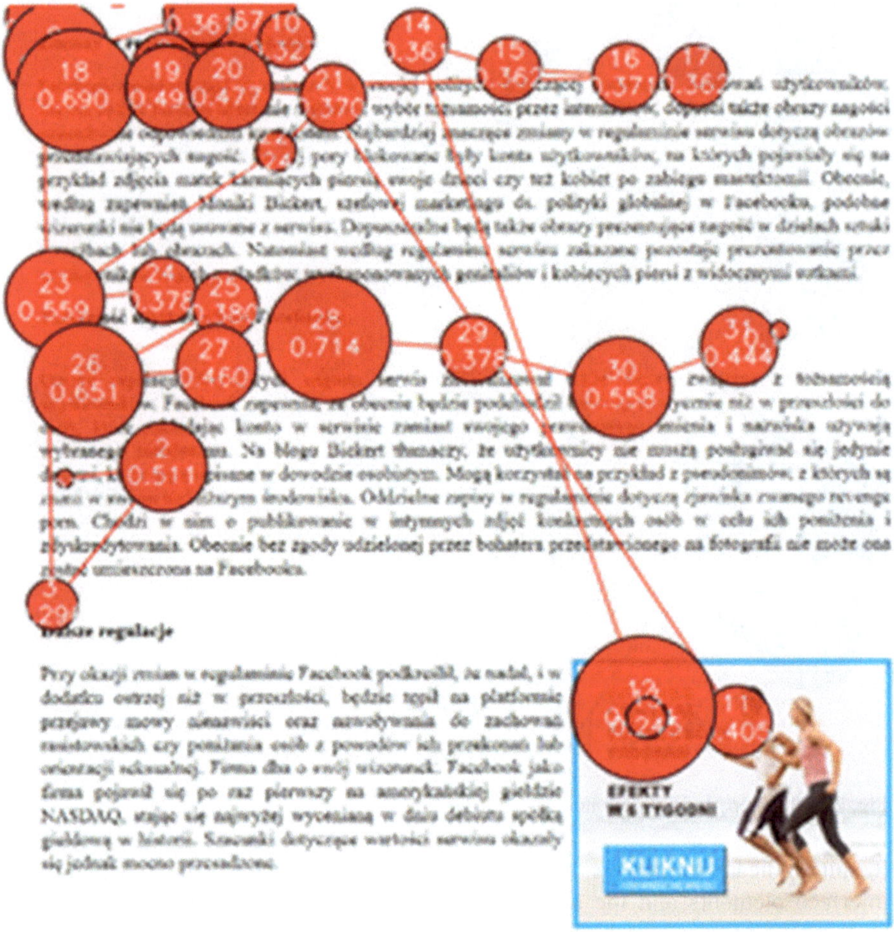

Fig. 20.7 Scan path for the variant 4—1 user

variables size, location and intensity was verified if the higher the value of these variables translates into higher values correlated dependent variables. Ads with the largest size and located in the upper part of the site were more effective than their counterparts with lower values. The highest intensity of colour was a deterrent to users who are more likely to look at advertising with an average colour saturation. It is possible that too sharp colour was associated with spam in the form of intrusive ads, which automatically led to replying to the ad. The analysis results do not indicate clearly that all the relationships in the model were significant. This may be due to the small study sample. However, it should be noted that the results obtained are varied. This indicates that the values of the independent variables affect the behaviour of users. This gives information on possible design solutions. The value of building blocks for advertisements can be selected in such a way as to maximize

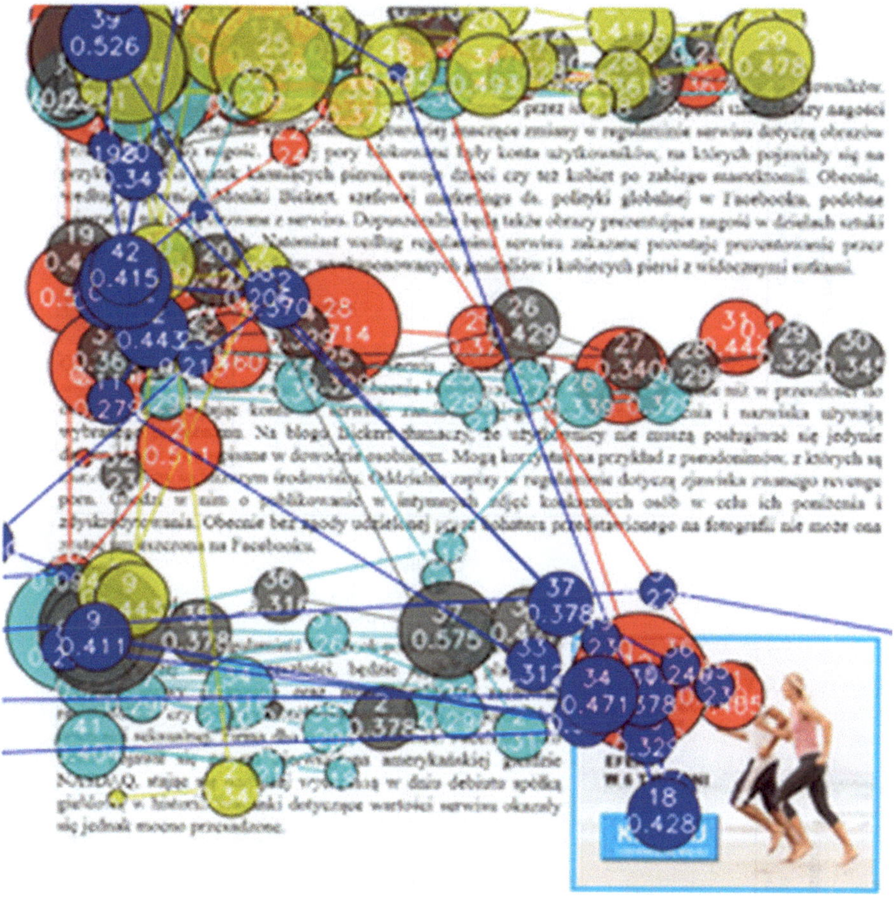

Fig. 20.8 Scan path for the variant 4—5 users

the selected value of the dependent variables. For example, based on the cases examined, in order to maximize the number of users who have turned their attention to advertising the most desirable combination of traits is the colour at level 2, level 1 location and size at level 1. According to the analyses, the combination gave the highest number of individual visits (62.5 %). Carrying out the experiment allowed a better understanding of how users perceive marketing messages. The study in a lab environment gives the opportunity to better match the marketing message to the user. It also allows for optimal decisions based on theoretical knowledge supported by experimental results. All of this translates into increased interest in this branch of economics relating mainly to human emotions. Future research in the field of economics will largely relied on such experiments that quickly and easily are able to provide reliable information on the phenomenon studied. In addition, it will be important to take into account trends in the design of personalized ads referring to the emotions of users which can bring online advertising into a new dimension.

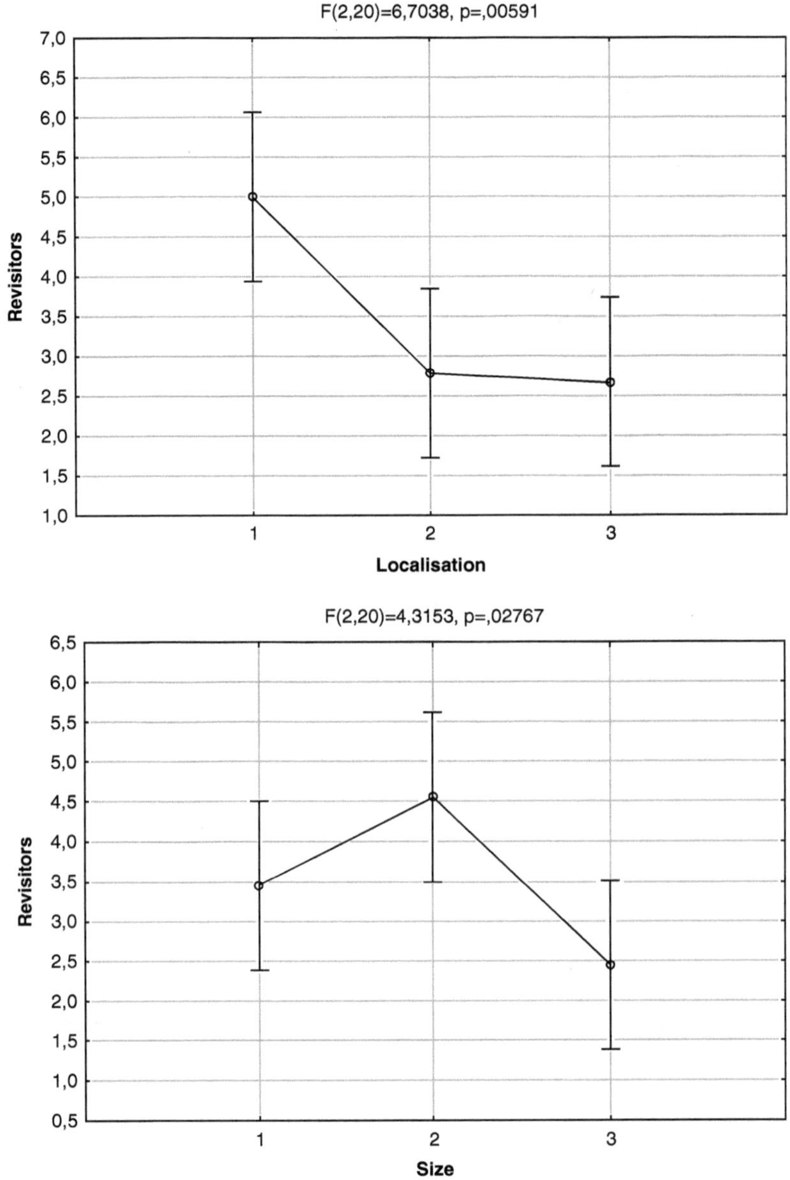

Fig. 20.9 Charts of factors significance

Table 20.4 ANOVA analysis used design variants

Factor	SS	df	MS	*F*	*p*
(1)Localization	24.5000	1	24.50000	11.78156	0.003177
Localization (Q)	6.6852	1	6.68519	3.21477	0.090787
(2)Size (L)	4.5000	1	4.50000	2.16396	0.159548
Size (Q)	15.5741	1	15.57407	7.48926	0.014056
(3)Persuasion (L)	2.7222	1	2.72222	1.30906	0.268420
Persuasion (Q)	2.2407	1	2.24074	1.07753	0.313791
1L by 2L	6.7500	1	6.75000	3.24594	0.089363
1L by 3L	0.3333	1	0.33333	0.16029	0.693873
2L by 3L	4.0833	1	4.08333	1.96359	0.179121
Error	35.3519	17	2.07952		
Total SS	102.7407	26			

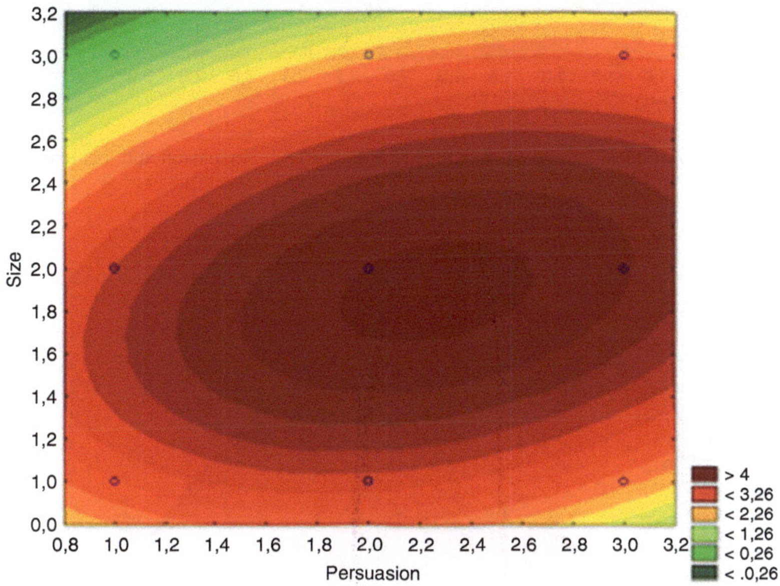

Fig. 20.10 Two-dimensional chart showing relation between size and persuasion

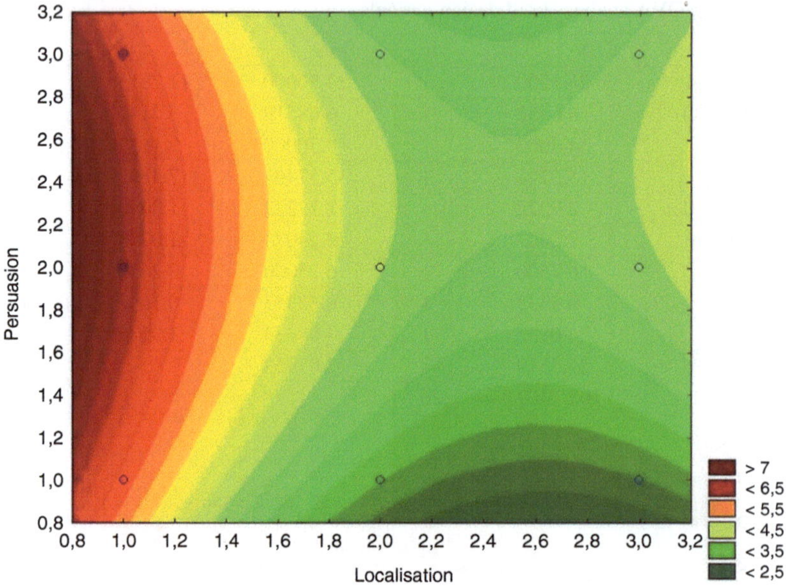

Fig. 20.11 Two-dimensional chart showing relation between persuasion and localization

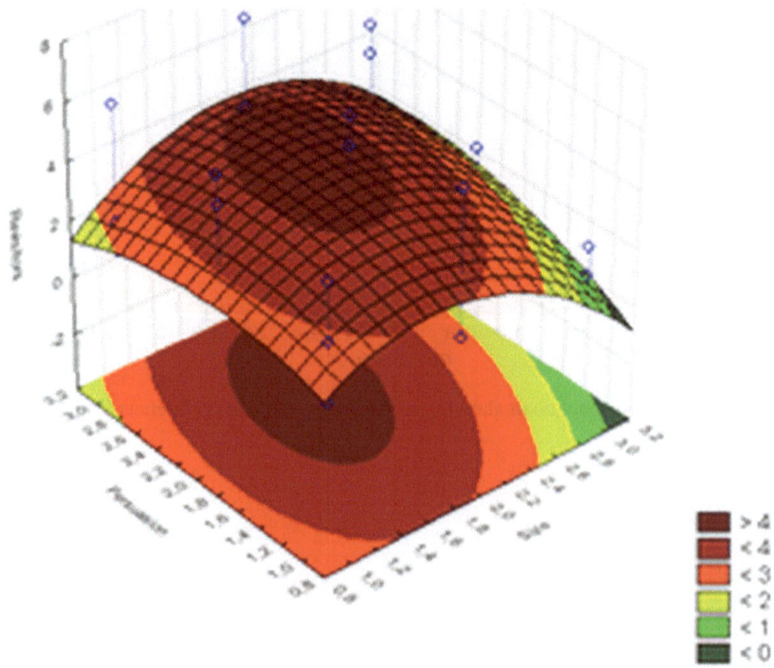

Fig. 20.12 Space chart for revisitors VS size VS persuasion

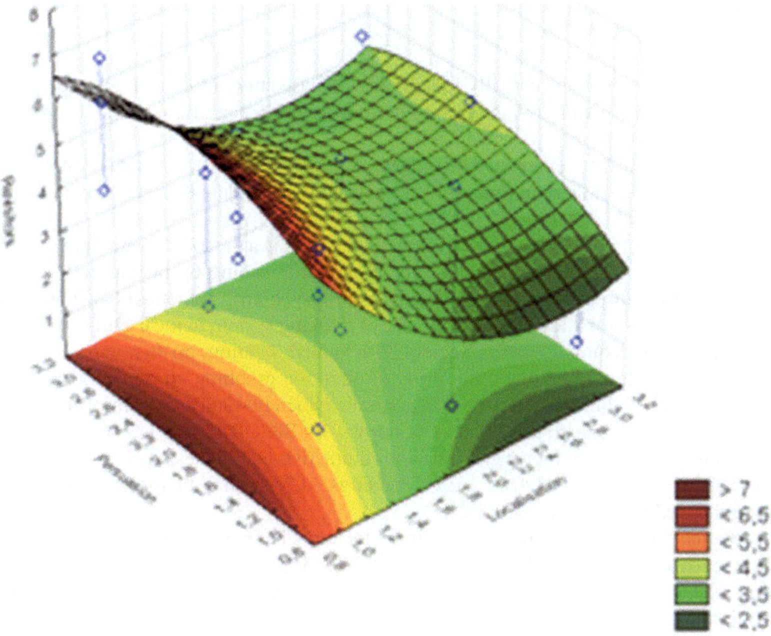

Fig. 20.13 Space chart for revisitors VS persuasion VS localization

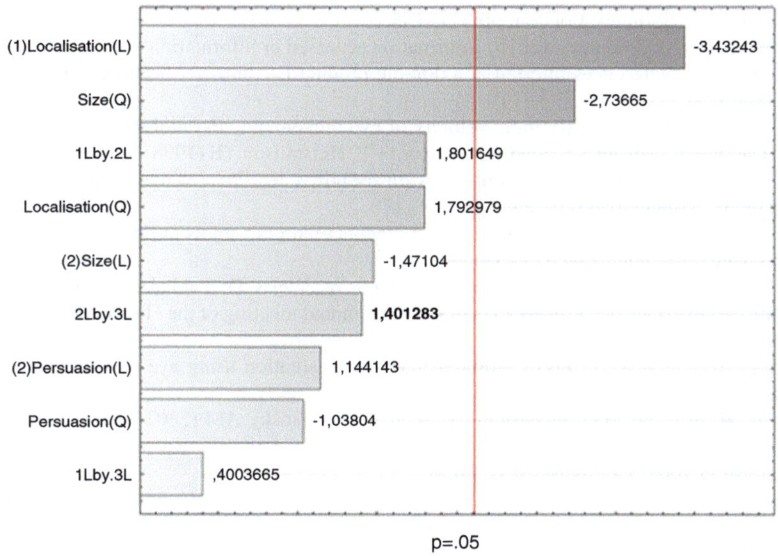

Fig. 20.14 Pareto effects chart

References

Albert W (2002) Do web users actually look at ads? A case study of banner ads and eye tracking technology. In: Proceedings of the eleventh annual conference of the usability professionals' association

Anliker J (1976) EyeMovements: On-LineMeasurement, Analysis, and Control. In: Eye Movements and Psychological Processes, Montyand RA, Senders RA (eds) Lawrence Erlbaum Associates. Hillsdale, NJ, pp. 185–202

Arolt V, Lencer R, Nolte A (1996) Eye tracking dysfunction is a putative phenotypic susceptibility marker of schizophrenia and maps to a locus on chromosome 6p in families with multiple occurrence of the disease. Am J Med Genet (Neuropsychiatric Genetics) 67(6):564–579

Benel DCR, Ottens D, Horst R (1991) Use of an eye tracking system in the usability laboratory. In: Proceedings of the Human Factors Society 35th annual meeting, pp 461–465

Benway JP (1998) Banner blindness: the irony of attention grabbing on the world wide web. In: Proceedings of the Human Factors and Ergonomics Society 42nd annual meeting, pp 463–467

Bolt RA (1981) Gaze-orchestrated dynamic windows. In: SIGGRAPH '81 Proceedings of the 8th annual conference on computer graphics and interactive techniques, pp 109–119

Bolt RA (1982) Eyes at the interface. In: Proceedings ACM human factors in computer systems conference, ACM Press, pp 360–362

Calisir F, Karaali D (2008) The impacts of banner location, banner content and navigation style on banner recognition. Comput Hum Behav 24(2):535–543

Cornsweet TN, Crane HD (1973) Accurate two-dimensional eye tracker using first and fourth Purkinje images. J Opt Soc Am 63(8):921–928

Cowen L (2001) An eye movement analysis of web-page usability. Unpublished Master's thesis, Lancaster University, UK

Cowen L, Ball LJ, Delin J (2002) An eye movement analysis of web page usability. In: Faulkner X, Finlay J, Detienne F (eds) People and computers XVI - memorable yet invisible, Proceedings of HCI 2002. Springer, London, pp 317–335

Currim IS, Mintz O, Siddarth S (2015) Information accessed or information available? The impact on consumer preferences inferred at a durable product E-commerce website. J Interact Mark 29:11–25

Dodge R, Cline ST (1901) The angle velocity of eye movements. Psychol Rev 8(2):145–157

Ellis S, Candrea R, Misner J, Craig CS, Lankford CP, Hutshinson TE (1998) Windows to the soul? What eye movements tell us about software usability. In: Proceedings of the usability professionals' association conference, pp 151–178

Fitts PM, Jones RE, Milton JL (1950) Eye movements of aircraft pilots during instrument landing approaches. Aeronaut Eng Rev 9(2):24–29

Glenn F, Iavecchia H, Ross L, Stokes J, Weiland W, Weiss D, Zaklad A (1986) Eye-voice-controlled interface. In: Proceedings of the 30th annual meeting of the Human Factors Society, pp 322–326

Goldberg HJ, Kotval XP (1999) Computer interface evaluation using eye movements: methods and constructs. Int J Ind Ergon 24:631–645

Goldberg JH, Stimson MJ, Lewenstein M, Scott N, Wichansky AM (2002) Eye tracking in web search tasks: design implications. In: Proceedings of the eye tracking research and applications symposium 2002 NY, ACM Press, pp 51–58

Thaker GK, Wonodi I, Avila MT, Hong LE, Stine OC (2004) Catechol O-methyltransferase polymorphism and eye tracking in schizophrenia. A preliminary report. Am J Psychiatry 161 (12):2320–2322

Hartridge H, Thompson LC (1948) Methods of investigating eye movements. Br J Opthalmol 32:581–591

Hernández-Méndez J, Muñoz-Leiva F (2015) What type of online advertising is most effective for eTourism 2.0? An eye tracking study based on the characteristics of tourists. Comput Hum Behav 50:618–625

Horsley M (2014) Eye tracking as a research method in social and marketing applications. In: Eliot M, Knight BA, Reilly R, Horsley M (eds) Current trends in eye tracking research. Springer International Publishing, New York, pp 179–182

Jacob RJ (1991) The use of eye movements in human-computer interaction techniques: what you look at is what you get. Trans Inf Syst 9(2):152–169

Jacob RJ, Karn KS (2003) Eye tracking in Human-Computer Interaction and usability research: ready to deliver the promises. In: Hyönä J, Radach R, Deubel H (eds) The mind's eye: cognitive and applied aspects of eye movement. Elsevier, Oxford, pp 573–605

Jankowski J, Wątróbski J, Ziemba P (2015) Modeling the impact of visual components on verbal communication in online advertising. In: Nunez M (ed) ICCCI 2015, Part II, vol 9330, Lecture notes in artificial intelligence. Springer, Heidelberg, pp 44–53. doi:10.1007/978-3-319-24306-1_5

Jankowski J (2013a) Modeling the structure of recommending interfaces with adjustable influence on users. In: Proceedings of 5-th Asian conference on intelligent information and database systems, vol 7803, Lecture notes in computer science. Springer, Heidelberg, pp 429–438

Jankowski J (2013b) Balanced approach to the design of conversion oriented websites with limited negative impact on the users. In: Proceedings of 5-th international conference on computational collective intelligence technologies and applications, vol 7803, Lecture notes in computer science. Springer, Heidelberg, pp 527–536

Jankowski J (2013c) Increasing website conversions using content repetitions with different levels of persuasion. In: Proceedings of 5-th Asian conference on intelligent information and database systems, vol 7803, Lecture notes in computer science. Springer, Heidelberg, pp 439–448

Judd CH, McAllister CN, Steel WM (1905) General introduction to a series of studies of eye movements by means of kinetoscopic photographs. In: Baldwin JM, Warren HC, Judd CH (eds) Psychological review, monograph supplements, vol 7. The Review Publishing Company, Baltimore, MD, pp 1–16

Just MA, Carpenter PA (1978) Inference processes during reading: reflections from eye fixations. In: Senders JW, Fisher DF, Monty RA (eds) Eye movements and the higher psychological functions. Wiley, Hillsdale, pp 157–174

Just MJ, Carpenter PA (1980) A theory of reading: from eye fixations to comprehension. Psychol Rev 87(4):329–354

Lapa C (2007) Using eye tracking to understand banner blindness and improve website design. Thesis. Rochester Institute of Technology

Levine JL (1981) An eye-controlled computer. Research report RC-8857. IBM Thomas J. Watson Research Center, Yorktown Heights, NY

Lohse G (1997) Consumer eye movement patterns on yellow pages advertising. J Advert 26 (1):61–73

Mackworth JF, Mackworth NH (1958) Eye fixations recorded on changing visual scenes by the television eye-marker. J Opt Soc Am 48(7):439–444

Mackworth NH, Thomas EL (1962) Head-mounted eye-marker camera. J Opt Soc Am 52 (6):713–716

Maughan L, Gutnikov S, Stevens R (2007) Look more, like more: the evidence from eye tracking. J Brand Manag 14(4):335–342

Monty RA, Senders JW (1976) Eye movements and psychological processes. In: National Research Council Washington DC Committee on hearing bioacoustics and biomechanics. ACM Press, pp 573–605

Poole A, Ball LJ (2006) Eye tracking in human-computer interaction and usability research: current status and future prospects. In: Ghaoui C (ed) Encyclopedia of human computer interaction. Interaction Design Foundation, Aarhus, pp 211–219

Ramalingam V, Palaniappan B (2006) Measuring advertisement effectiveness a neural network approach. Expert Syst Appl 31(1):159–163

Reutskaja E, Nagel R, Camerer CF, Rangel A (2011) Search dynamics in consumer choice under time pressure: an eye-tracking study. Am Econ Rev 101(2):900–926

Robinson H, Wysocka A, Hand C (2007) Internet advertising effectiveness: the effect of design on click-through rates for banner ads. Int J Adv Rev Marketing Commun 26(4):527–541

Rösler A, Ulrich C, Billino J, Sterzer P, Weidauer S, Bernhardt T, Steinmetz H, Frölich L, Kleinschmidt A (2004) Effects of arousing emotional scenes on the distribution of visuospatial attention: changes with aging and early subcortical vascular dementia. J Neurol Sci 229:109–116

Roth AE (1993) The early history of experimental economics. J Hist Econ Thought 15(2):184–209

Roth SP, Tuch AN, Mekler ED, Bargas-Avila JA, Opwis K (2013) Location matters, especially for non-salient features–an eye-tracking study on the effects of web object placement on different types of websites. Int J Hum Comput Stud 71(3):228–235

Sanders J, Fisher D, Monty R (1978) Eye movements and the higher psychological functions. Lawrence Erlbuam Associates, Hillsdale

Sibert JL, Gokturk M, Lavine RA (2000) The reading assistant: eye gaze triggered auditory prompting for reading remediation. In: Proceedings of the thirteenth annual ACM symposium on user interface software and technology.

Starker I, Bolt RA (1990) A gaze-responsive self-disclosing display. In: 'CHI '90 Proceedings', ACM, pp 3–9

Tinker M (1931) Apparatus for recording eye movements. Am J Psychol 43(1):115–118

Tzanidou E (2003) Eye tracking as a complementary, usability evaluation technique for E-commerce sites. In: Proceedings of the workshop on 'Exploring The Total Customer Experience (TCE): Usability Evaluations of (B2B) e-commerce Environments' - INTERACT 2003

Vertegaal R (1999) The GAZE groupware system: mediating joint attention in multiparty Communications collaboration. In: CHI '99 Proceedings of the SIGCHI conference on human factors in computing systems, pp 294–301

Ware C, Mikaelian HT (1987) An evaluation of an eye tracker as a device for computer input. In: Proceedings of the ACM CHI + GI'87 human factors in computing systems conference. ACM Press, New York, pp 183–188

Yuan X, Guo M, Ren F, Peng F (2014) Usability analysis of online bank login interface based on eye tracking experiment. Sens Transduc 165(2):203–212

Zhai S, Morimoto C, Ihde S (1999) Manual and gaze input cascaded (MAGIC) pointing. In: CHI '99 Proceedings of the SIGCHI conference on human factors in computing systems, pp 246–253

Ziemba P, Jankowski J, Wątróbski J, Becker J (2015a) Knowledge management in website quality evaluation domain. In: Nunez M et al (eds) ICCCI 2015, Part II, vol 9330, Lecture notes in artificial intelligence. Springer, Heidelberg, pp 75–85. doi:10.1007/978-3-319-24306-1_8

Ziemba P, Jankowski J, Wątróbski J, Wolski W, Becker J (2015b) Integration of domain ontologies in the repository of website evaluation methods. In: Proceedings of the federated conference on computer science and information systems. Annals of computer science and information systems 5, pp 1585–1595. doi:10.15439/2015F297

Ziemba P, Piwowarski M, Jankowski J, Wątróbski J (2014) Method of criteria selection and weights calculation in the process of web projects evaluation. In: Hwang D et al (eds) ICCCI 2014, vol 8733, Lecture notes in artificial intelligence. Springer, Heidelberg, pp 684–693

Chapter 21
The Study of Advertising Content with Application of EEG

Agata Wawrzyniak and Barbara Wąsikowska

Abstract The character and form of the commercial message have a decisive influence on its reception by potential clients. The appropriate preparation of advertising spots and all promotional materials significantly increases the chances of its positive reception and arouses consumer interest in a product or service. The study of advertising content and its influence can be carried out using different research methods. This chapter presents one of the modern approaches to analysis of advertising content, i.e. with application of the electroencephalography (EEG). The primary objective of the study was to identify features which should be characteristic of an advertisement answering the current situation on the market and meeting the expectations of the customer.

Keywords Marketing research • Electroencephalography • Advertising content

21.1 Introduction

Modern marketing strategies require from entrepreneurs something more than just creating new products or services, which are easily available, with competitive prices. They need to communicate with their current and prospective clients. For the majority of marketing specialists the main issue is not whether to communicate but rather how, when, with whom and how often. In order to reach target clients effectively and affect their shopping decisions, they creatively apply various forms of communication, including mass (non-personal) communication, whose essential instrument is advertising. Advertising still remains one of the main elements of any marketing campaign. Even in today's very demanding media environment, good advertisement may bring considerable benefits.

Currently people are surrounded by advertisements almost everywhere and it is easier to list places where there are no advertisements, than those where

A. Wawrzyniak (✉) • B. Wąsikowska
Department of Computational Methods in Experimental Economics,
Faculty of Economics and Management, Institute of IT in Management,
University of Szczecin, Mickiewicza 64, 71-101 Szczecin, Poland
e-mail: agataw@wneiz.pl; barbara.wasikowska@wneiz.pl

K. Nermend, M. Łatuszyńska (eds.), *Selected Issues in Experimental Economics*,
Springer Proceedings in Business and Economics, DOI 10.1007/978-3-319-28419-4_21

advertisements are present. Consumers have at their disposal hundreds of television channels, thousands of newspapers and magazines and millions of Internet websites. In all those places they encounter advertisements in one form or another. The reasons for advertisements' ubiquity seem obvious. The main goal of an advertisement is to persuade people to purchase various goods and use all kinds of services. The character and form of an advertising message play a crucial role in perception of the message by the potential clients. Appropriate preparation of commercials and other promotional materials significantly increases the chance that clients will respond to it positively and will arouse their interest.

The study of communicative effectiveness, also known as the study of advertising content, aims at determining whether a particular advertisement is effective. Marketing specialists should perform such studies both before and after the advertisement is placed in the media (Kotler and Keller 2012). The study of advertising content and their influence may be carried out with the use of various research methods. This chapter presents one of the most modern approaches to the study of advertising content, i.e. the study with the application of electroencephalography (EEG). The aim of the study was to identify the characteristics of an advertisement which would relate to the current market situation and meet the clients' needs.

21.2 The Effect of Advertising on Purchasing

A lot of decisions concerning shopping are made under the influence of advertising. According to Kotler, advertising is any form of non-personal presentation and promotion of ideas, goods or services by an identified sponsor via press, including newspapers and magazines; transmission media, including radio and television; networks, such as telephone, cable, satellite or wireless network; media such as magnetic tape, video tape, CD-ROM and Internet website; and also visual media, including billboards, labelling and posters (Kotler and Keller 2012). Advertising is therefore distinguished by such characteristics as paid form, direct indication of the sender of the message and purely communicative character of its influence on recipients. The influence of an advertisement may be direct (a client encounters an advertisement and therefore makes a purchase) or indirect (a client purchases something because it has been purchased by other people—usually family or friends—who had encountered a particular advertisement). Promotional activities contribute to brand equity and drive sales in many ways: by creating brand awareness, shaping its image in consumers' minds, creating positive judgements and feelings towards the brand and reinforcing clients' loyalty.

As an instrument of marketing communication, advertising has a significant range (e.g. national and international advertisements) and frequency (e.g. TV, radio or Internet advertisements), is highly expressive (especially in the case of audio-visual advertisements which use the highest number of means of expression), can attract attention and is relatively easy to control in terms of implementation. One of the advantages of advertising is a relatively low unit cost of reaching recipients.

This quality is, however, virtually eliminated by the fact that seeing an advertisement only once has a negligible effect on the recipient and therefore the advertisement needs to be repeated frequently, which significantly increases the costs. The main disadvantages of advertisements are the lack of message flexibility, varied degree of selectivity—dependent on the medium—in reaching recipients and the fact that its effect is only indirect on recipients' behaviour, which makes it difficult to estimate its impact (Woźniczka 2012).

Among the primary effects of advertising as an instrument of marketing communication one can distinguish:

1. Economic effects, also known as marketing effects, including material and financial effects of advertising activities
2. Behavioural effects, relating to stimulating particular market behaviours of the recipients of an advertisement
3. Communicative effects, referring to memory, cognitive, affective and volitional reactions of recipients to advertising messages
4. Media effects, consisting in ensuring that advertisements effectively reach target audiences of marketing communication of an organisation (see Table 21.1)

One of the most cohesive concepts of effects and purposes of advertising has been created by Rossiter and Percy. The starting point of their description of advertising effects was a sequence of six steps of advertising effects, including exposure to advertising content, processing the message, building communication effects and market position of the brand, causing target audience actions (these are the so-called buyer response steps) as well as achieving particular sales level, market share and brand value and also making profit. The final two steps in the six-step effect sequence are aggregate effects on the market or company levels. Therefore this sequence covers, respectively media, communicative, behavioural and economic effects, joining them into a series of interdependent steps (see Fig. 21.1).

Table 21.1 Basic types of advertising effects (Woźniczka 2012)

Types of effects	Selected detailed effects
Economic (marketing) effects	Sales Market share Financial gain Return on advertising costs
Behavioural effects	Keeping current clients Acquiring new purchasers Increase in the volume of purchases Increase in the frequency of purchases
Communicative effects	Brand awareness Attitude towards the brand Intention to purchase brand's products
Media effects	Advertising reach Advertising frequency Intensity of advertising in media

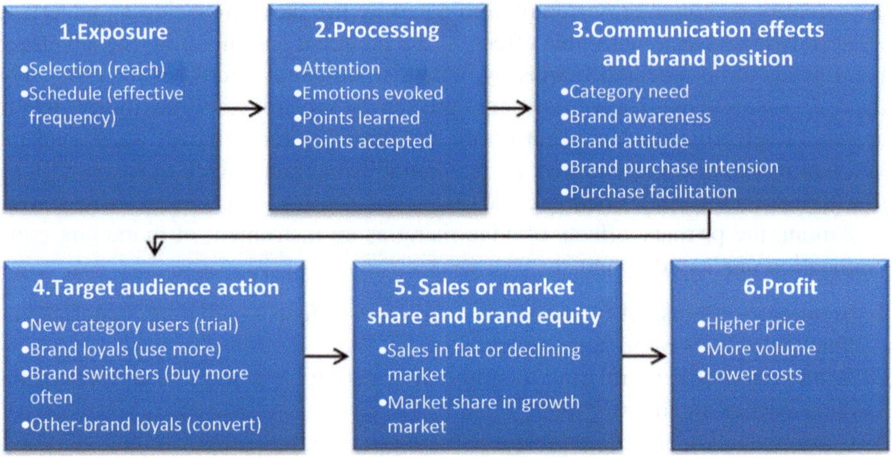

Fig. 21.1 Six-step sequence of advertising effects [source: authors' own elaboration based on Rossiter and Percy (1997)]

Despite these positive remarks, the effectiveness of advertising should not be overrated. It is worth emphasising that advertising is usually the most effective before the prospective client's first contact with a product, when the advertisement entices the client to try it out. After this, the client's opinion regarding the product's quality is of essential importance. The influence of advertising is stronger for products whose aesthetic and functional qualities cannot be assessed immediately, at a shop, before the products are bought and used, than when advertisements present products whose quality may be checked immediately. It is therefore more effective in the case of washing powder than clothes. The results of marketing research indicate that advertising in so-called mature industries, those whose products have been on the market for a long time (e.g. household appliances), is far less significant than in relatively young industries (e.g. mobile phones). Mature industries count more on clients' awareness of the quality of given products whereas in younger industries, where there is no sufficient data as to the advantages and disadvantages of products offered, the influence of advertising is greater.

A product or a service may be, obviously, sold also without advertising. Such is the case with ships or narcotics. Situations in which advertising proves totally ineffective are also highly interesting. Despite the advertisers' efforts, approximately 80 % of all new products fail or bring worse results than expected (Martin 2008). Although this index varies depending on the industry and the type of service, the overall results concerning products and services provide a thought-provoking example of costs which were borne in vain. Advertising does not help sales if an advertising campaign is badly prepared and sometimes advertising is ineffective in view of demographic, cultural and sociological phenomena or market rules, such as the recent faux pas with clothing giant Zara, which produced a "sheriff" shirt with stripes and yellow star, reminiscent of the Holocaust.

One should also remember that a large number of consumers think that advertising has no effect on them whatsoever and their purchasing decisions are entirely rational. Another widespread belief states that the more intelligent a given person, the less often he/she succumbs to illusions. Research however shows that well-educated people, despite their declared scepticism and doubtfulness towards advertising messages, do not behave according to these attitudes. Intelligent and well-educated people may know that they are frequently manipulated by advertisements, but still they purchase advertised products (Pratkanis and Aronson 2001). Social psychology experiments also show that critical recipients of advertisements are not willing to make purchases directly after seeing advertising messages. After some time, however, they behave as though they have forgotten where the information about products has come from and make the purchase.

21.3 Determinants of Marketing Communication Effectiveness

Marketing communication refers to various methods by which companies try to inform and persuade consumers and remind them—directly or indirectly—about products and brands they have to offer (Kotler and Keller 2012). Due to this recurring nature of information, or promoting new products, companies intentionally communicate and build relationships with clients, to "establish a community"—creating ownership and loyalty. Marketing communication also serves consumers in that it informs them how and why they should use a particular product, who it is for and who the producer is. Consumers may be, for instance, under the influence of advertising, encouraged to try out or use a given product or service.

Advertising, as one of the basic instruments of marketing communication, carries out mostly communicative tasks, i.e. causes psychological reactions of recipients to the message. The starting point in analysing these reactions is usually the model of marketing communication. The process of communication in the context of marketing is presented by means of the typical model, based on the classic Shannon-Weaver model, which involves signal, its transmitter and receivers, encoding and decoding processes, communication channel and noise disturbing the reception of the signal (see Fig. 21.2).

A construct crucial to analyse communicative effects is the Hierarchy of Effects Model, presenting a sequence of stages in the process of creating the effects. A significant number of models of communicative effects have been created since the beginning of the twentieth century and they have been widely discussed in scientific literature (Strong 1925; Lavidge and Steiner 1961; Rogers 1962; Ehrenberg 1974; Vaughn 1986; van Raaij 1989; Barry and Howard 1990; Dutka 1995; Rossiter and Percy 1997; Shimp 1997; Ambler 2000; Woźniczka 2012). Table 21.2 presents a synthetic overview of chosen models. At this point it is worth mentioning that criticism and verification of the models refer mostly to the

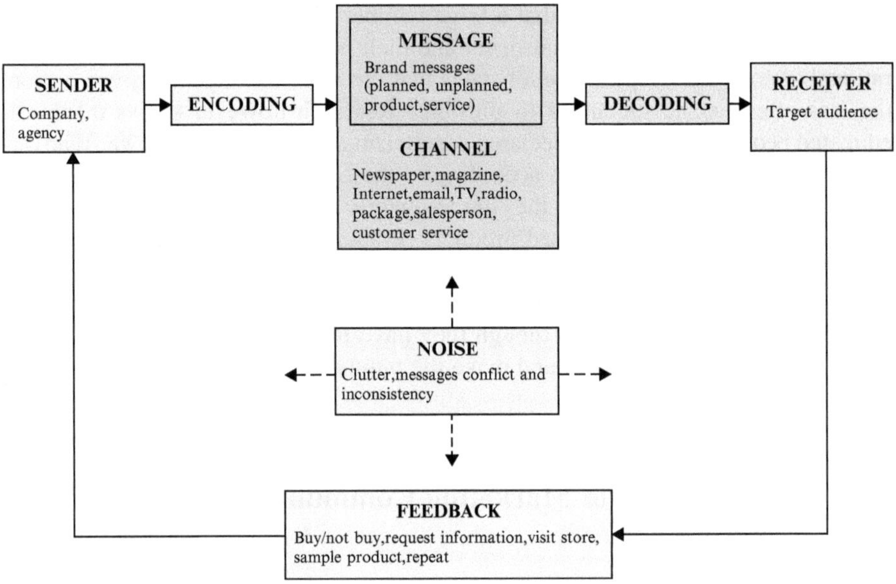

Fig. 21.2 Marketing communication process [source: authors' own compilation on the basis of Weaver and Shannon (1963), Duncan (2005)]

types of recipients' reactions, number and sequence of stages and their significance to the final evaluation of the effectiveness of advertising activities.

When perusing literature concerning the effectiveness of marketing communication—including advertising—one may notice that, among many factors, authors dedicate the most attention to the problem of the choice of a right target group, the adaptation of advertising content, cultural specificity and the choice of media and frequency of advertising.

The definition of advertising, quoted earlier in this chapter, indicates that advertising is not always addressed to everybody. It is usually aimed at a certain part of society, so-called target groups, with their specific demographic characteristics and psychological factors, such as attitudes, beliefs or personalities. The primary factors in determining advertisement's success are accurately and precisely defining the target group and constructing the advertising message in such a way that it would reach the target group. The message does not have to be accepted and deemed credible by all recipients. It should reach the demographic group for which it was designed. One of the factors taken into consideration when specifying the target group is the generational affiliation. The language and imaging of advertisements aimed at the older generation will be different from the construction of an advertisement aimed at middle-aged people. In yet another way companies will try to attract teenagers and this in turn will differ from advertisements targeting children. Another important element when establishing the group of recipients is their educational background and social status. Advertising messages relating to specialist subjects, the promotion of products for particular industries or dealing

Table 21.2 Selected models of hierarchy of communicative effects of advertising [source: authors' own compilation on the basis of Strong (1925), Lavidge and Steiner (1961), Rogers (1962), Dutka (1995), Rossiter and Percy (1997), Barry and Howard (1990)]

	Models					
Phases	AIDA Model (E.S. Elmo Lewis 1990)	DAGMAR/ACCA Model (R.H. Colley 1961)	Lavidge and Steiner Model (R.J. Lavidge, G.A. Steiner 1961)	New Adopter Hierarchy/AIETA Model (E.M. Rogers 1962)	ACALTA Model (T.S. Robertson 1971)	Rossiter and Percy Model (J.R. Rossiter, L. Percy 1997)
Cognitive phase	Attention ↓	Awareness ↓ Comprehension ↓	Awareness ↓ Knowledge ↓	Awareness ↓	Awareness ↓ Comprehension ↓	Category need ↓ Brand awareness ↓
Affective phase	Interest ↓ Desire ↓	Conviction ↓	Liking ↓ Preference ↓ Conviction ↓	Interest ↓ Evaluation ↓	Attitude ↓ Legitimation ↓	Brand attitude ↓ Brand purchase intention ↓
Conative phase	Action	Action	Purchase	Trial ↓ Adoption	Trial ↓ Adoption	Purchase facilitation

with niche, hermetic subjects will have a different construction. The means of expression and imaging will also be influenced by whether a given product will be sold to parents, young couples, people with health issues, members of particular professional groups, students, pupils or people connected with a specific industry. When considering the target group, one should also take into consideration the financial situation of prospective recipients and to what extent the particular services or products might be needed by those people. One should, however, point out here that aiming advertising message at particular social groups may also limit the effectiveness of an advertisement. Teenagers watching a commercial for breakfast cereal aimed at younger children may not want to try out this product.

Another factor influencing the effectiveness of advertising messages is adaptation. The notion of adaptation in the field of advertising has quite a broad meaning. It refers to the relation between at least two elements significant in the process of creating recipient's attitude to goods and services presented in an advertisement (Doliński 2007). For instance, adaptation may refer to relations between the character of the product and client's personality. In order for an advertisement to be effective, it must be adapted to the audience and transfer the information that is the most important for the client. This can be achieved by creating quality contents. The message which a company wishes to pass to a client should be of high substantive quality. In other words, it should offer clients something that would simply interest them and broaden their knowledge. This way prospective clients will take an interest in the offer out of their own free will.

The concept of adaptation may also refer to relationship between the method of purchasing and the character of an advertisement. The method of shopping undoubtedly depends on multiple factors but one of the most important is the type of goods purchased. R. Vaughn divides the shopping process into two types: the one where thinking is essential and the one where feeling or emotion is the predominate factor. He also assumes that client's involvement in doing shopping is also important. It is illustrated by the FCB Grid (i.e. Foote, Cone and Belding Product Category Classification Scheme). According to R. Vaughn, people's involvement in buying cars, housing estates or furniture is highly based on rationality. They are also highly involved in buying jewellery, toiletries and clothes but they do it emotionally. Low involvement level but high rationality accompany shopping for food and household chemicals, whereas buying cigarettes, candy and alcohol is connected with low involvement and following one's emotions (Vaughn 1980). These relations are presented in Table 21.3.

Table 21.3 Product categories in the FCB Grid [source: authors' own elaboration based on Vaughn (1986)]

	Rational purchase	Emotional purchase
High involvement	Products: cars, houses, washing machines, medicines Advertising: informative	Products: jewellery, cosmetics, fashion apparel Advertising: affective
Low involvement	Products: food, household items Advertising: habitual	Products: cigarettes, sweets, alcohol Advertising: satisfying

An advertisement is effective if it persuades a client to buy certain products. Since in the four presented cases determinants of a purchase are different, the character of an advertisement should depend on the product that is being advertised. The advertisement of goods which are bought rationally and with high involvement (e.g. house or a car) should be factual and filled with detailed information about the product (facts, figures, parameters, charts, tables). With relation to products which are bought with lower involvement level, but also mostly rationally (e.g. washing powder, dishwashing liquid), advertisements should emphasise those qualities of the product which point to its objective advantage over analogical products from different companies. The level of detail does not have to be great; often it is enough to come up with a catchy slogan or to mention a specific name of an ingredient which is present only in this particular product. When it comes to products which are connected with buyer's high involvement and emotionality (e.g. clothes, cosmetics), it is important for an advertisement to emphasise positive mood and create a specific atmosphere. In case of the last category, in which products are bought with high emotional level but low involvement (e.g. candy, stimulants), advertisements should appeal to highly emotional stereotypes and underscore the fact that buying a given product proves client's good taste. For instance, chocolate producers appeal mostly to recipients' feelings, everyday emotions and "spiritual" needs. Emotional states most widely associated with chocolate are joy, happiness, relaxation, carelessness and love. Therefore such warm, positive emotion images accompany the consumption of candy in advertisements. As a result, the ineffectiveness of a given advertisement may stem from using rational arguments where emotional ones would be more fitting and vice versa.

Paying attention to cultural differences is of the utmost importance in the world of marketing, as these differences may severely obstruct marketing communication. The effectiveness of an advertisement is closely connected with how well cultural differences have been taken into account. In many commercials, one may see the effects the culture has on the advertising message. Cultural elements are present in words, gestures, imaging or music. There are some types of advertisements which are directly originated in cultural norms. For instance, American advertisements are simple and easy to remember. The form of friendly conversation is connected with aggressive promotion. The advertisement must show how different a given product is in comparison with the rest (the American market is one of the most competitive ones). When entering foreign markets, one should remember that there are visible and invisible elements in any culture. Cultural knowledge cannot be limited to daily customs, tradition, language and art. One should also take into consideration the following: the level of directness of communication, the tendency to take risks, the effectiveness of emotional and rational arguments and the collectivist and individualist values. It is important for an advertisement to notice not only cultural differences, but also similarities. The success of international advertising campaigns should be created with the awareness of and sensitivity to cultural differences. It should also be emphasised that high intercultural competencies not only prevent gaffes, mistakes or cultural inadequacies in marketing actions, but also create added value, competitiveness and allow companies and businesses to reap the benefits of synergy.

Significant determinants of the effectiveness of an advertisement are as follows: an appropriate choice of media by which the message will reach recipients and the frequency of a given advertisement. The choice of media consists of identifying the most cost-effective media which will allow to achieve a desired number and type of interactions with recipients. A media planner must know the possibilities of basic types of media in terms of their reach, frequency and strength of impact. Main advertising media, together with their costs, advantages and limitations, have been discussed in an earlier study (Kotler and Keller 2012). Advertisers should make their decisions relating to a media plan after considering such factors: the media habits of target audience, the characteristics of a product/service, requirements of communication and costs. Apart from the problem of choosing media, there is also the issue of frequency with which a given advertisement will appear. It is connected with the so-called mere exposure effect. In his studies on this phenomenon, R. Zajonc presented his respondents a series of objects (human faces, geometric shapes, words, tunes) with some of the objects appearing in the series only once and some appearing multiple times. The study underscored the direct correlation between liking a product and the frequency of seeing it (Zajonc 2001; Monahan et al. 2000). One can therefore conclude that repeated exposure to an object may be sufficient to like this object. In studies of advertising effectiveness, mere exposure effect has been observed, irrespective of whether the experiment participants were directly asked to watch advertisements or came into contact with an object apparently incidentally (Perfect and Askew 1994; Perfect and Heatherley 1997). This effect has been confirmed many times by various types of studies, including psychological studies, that provoke a widespread debate on bilateral connections between intellectual cognition and emotional life in humans. M. Sutherland, a prominent researcher of advertising from the perspective of experimental psychology, emphasises that an advertisement is like a feather. When it is repeated, small, even imperceptible effects may create a larger, noticeable difference between goods. Additionally, if a certain message is repeated without contradiction, our brains seem to treat it as a proof that something is probable, possible or true (the truth effect) (Sutherland 2009).

21.4 Psychological Mechanisms of Advertising

The developments in marketing research, especially neuromarketing, have resulted in an increased interest in advertising and, more precisely, its psychological and neuronal aspects. Scientists have appreciated the role of memory, attention (Heath and Nairn 2005), emotion (Doliński 2007) and even mirror neurons (Lindström 2008) in the perception of advertising in a consumer's mind. The knowledge of advertising psychology and consumer behaviour allows marketing experts to understand the psychological conditioning of advertising effectiveness and therefore to construct more effective advertising messages. This issue has been present in scientific research for a long time—many academic textbooks, papers and monographs have been published on this subject. At the same time, advertising psychology studies have become increasingly popular in advertising practice, which has begun to pay more attention to the theoretical justification of the effectiveness of constructed advertising strategies. The knowledge of psychology and practical skills relating to creating strategy, choosing media and creating or evaluating advertisements from the psychological point of view allows one to predict the effectiveness of a given marketing campaign with high accuracy.

Cognitive psychology comes to the aid in explaining many issues connected with the influence of marketing and advertising actions on a client. It is a branch of psychology concerned with the process of human cognition of the environment—creating knowledge of the environment which may later be used in behaviour. Cognitive activity is defined as processing of information by the brain and therefore one can say that cognitive psychology is a study of organisation and functioning of the brain. Cognitive psychology studies cognitive processes relating to perception, attention, memory and reasoning (information processing) (Hayes and Stratton 2012).

Perception is a term describing a set of processes affecting the creation of subjective images of reality. Each person has certain genetic perceptive capabilities already at the moment of birth, which evolves during the course of one's life, developing with life experiences. Perception is the main stage of processing information perceived by the senses. Human beings, as a species, have highly specialised and complex sensory organs, reacting to multiple stimuli from the environment (Kardes et al. 2011). The process of perception involves not only data received from the environment at a given moment but also individual characteristics relating to a person's memory, the course of one's learning process or personality structure. Thanks to perception, an individual may create an orderly, systematised and cohesive image of reality. Also advertisements, which in some measure force the recipient to show cognitive involvement in order to read the message, are highly effective and frequently produce the desired effect. The way an advertisement is presented (i.e. its form) is as important as its content. With the knowledge of techniques influencing cognitive processes, advertisers can shape or profoundly influence attitudes or preferences concerning a product of service.

Attention is one of the elementary cognitive processes whose most important tasks are selecting information and preventing the cognitive system from being overloaded with data (Kardes et al. 2011). Attention highly influences people's thinking, behaviour and feeling and also plays a significant role in learning processes. It is attention that decides whether an advertisement a person has just watched will stay in memory or not. In other words, one may see the same advertisement hundreds of times but if it is not perceived (i.e. the recipient does not process information connected with the advertisement) but merely watched, the recipient will not remember the advertisement, the product or the price. This is why advertising triggers (scantily clad women, children and cute animals) connected to an advertised product are effective in attracting and keeping the attention of recipients. This is also why the aforementioned AIDA model starts with attention.

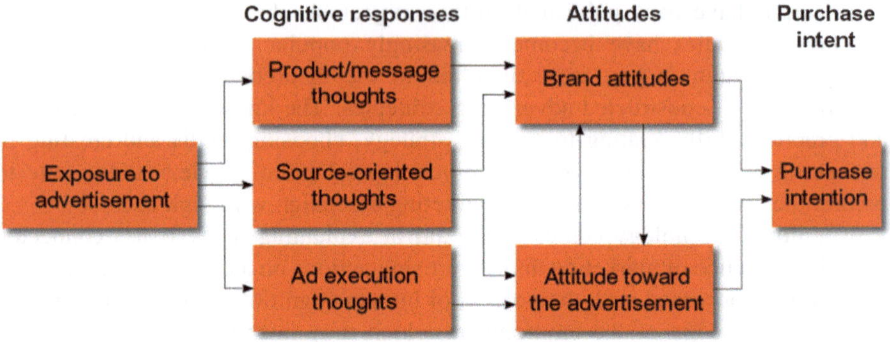

Fig. 21.3 The model of cognitive response [source: Belch and Belch (2003)]

Memory is the ability of an individual which consists of registration, storage and retrieval of particular stimuli. Memory is characterised by permanence, fidelity speed of remembering and speed of recalling information. Memory is also significant from the point of view of marketing—one should create the message in such a way that it will be remembered for a long time. Clients receive a lot of stimuli from various sources and their specific characteristics determine whether they are remembered or not. Results of memory research are useful in creating marketing strategies. Certainly, a key role in remembering an advertisement is not only how frequently it is presented, but also by the manipulation of memory cues.

The cognitive response approach has been widely used in research by both academics and advertising experts. Its focus has been to determine the types of responses evoked by an advertising message and how these responses relate to attitudes toward the ad, brand attitudes and purchase intentions. Figure 21.3 depicts the three basic categories of cognitive responses researchers have identified—product/message, source oriented and ad execution thoughts—and how they may relate to attitudes and intentions (Belch and Belch 2003).

21.5 The Application of EEG in the Study of Advertising Content

As part of the evolution of marketing, studies over the functioning of the human brain are conducted. As a result of those studies, the second half of 1990s saw the birth of a new discipline—neuromarketing. Studies carried out in this new branch allow us to know clients better and more precisely, and thanks to this—to prepare appropriate offers of products and services. Neuromarketing deals with how client's brain reacts to advertising message (Preuss 2010; Renvoise and Morin 2011; Vecchiato et al. 2014; Wąsikowska 2013; Zurawicki 2010). One of the methods applied in this discipline is electroencephalography (EEG). EEG is a method of recording changes in the electrical activity of the cerebral cortex. The recording is made with the use of special electrodes attached to the surface of the scalp by a gel or a paste or by electrodes attached to a cap which is then put on the head (Fig. 21.4).

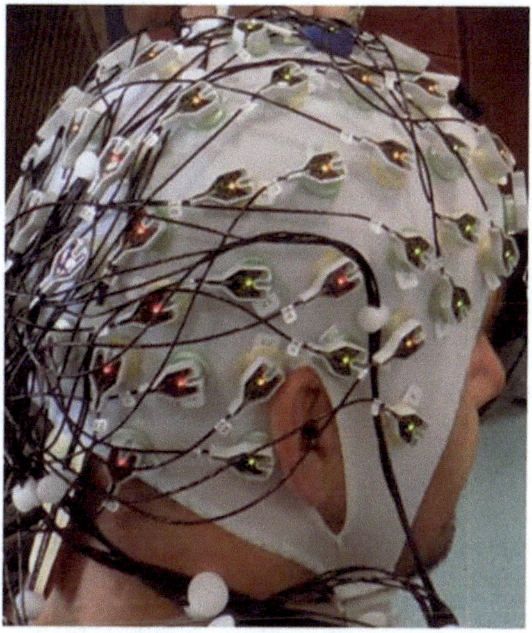

Fig. 21.4 A cap with active EEG electrodes (photo: B. Wąsikowska)

By recording and analysing respondent's brainwaves one can learn, for instance, which stimuli in an advertisement cause a positive or negative emotional reaction. One may also observe in real time the respondent's attention or the processes of emotional involvement in any second of a given advertisement. With the use of EEG, the advertisements may be analysed in three ways (Ohme and Matukin 2012):

1. Referential analysis—which compares characteristic advertisements for a whole category of products: A group of advertisements is chosen, which show various methods of presenting a brand or a product.
2. Vertical analysis—consists of dividing an advertisement into images and sounds: During the study, respondents' reactions to separately presented background music, voiceover and images are observed. Then the layers are integrated and changes in reactions observed. Therefore, one can see what has the biggest influence on the final effect of an advertisement: sound or images.
3. Horizontal analysis—an advertisement is analysed in terms of alternative ways of presenting a product or its uses. As respondents watch various versions of an advertisement of the same products, analysts check and determine which version creates the most positive reactions.

Currently, on the basis of the brainwave analysis, experts can describe an advertisement to a fraction of a second; point to scenes generating the highest emotional involvement; describe reactions to images, sound, words and special effects; and recommend the background music that is the best for reinforcing the message. In addition to all these, specialists can even determine the best way to display logo and packaging, determine whether the opening scene has the potential to make an advertisement stand out in a commercial break and decide which ending will be best to stimulate buying behaviour.

21.6 An Analysis of an Advertisement with the Use of EEG: An Example

Below authors present an example of the application of EEG in analysing advertising content. Forty-five healthy people participated in the experiment—students aged from 20 to 24. The study was conducted in the Laboratory of Cognitive Neuroscience, located at the Faculty of Economics and Management of the University of Szczecin.

Brainwaves were recorded with the use of a 19-channel electroencephalograph KT88-2400 (Digital Electric Activity Mapping) from Contec Medical Systems. Gold-plated cup-shaped electrodes were used to record signals, and Ten20 paste to attach electrodes to the scalp. Electrodes were attached to the scalp at seven points: Fp1, Fp2, F3, F4, F7, F8 and Fz (according to the international 10–20 system). A unipolar recording of brain electrical signals was performed. The reference point was the left earlap. Additionally, an ECG electrode was attached to the left wrist of each respondent and three EDA electrodes on the phalanges of fingers of the non-dominant hand in order to study electrodermal activity. Electrodermal activity was measured with the use of Neurobit Optima 4 device (Fig. 21.5).

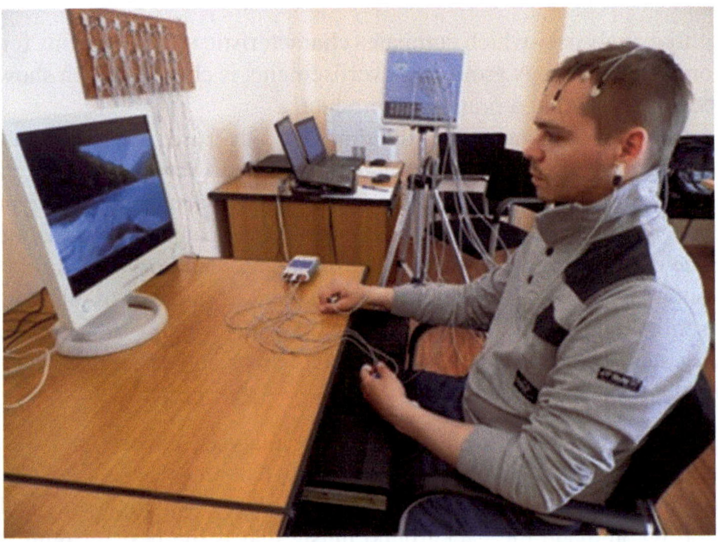

Fig. 21.5 Recording of EEG, EDA and ECG signals while the participant watches a film with advertising breaks (photo: B. Wąsikowska)

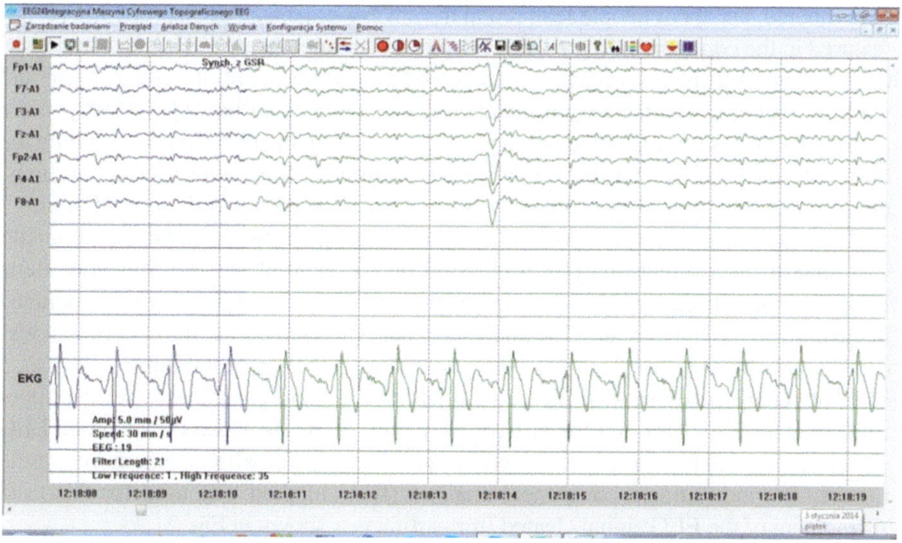

Fig. 21.6 Sample EEG and ECG recordings (source: authors' own elaboration)

Each participant watched a half-hour documentary interrupted with three advertising breaks. The film was shown on a 17-in. LCD monitor with 1280 × 1024 resolution and refresh rate of 60 Hz. The respondents sat ca. 80 cm from the monitor. Sound was emitted from Creative SBS260 speakers. Each of the advertising breaks consisted of 4 commercials, which means that 12 advertisements were presented in total. The first break contained commercials of yoghurts, the second—mineral water and the third—cars. Data was recorded both during the film and the advertisements. A sample EEG and ECG recording is presented in Fig. 21.6.

Directly after finishing the main part of the study, the participants were asked to take part in a survey. The survey was conducted as a direct interview with the use of an electronic questionnaire. The questionnaire was in the form of an Excel spreadsheet with pre-prepared questions. The first part of the interview consisted of demographic questions and four questions concerning the film. Demographic questions focused on obtaining data concerning demographic characteristics of respondents, e.g. age and sex. The study omitted questions referring to education, profession or marital status, due to the fact that all respondents were students and therefore their answers would have been identical.

The second part of the interview consisted of questions concerning advertising breaks. The first question related to commercials, focused on detecting which of the brands and products presented had been remembered by the participant (Q. 1. "You have just watched a film. During the projection you were shown some commercials (12 commercials in total). Do you remember the commercials you saw? Which commercials do you remember?"). The respondents' task was to enumerate brands and products which they remembered when they were watching the film (if a person did not remember any commercials, one should proceed to question 3). Then the researcher asked the respondents to give details about the plot of commercials they remembered, i.e. about people featured in the advertisements, places, props and scenes featured in the commercial (Q. 2 "Tell the plot of commercial A"). The next stage was to check whether the respondent remembered the advertisement of a given brand and while watching it whether they remembered seeing the ad earlier (Q. 3 "Did you see the advertisement for this brand while you were watching the film? When watching the film, did you recall seeing this advertisement before?"). For both of these questions, the respondent may have answered "Yes" or "No". The entire study took 45 min.

The next step of the study was the analysis of data gathered during the experiment. The advertising content analysis was based on the example of the Mercedes-Benz E-class car advertisement. This commercial was one of the four advertisements included in the third advertising break.[1] The analysis of data gathered during the experiment was carried out with the use of our own program made in Python programming language. The data analysis began with filtering signals with a band-pass filter, with the upper frequency limit of 2 Hz and lower frequency limit of 30 Hz. Then the recorded EEG signal was cleared from artifacts caused by eye blinking, eye-ball movements or muscle tremor. The independent component analysis (ICA) method was used for this task. A fragment of the EEG signal cleared from artifacts is shown in Fig. 21.7.

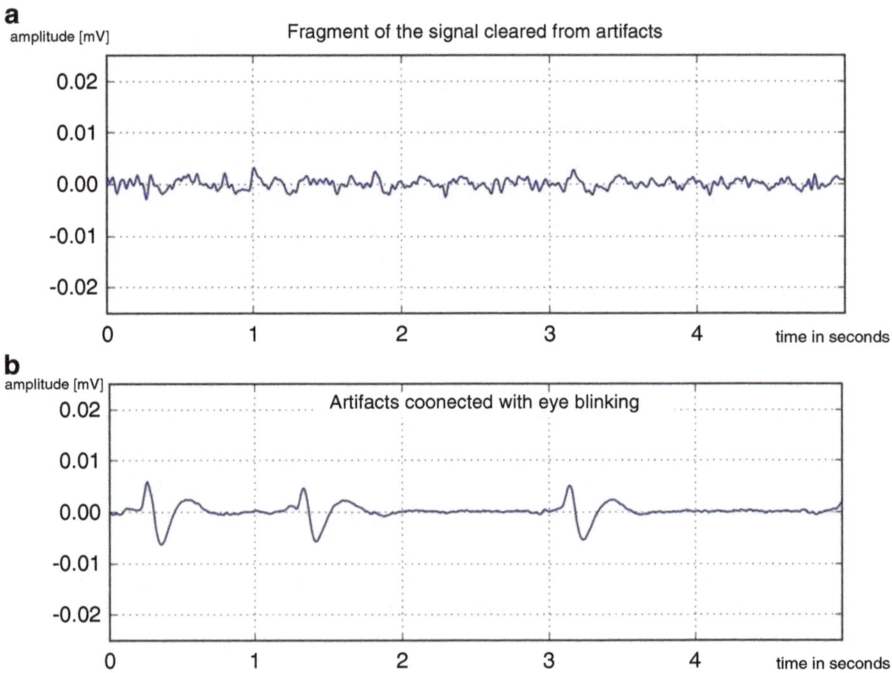

Fig. 21.7 (**a**) Fragment of the signal cleared from artifacts, (**b**) examples of artifacts connected with eye blinking (source: authors' own elaboration)

[1] The entire commercial is available on YouTube: https://www.youtube.com/watch?v=nFflUuGiSWw

Fig. 21.8 The initial scenes of the Mercedes-Benz E-Class car commercial (source: authors' own compilation on the basis of https://www.youtube.com/watch?v=nFflUuGiSWw)

Fig. 21.9 The middle scenes of the Mercedes-Benz E-Class car commercial (source: authors' own compilation on the basis of https://www.youtube.com/watch?v=nFflUuGiSWw)

After the EEG signal of all respondents had been cleared, the signal was averaged. The purpose of signal averaging was to pick up from the EEG recording all strong and characteristic reactions to the given commercial. Averaged signals were analysed in 5-s windows. In this way all scenes from Mercedes-Benz E-Class car commercial were analysed.

The commercial begins with a scene in which a respondent sees a black car going along a snowy road through a forest (Fig. 21.8). Then, next to the driver, in the passenger seat, the Grim Reaper appears, holding a scythe. The driver looks at the Grim Reaper surprised and frightened.

Death turns his head to the driver and with a triumphant smile says "Sorry . . .". At that moment, the driver turns his head to the road and sees a giant tree trunk hanging just in front of him. The driver brakes sharply and manages to avoid the crash. There is no collision. Now it is the man who turns his head towards the Grim Reaper and with an equally triumphant smile he says, "Sorry" (Fig. 21.9).

In the last scene of the commercial we see the front of the car, its make and a sign "Detects threats and increases braking force. Brake Assist System BAS PLUS" (Fig. 21.10).

When analysing individual scenes of the commercial with the averaged EEG recording, one can clearly see that the tree trunk appearing suddenly in front of the car causes a violent reaction in the respondents (Fig. 21.11).

Fig. 21.10 The last scene of the Mercedes-Benz E-Class car commercial (source: https://www.youtube.com/watch?v=nFflUuGiSWw)

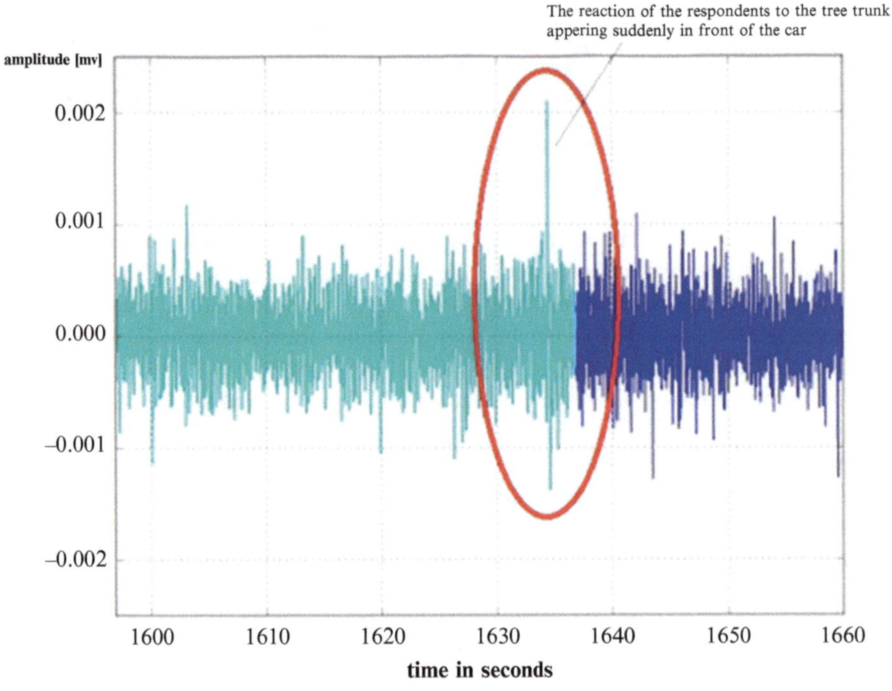

Fig. 21.11 The averaged EEG recording (source: authors' own elaboration)

This fact is confirmed by the electrodermal activity (EDA) recordings. A sample recording is presented in Fig. 21.12. When analysing the diagram, one can clearly see how the tension of the respondent grows, to reach its peak in the above-mentioned scene.

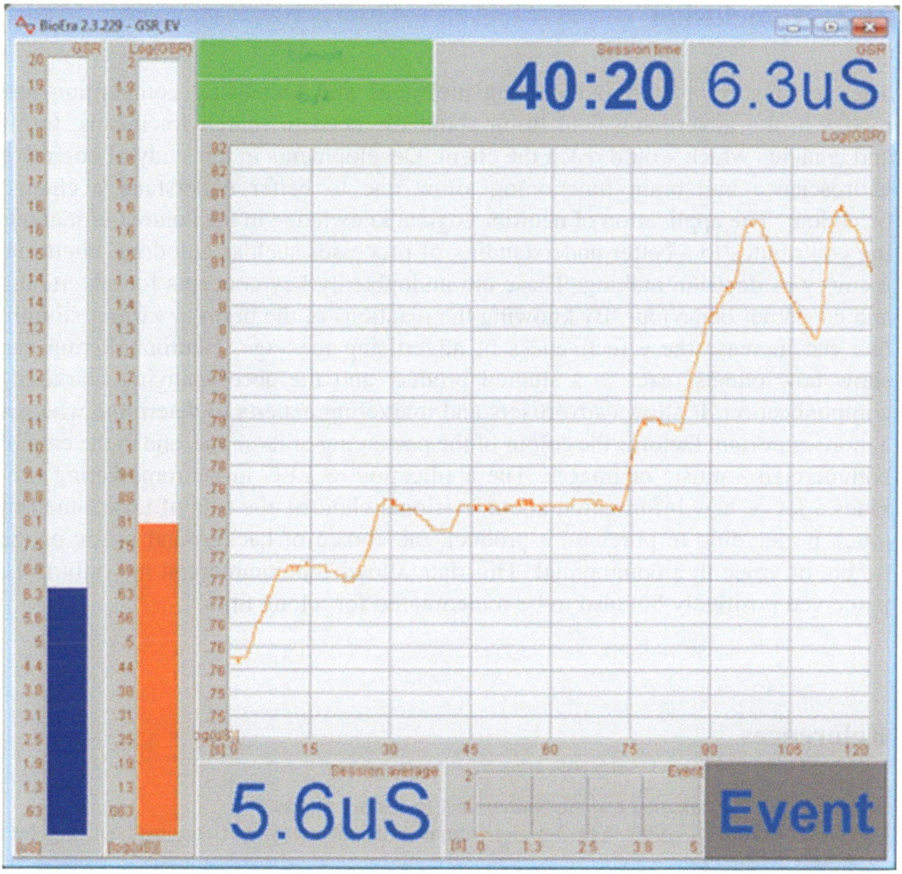

Fig. 21.12 A sample electrodermal activity (EDA) recording (source: authors' own elaboration)

The above results were confirmed also by surveys conducted directly after the study. Among all the advertisements watched, it was the Mercedes-Benz commercial that was best remembered because of the emotions it had evoked in the respondents. In some of the respondents the emotions were negative, while others were absolutely delighted. However, both groups remembered it perfectly.

The conducted research has shown that in order for a commercial to be remembered, it:

1. Should not be too long
2. Should not be boring
3. Should be interesting enough to draw the attention of the audience
4. Should evoke emotions (preferably positive emotions)
5. Should be understandable to the client and inform about the advantages of the product
6. Should clearly present the company's logo, catch phrase or slogan (preferably in the middle of the screen)

21.7 Conclusion

The growing number of advertising messages and increasing competition and modes in the advertising field bring about the need to search for means, forms and contents which would reach the client. Developments in the study of cognitive neuroscience and brain functioning allow one to better understand a clients' behaviour. The application of neurobiological knowledge in the context of marketing contributes to a better understanding of processes such as emotions, attention, memory or decision-making. These are undoubtedly key concepts for advertising and consumer behaviour. By knowing the reactions of the brain to various stimuli, one can increase the effectiveness of advertising message. Neuromarketing can show how clients react to a studied product and the accompanying marketing communication. It allows advertisers and marketing experts to determine whether a more important factor is the colour of the packaging or its shape, and in the case of commercials—music or images. The application of EEG in neuromarketing provides a lot of new information about irrational choices, the role of taste, smell or touch in deciding to purchase a product, the choice of background music or the timbre of voice in a commercial. This data allows the commercial not only to be perceived positively but also to be remembered for a long time.

References

Ambler T (2000) Marketing and the bottom line. Pearson, London

Barry TE, Howard DJ (1990) A review and critique of the hierarchy of effects in advertising. Int J Advert 2:121–135

Belch GE, Belch MA (2003) Advertising and promotion. An intergrated marketing communication perspective. The McGraw-Hill Companies, New York

Best Commercial: Mercedes-Benz E-class "Sorry". https://www.youtube.com/watch?v=nFflUuGiSWw. Accessed 15 Jul 2015

Doliński D (2007) Emotional see-saw. In: Pratkanis AR (ed) The science of social influence. Advances and future progress. Psychology Press, Philadelphia, PA, pp 137–153

Duncan T (2005) Principles of advertising and IMC. McGraw Hill, Boston, MA

Dutka S (1995) DAGMAR, defining advertising goals for measured advertising results. NTC Business Books, New York

Ehrenberg ASC (1974) Repetitive advertising and the consumer. J Advertising Res 14(2):25–34

Hayes N, Stratton P (2012) A sudent's dictionary of psychology. Routledge, London

Heath R, Nairn A (2005) Measuring affective advertising: implications of low attention processing on recall. J Advertising Res 45:269–281. doi:10.1017/S0021849905050282

Kardes FR, Cline TW, Cronley ML (2011) Consumer behavior: science and practice, Internationalth edn. South Western College, Cengage Learning, Mason

Kotler P, Keller KL (2012) Marketing management, 14th edn. Prentice Hall, Upper Saddle River, NJ

Lavidge RJ, Steiner GA (1961) A model for predictive measurements of advertising effectiveness. J Marketing 25(6):59–62

Lindström M (2008) Buyology: truth and lies about why we buy. Doubleday, New York

Martin N (2008) Habit. The 95% of behaviour marketers ignore. Pearson Education, Inc. Publishing, Upper Saddle River, NJ

Monahan JL, Murphy ST, Zajonc RB (2000) Subliminal mere exposure: specific, general, and diffuse effects. Psychol Sci 11:462–466

Ohme R, Matukin M (2012) A small frog that makes a big difference: brain wave testing of TV advertisements. IEEE Pulse 3(3):28–33. doi:10.1109/MPUL.2012.2189169

Perfect TJ, Askew C (1994) Print advertisements: not remembered but memorable. Appl Cogn Psychol 8:693–703

Perfect TJ, Heatherley S (1997) Preference for advertisements, logos and names: the effect of implicit memory. Psychol Rep 80:803–808

Pratkanis AR, Aronson E (2001) Age of propaganda: the everyday use and abuse of persuasion. W. H. Freeman & Co., New York

Preuss R (2010) Neuromarketing. Validity and deploy within marketing. Lap Lambert Academic Publishing, Saarbrücken

Renvoise P, Morin C (2011) Neuromarketing. Understanding the buy buttons in your customer's brain. SalesBrain LLC, Nashville

Rogers EM (1962) Diffusion of innovation. Free Press, New York

Rossiter JR, Percy L (1997) Advertising communication and promotion management. McGraw-Hill, New York

Shimp TA (1997) Advertising and promotion and supplemental aspects of integrated marketing communication. Dryden Press, Fort Worth

Strong EK (1925) The psychology of selling and advertisement. McGraw-Hill, New York

Sutherland M (2009) Advertising and the mind of the consumer: what works, what doesn't, and why. Allen & Unwin, Crows Nest

van Raaij WF (1989) Economic news, expectations and macro-economic behaviour. J Econ Psychol 10(4):473–493

Vaughn R (1980) How advertising works: a planning model. J Advertising Res 20(5):27–33

Vaughn R (1986) How advertising works: a planning model revisited. J Advertising Res 26 (1):57–65

Vecchiato G, Maglione AG, Cherubino P, Wąsikowska B, Wawrzyniak A, Łatuszyńska A, Łatuszyńska M, Nermend K, Graziani I, Leucci MR, Trettel A, Babiloni F (2014) Neurophysiological tools to investigate consumer's gender differences during the observation of TV commercials. Comput Math Method M, Article ID 912981. doi:10.1155/2014/912981

Wąsikowska B (2013) Contemporary data exploration technologies in marketing. In: Szewczyk A, Krok E (eds) Studia informatica 32. Wydawnictwo Naukowe Uniwersytetu Szczecińskiego, Szczecin, pp 137–151

Weaver W, Shannon CE (1963) The mathematical theory of communication. University of Illinois Press, Chicago

Woźniczka J (2012) Efekty reklamy i ich pomiar (Advertising Effects and Their Measurement). Wydawnictwo Uniwersytetu Ekonomicznego we Wrocławiu, Wrocław

Zajonc RB (2001) Mere exposure: a gateway to the subliminal. Curr Dir Psychol Sci 10:224–228

Zurawicki L (2010) Neuromarketing. exploring the brain of the consumer. Springer, New York

Chapter 22
Neuroelectrical Indexes for the Study of the Efficacy of TV Advertising Stimuli

Patrizia Cherubino, Arianna Trettel, Giulia Cartocci, Dario Rossi, Enrica Modica, Anton Giulio Maglione, Marco Mancini, Gianluca di Flumeri, and Fabio Babiloni

Abstract In this chapter, we present the findings of an experiment aimed to investigate cognitive and emotional changes of cerebral activity during the observation of TV commercials. In particular, we recorded the electroencephalographic (EEG), galvanic skin response (GSR) and heart rate (HR) from a group of 24 healthy subjects during the observation of a series of TV advertisements. The group was equally divided also by gender (male, female) and age (young, old). Comparisons of cerebral and emotional indices previously defined have been performed to highlight gender differences between TV commercial and scenes of interest of specific commercials. Findings show how EEG methodologies, along with the measurements of autonomic variables, could be used to obtain information not obtainable otherwise with verbal interviews. These cerebral and emotional indexes could help to analyze the perception of TV advertisements according to the consumer's gender and age.

Keywords EEG • HR • GSR • TV commercials • Neuromarketing

P. Cherubino (✉)
Department of Economics and Marketing, IULM University, Milan, Italy

BrainSigns srl, Via Sesto Celere 7/C, 00152 Rome, Italy

Department of Molecular Medicine, University of Rome Sapienza, Viale Regina Elena 291, 0016 Rome, Italy
e-mail: patrizia.cherubino@brainsigns.com

A. Trettel • M. Mancini
BrainSigns srl, Via Sesto Celere 7/C, 00152 Rome, Italy
e-mail: arianna.trettel@brainsigns.com

G. Cartocci • D. Rossi • E. Modica • A.G. Maglione • G. di Flumeri • F. Babiloni
BrainSigns srl, Via Sesto Celere 7/C, 00152 Rome, Italy

Department of Molecular Medicine, University of Rome Sapienza, Viale Regina Elena 291, 0016 Rome, Italy
e-mail: fabio.babiloni@uniroma1.it

K. Nermend, M. Łatuszyńska (eds.), *Selected Issues in Experimental Economics*, Springer Proceedings in Business and Economics, DOI 10.1007/978-3-319-28419-4_22

22.1 Introduction

Recently, a rapidly growing approach within consumer research has developed under the label of "consumer neuroscience". Its goal is to use insights and methods from neuroscience to enhance the understanding of consumer behaviour. The application of neuroscience to consumer psychology has gained popularity over the past decade in academic research and business practice. The birth of the field of consumer neuroscience has generated wide-ranging, ongoing debates of whether this hybrid field benefits its parent discipines (consumer psychology and neuroscience) and, within them, what forms these benefits might take (Ariely and Berns 2010; Kenning and Plassmann 2005). In fact, the goal of consumer neuroscience is to adapt methods and theories from neuroscience combined with behavioural theories to develop a neuropsychologically sound theory to understand the consumer behaviour.

In these last few years, findings from the consumer neuroscience experiments have deconstructed the picture of perfectly rational humans, which are deliberating their choices by weighting costs and benefits until a deliberative equilibrium is reached. Although humans are definitely capable of conscious deliberation, many, if not most economically relevant decision processes are characterized by certain other features: first, they rely on automatic, fast and effective cognitive processes, which are not under direct volitional control (Bargh and Chartrand 1999). Second, they are under the influence of unrecognized and finely tuned affective mechanisms, which often play a decisive role in action (Damasio 1998; Davidson et al. 1999; Panksepp 2004). Third, many of these processes have been shaped by evolution in order to serve social purposes (Adolphs 2003; Brothers 1990; Cacioppo et al. 2002).

The term "neuromarketing" refers to practitioner and commercial interest in neurophysiological tools, such as eye tracking, skin conductance, electroencephalography (EEG) and functional magnetic resonance imaging (fMRI), to conduct company-specific market research. Neuromarketing has received considerable attention in the corporate world, and the growth of neuromarketing companies over the last decade has been impressive (Plassmann 2012). More properly, neuromarketing can be defined as the field of study that applies the methodologies of the neuroscience to analyze and understand the human behaviour related to market and economic exchanges (Lee et al. 2007). Hence, the contribution of neuroscientific methods becomes significant for the knowledge of the human behaviour in the marketing scope. Moreover, another interesting issue is overcoming the dependence from the verbal answering nowadays used on testing subjects in traditional marketing researches where insights and indicators depend on the good-faith and accuracy of the experimental subject reporting his own sensations and opinion to the experimenter. Instead, the use of the brain imaging technique can distinguish the subject's cognitive and emotional experiences (verbally expressed during the interviews) from the activations of cerebral areas related to different, and unconscious, mental states. Interesting experimental evidences suggest that the use of the brain imaging, in a near future, could be placed side by side to classical tests today largely used in the marketing sciences (Vecchiato et al. 2013).

22.2 The Rationale Behind the Present Chapter

In these last few years we have assisted to an increased interest in the use of brain imaging techniques for the analysis of brain responses to the commercial advertisements or for the investigation of the purchasing attitudes of the subjects (Ioannides et al. 2000; Knutson et al. 2007; Astolfi et al. 2008a; Morris et al. 2009; Vecchiato et al. 2014). The interest is justified by the possibility to correlate the particular observed brain activations with the characteristics of the proposed commercial stimuli, in order to derive conclusions about the adequacy of such ad stimuli to be interesting or emotionally engaging. Standard marketing techniques, so far employed, involved the use of an interview and the compilation of a questionnaire after the exposition to novel commercial ads before the massive launch of the ad itself (ad pre-test). However, it is now recognized that often the verbal advertising pre-testing is flawed by the respondents' cognitive processes activated during the interview, being the implicit memory and subject's feelings often inaccessible to the interviewer that uses traditional techniques (Zaltman 2003). In addition, it was also suggested that the interviewer on this typical pre-testing interviews has a great influence on what respondent recalls and on the subjective experiencing of it (McDonald 2003; Franzen and Bouwman 2001). Taking all these considerations in mind, researchers have attempted to investigate the signs of the brain activity correlated with an increase of attention, memory or emotional engagement during the observation of such commercial ads. Researchers within the consumer neuroscience community promote the view that findings and methods from neuroscience complement and illuminate existing knowledge in consumer research in order to better understand consumer behaviour (e.g. Solnais et al. 2013; Ambler et al. 2000; Klucharev et al. 2008; Summerfield and Mangels 2005; Russell and Barret 1999; Werkle-Bergner et al. 2006; Klimesch 1999).

It is very well known that the hemodynamic measurements of the brain activity allow a level of localization of the activated brain structures on the order of cubic mm, being capable to detect activations also in deep brain structures such as amygdala and nucleus accumbens. However, the lack of time resolution, due to the delay of the cerebral blood flow's increment after the exposition to the stimuli, make the fMRI unsuitable to follow the brain dynamics on the base of its subseconds activity. The use of EEG allows following the brain activity on a millisecond base, bearing in mind that the recorded EEG signals are mainly due to the activity generated on the cortical structures of the brain. In fact, the electromagnetic activity elicited by deep structures advocated for the generation of emotional processing in humans is almost impossible to gather from usual superficial EEG electrodes (Nunez 1995; Urbano et al. 1998). However, nowadays high-resolution EEG (hrEEG) technology has been developed to enhance the poor spatial information content of the EEG activity in order to detect the brain activity with a spatial resolution of a square centimetres and the unsurpassed time resolution of milliseconds (Nunez 1995; Bai et al. 2007; He et al. 1999; Dale et al. 2000; Babiloni et al. 2005).

It has underlined that the positive or negative emotional processing during the observation of the commercial ads is an important factor for the formation of stable memory traces (Kato et al. 2009). As we know, from cognitive psychology, emotions play an important role for memory processes: they can help us to learn and to remember (Erk et al. 2002). Hence, it became relevant to infer the emotional engage of the subject by using indirect signs for it. In fact, indirect signs of emotional processing could be gathered by picking variations of the activity of the anatomical structures linked to the emotional processing activity in humans, such as the activity of sweat glands on the hands and/or the variation of the heart rate (Baumgartner et al. 2006). Such gathering could be performed also along with the tracking of the variations of the prefrontal and frontal cortex (PFC and FC, respectively; Davidson and Irwin 1999).

In particular, by monitoring autonomic activity using devices able to record the variation of the skin conductivity (Galvanic Skin Responses, GSR) and the heart rate (HR) it is possible to assess the "internal" emotional state of subjects, measuring variables of the autonomic nervous system (Mauss and Robinson 2009). In fact, Galvanic Skin Response (GSR) activity is actually viewed as a sensitive and convenient measure of indexing changes in sympathetic arousal associated with emotion, cognition and attention (Critchley 2002). Studies using functional imaging techniques (Critchley 2002; Nagai et al. 2004) have related the generation and level of electrodermal activity to specific brain areas. These specific regions are the ventromedial prefrontal cortex, orbitofrontal cortex, left primary motor cortex, and the anterior and posterior cingulate, which have been shown to be associated with emotional and motivational behaviours. Such as findings indicate the close association between peripheral and central measures of arousal, re-emphasize the close connections between electrodermal activity, arousal, attention, cognition and emotion. In addition, the link between the heart rate (HR) or the Heart Rate Variability (HRV) and the sympatho-vagal balance has been also suggested in literature (Malik et al. 1996; Malliani 2005; Montano et al. 2009).

In addition, the PFC region is structurally and functionally heterogeneous but its role in emotion is well recognized (Davidson 2002). EEG spectral power analyses indicate that the anterior cerebral hemispheres are differentially lateralized for approach and withdrawal motivational tendencies and emotions. Specifically, findings suggest that the left PFC is an important brain area in a widespread circuit that mediates appetitive approach, while the right PFC appears to form a major component of a neural circuit that instantiates defensive withdrawal (Davidson 2000, 2004).

The idea behind the present chapter is to illustrate the potential of EEG techniques when applied to the analysis of brain activity related to the observation of TV commercials. In particular, we want to describe how by using appropriate statistical analysis it could be possible to recover significant information about scalp areas engaged, along with variations of the activity of the autonomous nervous system, by particular scenes inserted within the TV commercial analyzed (Young 2002). In the last 2 years, we have conducted and published several studies showing how it is possible to detect hidden signs of the memorization process and emotional engagement, such as pleasantness perceived while watching an advertisement, by employing neurophysiological recordings (Astolfi et al. 2007, 2008, 2009; Vecchiato et al. 2010, 2011).

In particular, we were interested in analyzing the brain activity occurring during the "naturalistic" observation of commercial ads intermingled in a random order in a documentary. To measure both the brain activity and the emotional engage of the healthy subjects investigated, we conducted several experiments in order to use simultaneous EEG, GSR and HR measurements during the observation of TV commercials. We linked significant variation of EEG, GSR and HR measurements with the emotion and pleasantness of the presented stimuli, as successively resulted from the subject's verbal interview. In order to do that, different indexes were employed to summarize the cerebral and autonomic measurements performed, later used in the statistical analysis.

The aim was to recreate, as much as possible, a "naturalistic" approach to the task, in which the observer is viewing the TV screen without particular goals in mind. In fact, the subjects were not instructed at all on the aim of the experiment, and they were not aware that an interview about the proposed TV commercials would be generated at the end of the task.

In particular, the experimental questions we wanted to answer in the present studies are the following:

1. Is it possible to track the cerebral activity, frame by frame, of subjects watching TV commercials?
2. Are there particular EEG activities in the spectral domain that correlates with the pleasantness perceived by the subjects?
3. Are there particular autonomic indexes, derived from GSR and HR recordings, that correlate with the pleasantness of the commercials perceived by the subjects and for different sub-group?
4. Is there exist any EEG frontal asymmetrical activity when we are watching pleasant and unpleasant commercial advertisements?

22.3 An Overview on the EEG Technique

Information about the brain activity can be obtained by measuring different physical variables arising from brain processes, such as the increase in consumption of oxygen by the neural tissues or a variation of the electric potential over the scalp surface. All these variables are connected in direct or indirect way to the neural ongoing processes and each variable has its own spatial and temporal resolution. Hence, the different neuroimaging techniques are then constrained by their spatio-temporal resolution, depending on the monitored variables. Human neocortical processes involve temporal and spatial scales spanning several orders of magnitude: from the rapidly shifting somatosensory processes characterized by a temporal scale of milliseconds and a spatial scale of few square millimetres, to the memory processes, involving time periods of seconds and spatial scale of square centimetres. Today, no neuroimaging method provide a spatial resolution on a millimetre scale and a temporal resolution on a millisecond scale at the same time.

Electroencephalography is an interesting technique characterized by a high temporal resolution, on the millisecond scale, adequate to follow a particular kind of brain activity (to deepen this topic, far from the goal of the present book, we suggest Michel and Murray 2012; Hallez et al. 2007; Michel et al. 2004; for a review). Unlikely, this technique has a relatively modest spatial resolution, beyond the centimetre, because of the inter-sensor distances and the fundamental laws regulating the electromagnetism (Nunez 1995). The simultaneous activation of an entire population of neurons can generate an electric signal detectable on the head surface with electrodes placed on the scalp. In order to estimate the cortical activity, the EEG signal has to be measured in different scalp sites; the most common measurement system is the international montage 10–20. Generally, the standard EEG analysis, using 20–30 electrodes, brings to a spatial resolution of about 5÷7 cm. It might be argued that such spatial resolution could be not enough to solve the scientific issues related to standard clinical investigations. In fact, researchers have developed a body of techniques called "high resolution EEG techniques" that allow to move up to 2 cm of spatial resolution with the use of 64–128 electrodes (Nunez 1995). However, a low spatial resolution of 5–7 cm is sufficient in the case experiments are aimed to differentiate the activity of the right and left PFC as in a typical "neuromarketing" experiments (Davidson et al. 1994; Vecchiato et al. 2014). In the following, we provide an example of the use of the unbalance for the activity of left and right prefrontal cortex for the analysis of a TV advertising.

22.4 Methodology of a Typical Neuromarketing Experiment

In the investigated ecologic situation, as Fig. 22.1 shows, our experimental subjects are asked to comfortably have a seat in front of a computer screen by means of which we present a documentary. A train of two commercial breaks is inserted within it, which are our stimuli of interest. The cerebral signals gathered during the observation of the documentary will be used to generate a suitable baseline for each subject's cerebral activity. In the interview, subjects were asked to recall the commercial clips they remember, tell if they are consumers or not of the products advertised and express the degree of pleasantness perceived. In such a way, we divide the signals of the recorded population into different datasets that will be compared for analysis.

Specifically, subjects were comfortably seated on a reclining chair, in an electrically shielded, dimly lit room. A 10-channels EEG system (BrainAmp, Brainproducts GmbH, Germany) was used to record the electrical potentials,

Fig. 22.1 Picture shows the experimental set-up of our neuromarketing studies. The subject is seated in front of a computer screen on which a neutral documentary is running. We inserted a series of commercial breaks within, each consisting of several TV advertisements, which will be our stimuli

according to an extension of the 10–20 international system. Recordings were initially extra-cerebrally referred and then converted to an average reference off-line. We collected the EEG activity at a sampling rate = 256 Hz while the impedances kept below 5 kΩ. Each EEG trace was then converted into the Brain Vision format (BrainAmp, Brainproducts GmbH, Germany) in order to perform signal pre-processing such as artefacts detection, filtering and segmentation. Raw EEG traces were first band-pass-filtered (high pass = 2 Hz; low pass = 47 Hz), and the independent component analysis (ICA) was then applied to detect and remove components due to eye movements and blinks that could afflict the estimation of the EEG power spectra on the prefrontal areas.

These EEG traces were then segmented to extract the cerebral activity during the observation of the TV commercials and the one associated to the documentary (baseline period). Then, this dataset has been further segmented into one-second length trials . Only artefacts-free trials have been considered for the following analysis.

The waveform was then subjected to the time-varying spectral analysis by computing the Power Spectral Density (PSD) in the different frequency bands normally used in the EEG analysis, i.e. theta (4–7 Hz), alpha (8–12 Hz), beta (13–24 Hz) and gamma (24–45 Hz).

For each recorded subject, the statistical significance of the spectral values during the observation of the TV commercials was then measured against the activity evaluated during the observation of the documentary. This was obtained by computing a time-varying *z*-score variable for each subject in the analyzed frequency band of interest. The mean and the standard deviation for such *z*-score variable was estimated by taking into account the documentary period, while the time-varying values of the spectral power during the observation of the TV commercial for each dipole were employed.

Different indexes related to the perception of the TV commercial advertisings have been estimated. In particular, we estimate the index related to the approach–withdrawal theory previously proposed by Davidson and colleagues (Davidson et al. 1994; Vecchiato et al. 2012).

Each EEG trace has been band pass filtered in order to isolate the spectral components in the alpha band from the whole EEG spectrum. The filtered traces have been used to calculate the Global Field Power (GFP; Lehmann and Skrandies 1980). We used the frontal electrodes to compute the GFP indexes in this study, by selecting the electrodes F7, F3, Fp1, Fz, Fp2, F4, F8 of the International 10–20 montage. Such selection was performed to evaluate the approach–withdrawal index (AW index).

The formula that defines the AW index is the following:

$$AW = GFP_{\alpha\_right} - GFP_{\alpha\_left} \tag{22.1}$$

where the GFP_{α_right} and GFP_{α_left} stand for the GFP calculated among right (Fp2, F4, F8) and left (F7, F3, Fp1) electrodes, in the alpha band, respectively. The AW index was then normalized returning a *z*-score values across all the experiment for each subject. In fact, such index has been defined by taking into account the frontal EEG asymmetry's theory by Davidson and co-workers.

The use of the autonomic variables related to the heart rate (HR) and the cutaneous impedance (Galvanic Skin Response; GSR) allow estimating an index that is related to the perceived emotions of the sensory stimuli. In particular, such index has been called the emotional index (EI) and it was clearly described previously (Vecchiato et al. 2015). The AW index and EI were used to describe quantitatively the perception of the tested advertising as presented in the following.

22.5 Case Study: When a Laugh Can Be Dangerous (or Not)

22.5.1 Population Target and TV Commercial

The whole experimental sample was formed by 24 subjects (25–54 years, 12 women), which will be in the following divided in two subgroups (younger adults and older adults) differing by age. Written informed consent was obtained from each subject after the explanation of the study. The procedure of the experimental task consisted in observing a 17 min long documentary in which we inserted two commercial breaks, after five and 12 min from the beginning of the movie, respectively. Each commercial break was formed by seven commercial

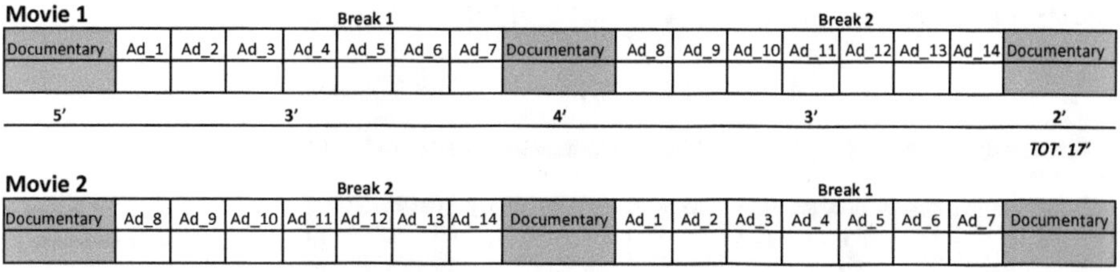

Fig. 22.2 Picture presents the schema describing the video stimulation for this study. *Grey boxes* indicate the time slots related to the portions of documentary, whereas the *white boxes* are related to the time slots of the TV commercials. Durations in minutes and seconds, for documentary and spots respectively, are also indicated

video-clips of different length (30″, 20″ and 15″). The TV commercial we use here for case study was unknown to the subjects and it has been showed only once during the experiment. Randomization of the occurrence of the all commercial videos within the documentary was made to remove the order effect as possible confounding effect (Movie 1 and Movie 2). The schema of the video sequence is shown in Fig. 22.2.

The specific advertisement tested was the one aired by Air Action Vigorsol, a famous brand and type of chewing gum, which has as protagonists a pair of lovers who live far away from each other. The TV commercial can be watched at the following link: http://www.youtube.com/watch?v=o8RCOb3WQOs.

The specific feature of the present advertisement consists in generating an exhilarating climax with some relative "strong" images that it was hypothesized a priori that could be appreciated quite differently by the experimental sample. To test such hypothesis the advertisement has been divided into five time intervals showing different key scenes of the video-clip (as shown in Fig. 22.3) in which we estimated the AW and EI for all the subjects investigated. Each subject at the end of the experiment explicit rates the advertising with a score from 1 to 9. In the following the scores given by the subjects allowed to us to divide the experimental sample in two subgroups, the subjects that liked much the TV spot (LIKE group) and the subsample that did not like the TV spot (DISLIKE group). For both of these groups we estimated the averaged AW and EI variables.

22.5.2 *Behavioural Results*

The recording of the neurometric response included the detection of the EEG signals, HR (Heart Rate) and GSR (Galvanic Skin Response) parameters on a sample of 24 subjects (39.56 ± 8.11 years; 12 men) that rated the TV commercial with a pleasantness score distribution with median = 7 and an interquartile range (iqr) of 6. The experimental subjects have been divided in two subgroups differing by age (10 younger adults: 31.33 ± 3.31; 14 older adults: 44.86 ± 5.24; Student's $t = 7.57, p < 0.01$). Younger adults resulted rating the proposed advertisement with

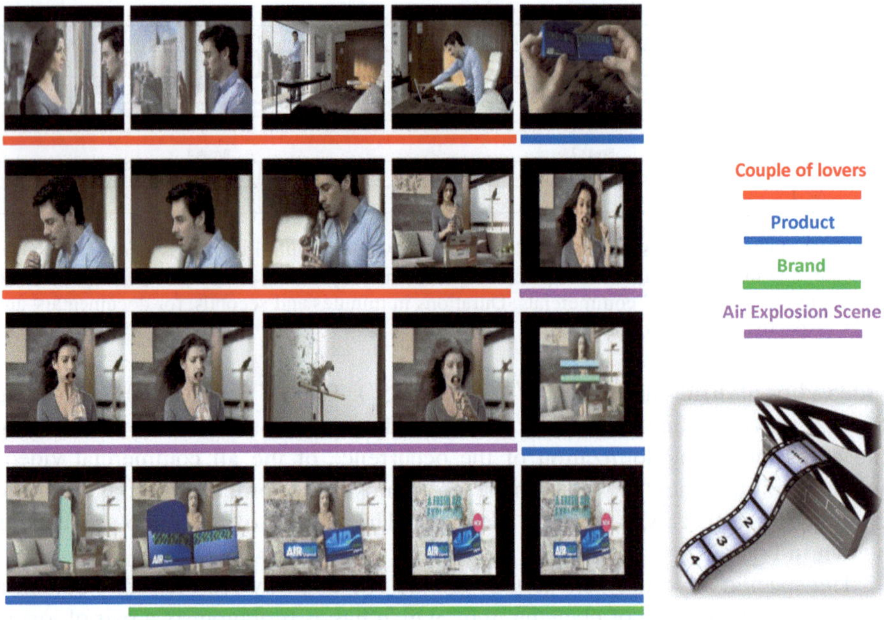

Fig. 22.3 Frame sequence of the Air Action Vigorsol TV commercial for each second of the video-clip. The underlying colours highlight the different scenes in which it is possible to divide the advertisement, as the legend on the right shows. In such segments the average values for the estimated indices were computed

higher pleasantness score (median = 8 and iqr = 1) with respect to the older adults (median = 3.5, iqr = 5; Kolmogorov–Smirnov test: $d = 0.78$, $p < 0.01$). Later, as previously described we divided the whole experimental sample in LIKE and DISLIKE groups according to the pleasantness score they gave during the interview (LIKE: median = 8, iqr = 1.5; DISLIKE: median = 1, iqr = 1.5; Kolmogorov–Smirnov test: $d = 1$, $p < 0.01$).

22.5.3 Cerebral Indices

By analyzing the AW and EI, shown in Fig. 22.4, it was evident that the investigated commercial video arouses different responses with respect to the two used indices (AW and EI). In particular, as far as concerning all the investigated samples, the final frames elicited high value related to the approach–withdrawal index.

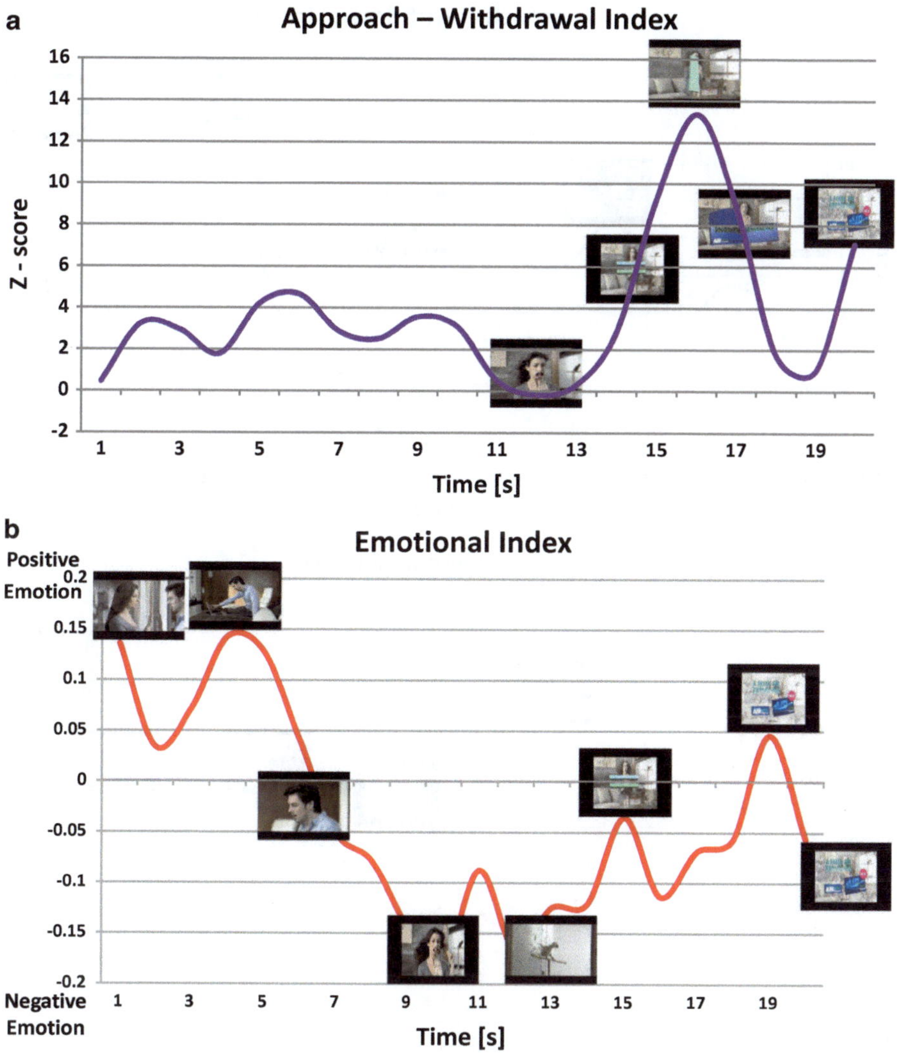

Fig. 22.4 Picture presents the average approach–withdrawal (**a**) and emotional (**b**) profiles, across the entire experimental sample, related to the observation of the Air Action Vigorsol TV commercial. Both the horizontal axis describes the time evolution of the clip (from 1 to 20 s). The vertical axis of the considered approach–withdrawal index describes the amplitude of the variable in *z*-score values. Vertical axis of the emotional index indicates positive emotion from 0 to 0.15 values and negative emotions for values from 0 to −0.2 values. Note that the zero value is the average value of the analyzed index during the baseline phase. Particular frames of the advertisement are showed on the AW and EI waveforms

22.5.4 *The Reaction of Younger and Older Adults*

The negative effects measured for the emotion on the opening of the bottle in the video-clip has been reported as the average value for the whole experimental

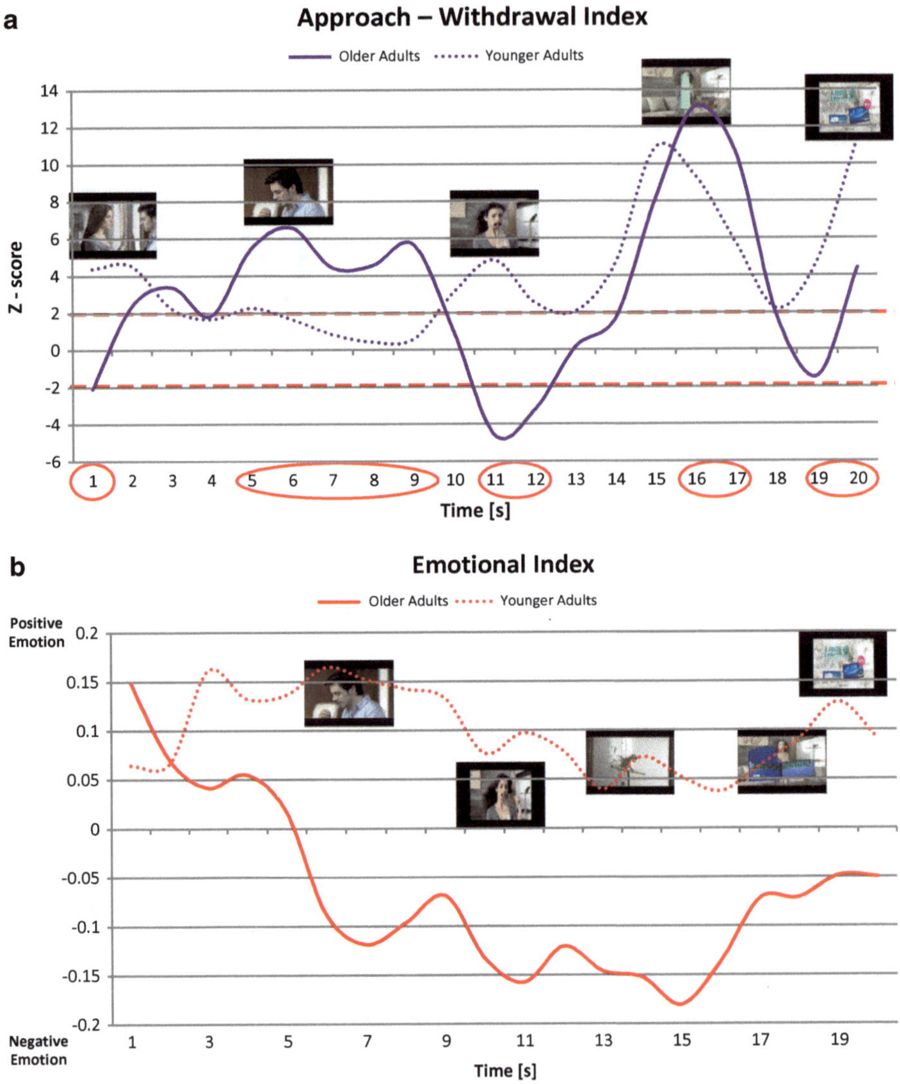

Fig. 22.5 Picture presents the average approach–withdrawal (**a**) and emotional (**b**) profiles across the two analyzed sub-targets, older adults (*continuous line*) and younger adults (*dotted line*), related to the observation of the Air Action Vigorsol TV commercial. Both horizontal axes describe the time evolution of the clip (from 1 to 20 s). The vertical axis of the considered approach–withdrawal index describes the amplitude of the variable in *z*-score values. Dotted lines at $z = -2$ and $z = 2$ indicate the thresholds of statistical significance ($p < 0.05$) between the single waveforms and the level related to the documentary. Instead, red circles in the horizontal axis highlight statistically significant differences between the two groups, older adults and younger adults ($p < 0.05$, Bonferroni corrected). Vertical axis of the emotional index indicates positive emotion from 0 to 0.15 values and negative emotions for values from 0 to -0.2 values. A zero level of the EI or AW estimators represents the average value for that estimators during the documentary seen before the TV commercial analyzed. Particular frames of the advertisement are showed on the AW and EI waveforms

sample. However, it is possible to prove that such effect was sensitive to the age of the sample subjects. In particular, Fig. 22.5 shows the results in terms of AW (A) and EI (B) estimators related to the two age-generated subgroups, younger and older adults. According to the variations of the AW index, older adults present an increase of activation in the initial part of the commercial (story telling), whereas younger adults show a similar increment in the middle of the spot (funny scenes). The emotional index, except for the initial part, is always higher for younger adults. In particular, the average EI values for the younger adults if 0.09 ± 0.04 while for the older adults shows a level of -0.06 ± 0.08 (Student's $t = 10.57, p < 0.01$). This result is in agreement with the subjects' behavioural ratings as it is possible to appreciate in the previous section.

The entire experimental sample has been also divided according to the pleasantness score in order to form the LIKE and DISLIKE groups. These two sub-targets have been further analyzed to highlight difference in terms of AW and EI in particular time segments of the TV commercial. Figure 22.6 shows the variation of AW (A) and EI (B) for the defined time intervals. As to the AW index, data highlights a statistically significant difference for two segments (Air Explosion Scene, Brand). Instead, the EI does not present statistically significant differences between the Like and Dislike groups across the time segments. However, it is possible to appreciate how the Like group present higher values of EI in all the specific time intervals.

22.6 Discussion

The analysis of the approach–withdrawal and the emotional indexes returned, at least apparently, discordant interpretation. The difference between them is evident in terms of emotional reaction to the spot (as indicated by the EI), whereas there is a difference in terms of neuroelectrical reaction to the spot, just in the central scene, according to the AW index. In particular, as to the approach–withdrawal index, the older adults prefer the initial part, when the story is told. At the seconds 11″–15″, when the humour of the TV commercial comes on in the scenes, they watch the ad with more detachment, while the younger adults are more interested. In fact, what we can observe that at first sight the cerebral approach–withdrawal index is characterized by positive values, whereas the analysis of autonomic signals through the emotional index show negative emotions. The interpretation of this phenomenon has to be read in the different nature of the two indices. The former mostly highlights the cerebral attractiveness or the rejection towards a stimulus; the latter shows the experienced internal state, through the cardiac and cutaneous "body markers". We could speculate interpreting the described results as a sign of high cerebral curiosity but an emotional detach of the gathered sample related to the TV commercial analyzed.

Results suggest that the ugly scenes of the TV commercial elicit negative peaks of emotions but high peaks of AW index (e.g. approach tendency). A possible

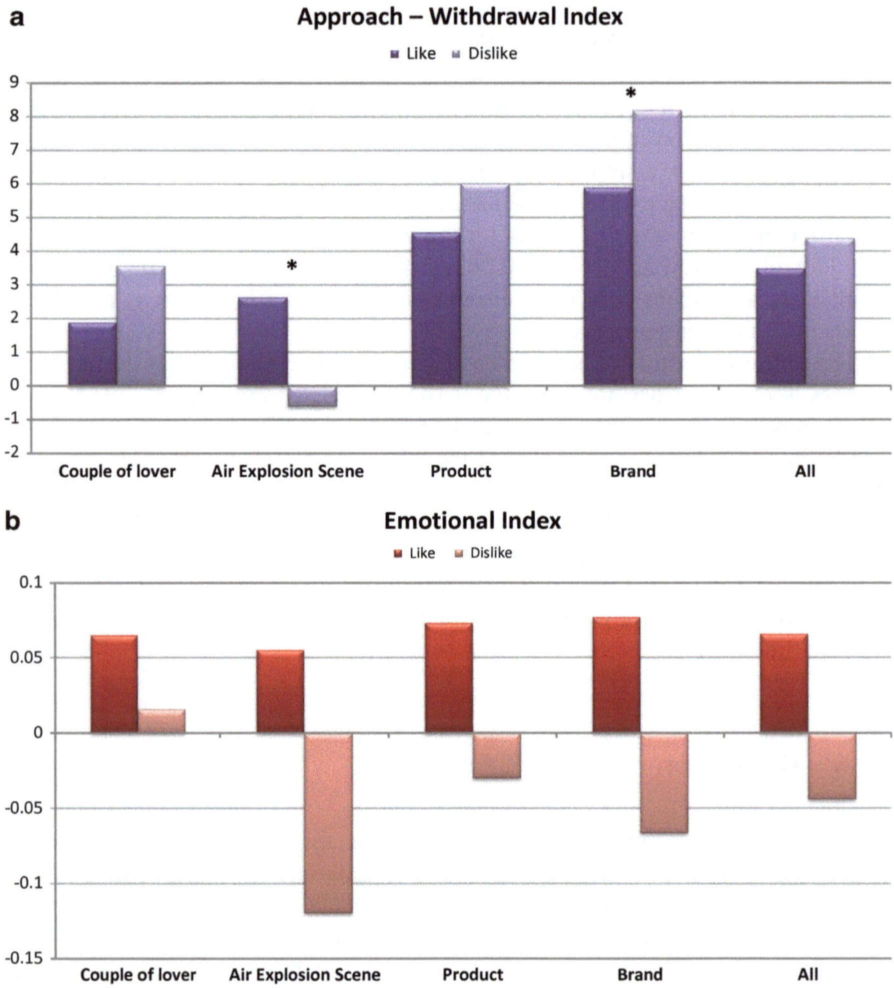

Fig. 22.6 Picture presents the average approach–withdrawal (**a**) and emotional (**b**) indices calculated within particular segments of interest of the Air Action Vigorsol TV commercial for the two analyzed sub-targets, LIKE and DILIKE. On the horizontal axis, the labels of the particular segments are shown. The vertical axis of the considered Approach–Withdrawal index describes the amplitude of the variable in z-score values. Vertical axis of the emotional index indicates positive emotion from 0 to 0.15 values and negative emotions for values from 0 to −0.2 values. A zero level of the EI or AW estimators represents the average value for those estimators during the documentary seen before the TV commercial analyzed. Statistically significant differences in the time segments are highlighted with the symbol *

interpretation is that such scenes are able to elicit interest from the subjects although the sudden events depicted in the video generated a negative emotions.

These considerations could be enforced after analyzing the results of the two different subgroups: younger adults and older adults. Specifically, the former group not only shows higher values of the approach–withdrawal index, when compared to the latter, but also highlights a positive emotion waveform. In this case, it appears that only the older adults have been negatively impressed by some ugly scenes of the clip. Younger adults, instead, perceive the commercial with a positive emotion along its whole length. From these last considerations, we can argue that the analyzed advertisement resulted particularly convincing and effective for the investigated younger sample. In addition, the analysis in different time segments between the LIKE and DISLIKE groups highlighted the presence of particular short periods in the advertisement in which the major part of the effects are generated. The analysis and consideration presented here for the specific TV Commercial analyzed could be applied also to all the other spots of the commercial break used in the experiment. However, we do not provide such results because the space limitations.

Overall, the biometric EEG, HR and GSR recordings returned neurometric indexes linked to the variation of the interest and emotional involvement of the two experimental groups investigated. Variation of such indices along the adopted time segments returned information about the ads perception, scene by scene, on the total sample of recorded subjects and on sub-samples of such group. This information may be analyzed by providing interesting indications about the efficacy of the different frame sequences or observing original insights related to cognitive and emotional variables. In addition, these tools could provide a rational schema useful to guide a reduction of the ads in time, which is often implemented in advertising campaigns after the first detailed creative production. In fact, this reduction can be performed by pointing out the most (less) performing scenes which could be preserved (cut) of a possible time-frames reduction. Such time reduction could be specifically performed and differently adapted to men and women, to young and adult and any other sub-groups of interest.

Acknowledgments The grants provided to Fabio Babiloni by the Italian Ministry of University and Education under the PRIN 2012 and that provided by the Ministry of Foreign Affairs for the bilateral relation between Italy and China for the project "Neuropredictor" are gratefully acknowledged.

References

Adolphs R (2003) Cognitive neuroscience of human social behaviour. Nature Reviews. Neuroscience 4(3):165–178

Ambler T, Ioannides A, Rose S (2000) Brands on the brain: neuro-images of advertising. Bus Strat Rev 11(3):17–30

Ariely D, Berns GS (2010) Neuromarketing: the hope and hype of neuroimaging in business. Nat Rev Neurosci 11(4):284–292

Astolfi L, Vecchiato G, De Vico Fallani F, Salinari S, Cincotti F, Aloise F, Mattia D et al (2009) The track of brain activity during the observation of TV commercials with the high-resolution EEG technology. Comput Intell Neurosci 652078

Astolfi L, De Vico Fallani F, Salinari S, Cincotti F, Mattia D, Marciani MG, Soranzo R, Babiloni F (2008a) Brain activity related to the memorization of TV commercials. Int J Bioelectromegn 10(2):1–10

Astolfi L, De Vico Fallani F, Cincotti F, Mattia D, Bianchi L, Marciani MG, Salinari S, Colosimo A, Tocci A, Soranzo R, Babiloni F (2008b) Neural basis for brain responses to TV commercials: a high-resolution EEG study. IEEE Trans Neural Syst Rehabil Eng 16 (6):522–531

Astolfi L, Cincotti F, Mattia D, Marciani MG, Baccala LA, De Vico Fallani F, Salinari S, Ursino M, Zavaglia M, Ding L, Edgar JC, Miller GA, Bin H, Babiloni F (2007) Comparison of different cortical connectivity estimators for highresolution EEG recordings. Hum Brain Mapp 28(2):143–157

Bargh JA and Chartrand TL (1999) The unbearable automaticity of being. American Psychologist 54 (7):462–479

Baumgartner T, Esslen M, Jancke L (2006) From emotion perception to emotion experience: emotions evoked by pictures and classical music. Int J Psychophysiol 60(1):34–43

Brothers L (1990) The social brain: A project for integrating primate behavior and neurophysiology in a new domain. Concepts in Neuroscience 1:27–51

Cacioppo JT et al (2002) Foundations in Social Neuroscience, illustrated edn. The MIT Press

Critchley HD (2002) Electrodermal responses: what happens in the brain. Neuroscientis 8(2):132–142

Damasio AR (1998) Emotion in the perspective of an integrated nervous system. Brain Res Rev 26:83–86

Davidson RJ et al (1999) Regional brain funcion, emotion and disorders of emotion. Current Opinion in Neurobiology 9(2):228–234

Davidson RJ (2004) What does the prefrontal cortex "do" in affect: perspectives on frontal EEG asymmetry research. Biol Psychol 67(1–2):219–233. doi:10.1016/j.biopsycho.2004.03.008

Erk S, Spitzer M, Wunderlich AP, Galley L, Henrik W (2002) Cultural objects modulate reward circuitry. Neuroreport 13(18):2499–2503. doi:10.1097/01.wnr.0000048542.12213.60

Ioannides AA, Lichan L, Theofilou D, Dammers J, Burne T, Ambler T, Rose S (2000) Real time processing of affective and cognitive stimuli in the human brain extracted from MEG signals. Brain Topogr 13(1):11–19

Kenning P, Plassmann H (2005) NeuroEconomics: an overview from an economic perspective. Brain Res Bull 67:343–354

Klimesch W (1999) EEG alpha and theta oscillations reflect cognitive and memory performance: a review and analysis. Brain Res Rev 29(2–3):169–195

Knutson B, Rick S, Wimmer GE, Prelec D, Loewenstein G (2007) Neural predictors of purchases. Neuron 53(1):147–156. doi:10.1016/j.neuron.2006.11.010

Lee N, Broderick AJ, Chamberlain L (2007) What is "neuromarketing"? A discussion and agenda for future research. Int J Psychophysiol 63(2):199–204

Lehmann D, Skrandies W (1980) Reference-free identification of components of checkerboard-evoked multichannel potential fields. Electroencephalogr Clin Neurophysiol 48:609–621

Mauss IB, Robinson MD (2009) Measures of emotion: a review. Cognit Emot 23(2):209–237. doi:10.1080/02699930802204677

Nagai Y, Critchley HD, Featherstone E, Fenwick PBC, Trimble MR, Dolan RJ (2004) Brain activity relating to the contingent negative variation: an fMRI investigation. Neuroimage 21 (4):1232–1241. doi:10.1016/j.neuroimage.2003.10.036

Panksepp J (2004) Affective Neuroscience: The Foundations of Human and Animal Emotions, 1st edn. Oxford University Press, USA

Plassmann H, Ramsøy TZ, Milosavljevic M (2012). Branding the brain: A critical review and outlook. Journal of Consumer Psychology 22(1):18–36. http://doi.org/10.1016/j.jcps.2011.11.010

Russell JA, Barrett LF (1999) Core affect, prototypical emotional episodes, and other things called emotion: dissecting the elephant. J Pers Soc Psychol 76(5):805–819

Solnais C, Andreu-Perez J, Sánchez-Fernández J, Andréu-Abela J (2013) The contribution of neuroscience to consumer research: a conceptual framework and empirical review. J Econ Psychol 36:68–81

Summerfield C, Mangels JA (2005) Coherent theta-band EEG activity predicts item-context binding during encoding. NeuroImage 24(3):692–703. doi:10.1016/j.neuroimage.2004.09.012

Vecchiato G, Cherubino P, Maglione AG, Herrero MTE, Marinozzi F, Bini F, Trettel A, Babiloni F (2015) How to measure cerebral correlates of emotions in marketing relevant tasks. Cogn Comput. doi:10.1007/s12559-014-9304-x

Vecchiato G, Cherubino P, Trettel A, Babiloni F (2013) Neuroelectrical brain imaging tools for the study of the efficacy of TV advertising stimuli and their application to neuromarketing. Springer, Heidelberg

Vecchiato G, Wanzeng K, Maglione AG, Daming W (2012) Understanding the impact of TV commercials: electrical neuroimaging. IEEE Pulse 3(3):42–47. doi:10.1109/MPUL.2012.2189171

Vecchiato G, Toppi J, Astolfi L, De Vico Fallani F, Cincotti F, Mattia D, Bez F, Babiloni F (2011) Spectral EEG frontal asymmetries correlate with the experienced pleasantness of TV commercial advertisements. Med Biol Eng Comput 49(5):579–583. doi:10.1007/s11517-011-0747-x

Vecchiato G, Astolfi L, De Vico Fallani F, Cincotti F, Mattia D, Salinari S, Soranzo R, Babiloni F (2010) Changes in brain activity during the observation of TV commercials by using EEG, GSR and HR measurements. Brain Topogr 23(2):165–179. doi:10.1007/s10548-009-0127-0

Werkle-Bergner M, Müller V, Li SC, Lindenberger U (2006) Cortical EEG correlates of successful memory encoding: implications for lifespan comparisons. Neurosci Biobehav Rev 30 (6):839–854. doi:10.1016/j.neubiorev.2006.06.009

Young C (2002) Brain waves, picture sorts, and branding moments. J Advert Res 42(4):42–53. ISSN 0021-8499

Zaltman G (2003) How customers think: essential insights into the mind of the market, 1st edn. Harvard Business Press, Cambridge, MA

Chapter 23
EEG Frontal Asymmetry Related to Pleasantness of Olfactory Stimuli in Young Subjects

Gianluca Di Flumeri, Maria Trinidad Herrero, Arianna Trettel, Patrizia Cherubino, Anton Giulio Maglione, Alfredo Colosimo, Elisabetta Moneta, Marina Peparaio, and Fabio Babiloni

Abstract It is widely known, in neuroscientific literature, that the brain prefrontal cortex activity asymmetry is closely linked with the pleasantness emotion experienced by the subject during a sensorial stimulation. Thus, from the electroencephalographic (EEG) signal it is possible to estimate the approach/withdrawal index, and this index has been largely investigated and validated in scientific literature, regarding visual and acoustic stimuli. In this work, we present an innovative study aimed to prove, in a systematic way, that such brain AW index is actually correlated with the "pleasant" or "no-pleasant" perception also

G. Di Flumeri (✉) • A. Trettel
BrainSigns srl, Via Sesto Celere, 7c, Rome 00152, Italy
e-mail: gianluca.diflumeri@uniroma1.it; arianna.trettel@brainsigns.com

M.T. Herrero
Clinical and Experimental Neuroscience, Institute of Biomedical Research of Murcia (IMIB), School of Medicine, University of Murcia, Campus Mare Nostrum, Murcia 30100, Spain
e-mail: mtherrer@um.es

P. Cherubino
Department of Economics and Marketing, IULM University, Milan, Italy

Via Gigi Peronace, Soverato, CZ 88068, Italy
e-mail: patrizia.cherubino@brainsigns.com

A.G. Maglione
BrainSigns srl, Via Sesto Celere, 7c, Rome 00155, Italy

A. Colosimo
Department of Anatomical, Histological, Forensic Medicine and Orthopedic Sciences, Sapienza University of Rome, via Alfonso Borelli, Rome 50-00161, Italy

E. Moneta • M. Peparaio
The Agricultural Research Council – Food and nutrition Research Center (CRA-NUT), Via Ardeatina, Rome 546-00178, Italy

F. Babiloni
Department of Molecular Medicine, Sapienza University of Rome, Via di Macchia Palocco 107a, Rome, Italy

K. Nermend, M. Łatuszyńska (eds.), *Selected Issues in Experimental Economics*, Springer Proceedings in Business and Economics, DOI 10.1007/978-3-319-28419-4_23

of olfactory stimuli, conveniently produced by standardised methods in the sensory specific scientific literature. In particular, we recorded the electroencephalographic (EEG) signal from a group, gender balanced, of 24 healthy and no-smokers subjects during the perception of ten different smells, presented by means of the "Screening test-odour identification" set (Sniffin' sticks, Burghart). The cerebral AW indexes of all the subjects, for each odorous stimulus, were compared with the appreciation numeric score assessed by the subject during the experiment, by performing a statistical correlation test. Findings show that it is possible to evaluate the pleasantness or no-pleasantness of odorous substances by means of the analysis of EEG signals collected during the presentation of such substances, making way for new applications of such measure kind in experimental environments more and more ecological, as the typical ones of the marketing research areas.

Keywords EEG • PFC • Alpha asymmetry • Approach–withdrawal • Emotions • Motivations • Pleasantness • Neuromarketing

23.1 Introduction

As it is well known in the neuroscientific field, there is a strong relationship between the human brain prefrontal cortex (PFC) activity and motivational processes. In particular, there are evidences about the PFC activity lateralization, with left hemisphere activity increasing for "approach" attitude to emotions, while right hemisphere activity increasing for "withdrawal" attitude. This kind of phenomenon, i.e. the asymmetry of PFC activity, in the scientific literature is called "Approach/Withdrawal motivation" (Davidson 1999), and it has been largely employed as a significant index of positive or negative attitudes of subjects in front of the sensory perception proposed.

By means of electroencephalographic (EEG) techniques, the approach/withdrawal (AW) signal can be estimated as the EEG signal spectral power difference, in the alpha band (8–12 Hz) between the right and left prefrontal cortex (Davidson et al. 1990). Thus, it is possible to estimate in the human such appreciation or avoidance indicators of sensory stimuli by means of some quite simple processing of the EEG signal recorded simultaneously with the proposition of the sensory stimulus.

The AW index is known to be positive in reaction to a sensorial stimulus perceived as "appreciable" by the experimental subject, whilst it will be negative in reaction to a sensorial stimulus perceived as "no appreciable". In particular, this index has been widely investigated and validated in scientific literature, regarding visual (Jackson et al. 2000, 2003; Kong et al. 2013) and acoustic (Schmidt and Trainor 2001; Vecchiato et al. 2012) stimuli.

On the contrary, it has not yet been validated in a systematic way regarding the olfactory stimuli. In fact previous studies just contrasted a couple of smells

(Kim and Watanuki 2003), whilst it becomes clear that there is the need to validate the brain AW index in reaction to a larger number of olfactory stimuli and in a more controlled experimental conditions.

Hence, this study has the aim to prove in a systematic way that such brain AW index is actually correlated with the "pleasant" or "no-pleasant" perception of olfactory stimuli, conveniently produced by standardised methods in the sensory specific scientific literature.

The results are presented and discussed in the form of a comparison between the AW index values and the experimental subjects evaluation explicit scores, collected by a questionnaire, for the whole proposed smells sample.

23.2 Materials and Methods

23.2.1 Experimental Design

Twenty-four healthy and nonsmoker subjects, gender balanced (25 ± 2.6 years), were recruited for this study. Informed consent was obtained from each subject after explanation of the study, which was approved by the local institutional ethics committee.

For each subject, his own olfactory sensitivity had previously been established through the validated method "Threshold odour test" (Sniffin' sticks; Heinrich Burghart Elektround Feinmechanik GmbH, Wedel, Germania) (Kobal et al. 1996; Hummel et al. 1997).

The "Sniffin' Sticks" is a test of nasal chemosensory performance based on pen-like odour dispensing devices. It comprises three tests of olfactory function, namely tests for odour threshold, odour discrimination and odour identification. In particular about the odour threshold identification, using a triple-forced-choice paradigm, detection thresholds were determined by employing a single staircase method as described by Doty (1991). The subjects were blindfolded to prevent visual identification of the odorant containing sticks. Three sticks were presented to each subject in a randomised order, two contained only the odourless solvent (propylene glycol in water, 4 %) and the other the odorant (2-phenylethanol) at a particular dilution in the same solvent. The task of the subject was to indicate the stick with the odorant. Presentation of the triplets to a subject occurred every 20 s, until they had correctly discerned the odorant in two successive trials which triggered a reversal of the staircase. The geometric mean of the last four staircase reversal points of a total of seven reversals was used as the threshold estimate.

By means of this method, the 24 subjects involved in this study were selected within a subjects larger sample. These subjects showed an olfactory sensitivity coherent to the age range considered (2-phenylethanol maximum concentration threshold = 0.063 %).

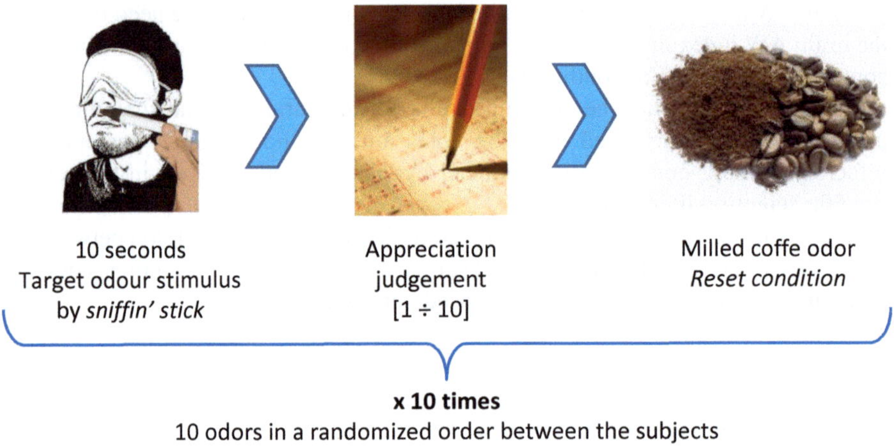

Fig. 23.1 Schematic representation of the experimental task described in the paragraph

The experimental task (Fig. 23.1) consisted in presenting to each subject 10 different smells, with an over-threshold concentration, selected within the "Screening test-odour identification" set (Sniffin' sticks, Burghart). In particular, the olfactory stimuli consisted in the following essences: Rose, Banana, Mint, Leather, Cloves, Orange, Pineapple, Fish, Mould, Mushrooms. The odour presentation order was randomised between the subjects in order to prevent the sequence effect as possible confounding effect. The subjects were blindfolded to prevent visual identification of the odorant containing sticks. For each odour presentation, the cap was removed by the experimenter for ~3 s and the stick tip was placed ~2 cm in front of both nostrils (Hummel et al. 1997). In the time between the odours presentation the subject was free to open his eyes; in this time interval a questionnaire was submitted to the subject, who had to produce his explicit smell appreciation judgement, with a numeric score between 1 and 10 (1 as the worst and 10 as the better judgement in terms of smell appreciation). After the questionnaire and before the following odour presentation, the coffee odour, by means of some milled coffee, was presented to the subject in order to neutralise the previous odour.

23.2.2 EEG Signal Recording and Processing

The EEG data was collected, for each subject during the whole experiment, by a portable 64-channel system (BE+ and Galileo software, EBneuro, Italy), at a sampling rate of 256 Hz; impedances kept below 10 kΩ. Nineteen electrodes (Fz, Cz, Pz, Fp1, Fp2, F3, F4, F7, F8, C3, C4, P3, P4, P7, P8, T7, T8, O1, O2) were located on a cap according to the 10–20 international system. FCz was used as reference, AFz as ground.

Each EEG trace was then converted into the Brain Vision format (BrainAmp, Brainproducts GmbH, Germany) in order to perform signal pre-processing such as artefacts detection, filtering and segmentation. Thus, raw EEG traces were first band pass filtered (high pass = 2 Hz; low pass = 40 Hz), and the Independent Component Analysis (ICA) was then applied to detect and remove components due to eye movements, blinks, and muscular artefacts. Subsequently, the pre-processed EEG signals have been transformed by means of the Common Average Reference (CAR). In the end, for each subject the Individual Alpha Frequency (IAF) was calculated on the 60-s Closed Eyes segment, recorded at the beginning of the experimental task, in order to define the EEG bands of interest according to the method suggested in the current scientific literature, i.e. each band is defined as "IAF $\pm$ x," where IAF is the Individual Alpha Frequency, in Hertz, and x an integer in the frequency domain (Klimesch 1999).

23.2.3 Brain Approach/Withdrawal Index

From the pre-processed EEG data, each channel was filtered in the Alpha band, defined as [IAF-4, IAF+2] according to the IAF definition. Then, the asymmetry of the EEG signal power was evaluated in the Alpha band on the electrodes above the prefrontal and orbitofrontal cortex. The estimation of such asymmetry is called "Approach/Withdrawal (AW) Index". In particular, it is defined as follows:

$$\mathrm{AW} = \frac{1}{N_P}\sum_{i\in P} x_{\alpha_i}^2(t) - \frac{1}{N_Q}\sum_{i\in Q} y_{\alpha_i}^2(t) = \mathrm{AveragePower}_{\alpha_{\mathrm{right,\,frontal}}} - \mathrm{AveragePower}_{\alpha_{\mathrm{left,\,frontak}}} \tag{23.1}$$

where $x_{\alpha,i}$ and $y_{\alpha,i}$ are the i-th EEG channel in the Alpha band, collected from the frontal right electrodes $P = \{\mathrm{Fp2,F4,F8}\}$ and the frontal left ones $Q = \{\mathrm{Fp1,F3,F7}\}$. Thus, for each frontal site (i.e. P and Q) the Global Field Power (Vecchiato et al. 2012) was estimated, where the N_P e N_Q values are the cardinality of the two electrodes set. Therefore, the AW index zero value represent an experimental condition where the left and right PFC activity values are equivalent.

For each subject for each olfactory stimulus, the AW signal was calculated. Then, it was averaged along the 10 s of the stimulation. In conclusion, the correlation value was estimated between the mean AW value and the subjects evaluation explicit score.

23.3 Results

The Fig. 23.2 shows the distribution of appreciation scores attributed by the subjects during the experimentation at the odorous stimuli employed. The vertical bars refer to the appreciation average stated scores obtained by the subjects' whole experimental sample for each odorous substance, indicated along the abscissa axis.

It shows that the fish smell scored the worst evaluation (a mean value of 2.1), on the contrary the Rose, Banana and Mint smells scored the betters. The red line in the graphic refers to the pleasantness threshold, as the total mean score for all the odorous stimuli, equal to 6.1.

The Fig. 23.3 shows the distribution of the AW index values estimated in the subjects experimental sample during the odorous stimuli presentation. For each odour, the AW value was averaged along the whole subjects sample. On the ordinate axis, the AW scores, where a positive value refers to the approach motivation (i.e. appreciation), whilst a negative value refers to the withdrawal motivation (i.e. rejection) towards the specific odorous stimulus (Davidson et al. 1990).

The Pearson's correlation coefficient between the appreciation stated mean scores and the brain AW mean indexes was estimated, in order to verify the validity of this index in response to olfactory stimuli.

The Fig. 23.4 shows the scatterplot graphic for the ten odorous substances used in this experiment. This graphic type is very useful to highlight the correlation between two variables, in this case the appreciation stated mean scores and the brain AW mean indexes.

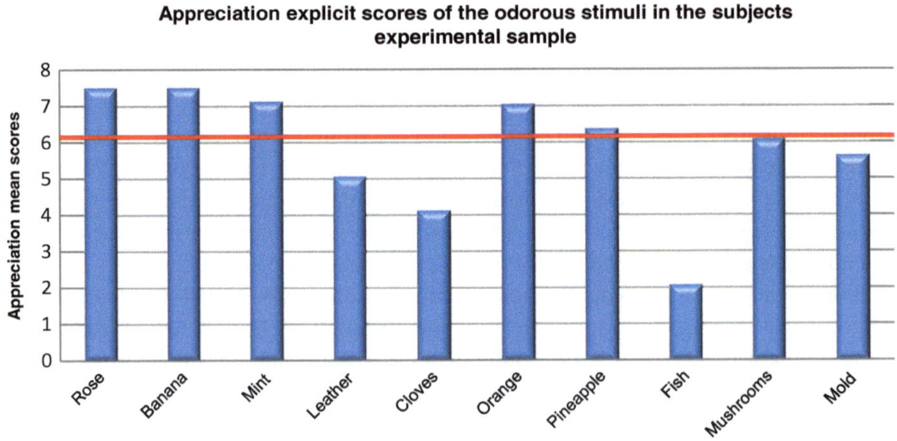

Fig. 23.2 The graphic shows the mean values of explicit appreciation (range between 1 and 10) stated by the subjects experimental sample during the experimentation for each odorous substance. The *red line* refers to the total mean score, equal to 6.1. It is evident that the Rose, Banana, Mint, Orange and Pineapple smells are above this threshold

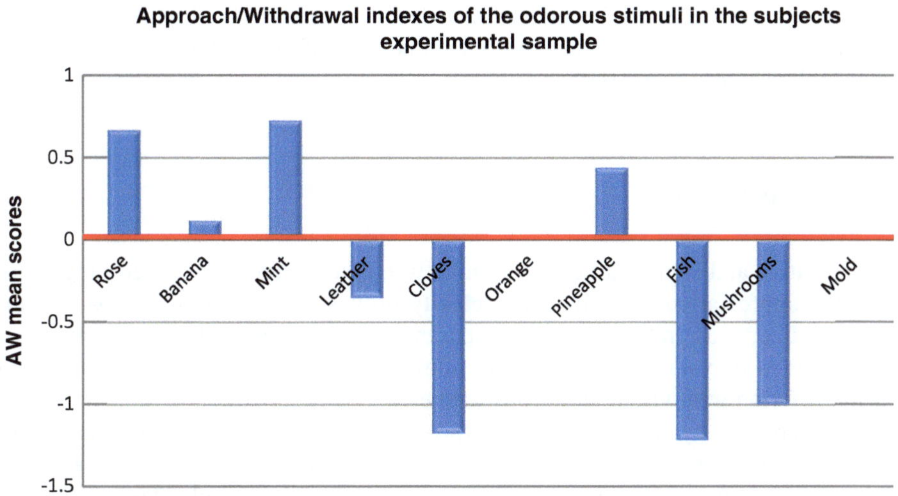

Fig. 23.3 The graphic shows the mean values of the Approach/Withdrawal (AW) index estimated, in the subjects experimental sample, from the electroencephalographic data collected during the odour presentation. The *red line* corresponds to the AW index zero value, i.e. the indifference situation towards the stimulus. A positive value refers to the approach motivation (i.e. appreciation), whilst a negative value refers to the withdrawal motivation (i.e. rejection) towards the specific odorous stimulus. It is evident that the Rose, Banana, Mint, Pineapple and Mould smells are above this zero level

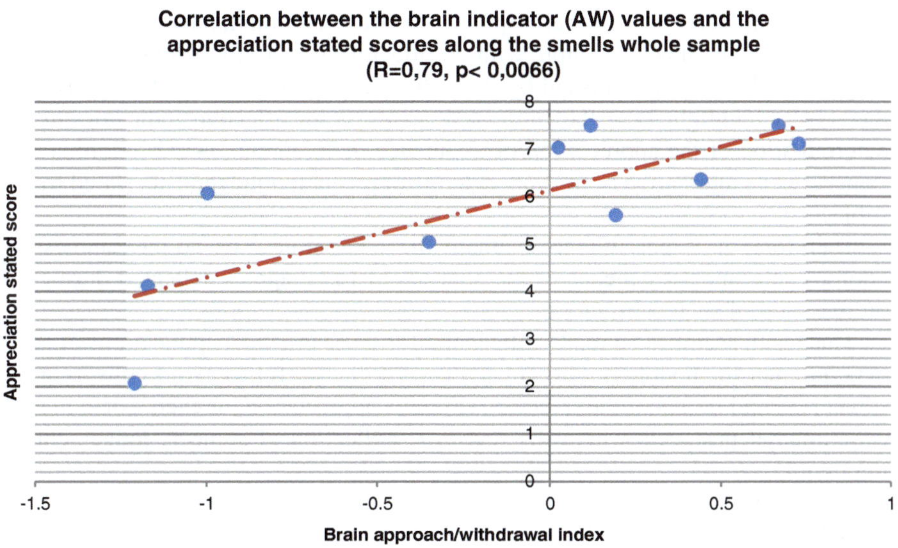

Fig. 23.4 The figure shows the scatterplot between the brain AW index, along the abscissa axis, and the appreciation stated score, between 1 and 10, on the ordinate axis. Each dot in the graphic refers to a specific odorous stimulus used in the experiment. The estimated correlation coefficient R is equal to 0.79, with a statistical significance of $p < 0.006$

The estimated Pearson's correlation index R is equal to 0.79, with a statistical significance index p lower than 0.006, thus largely inferior to the statistical significance threshold, i.e. $p = 0.05$.

23.4 Discussion

The positive and significant correlation between the appreciation stated judgement and the appreciation brain indicator clearly proves that the brain approach/withdrawal theory, as indicator of the pleasantness experienced toward a stimulus, continues to be valid also for odorous stimuli, in addition to the widely accepted demonstration with visual and acoustic ones.

Furthermore, by means of the interpolation line in Fig. 23.4 it is possible to appreciate how the brain AW index zero value (indifference towards the smell presented) corresponds approximately to the same threshold level obtained from the appreciation scores assessed by the experimental subjects. In particular, this level is equal to 6.1, is that the threshold to discriminate the pleasant from the no-pleasant stimuli corresponds for both the indicators.

23.5 Conclusions

In the present work, the cerebral responses to olfactory stimuli have been studied in a healthy young subjects sample with an olfactory sensitivity coherent to the age range considered, as established by the previous analysis performed. In particular, the results highlight how the brain AW index is an effective indicator for the determination of the appreciation or avoidance motivations towards odorous substances, as an alternative or in support to the appreciation judgements stated by the subjects.

Therefore, it is possible to evaluate the pleasantness or no-pleasantness of odorous substances by means of the analysis of EEG signals collected during the presentation of such substances.

This result seems to be really interesting for those practical applications of these experimental methodologies where it should to be useful to avoid collecting the subjects verbal scores of the olfactory stimulus appreciation, or even worse in such experimental protocols where the real time collection of subjects judgements is impossible.

In addition, another important application of these methodologies could be in the food sciences field, since it should be very useful to better understand how the smells influence the consumers in their food choice. Furthermore, the awareness about the brain motivational processes towards the food could be used to improve the quality of the nutrition, making it more and more pleasant and healthy at the same time.

In conclusion, the brain activity measure use during the olfactory stimuli perception makes way for new applications of such measure kind in experimental environments more and more ecological.

Acknowledgments The grants provided to Fabio Babiloni by the Italian Ministry of University and Education under the PRIN 2012 and that provided by the Ministry of Foreign Affairs for the bilateral relation between Italy and China for the project "Neuropredictor" are gratefully acknowledged.

References

Davidson RJ (1999) Neuropsychological perspectives on affective styles and their cognitive consequences. In: Dalgleish T, Power MJ (eds) Handbook of cognition and emotion. Wiley, New York, NY, USA, pp 103–123

Davidson RJ, Ekman P, Saron CD, Senulis JA, Friesen WV (1990) Approach-withdrawal and cerebral asymmetry: emotional expression and brain physiology: I. J Pers Soc Psychol 58 (2):330

Doty RL (1991) Olfactory system. In: Getchell TV, Doty RL, Bartoshuk LM, Snow JB Jr (eds) Smell and taste in health and disease. Raven, New York, p 1803

Hummel T, Sekinger B, Wolf SR, Pauli E, Kobal G (1997) Sniffin' sticks: olfactory performance assessed by the combined testing of odor identification, odor discrimination and olfactory threshold. Chem Senses 22(1):39–52

Jackson DC, Malmstadt JR, Larson CL, Davidson RJ (2000) Suppression and enhancement of responses to emotional pictures. Psychophysiology 37:515–522

Jackson DC, Mueller CJ, Dolski I, Dalton KM, Nitschke JB, Urry HL, Rosenkranz MA, Ryff CD, Singer BH, Davidson RJ (2003) Now you feel it, now you don't frontal brain electrical asymmetry and individual differences in emotion regulation. Psychol Sci 14(6):612–617

Kim YK, Watanuki S (2003) Characteristics of electroencephalographic responses induced by a pleasant and an unpleasant odor. J Physiol Anthropol Appl Human Sci 22(6):285–291

Klimesch W (1999) EEG alpha and theta oscillation reflect cognitive and memory performance: a review and analysis. Brain Res Rev 29(2):169–195

Kobal G, Hummel T, Sekinger B, Barz S, Roscher S, Wolf S (1996) Sniffin' sticks: screening of olfactory performance. Rhinology 34:222–226

Kong W, Zhao X, Hu S, Vecchiato G, Babiloni F (2013) Electronic evaluation for video commercials by impression index. Cogn Neurodyn 7(6):531–535

Schmidt LA, Trainor LJ (2001) Frontal brain electrical activity (EEG) distinguishes valence and intensity of musical emotions. Cognit Emot 15(4):487–500

Vecchiato G, Maglione AG, Scorpecci A, Malerba P, Marsella P, Di Francesco G, Vitiello S, Colosimo A, Babiloni F (2012) EEG frontal asymmetry related to pleasantness of music perception in healthy children and cochlear implanted users. In: Engineering in medicine and biology society (EMBC), 2012 annual international conference of the IEEE, San Diego, CA, pp 4740–4743

Index

K. Nermend, M. Łatuszyńska (eds.), *Selected Issues in Experimental Economics*, Springer Proceedings in Business and Economics, DOI 10.1007/978-3-319-28419-4

MIX
Papier aus verantwortungsvollen Quellen
Paper from responsible sources
FSC® C105338
www.fsc.org

If you have any concerns about our products,
you can contact us on
ProductSafety@springernature.com

In case Publisher is established outside the EU,
the EU authorized representative is:
Springer Nature Customer Service Center GmbH
Europaplatz 3, 69115 Heidelberg, Germany

Printed by Libri Plureos GmbH
in Hamburg, Germany